Martha de la Cal was born near Kansas City, Missouri, and read psychology at the University of Kansas City. After marrying, she moved to Havana, Cuba, and took a PhD in clinical psychology at the University of Vilanova there. With two friends Martha de la Cal founded the Lafayette School and also began her career as a journalist, writing for McGraw-Hill World News and the *Times of Havana*. Leaving Cuba two years after the Revolution, she and her family travelled in South America before moving to Madrid, where she helped to found the American School. Martha de la Cal went to live in Lisbon in 1966 and has since been a full-time journalist there, first for McGraw-Hill World News and, since 1972, for *Time* magazine, covering the 1974 Revolution in Portugal in detail. She also now writes on Portuguese affairs for *The Times* of London and does travel pieces for several magazines, including *Orient Express*. She has travelled extensively in Europe, North Africa and Asia and has six children and six grandchildren.

Other Collins Independent Travellers Guides include:

Greek Islands by Victor Walker (**Revised edition**)
Mainland Greece by Victor Walker
Morocco by Christine Osborne
Provence, Languedoc & Côte d'Azur by John Ardagh
South-west France by Rex Grizell
Rome, Umbria and Tuscany by Derek Wilson
Southern Italy by Ian Thomson
Spain by Harry Debelius (**Revised edition**)
Soviet Union by Martin Walker
Turkey by Daniel Farson (**Revised edition**)

COLLINS

INDEPENDENT TRAVELLERS GUIDE

PORTUGAL

MARTHA DE LA CAL

Revised Edition

Series Editor Robin Dewhurst

HarperCollins*Publishers*

Note

Whilst every effort has been made to ensure that prices, hotels and restaurant recommendations, opening hours and similar factual information in this book are accurate at the time of going to press, the Publishers cannot be held responsible for any changes found by readers using this guide. In particular, telephone codes in Portugal can vary from region to region and may differ from those given in the book, depending on the area from which you are dialling. In case of difficulty, check with the operator for local and long distance codes.

For all my children, who have travelled with me around the world.

HarperCollins Publishers
London

First published in 1988
Reprinted 1988
Revised edition 1991
© Martha de la Cal 1988, 1991

Maps by Jillian Luff of Bitmap Graphics

Cover photographs: **front** *Viana do Castelo, Santa Luzia (Tessa Musgrave);* **back** *traditional tiled house (William Kennedy, The Image Bank).*

A CIP catalogue record for this book is available from the British Library.

ISBN 0 00 412589 4

Typeset by Ace Filmsetting Ltd, Frome, Somerset
Printed and bound in Great Britain by Mackays of Chatham

Contents

Introduction   7
History   12
Portugal Today   25
The Weather and When to Go   32
Travelling Around   33
Where to Stay   41
Eating and Drinking   45
Entertainment   49
Sport   52
Shopping   53
General Basics   54

GAZETTEER

The Minho   66
The Douro   110
Trás-os-Montes   144
The Beiras   170
Estremadura   212
The Ribatejo   272
The Alentejo   286
The Algarve   326

Index   349

Introduction

Portugal could be several countries in one: the very different north and south, roughly divided by the River Tagus, which flows diagonally south-west from the Spanish border to join the Atlantic Ocean; the densely populated, well-developed coast in sharp contrast to the sparsely peopled, backward interior; the smart world of the extremely rich which lies side by side with the depressing shanty-town world of the extremely poor; and the modern, European Portugal of the cities that coexists with the prehistoric and medieval Portugals that seem to persist in a fabulous time-machine.

Portugal sits back to back with Spain on the Iberian Peninsula, cut off from the rest of Europe. It is bordered by Spain on the north and east and the Atlantic Ocean on the south and west. Portugal's justifiable fear over the ages that it would be gobbled up by its larger and more powerful neighbour was one of the reasons it turned to the sea and the lands beyond.

Even today the two countries do not live easily as neighbours. It is interesting to note that along their 1,000 km frontier there are few areas of transition where physical types, customs and language intermingle as they do along borders in other European countries. The exception is in the north between Trás-os-Montes and Spanish Galicia, where the languages tend to blend into one. Everywhere else a strict line is drawn between the Spaniards on one side and the very different Portuguese on the other. This is very apparent to anyone crossing the border.

The land

The north, with Oporto as its centre, is, to a great extent, mountainous and green, except for the remote north-east behind the mountains where rainfall does not reach. The south, dominated by Lisbon (even though Lisbon sits on the north side of the River Tagus), tends to be flat and dry, except for the tiny Monchique mountain range that separates the Algarve coast from the rest of the country.

In the north, the land is mostly divided into small subsistence farms, belonging to individual farmers who jealously guard their ownership and resist any attempt to bring them together into co-operatives to increase production. In many parts of the north, each owner encloses his plot of ground within laboriously hand-constructed walls of granite stones – some in artistic patterns that indicate a latent artist lost to the soil – giving the entire countryside a chequered appearance. The process of fragmentation continues, because the inheritance laws divide property equally between all descendants – and families tend to be large.

Further east from the coast towards Spain or south towards Lisbon, there are larger farms and even a few large estates, but they too are family holdings kept for many generations.

The south between the River Tagus and the Algarve coast is a rolling plain where low-yield wheat is grown. Tens of thousands of cork and olive trees stand out against the landscape. The land is divided into vast estates. Before the 1974 Revolution in Portugal most of these belonged to absentee landlords, who kept them as private hunting preserves and employed seasonal workers to harvest the cork and olives as well as wheat. Those itinerant workers owned no land and were very poor. After the Revolution, the Communist Party led the farmworkers in occupying the estates and forming co-operatives. Subsequent governments have handed back to former owners all but 120,000 hectares of the 1.2 million confiscated, and in 1990 parliament voted to do away entirely with the agrarian reform.

North and south

The people in the north tend to be more friendly and helpful than those in the south. Waiters are more attentive, shop assistants are more polite and everyone there seems more anxious to show the tourist around. Perhaps the difference stems from the fact that the south – especially Lisbon and the Algarve – has been the centre of tourism for a much longer time. Tourism is still relatively new in the north.

The north is very proud of being 'the cradle of the Portuguese nation'. It was in the north, in 1139, that Dom Afonso Henriques, having driven out the Castilian Spaniards, declared himself King Afonso I of Portugal. He established a kingdom betweeen the Minho and Mondego rivers and proceeded to reconquer the rest of the north from the Moors.

The northern nobility, with names like Lencastre, Bragança, Guimarães, Calheiros and others that pre-date Portugal as a nation or were created at its birth, are very jealous of their ancestry and the antiquity of their titles. They tend to look down on the aristocracy of Lisbon, whose titles may date from only two or three centuries ago.

The north is more conservative and traditional in its outlook than the south. The Catholic Church and the conservative political parties tend to dominate. The very powerful Archbishop of Braga, which has been the centre of Catholicism since Roman times, and the village priests have exerted great influence over the thinking and the lives of the people for hundreds of years. This accounts for the incredible number of churches in every village and every city in the north, rich in Romanesque, Gothic, Baroque and Manueline architecture and splendid religious treasures dating back over the centuries to before the founding of the country and even to Roman times.

The south is more free-thinking and liberal. The religious orders were expelled early from the south, and the priests – except worker priests – have little influence there. With the exception of Lisbon, Évora, Beja and Setúbal in the Alentejo region and Tavira and a few more towns in the Algarve, the south has few churches worthy of artistic note.

Politically the south is left wing. The Alentejo was the focal point for the Communist struggle against the dictatorship for half a century. After the dictatorship was overthrown in 1974, the Communists remained strong there, obtaining more than half the vote in elections and controlling local governments. Their support has, however, declined somewhat recently.

Oporto, the northern capital, has always been a bustling trade and industrial centre at the mouth of the River Douro, dealing traditionally in textiles, port and agricultural products, while Lisbon, the southern capital, has been the political and cultural centre – the seat of the nation's government and parliament and the home of many museums, art galleries, symphony orchestras, the opera and European-type entertainment.

The northerners boast that they are hard-working and industrious, while people in Lisbon tend to be a bit lazy, given to talking a lot, having fun and accomplishing little. A popular saying sums up this attitude: 'Braga prays, Oporto works and Lisbon plays.'

Northern industries – the great majority privately owned –are, on the whole, doing better than those in the south. Northern textiles account for a large part of the country's exports. The ready-made clothing and the shoe industries have really taken off in recent years. Port continues to hold its own.

Southern industries – most of them, such as steel, shipbuilding and chemicals, state-owned – went seriously into debt, causing the country's national debt to reach astronomic heights. They are being privatized and sold off. An exception, of course, is the tourist industry, which is flourishing.

Much of the far north, in spite of its pockets of healthy industry, is more backward than anything to be found in the south. The inland mountain villages far from the coast were, until recently, virtually cut off from the rest of the country, without roads, electricity or running water. Many are still isolated during the winter and many still have no running water. The people live in close contact with their livestock, on which they depend for most of their necessities.

Pre-Celtic and Celtic ways and beliefs persist in some areas. There are traces of ancient devil worship in some rituals. People regularly consult the local *bruxas* (witches) and *curandeiros* (medicine men) about their health, love-life, and future, to put a spell on someone or to have one removed. Farm tools and other utensils are right out of the Old Testament. Many still lead a communal life, in which land, forests and animals are held and worked in common and the village elders rule and hand out each person's duties for the day. This way of life probably originated with the Iberian tribes of prehistory.

National characteristics

The Portuguese tend to be gentle, mild-mannered people. They refer to themselves as the country of *brandos costumes* (gentle ways) and are proud of the fact that they abolished the death penalty in 1867, carried out a virtually bloodless revolution in 1974, and do not kill the bull in bullfights.

They also tend to be sentimental – a trait which can lead them to carry their 'gentle ways' a bit too far and be over-lenient with criminals. A common Portuguese reaction to the fears of even a multiple murderer is a sympathetic murmur of 'poor thing' (*coitadinho*).

Their sentimentality, combined with a certain amount of melancholy, has produced their national music – the *fado*, songs of unrequited love, homesickness or despair, wailed to guitars.

They are also passive and reserved and somewhat introverted. They find it difficult to say an outright 'no'. You might find this somewhat frustrating if you want a question answered in a hurry.

Many Portuguese are rather simple and uneducated. There are very high rates of illiteracy, especially in the countryside, where, until recently, the outside world did not penetrate.

Most Portuguese still cling to traditional values, such as the central importance of home and family. Things are changing a bit with the younger generation, but still several generations of one family may live together in one house, with the young taking care of the old. They very much keep to themselves in their homes and do not often invite other people in.

This does not mean, however, that they are unfriendly. On the contrary, the Portuguese are very friendly and tolerant. Portugal is one of the few countries where a tourist does not feel like a foreigner. The Portuguese tend to accept visitors and their peculiarities without comment.

Most Portuguese are very helpful to foreign tourists. You will often find that someone you have asked for directions will drop whatever task he is engaged in to become your self-appointed guide.

Recent developments

During the 1960s and 1970s, the composition of the population began to change. In the 1960s nearly 1.5 million Portuguese emigrated to northern Europe, and about 40,000 Cape Verde Islanders came in to fill the jobs left vacant. The Cape Verde Islanders are now very much a part of the scene, on building sites and in the shanty towns on the outskirts of cities, particularly Lisbon. These shanty towns resemble African villages: at first it can be rather startling, in a European country, to see exotically dressed and turbaned women pounding meal in large African mortars or washing clothes in open tanks. There are also Cape Verdian restaurants and night clubs.

One result of the 1974 Revolution was the sudden decolonization of Portugal's widespread empire. This in turn brought about a rapid influx of nearly one million *retornados* (returnees), and 200,000 Portuguese troops who had been fighting the twelve-year colonial war in Africa. Many of the *retornados* were Black African or Asian. Other thousands were Timorese who fled the civil war in East Timor that followed the Portuguese withdrawal and the invasion by Indonesia in 1975.

Surprisingly, all of these different groups have been integrated into Portuguese society with very few problems. They have, in fact, with their drive and determination, given a new dimension to Portuguese life. They have opened shops, restaurants and small industries which have greatly contributed to the economy.

The 1980s saw the return of an increasing number of emigrants from northern Europe and Brazil. They are returning at the rate of 40,000 per year. Many of them are bringing with them new skills acquired in the more advanced countries and applying them in Portugal. They are, however, faced with a serious problem: often their children, born abroad, do not adjust well to Portugal, preferring the life-styles of France or Germany.

The super-rich, who fled Portugal after the Revolution for more congenial settings in Paris or Rio, have now also returned, brightening up the scene in new, smart pubs, restaurants and discos such as Fragil in Lisbon, or throwing extravagant parties in their palaces and beach-side mansions in Cascais and Estoril.

You can expect, then, a land of contrasts in Portugal. Whether you want to see evidence of the old country of the navigators, sample the sophistication of cities such as Lisbon, laze on a beach in the Algarve or tour the remote mountain regions in the north, you are guaranteed an interesting and enjoyable holiday.

History

Recent History

The history of each region, and particularly that of Lisbon and Oporto, is described in detail in the Gazetteer. The following section is intended as a brief guide to Portugal's more recent history only.

King assassinated

In 1908, after years of political crises and the rise and fall of successive governments, combined with a severe economic depression, a group of political radicals shot and killed King Carlos and his elder son as they were riding through the Praça do Comércio in Lisbon in an open carriage with the queen and their younger son. It was the first regicide in Portugal's history. The younger son Manuel attempted to govern, but found it impossible. He and his mother and sister departed for England in 1910.

Rebellion

There followed attempted coups, counter-coups and governments of all kinds between 1912 and 1917. Not even the First World War ended the confusion.

First World War

Portugal entered the war mostly to protect its African colonies. It requisitioned thirty-six German ships stationed in the harbour at Lisbon. Two divisions of 40,000 men were sent to France.

Corporate State

The chaos that followed the war lasted for seven years. There were constant strikes and sixteen different governments in two years. Organized crime and secret societies were the order of the day. A Prime Minister and other ministers were assassinated. The escudo lost its value and big swindlers robbed the treasury of money. The Army decided to take over. The prestigious General Gomes da Costa marched with his troops down from Braga into Lisbon on 3 June 1926. General Carmona was named President and later re-elected three times until he died in office in 1951.

Dr António de Oliveira Salazar, a professor of economics from Coimbra University, accepted the post of Minister of Finance in 1928 on the condition that he would be given a free rein. No other minister was allowed to spend any money without consulting him. By levying taxes and cutting expenditure, he turned deficits into profits. He devoted these to public works, rearmament, communications, ports, irrigation projects, health and education. He grew wheat to cut down on imports. In 1932, Salazar became Prime Minister. He wrote a new constitution which included the overseas territories. The government had two houses: a National Assembly, which was directly elected, and a corporate chamber made up of representatives from all aspects of Portuguese life. There would be no strikes or lock-outs.

Spanish Civil War

A great deal of concern was felt in Portugal when the Communists took over in Spain during the Spanish Civil War, and in 1936 Salazar severed relations with Madrid. When the war ended and Franco was in power, he concluded a treaty of friendship – the Iberian Pact – with the Franco régime, with each pledging to come to the defence of the other in case of attack.

Second World War

Portugal managed to remain neutral in the Second World War. Secret agents of every nation spied on each other in Lisbon, and royalty and the rich from every European country sat out the war on the beaches of Estoril and Cascais or in the casino. Thousands of Jewish refugees swarmed into Portugal seeking passage to America. The Portuguese government was constantly worried that the Germans might invade by coming through Spain. This never happened. When it looked as if Hitler was losing, Salazar agreed to give Britain the use of the Azores to defend the Atlantic. He was also forced to stop the sale of vital wolfram to the Germans. After the war Salazar built a new fleet of fifty-one ships with money he had borrowed from Britain. He built bridges, dams and electrical lines.

In the 1950s Portugal lost a good part of its territories in Asia when India invaded and took Goa. There was also agitation in Africa by left-wing independence groups.

Repression

A one-party system developed under which opponents of the government were lumped into the same category as dangerous revolutionaries. Most parties that were allowed to form just before the elections dropped out because they were persecuted by the police. One presidential candidate was General Humberto Delgado, who stood against Admiral Amerigo Thomás in 1958. Thomás got 77 per cent of the vote and the opposition cried fraud. Some time later, Delgado was found dead near the Spanish border, supposedly murdered by the secret police. The Communist Party was outlawed and suspected members jailed. Labour organizers also went to prison. Students who protested were brutally suppressed. All newspapers, plays, radio and television were censored. All power and money were in the hands of an elite of twenty families, who controlled all banking and industry, in conjunction with the government and the Catholic Church.

War in Africa

In 1962, war broke out in Africa as Communist-trained guerrillas came over the borders into Angola. An identical thing happened in Mozambique a year later. The war lasted for thirteen years until the Armed Forces revolution in Lisbon. The wars in Africa caused Portugal to make a belated effort to maintain its empire by pouring in money for dams, roads, electricity, ports and other improvements. Portugal is still paying for some of the international loans contracted at that time.

The war became very unpopular with young people, who saw all of their opportunities for an education and a career slip away. Military service, virtually without pay, was evaded when possible – many ran away to Sweden or France. There were demonstrations in the university and in the streets. Students were killed or arrested by the police. Still the war dragged on.

Marcelo Caetano In 1968, Salazar fell from a chair and went into a coma. Later he was replaced by Professor Marcelo Caetano, a law professor from Lisbon University. Everyone believed that there would be an easing up in the repression. Young intellectuals like Francisco Pinto Balsemão and Francisco Sá Carneiro joined the National Assembly hoping to bring about change from within. It was useless. Neither they nor Marcelo Caetano could do anything about the entrenched conservatives in the military, the Church and banking and industry.

Movement of the Armed Forces The young officers in the military, especially those who were conscripts, became more and more fed up with the war and with unfair pay. They had also been in contact so long with the Marxist guerrillas whom they were fighting in Africa, all Portuguese-speaking like themselves, that they had become sympathetic with their cause. The 'Young Captains', as they were called, began to meet and plot the overthrow of the regime. There were about two hundred of them, but there were three real leaders: Major Vitor Alves (now a lieutenant-colonel in the Reserve); Captain Vasco Lourenço (a colonel on active duty); and Captain Otelo Saraiva de Carvalho (now a lieutenant-colonel condemned to an eighteen-year prison sentence for organizing a radical left terrorist organization in 1980 that bombed, robbed banks and assassinated in an attempt to bring about an armed insurrection). The 'Young Captains' called themselves the Movement of the Armed Forces, or MFA. They drew up a programme that guaranteed the re-establishment of democracy, free elections, independence for the overseas territories and many other reforms. The 'Young Captains', who formed the Council of the Revolution, promised in their programme and in the constitution that was later drawn up that they would withdraw from politics as soon as democracy was assured. True to their word, they did, a most uncommon thing after a military coup.

The Generals Meanwhile, the military commander of Guinea-Bissau, General António de Spinola, wrote a book outlining a peace and development plan for Guinea-Bissau. The régime in Lisbon was becoming jittery. The secret police (the PIDE) were cracking down. Prime Minister Caetano called all the generals to Lisbon to take an oath of allegiance to the régime. General Spinola and General Costa Gomes (now a member of the World Peace Organization) did not take the oath.

14

Caldas da Rainha

After an aborted attempt in Caldas da Rainha on 16 March 1974, the captains pulled off their coup in Lisbon on 25 April. The conspirators brought their forces and tanks into Lisbon and all of the units finally joined in. The only shots fired were at the headquarters of the hated secret police, who fled or surrendered. The 'Young Captains' were idealists and were very proud of their democratic programme. A group of them stopped in the street to show it to me as their tanks whizzed by and their gun emplacements were being set up.

Junta of National Salvation

A military junta of national salvation was set up immediately with General Spinola as President. Prime Minister Caetano and President Amerigo Thomás had been escorted to a plane that took them to exile in Brazil.

People

There was jubilation everywhere. Whole Portuguese families piled into their cars to follow the tanks around, often getting in the way. The revolutionary song *Grândola Vila Morena* blared from every loudspeaker. At the Caxias prison outside Lisbon, crowds gathered to wait for the political prisoners to be released. Otelo Saraiva de Carvalho had truckloads of red carnations driven into Lisbon. They sprouted from rifle barrels and lapels and became the symbol of the Revolution. On Labour Day, 1 May, a million people came to Lisbon to march.

Deterioration

Then things began to fall to pieces. Ministers who had been appointed from all of the parties – which had been hastily formed the day after the Revolution, except for the well-organized Communists, who had been operating in Portugal for forty-eight years – resigned because they thought the Communists and the radical left were taking over. They were. The Communists organized trade unions and brought hundreds of thousands into the street to strike. There were six provisional governments in two years. It began to look like a repeat of every attempt to form a republican government in the past hundred years.

Decolonization

Socialist Mário Soares was Foreign Minister and was set on decolonizing Portugal's African territories. He travelled around Africa consulting leaders of the other African countries. His aim was self-determination and elections for them. That didn't happen. With the aid of left-wing Portuguese military officers and Cubans, Marxist-Leninist liberation movements took over in every territory, where they still remain.

Retornados

Following the takeovers in Africa, civil war broke out. A million refugees streamed out of Angola and Mozambique in international airlifts or on fishing boats or any other transport they could find. They were white Portuguese, Black Africans from Angola and Mozambique, Indian traders and Timorese from East Timor. They represented a tenth of the population of Portugal, but somehow the country coped. These *retornados* (returned ones) were housed in luxury hotels, camps, empty houses and everywhere else imaginable. Amazingly, they were absorbed into the country's life.

Palace coup

Some disgruntled right-wingers and conservatives attempted to stage a march on the Palace on 28 November 1974, to show support for President General Spinola, who was horrified by what he considered a Communist takeover. They were stopped by left-wingers and radicals and General Spinola resigned, being replaced by the left-wing General Costa Gomes, who appointed the Communist-leaning Colonel Vasco Gonçalves Prime Minister.

Counter coup

On 11 March 1975, the Communists used the pretext that General Spinola was about to stage a counter coup, to gain control, nationalize industries – including banks and transport – and lead workers into occupying the lands in the Alentejo and set up co-operatives.

Elections

On 25 April, a year after the first coup, there were elections for a Constituent Assembly to write a constitution. Twelve political parties presented themselves. The Socialists under Mário Soares obtained the most votes with 37.8 per cent. The Communists polled 12.5 per cent. The Assembly wrote a Marxist-Leninist constitution under intimidation. Everyone was afraid to admit that he was not a leftist. Even the fashion for clothes had become 'radical chic' – jeans, boots and khaki jackets – and everyone went around in old, junky cars.

Violence

In the summer of 1975, things got very hot. There were clashes in the street between the radical left and the conservative right. The military security forces, COPCON, under the now avowedly radical left populist Brigadier-General Otelo Saraiva de Carvalho (promoted from captain), arrested around 125 'fascists' and 'capitalists' and held them without charges for several months in prison. Workers took over factories, hospitals, schools, university and occupied empty houses and apartment blocks. The Brigadier-General and Revolutionary Brigade leader Isabel do Carmo were handing out guns to workers and soldiers for an armed insurrection. Political parties were wrecking and burning each other's headquarters.

25 November

On 25 November 1975 the radical armed insurrection began, but the moderate officers and political parties under the command of General Ramalho Eanes were waiting for them. The Communists who had ventured into the street hastily withdrew. The extremists who held out were dealt with and that ended the 'revolution'.

President Eanes

All the moderate political parties obligingly supported General Eanes in the presidential election, which he won by a large majority. He was re-elected in 1980. The military was brought under control. He three times appointed the socialist Mário Soares as Prime Minister. After a conservative Democratic Alliance of Social Democrats, Christian Democrats and Monarchists obtained a majority in parliament in 1979, he appointed Francisco Sá Carneiro Prime Minister, who was killed in a plane crash while in office.

Revolving governments

Governments rose and fell with alarming regularity until 1987, when the right-of-centre Social Democrats headed by Aníbal Cavaco Silva won a majority in parliament. In two years they dismantled most of the things established under the constitution after the Revolution, and the constitution was changed to wipe out any mention of socialism. They did away with the agrarian reform and are privatizing all nationalized industries by selling them off and using most of the profits to reduce the national debt. Newspapers, radio and television are also being denationalized.

Architecture

The people of Portugal have always excelled in architecture. They have used stone since Celtic and Roman times for carving and building – probably because of the great abundance of granite and limestone. Portugal has been called 'The Stone Land'.

Prehistoric: For 1,000 years between 800 BC and AD 200, there existed in the north of Portugal a civilization called *castreja* living in fortified hill towns, the smaller of which are known as *castros*, the larger ones as *citânias*. The towns were built on the tops of high, stony hills, or against the sides at the summit. A *castro* or *citânia* would often have as many as three different sets of stone walls, for protection and to keep in the flocks, and were often backed by a wide rampart with a field of pointed granite slabs (*pedras fincadas*) sticking up to make it difficult for people or horses to cross. As a further protective measure, the town would also be surrounded by a series of moats, some of them as much as 7 or 8 m deep, and very wide. All the *castros* were either built on a river or stream or had springs within the walls.

The inhabitants of the *castros* were a mixture of native tribes and Indo-Europeans – mostly Celts – who had infiltrated the Peninsula in around 1000 BC. The number of people in most *castros* was small: sometimes they were all of the same family, or just a few families from one clan. However, some of the larger *citânias* contained up to two hundred houses within a series of walled enclosures. They were herdsmen and warriors with a dominate nobility and serfs, who also lived by raiding the nearby valleys.

Each house was built of granite stones set together in a circular, oval or rectangular shape: the round houses were the most common, and the average diameter of the round houses was about 5 m. Each house had a cone-shaped thatched roof held up by a pole set in a large stone in the centre of the house. Some of the remaining walls of the round houses have no doors, which has perplexed archaeologists. It is thought that they must have had openings near the roof entered by retractable ladders. Other houses did have doors and it is still possible to see where the wooden hinges fitted.

Several *castros* and *citânias* have been partially excavated, and it is possible to visit them. Many are in rather inaccessible places, and you have to clamber up rocky roads or ox tracks to reach them. Information on the whereabouts of the *castros* and *citânias* is available at Regional Tourist Offices.

Roman: The Romans arrived in the second century BC and stayed for six hundred years, a legacy of which is the great number of Roman remains all over the country, including entire cities with columns, walls and mosaic floors. Most numerous of all, however, are the roads, bridges and aqueducts – as one would expect from the Romans.

The temple to Diana in Évora is from the second century BC and is the best-known piece of Roman architecture in the country. Conimbriga, near Coimbra, is a large, excavated city on a high hill, with foundations and walls of several houses, columns and mosaic floors. Idanha-a-Velha has a paleo-Christian church in which there are Roman inscriptions. There are the ruins of another Roman town at Medóbriga near Castelo de Vide. South of Lisbon on the Tróia Peninsula there is a sixth-century Roman chapel with walls covered with murals. Further south, near Santiago do Cacém, there is the ruined town of Miróbriga with houses, baths, basilica and Hippodrome. Near Belmonte in the north, an imposing three-storey Roman building of granite stands in the middle of an open field. On the Algarve at Milreu there is a large Roman villa made of brick with columns, mosaics and a ruined apse. Lisbon, which was called Osipon by the Romans, had many Roman baths and a theatre built in the time of Nero. Unfortunately, they are under the buildings of the Baixa, and are only opened at certain times.

Visigoth: Except for the seventh-century basilica in the church in Balsemão and vestiges in the Santo Amaro Chapel in Beja, there is very little left of Visigoth architecture. There is a combination of Visigoth and Byzantine in the seventh-century São Frutoso Chapel in Montel near Braga.

Arabic: Little is left of Arabic architecture either, except for its influence on local Algarve architecture. One example remaining is the parish church in Mértola, which was a mosque converted to a Christian church.

Mozarabic: The Christians dominated by the Arabs evolved a hybrid Mozarab style that is best illustrated in the church of São Pedro in Lourosa.

Romanesque: In the twelfth century, after Portugal had become a nation, there was a spate of building in the north and centre of the country. The builders of the churches came under the influence of the Order of Cluny in France. The great cathedrals of Braga, Lisbon and Coimbra are excellent examples of this period, and so is the town hall, *Domus Municipalis*, in Bragança. The Évora cathedral (1186–1283) illustrates the transition to the Gothic.

Gothic: Between the thirteenth and early sixteenth centuries the Gothic style was dominant. No tourist should miss seeing the

Alcobaça monastery (twelfth and thirteenth centuries), the Elvas temple (thirteenth century) or the Batalha monastery (fourteenth century).

Manueline: Manueline is Portugal's own style of architecture. It grew out of the triumphal jubilation of the Age of Discoveries in the sixteenth century. The architects – some of them Spanish and French – combined basic Gothic with representations of all the symbols imaginable of the Discoverers' sea voyages and the exotic places they had seen. Entwined ropes carved in stone climbed up pillars and surrounded windows encrusted with sea-shells, nets, flowers, leaves, ocean waves, military arms, anchors, armillary spheres, the Cross of Christ, and even the Order of the Garter bestowed on Henry the Navigator. The Jerónimos monastery and the Belém Tower in Lisbon best illustrate the style. The unfinished chapels at the Batalha monastery are also pure Manueline. The enormous window in the nave of the Convent of the Order of Christ in Tomar is the most flamboyant example. I have known people need a glass of brandy to restore them after their first sight of it. It is a style that takes a bit of getting used to, but it does grow on you.

Renaissance: This style was late in coming to Portugal, because there was such a preference for Manueline. Coimbra became the centre of the Renaissance movement in the latter part of the sixteenth century. The door on the Old Cathedral in Coimbra is a good example, as is the Cristo monastery in Tomar.

Mannerist: By the middle of the sixteenth century the Renaissance style had degenerated into Mannerism. The cathedrals of Leiria, Portalegre, Miranda do Douro and the New Cathedral in Coimbra are in the Mannerist style.

Baroque and Romantic: In the seventeenth and eighteenth centuries, architecture moved from the austere and classic to the Baroque. Great manor houses, including the famous Solar de Mateus near Vila Real, were built in the north, paid for with gold from Brazil. New, revolutionary ideas from the north of Europe caused a breakaway from traditional forms. The Portuguese Baroque incorporated gold work, painted ceilings and walls of decorative tiles encrusted with medallions, vases of flowers, and so forth. Some of the best examples are the Cleridges Church in Oporto, the Convent at Mafra, the Queluz Palace near Lisbon, the eighteenth-century aqueduct and the Estrela Basilica in Lisbon.

Neoclassic: Inspired by the French and Italians, the Portuguese took up Neoclassicism at the end of the eighteenth century. It dominated in the reconstruction of the vast area of Lisbon destroyed in the 1755 earthquake. The São Bento Palace, that houses Parliament; the Ajuda Palace and the São Carlos National Theatre are typical of the period.

Romantic: During this period, styles from classic antiquity to Manueline were revived. Ideas were also borrowed from Moorish art. The Pena Palace and the Palace of Monserrate in Sintra, as well as the Rossio railway station in Lisbon, are typical Romanticism. The Arabic Salon in the Oporto Stock Exchange is an extreme example.

Art nouveau: At the beginning of the twentieth century this new movement caught on in Lisbon, Coimbra and Leiria, where many houses were built in the art nouveau style.

During the 1940s, the modern Church of Our Lady of Fátima was built in Lisbon; in 1970 the Church of the Sacred Heart of Jesus and the Calouste Gulbenkian Museum were built.

Utilitarian: During the 1940s and 1950s, emphasis was on the utilitarian rather than the artistic, which accounts for the proliferation of public buildings and urbanization projects totally without personality that mar every city and town. During that period, ambitious city planners such as Duarte Pacheco constructed the wide avenues and large plazas seen today. Buildings were embellished in the nationalistic and monumental style favoured by Italians in the time of Mussolini, of whom the men of Dictator Salazar were great admirers. Efforts were made, however, to use a bit of imagination in some tourist projects and hotels – especially on the Algarve, where a huge pre-Revolution regional development plan controlled architectural style to keep it in harmony with the landscape and the Moorish heritage of the region. After the Revolution brought 'freedom' to the country, controls were removed and construction ran riot.

Shanty town: If all buildings and structures can be called architecture, then Portugal's shanty towns (*bairros de lata* or *barracas*) must be included. Thousands of them have been built on hillsides around towns and cities by the nation's poor. The building materials are packing cases, bits of tin, pieces of old cars, plastic, wooden planks, broken bricks and whatever else comes to hand. A great amount of inventiveness and creativity go into their building; and, not too surprisingly, the owners are often very proud of these structures they have built with their own hands – even if they have no sewage disposal facilities or running water.

Post-Modernist: One young architect is single-handedly transforming contemporary Portuguese architecture. He is Tomás Taveira, an avowed Post-Modernist, who thinks that buildings should say something, be colourful and be fun.

His most spectacular achievement is the eighteen-storey Amoreiras complex of apartments, business offices and shopping centre covering 250,000 sq. m that stands on a high hill in the west of Lisbon, near the eighteenth-century aqueduct. It is a combination of a castle and a medieval village, with three towers 'representing two medieval warriors escorting a damsel'. The towers, which are pink, grey, green, blue and ochre, are made of glass, aluminium and mirrors that reflect the light. The building's huge, brightly painted columns remind me of

Knossos on the island of Crete. People either love his work or hate it. It is the subject of constant controversy. It is worth a trip to Amoreiras, if only to form an opinion and take a stand.

Decorative tiles

Tiles (*azulejos*) have been a favourite decoration in Portugal since before the sixteenth century. The idea of using them on the outside as well as the inside of buildings came from the Moors, and the first tiles used in Portugal were *mudéjar*, imported from Seville in Spain in the fifteenth century to decorate palaces and churches.

Early in the sixteenth century, the Portuguese began to import and copy tiles from Italy, and later in the century to copy Flemish ones. By the seventeenth century they were making patterns of tiles that resembled Muslim rugs. The colours were predominantly blue and yellow, and the commonest motifs were flowers with leaves. Later, other colours were added along with birds and animals, reflecting those found in Portugal's new colonies in the Far East and in Africa.

During the eighteenth century the colours used were almost exclusively blue and white, and the tiles told stories. This was the greatest period for Portuguese tile-making. The most renowned of the tile artists was António de Oliveira Bernardes, who founded a famous school. The best-known productions of his school were sets of tiles depicting the city of Lisbon with its squares, buildings and waterfront and the life of the people at the time. These tiles are one of the greatest sources of information about the period and can be seen in Lisbon's tile museum (see below).

As the century progressed, styles became more and more elaborate and overloaded with decorations set on a bright blue field. A new style also emerged in which each tile had a separate design, usually flowers or birds or boats. Tiles imitating tapestries were also used to cover church walls – such as those in the Madre de Deus Church in Lisbon.

After the 1755 earthquake in Lisbon, when the Prime Minister, the Marquês de Pombal, was rebuilding the city, tiles were introduced that were more simple in design and were in pale colours on a white background. But by the middle of the nineteenth century, decorative, stylized tiles were once more being used on the outside of buildings – a style reimported from Brazil.

Examples of all of the styles of tile can be found in churches, universities, private houses, palaces, museums, on garden walls all over the country and even on the walls of railway stations in the most remote corners of Portugal. Some of the best tiles are in Coimbra University and the buildings in Guimarães.

There is an excellent tile museum in Lisbon: Museu Nacional do Azulejo, Madre de Deus 4. Tel. (01) 824132.

There is a revival in the use of decorative tiles in building. Period tiles are being reproduced, along with copies of sixteenth- to eighteenth-century porcelain, at various factories. Chiefly responsible for the renewed interest in tiles in this century were painters such as Jorge Barradas, Almada Negreiros, Maria Keil, Júlio Resende and Querubim Lapa.

Most of the tile factories are in Lisbon, and it is possible to visit them. They have retail outlets all around the country. Some of them will package and ship.

• Fábrica de Cerâmica Constância, 8-C Santo Domingo à Lapa. Tel. (01) 600017/663951.

• Fábrica de Cerâmica Viúva Lamego, 25 Largo Intendente Pina Marique. Tel. (01) 521401/575929.

• Fábrica Sant'Anna, 95 Rua do Alecrim (showrooms). Tel. (01) 322537.

96-C Boa Hora (factory). Tel. (01) 648035/638292.

• Santa Rufina – Azulejos e Cerâmicas, 9 A/B C-d-e Penafiel. Tel. (01) 876018.

• Cerâmica Artística Isabel Garcia, Terrugem – Sintra. Tel. (01) 9278509.

Painting

Painting in Portugal really dates from only the fifteenth century. Before that it was limited mostly to medieval illuminated manuscripts preserved in the churches, the archives of the Torre do Tombo and the Ajuda Palace Library in Lisbon. There is a twelfth-century mural in the São Francisco Church in Oporto and there are some vestiges of frescoes in Roman and Romanesque churches.

The most noteworthy example of fifteenth-century painting is to be found in the São Vicente de Fora panels by Nuno Gonçalves in the Museum of Ancient Art in Lisbon. The central theme is the adoration of Saint Vincent, the patron saint of Lisbon, and it is a tribute to the great personages of the Age of Discoveries. A well-known portrait of Prince Henry the Navigator is incorporated in it. Dark, rich colours – particularly dark reds – predominate.

From this period, there are also the triptych of Santa Clara (1486) in the Machado de Castro Museum and the portrait of Princesa Santa Joana in the Aveiro Museum.

In the sixteenth and seventeenth centuries, the portrait was the thing, and painters, especially in Lisbon and Évora, were greatly influenced by Flemish painters. There was an interesting half-Spanish woman who lived in Óbidos, Josefa de Óbidos (1634–84), who did still life and religious paintings.

In the eighteenth century the Portuguese painter Domingos Sequeira (1768–1834) had great success in Paris, London and Rome. His best-known painting is *The Painter's Children*.

Finally, in this century, some great modern painters emerged. Almada Negreiros (1883–1970) became the central figure of Modernism. He was a many-faceted genius, excelling in painting, murals, design, tiles, tapestry and glazing. In 1945 he painted the giant murals in Lisbon's docks. He also wrote novels. Art exhibitions are held by the Ministry of Culture in their Lisbon gallery named after him.

Many of Portugal's painters left the country during the fifty years of dictatorship, because they felt they could not express themselves freely. The Portuguese abstract painter Helena Vieira da Silva, who painted in Paris, introduced innovations and had great influence on the Paris School. She has frequent exhibitions in Lisbon now.

There has been a renaissance in Portuguese painting in the past few years. It was given impetus by the Gulbenkian Foundation in Lisbon, which granted scholarships to talented painters. In the 1960s the Gulbenkian Foundation also bought a large collection of British paintings that greatly influenced Portuguese painters. In 1983 the Foundation opened its Museum of Contemporary Art, which has an entire room devoted to Almada Negreiros. The Ministry of Culture has also opened two galleries in Lisbon – the Almada Negreiros Gallery, mentioned above, and another in the historic Foz Palace in the Praça dos Restauradores. There has also been the biggest movement in history to open mainly private galleries all around the country to show and sell paintings. Portuguese paintings are underpriced by international standards, so they are an excellent buy, both for their value as art and as a good investment.

The list of modern Portuguese painters is long and varied. It includes those who work in London and Paris, but show in Lisbon and are sold in local galleries; established painters, both men and women; and talented young artists.

I particularly like the work of José de Guimarães. His paintings are very original and colourful; his figures are sometimes infantile and not very pretty, but always imaginative. Another favourite is Nikias Skapinakis, a Portuguese of Greek extraction, whose work has moved from the abstract through a 'poster' period to abstract landscapes seen from above. They are 'an illusion of nature', he says. Another painter of great power is Júlio Pomar, who lives most of the time in Paris, but whose work is exhibited and sold in Lisbon. Paula Rego, who studied and lives in London, is also exhibited and sold in Lisbon.

It is also worth seeking out the work of the following painters. Gil Teixeira Lopes is a painter and engraver, whose work is figurative and abstract. Navarro Hogan paints traditional configurations, but without details or movement, in dark colours; his works have been described as 'paintings of silence'. Lima de Freitas paints classical themes in oil; Luis Noronha da Costa is very popular for his ingenious designs sprayed on to canvas. Eduardo Batarda uses sweeping white lines, with some colour, on large black canvases. Bual does abstracts of great quality. Cruzeiro Seixas, who lives on the Algarve, is a very interesting surrealist painter. Angelo Sousa specializes in 'minimal art'. Margarida Cepeda is a talented new painter. Júlio Resende paints brightly coloured watercolours. Jorge Oliveira does abstracts mostly in blues and reds. Nuno de Siqueira paints abstracts. Graça Morais does many strong paintings that show the influence of her origins in Trás-os-Montes, and also others that are much gentler.

Other names to look out for are: António Sena, Alvaro Lapa, António Dacosta, Pedro Portugal, Pedro Proença, Ilda David, Pedro Tudela, Paiva Raposo, Matilde Marçal, Manuel Cargaleiro and Martim Lapa.

Galleries

There are many reputable galleries in Portugal. There are galleries in the big hotels, but they do not necessarily show the country's best modern artists.

Commercial galleries

Galeria 111, Campo Grande 111–13, Lisbon. Tel. (01) 777418. The most well established.

Galeria de São Francisco, Rua Ivens 40, Lisbon. Tel. (01) 3463400. Shows a good selection of modern painters.

Galeria São Mamede, Rua da Escola Politécnica 161/75, Lisbon. Tel. (01) 673255/668691. Well known and reputable.

Galeria Comicos, 1-B Ten.Raul, Cascais, Lisbon. Tel. (01) 677794.

Galeria Quadrum, in the annexe to the Palácio Corucheus. Tel. (01) 779723.

Galeria A Janela Verde, Rua do Olival 9, Lisbon. Tel. (01) 600741.

Museum of Modern Art (Casa de Serralves), Rua de Serralves 977, Oporto. Holds temporary expositions of paintings, jewellery, photography and sculpture.

Exhibition galleries

The Almada Negreiros Gallery, Avenida da República 16, Lisbon, holds contemporary and retrospective exhibitions open to the public.

The Casino Estoril Gallery, in the central park in Estoril, holds exhibitions of modern Portuguese and other artists – often Brazilian.

The Centre of Contemporary Art in the grounds of the Gulbenkian Centre, with an entrance in Rua Marquês Sá da Bandeira, is the most important single collection of modern Portuguese art in the country. The exhibition is permanent, but the works are rearranged and rotated in order to display the large collection. It also has important foreign painting and sculpture.

The Gulbenkian Centre itself, in addition to its permanent museum collection, stages important art exhibitions. Entrance is from Avenida de Berna.

Portugal Today

To all outward appearances the Revolution is over – except for a few fading slogans and peeling posters on walls, but many things remain.

Freedom of speech

There is freedom of the press. You will see dozens of newspapers on the stands, far more than are needed; but then, after half a century of being muzzled, this is only to be expected. The problem is that many Portuguese interpret this freedom as meaning that while they are able to say what they like, others have no right to an opposing view. This makes cartoonists and comedians a bit wary, and you won't see any of the lampooning you see in Britain or the USA, for example.

Government

Portugal is a republic with a president and a national parliament elected by universal suffrage. The system is semi-presidential, with most governing power in the hands of the Prime Minister, who is appointed by the President taking into consideration the political composition of parliament. The President is elected for five years; members of parliament for four. The President can dissolve parliament and call elections if the situation warrants it. The Hondt proportional system made it extremely difficult for any political party to gain a majority until Social Democrat Cavaco Silva achieved it in 1987. All bills must go to the President for approval. He can veto them if they contravene the constitution.

1987 elections President Mário Soares

Socialist leader Mário Soares was elected President in 1987 with the votes of the Socialists and the Communists. Although the Communist Party does not like Mário Soares – in fact, they are enemies from way back – it told its comrades to vote for him because he was preferable to the very conservative Freitas do Amaral. Mário Soares spent a great amount of his campaign assuring his faithful that he was not soliciting the Communist vote, and he has spent a great deal of time since his election courting the moderates and the political right with an eye on 1991. When he was elected President, Mário Soares turned in his Socialist Party card and declared himself 'President of all the Portuguese'. He is running an open presidency, including an open palace at Belém where he holds concerts and other cultural events. He has several times moved his presidential seat to other towns to take it to the provinces and give the people there a look at how it operates. His first sortie was to Guimarães in the north where Portugal was first declared a nation under King Afonso Henriques. He is often seen with his wife at glittering galas among the rich and aristocratic. He travels constantly to Africa, the USA, the Soviet Union, France, Spain and so on. Mário Soares presents a striking contrast to his predecessor President Eanes, a taciturn man who had a sombre 'father' image. He was well respected, however, for his dedication to duty, his honesty and his self-abnegation.

President Soares was born in 1925. His father was a respected Republican who ran one of the most prestigious schools in Lisbon, which is still run by his family. At university, Mário Soares was a student leader who opposed the dictatorship. Several times he was jailed and exiled. He spent a great deal of time in exile on the island of São Tomé or in Paris. When he arrived back in Lisbon just after the Revolution in a train from Paris, an enormous, jubilant crowd was waiting for him at the station. A friendly, open man with few pretensions, he still lives in his modest flat by his school and only uses the Palace at Belém as an office and for entertaining. His wife, Maria Barroso, is a cultured woman whom he met at university and who ran the school while he was in exile. They have a son and a daughter and three grandchildren.

Cavaco Silva   The Prime Minister, Cavaco Silva, was born of a poor family in the Algarve at Loulé in 1939. A hard-working, conscientious man, he took his degree in economics and finance at the Higher Institute of Technology in Lisbon, where he became an assistant professor. In 1971 he went to England to study economics at York University under Professor Alan Peacock, obtaining his doctorate in 1974. In December 1975 he became professor of economics at the Catholic University in Lisbon. He joined the Social Democrat Party, becoming Minister of Finance in 1980 in Sá Carneiro's government. He gained complete control of the party after squabbling among the other leaders threatened to weaken the party. He is extremely dedicated and expects those around him to be the same. He is a supporter of an open market economy and of private industry, but is not above being pragmatic when necessary. He won the 50.22 per cent of the vote that the Social Democrats obtained in the June 1987 elections almost singlehandedly by his tireless campaigning. A shy man off the podium, he turns into a dynamic force the moment he takes the spotlight.

Political parties   There are five main political parties in Portugal. The right-of-centre Social Democrats were elected with 50.22 per cent of the vote in 1987 and will remain in power for four years with their leader Aníbal Cavaco Silva as Prime Minister. The party was founded in 1974 by Francisco Sá Carneiro (who was killed in a plane crash), Francisco Pinto Balsemão (who plays a very small part) and Magalhães Mota (who has now left the party).

The middle-of-the-road Socialists are the second largest party, obtaining 22.4 per cent of the vote in 1987, having dropped from first place after the Revolution. They recuperated in 1989 during the country's municipal elections. After an 'historic compromise' with the Communists, the Socialists and the Communists elected Socialist leader Jorge Sampaio Mayor of Lisbon. The party was founded in 1973 in West Germany by Mário Soares, the current President, who was in exile at the time.

The Democratic Renewal Party, which obtained only 4.91 per cent of the vote in 1987, was founded in 1985 by the followers of former President Ramalho Eanes, who counted on his popularity to pull down a large vote. They failed to do so.

The Communists, who, with the small Greens Party, polled 12.14 per cent of the vote in 1987, was founded long before the 1974 Revolution under the leadership of Álvaro Cunhal, a lawyer who spent many years of his life keeping a low political profile in the Alentejo or in the prisons of the secret police or in exile in the Communist Bloc countries. The party – usually considered the most hard-line in Europe – has been having considerable trouble adjusting to *perestroika*. It has split into several factions, closed its newspaper, *O Diario*, and chosen a younger man to succeed Cunhal (now in his late seventies) when he steps down.

The Christian Democrats, bastion of the hard-line right-wingers, dropped to a poor 4.44 per cent in the 1987 election. The party was founded in 1974 under the leadership of Diogo Freitas do Amaral, and was affiliated with the European Christian Democrats.

There have been strong indications that the ultra-right is gaining force in Portugal through the New Monarchist Party, closely allied to the National Front of Jean-Marie Le Pen in France. There have been several violent incidents with 'skinheads' in Lisbon and Oporto.

Economy

Portugal has been on the brink of economic disaster several times since the 1974 Revolution. It was hard hit by the oil crises and the rising dollar. Its foreign debt reached seventeen billion dollars and its balance of payments deficit three billion. Inflation galloped along at 30 per cent for years, though this has now dropped to 13 per cent and austerity measures have reduced the balance of payments deficit.

Poverty

However, there is still a lot of poverty and the gap between rich and poor is growing alarmingly. On the outskirts of every big town you will see shanty towns, where many people still live without mains water or sewers. Many farms are subsistence level and are worked only by old people as the young have fled to the cities seeking a better life, but many times find they must turn to crime or prostitution to survive. Old-age pensions are around 10,000 esc. per month – in a country where hamburger costs 1,200 esc. per kilo.

Wealth

In contrast, the rich who fled the Revolution are now back and flaunting their wealth. The aristocrats have taken to using their titles again. The middle classes have been hard hit by rising prices, taxes and rents. Only a few Portuguese can afford holidays.

The family

About the only thing that saves the middle classes and the poor is the family. Although it is falling to pieces fast, thanks to the influence of movies, TV, drugs and independence learned from abroad by young people, the family still remains a fairly solid institution in Portugal. Several generations live together, taking care of each other and sharing costs and duties. Old people usually live with the family and are taken care of. Young people live at home until they marry – and often after that, because of the dearth of cheap housing.

Women

Before the Revolution, a woman had very few rights in Portugal. Her husband got all of her possessions when she married unless a special dispensation was signed. He could open her mail, prevent her from taking their children out of the country without his permission and even kill her almost with impunity if he caught her committing adultery. And you would have been surprised by how many apparently well-educated men clung to this old order.

Immediately after the Revolution, this all changed – at least on the law books. Portugal has a new civil code giving rights to women that would put most other so-called advanced countries to shame. Women, according to the law, have absolute equality with men. They can become judges, join the police force, travel anywhere they like, have control over their children, buy property and so on. Parliament approved a law permitting abortion if a mother's life is in danger, or in case of rape, or if the child would be born defective. Of course, the laws will probably not reach the countryside for several generations. You still see women carrying enormous loads on their heads while their men walk along carrying nothing or you will see the man riding along on a donkey with the woman walking behind.

A women's liberation movement was started after the Revolution by a group of professional women, artists and writers, but they had little effect because the leftists considered them to be bourgeois dilettantes. The women who really made an impression were those in the trade unions. But even now, most women in Portugal earn less than a man doing the same job.

Crime

Crime, especially assaults with deadly weapons and petty crime, has risen alarmingly in Portugal since the Revolution. Many weapons were distributed to the population after the Revolution. Many of the 200,000 soldiers in the African wars brought their weapons home with them and knew how to use them. The police were too cowed by the Revolution and the open hostility of the populace to take much action, but now they are making up for this with renewed aggressiveness. Portugal also became wide open to drug smugglers because of the lack of police control, and thus it became a distribution centre for drugs. The high unemployment, at 10 per cent, made theft and prostitution commonplace. Crime rose in tourist areas, but the authorities have taken measures to bring it under control. You will be safer on city streets in Portugal than in most other countries.

Birthrate The birthrate is falling in Portugal, for several reasons: people get married later; there is a lack of housing; contraceptives are easy to get, whereas before the Revolution they were unavailable; husbands and wives now both work; the cost of living is so high that many young couples can't afford one child – much less two or three.

Homosexuality and unmarried couples The attitude towards homosexuals in Portugal is fairly tolerant, and little attention is paid to them unless they make themselves too obvious. However, there has been a rather large campaign about AIDS in Portugal which may have had some effect on this tolerance. There are gay bars, especially in Lisbon.

More and more couples live together without getting married, often in the house of the parents of one or the other. There is no stigma attached to it. Unmarried couples also lived together before the Revolution, because in those days there was virtually no divorce.

Women travelling alone Women travelling alone are not likely to come to harm in Portugal. If they are fairly good-looking or young, they may be bothered by men in the street making remarks, but unless they show interest, it probably won't be taken any further than that. There are many women who are doctors, journalists, policewomen, secretaries, or in public relations and other professions. They encounter few problems when travelling around, though the usual warnings about the danger of being robbed and keeping your car doors locked should be heeded.

NATO Portugal has been a member of NATO since it began. There are NATO bases in Portugal and in the Azores and Porto Santo. The US Air Force uses Lajes Airbase in the Azores for fuelling purposes. The airbase in Beja in the Alentejo is used by the West Germans.

The Portuguese are reviewing their military aims in view of what has happened in the Eastern Block countries.

Off the farm The big cities have become overcrowded, as you will notice if you try to walk through the streets during shopping hours. People have moved off the farms and into the cities because television and films have made them bored with country life. They also believe they can make more money in the city, which is usually not true. This exodus from the farms, especially in the north, has created a severe shortage of food. Portugal now imports 60 per cent of all its foodstuffs, causing a big drain on foreign exchange.

Nuclear A hot question in Portugal is whether or not to go nuclear. Portugal does not have any nuclear plants and must rely on hydroelectricity, oil-powered generators or energy imported from France. Opposers point out that Portugal is earthquake-prone and that the plants would pollute the rivers or the sea. Supporters see nuclear power as a way to save money. Portugal imports all of its crude oil, but does have large uranium deposits.

EEC Portugal joined the EEC in 1986, hoping to receive benefits to help its backward agriculture and to build up much-needed infrastructures – and also hoping that the competition would light a fire under the traditionally slow and overprotected Portuguese private industries and get them moving towards the modern age. Some good signs are already apparent. Farmers are seeking loans and putting in new crops. New roads are being built, including a highway in 1991 between Oporto and the Spanish border. The stock market has enjoyed a mini-boom, with new companies every day putting their shares on the market. Foreign companies are flocking in to invest, with the amount of investment doubling every year. Other effects are not so good. Portugal is in danger of being flooded with a deluge of Spanish products while it hasn't much to compete with on the Spanish market. Portugal's banking and financial sector is in danger of being overwhelmed by the giants of northern Europe. It is also concerned that the opening up of Eastern Europe will deflect EC funds and investment away from Portugal. To console themselves, the Portuguese can now buy whisky at a third of the price it was before joining.

Wine consumption

The Portuguese tend to enjoy their own good wine a little too much. The country has the highest wine consumption per capita in Europe, with people starting drinking when they are just children.

Standard of living

Appearances are deceptive when it comes to the way people live in Portugal. Shanty towns comprising houses made out of boards and bits of tin and some broken cement blocks certainly exist, but most families living there have colour televisions and many have cars. There is also a black market that accounts for about 25 per cent of the total economy, with people dealing in contraband and moonlighting for which they pay no taxes. They tend to flash their money around.

The minimum wage is currently 35,000 esc. per month with extra payments at Christmas and in summer. Each worker is entitled to a month's holiday a year and many long weekends, holy days and national days. Most people, however, earn an average of about 60,000 esc. per month – which is not much when you consider the cost of living. By comparison, in 1990 the President of Portugal earned 1.2 million esc. per month; the Prime Minister 643,000 esc. per month; the delegates 450,000 esc. per month. Even so, most families have someone who comes in every day or at least a few times a week to do some housework. That person will receive perhaps 350 esc. an hour.

All workers are covered by the social security system. They and their employers each contribute a sum each month which entitles them to free medical treatment and reduced prices on medicines. They have the right to retire at sixty-five, but the retirement benefits are quite small. Taxes are among the highest in Europe.

Young people

Young people in Portugal have many genuine worries about the future – they and women have the highest unemployment rate in the country. The government started a job training programme for young people in 1987, but results have been patchy.

Useful phrases

Sunday	*Domingo*	Where is the	*Onde fica o posto*
Monday	*Segunda-feira*	Tourist Office?	*de turismo?*
Tuesday	*Terça-feira*	Where is/are …?	*Onde fica …?*
Wednesday	*Quarta-feira*	museum	*museu*
Thursday	*Quinta-feira*	church	*igreja*
Friday	*Sexta-feira*	cathedral	*catedral/sé*
Saturday	*Sábado*	convent	*convento*
January	*Janeiro*	monastery	*monasteiro*
February	*Fevereiro*	palace	*palácio*
March	*Março*	fortress	*fortaleza*
April	*Abril*	ruins	*ruínas*
May	*Maio*	statue	*estátua*
June	*Junho*	fountain	*fonte*
July	*Julho*	park	*parque*
August	*Agosto*	square	*praça*
September	*Setembro*	city centre	*centro da cidade*
October	*Outubro*	supermarket	*supermercado*
November	*Novembro*	chapel	*capela*
December	*Dezembro*	art gallery	*galeria de arte*
1	*um*	bank	*banco*
2	*dois*	Do you speak	*Fala Inglês?*
3	*três*	English?	
4	*quatro*	How much is it?	*Quanto custa?*
5	*cinco*	What is the	*Quanto custa*
6	*seis*	fare to …?	*ir até …?*
7	*sete*	Take me to …	*Leva-me para …*
8	*oito*	Stop here,	*Para aqui, faz*
9	*nove*	please	*favor*
10	*dez*	What time do	*A que horas é*
20	*vinte*	you open/	*que abre/*
30	*trinta*	close?	*fecha?*
40	*quarenta*	Could you	*Podia fazer o*
50	*cinquenta*	please call me	*favor de chamar*
60	*sessenta*	a doctor?	*um médico?*
70	*setenta*	Can I take	*Posso tirar*
80	*oitenta*	photographs	*fotografias*
90	*noventa*	in here?	*aqui?*
100	*cem*	Where are the	*Onde é a casa*
1000	*mil*	lavatories?	*de banho?*
what time is it?	*que horas são?*	I am lost	*Perdi-me*
today	*hoje*	The bill, please	*A conta, por favor*
tomorrow	*amanhã*	Could you	*Poida fazer o*
yesterday	*ontem*	please call an	*favor de chamar*
this morning	*hoje de manhã*	ambulance?	*ambulância?*
this afternoon	*esta tarde*	Do you have any	*Tem ingares*
tonight	*hoje a noite*	vacancies?	*vagos?*

The Weather and When to Go

There are great differences in climate between the north and the south, and because of the influence of the Atlantic Ocean there are variations in weather from one day to the next anywhere in the country. It is always worth packing a sweater as well as your swimming costume.

The north has an Atlantic climate tempered by the Gulf Stream. It is very rainy near the coast – sometimes even in summer – but never extremely cold. Oporto has an average annual temperature of 14.4°C/58°F. Further inland, beyond the mountains that separate the Minho region and the Trás-os-Montes region and those that range north and south cutting through the Beira region, the climate is dry and cold in the winter, with below-freezing temperatures, and snow. In summer it is dry and extremely hot, with temperatures soaring above 40°C/104°F. In protected valleys there are isolated pockets that have Mediterranean-type microclimates where almonds, figs and citrus fruits can be grown.

The centre of the country has a climate transitional between Atlantic and Mediterranean. In general it has hot, dry summers and mild, rainy winters, but its chief feature is its unpredictability. Summer might begin in May and extend through September and October before the rains begin, or February might be sunny and warm enough for the beach. It is a matter of chance. Lisbon has an average annual temperature of 16.6°C/62°F.

The south has a Mediterranean climate, with long, hot summers and short, mild winters with little rain. The interior of the Alentejo region south of Lisbon often has extremely hot summers. The Algarve, which benefits from the effects of winds blowing in from North Africa, is hot in summer, warm in winter and almost always sunny. The climate lends itself to year-round tourism. The average annual temperature in Faro is 17.8°C/63°F.

Travelling Around

By air

Portugal's TAP-Air Portugal and its subsidiary LAR were state-owned but are being sold to private companies. They have excellent records, but fares are not cheap. You can get a flight out of Lisbon to almost any point in the world and there are regular flights on LAR between Lisbon, Covilhã, Viseu, Oporto, Vila Real, Chaves and Bragança. There are flights to Oporto and Faro on regular TAP airline flights, but flights to other, more remote cities are made in smaller aircraft. There are also regular flights to Funchal and Porto Santo in Portugal's Madeira islands and to Ponta Delgada and Horta in the Azores. Air Atlantis, a TAP subsidiary, operates out of Faro with flights to Lisbon, Oporto and Funchal. Portugalia, a private Portuguese airline, began regular internal flights to Faro, Oporto, Funchal and other cities in 1990.

Airports   Lisbon Airport is spacious, with tourist shops, restaurants, bars and news-stands; Oporto Airport is cramped, with a tiny café and a cramped bar, while the airport in Faro is adequate. You can change money, hire cars, obtain tourist information and make hotel reservations at the airports.

There is no airport landing or exit tax in Portugal.

By boat

From being the greatest sailing nation in the world with ships that ventured where no other had dared to go, Portugal has declined to a state where most of its merchandise is carried in foreign freighters and, with a few exceptions, its fishing is done from antiquated boats, including rowing boats. Its last ferries to England and Morocco closed down in the 1970s. However, in 1989 the Lusitanian Ferries began operating a car ferry out of Faro to Algiers in Morocco.

Luxury cruises   There is a foreign-owned boat, the *Funchal*, with an all-Portuguese crew which operates luxury cruises from Lisbon to the Canary

Islands, Madeira, Sardinia, Venice, Dubrovnik, Sicily, Turkey, Greece and the Greek islands. The ship has a swimming pool, gambling, dancing and a lovely dining room with excellent food. For reservations contact Europeia, Agencia Turistica, Avenida da Liberdade 233, 1200 Lisbon. Tel. (01) 536121.

River cruises and ferries

There are short cruises on the River Tagus at Lisbon and some of the rivers in the north of the country. There are regular excursions down the River Tagus to Cascais which leave from the Praça do Comércio. Boats also leave Lisbon every few minutes from Praça do Comércio and Cais do Sodré to cross the river to the towns on the south bank. There are also car ferries at Cais do Sodré to cross the river and the cost is approximately the same as the bridge toll. The ferry from the fluvial station by the Praça de Afonso de Albuquerque in Belém will take you across the river to Porto Brandão, a small village with good fish and shellfish restaurants and a splendid view of Lisbon and its monuments.

Passenger and car ferries at Setúbal take you across the River Sado to the beaches and resorts on the Tróia peninsula (see page 312).

Tourist boats carry passengers for day-long sightseeing trips up the River Douro from Oporto, through the valley where the grapes for making port are grown, to the town of Peso da Régua.

There are also tourist boats on the River Lima at Viana do Castelo, on the Cávado at Fão and on the Nabonne near Tomar. Consult the Regional Tourist Offices, hotels or travel agencies for the times of departure.

Nearly every town on the Algarve coast from Monte Gordo to Lagos offers excursions by boat all along the coast to other towns for sightseeing, and to deserted beaches for cook-outs.

Fishing boats

You can hire boats for deep-sea fishing at Sesimbra on the Setúbal Peninsula and in the Algarve. Most beach resorts also have boats for hire.

By bus

The cheapest way to travel in Portugal is by bus, and the majority of Portuguese use this form of transport. There are buses to take you nearly everywhere in the country. Most of these belong to the state-owned Rodoviário Nacional, but many companies such as Mundial de Turismo run excursions by bus to all the interesting places.

Discounts

Tourists can obtain passes for travelling in the cities for a fixed length of time at lower rates. Passes can be obtained in Lisbon at the metro stations in Praça dos Restauradores, the Santa Justa Elevator and the Rotunda in Praça Marquês de Pombal (see page 248). These entitle you to travel anywhere within the city limits by bus, train, metro, elevator and boat.

Bus terminals

The Rodoviário Nacional bus terminal in Lisbon is at Casal de Ribeiro 18.

The terminal in Oporto is at Rua Alexandre Herculano 366.

The terminal in Faro is at Avenida Dom Infante Henriques 76.

By car

You will see more and be more independent if you use your own car or hire one when you arrive in Portugal. If you are travelling from Britain, you can put your car on a ferry to Santander in northern Spain and then drive across to Portugal. If you bring your own car, you will need ownership papers and a 'green card' from your insurance company. Foreign driving licences are valid for six months in Portugal.

Car hire

You will find car hire prices in Portugal very expensive compared with Britain and terribly expensive compared with the United States. It would be best to arrange a fly-and-drive deal in your own country before you arrive.

Roads

Except for 200 km of autostrada that will take you halfway to Oporto and leave you stranded on a narrow highway full of trucks or take you comfortably to Setúbal in the south for 30 km before ending, most of the roads in Portugal are not very good.

Drivers

The drivers in Portugal are worse than the roads. They appear to combine a penchant for excessive speed with slow reflexes. They stop on the road at night without lights and fail to post a warning – which is particularly unnerving if the vehicle happens to be a two-ton truck. They blithely pass on hills and curves. I once came around a curve on a hill to encounter a car reversing down my lane! Portuguese drivers will do a U-turn unexpectedly on a main road or stop suddenly to hail a friend. They continuously fail to heed the 'If you drink, don't drive' campaigns and take to the road after several bottles of wine. Very few cars observe the zebra crossings for pedestrians, so be careful if you're driving that you don't get rammed from the rear if you stop or, if you're a pedestrian, that you don't get run over. Don't expect helpful behaviour from bus and lorry drivers: they are among the worst offenders. They pull out in front of you from side streets as though you were invisible. Beware of pedestrians, too: they walk in the road.

Portugal has the highest accident rate in Europe. It is said that more people are killed on the roads in a year than died in Portugal's African war. Be particularly careful on the 'Marginal', which is the coastal road between Lisbon and Cascais. Some foreign residents who have moved away have received as leaving presents T-shirts that read 'Survivor of the Marginal'.

Traffic regulations

International traffic regulations apply in Portugal.

The speed limit in built-up areas is 60 km per hour; outside towns it is 90 km per hour unless specified otherwise; and it is 120 km per hour on motorways. When towing a caravan or trailer, the limits are 50 km per hour in town and 70 km outside town and on motorways.

Insurance

You must obtain a 'green card' from your insurance company before you leave home, as third-party insurance is compulsory in Portugal. If you have an accident you and the other driver must immediately exchange insurance company names and policy numbers. The accident must be reported to the police before you can make a claim.

Breakdowns and accidents

If you break down or have an accident which leaves your car on the road, you must immediately display a red triangle at least 50 m before the site.

Members of foreign automobile clubs have reciprocal rights with the Automovel Clube de Portugal (ACP), which has a twenty-four-hour assistance service (*pronto socorro*). Telephone the Lisbon number (01) 775402 and they will come and tow you away. All major towns have a towing service. Telephone 115 for an ambulance or the police.

Petrol stations

Portuguese petrol stations are not open all the time. This may cause you real problems if you are driving around at night and have forgotten to fill your tank. Some of them close as early as 8 p.m. while others close at midnight, and some also close on Sundays. All-night stations are few and far between even on the main roads. The north and south autostradas have only one each. There is usually one station on duty somewhere, but you have usually run out of petrol before you can find it. It is prudent therefore always to fill up before dark and on Saturdays.

'Super' petrol is 97 octane and costs about 150 esc. per litre. Some petrol stations sell lead-free petrol: ask for a list and map at one of the state-owned Galp petrol stations.

Hitch-hiking

Only young people hitch-hike in Portugal, and drivers are wary of picking anyone up. Girls should never hitch-hike alone.

By taxi

Taxis in Portugal are not state-owned: some are owned privately and others belong to co-operatives, which accounts for the fact that the cars are all different makes and vintages. All are painted black and trimmed in green, with two small green lights on the roof on either side of a sign reading 'Taxi'. The green lights do not indicate that the taxi is vacant; this is the case only when the 'Taxi' sign is lit up. Taxis are easy to find in most places, except at lunchtimes when all the drivers seem to take their lunchbreak at the same time. They are also scarce when it rains and during the evening rush hour.

Prices

Taxis are relatively cheap in Portugal, but the system for calculating out-of-town fares is a complicated one which can lead to your being cheated by an unscrupulous driver. Within the city limits the fare is registered on the meter; outside it is by kilometre. Ask at your hotel or travel agency what they think the approximate price of an out-of-town trip should cost before you go or ask to see the driver's table of prices per kilometre. You are charged about 75 esc. extra per bag. When tipping, it is customary to round off the fare to the nearest amount that approximates to 10 per cent.

By train

Trains in Portugal are state-owned by Caminhos de Ferro Portugueses (CP). Most of the lines are single track with many level crossings, some of which are manned and others not. Some of the trains are old, slow and rattly, but there are new express trains to Braga, Oporto, Lisbon and the Algarve.

Main lines and stations

It is possible to travel to most main towns in Portugal by train. The international trains to Spain and France have sleeping cars and compartments. Second class ticket holders may pay extra for a bed in a compartment for six people.

Some of the trains between Lisbon, Oporto and Faro have air-conditioned coaches, with bar and restaurant facilities. You can take your car with you on trains to these destinations. In the summer season you must arrive at the station at least an hour and a half before the departure time to load your car, or you will find that it is left behind to follow on the next train while you cool your heels at your destination.

The train from Lisbon to Faro leaves from Barreiros, across the River Tagus estuary at Lisbon. The price of your train ticket also includes the price of the boat ticket, and the river crossing takes about half an hour.

There are restaurants, bars and news-stands in the Lisbon Santa Apolónia station, but none in the Campanhã station in Oporto. The Oporto station is small and inconvenient, and you must leave your baggage to go across the street if you want anything to eat or drink.

Commuter trains

There are very good commuter trains between Lisbon and Cascais that run all day from 5.30 a.m. until 2 a.m. They are fast and efficient and a good way to avoid the 'Marginal' if you want to get to the beaches, casino, restaurants, Estoril and Cascais. They leave Lisbon from the Cais do Sodre station near the River Tagus. Frequent trains leave the Rossio station for Queluz and Sintra, and some go as far as Óbidos.

Tickets

Tickets are sold at stations or through travel agents, and you must have a valid ticket before boarding the train. If you board without a ticket, you are liable to a minimum fine of 1,250 esc. Round-trip tickets have limited validity, so check with your travel agent or the station. You can change the date of your ticket by paying a minimal charge if you do it in advance. If you make a reservation and fail to turn up, you will probably recoup only 50 per cent of your fare. On international and express trains, you must have your reservation confirmed and your ticket stamped before you board the train, so arrive well in advance of the departure time.

Children up to four years of age do not pay provided they do not occupy a seat; otherwise they pay the second class fare. Between the ages of four and twelve children pay 50 per cent of the adult fare.

Tourists may obtain special non-transferable tourist passes which allow them to travel at cheaper prices anywhere in the country for periods of one, two or three weeks. The holder must travel with proper identification at all times or will be deemed to be a passenger without a ticket. There are several other types of discount for families, students, old people and so on. Enquire at any station for more details.

Scenic trains

There are six basic sightseeing routes in the north. Except for one that goes south to Aveiro by the sea and over to Santa Comba Dão through the Serra do Caramulo mountains, they are all north of the River Douro and follow its tributaries through the mountains. Most of the routes have spectacular views.

The Douro Line

There are three trains that travel the Douro Line (*Linha do Douro*) each day, following the River Douro from Oporto to Pocinho in the spectacular port wine region. The whole trip takes roughly five hours, but if you like you can break the journey by stopping at Régua or somewhere else along the line. You can get sandwiches and drinks on the train. The train leaves the São Bento station in Oporto and climbs through rather unexciting country for about an hour and a half before it gets to the top of the mountain range. It passes through a long tunnel: and suddenly there below you is the River Douro.

The train goes down to water level and follows the river. The river has been tamed now by dams so that it no longer tumbles over rocks in a mad rush to the sea as it did until the middle of this century. The little wooden river boats called *rabelos* (they had a big rudder and a large, square sail) that used to carry the barrels of port through the rapids down to the warehouses of Oporto have been replaced by trains, but you can still see river boats in the inlets and see the narrow, man-made ledges on the granite mountainsides where boatmen used to walk to tow the *rabelos* by ropes back up the river.

For hours you see the steep granite and schist mountainsides that look like pyramids terraced and planted with the port vineyards, and the stately, imposing manor houses belonging to the famous port families – Ferreira, Croft, Warre, Guimarães, Sandeman, Taylor – standing high above the river, and the little farmhouses and villages encrusted on its banks. You will also see big empty spaces where vineyards were not replanted after the phylloxera plague of 1868. These are *mortorios* (vine cemeteries), about which there is a certain amount of uneasy superstition.

At the railway stations you will see big wine storehouses open under the eaves for ventilation. At the station in Pinhão, you will see tiles on the walls depicting the entire process of port-making from planting to shipping. There are more tiles at the Pocinho station. At Régua, you will see evidence of all the activities involved in storing, buying and shipping the wine down to Oporto.

As the river continues towards Spain, it gets wilder and narrower, with small whirlpools. Here the boatmen used cows to tow their boats back up-river. This part of the Douro is a wildlife preserve where rare birds, such as black storks, have been spotted. There are wild flowers such as the *esteba* (rock roses that give a special flavour to the honey of the Douro region), rosemary, lavender and heather. There are orange, olive, cork, almond and juniper trees. Red carp jump in the river. There are also many abandoned tiny villages and stone houses.

The Vouga Line
The train on the Vouga Line (*Linha do Vouga*) is as famous in Portugal as the Orient Express or the Chatanooga Choo-Choo are elsewhere. Songs have been dedicated to it, and a folk-dance group named after it. It has been threatened with extinction innumerable times by the train company because they consider it economically unviable, but has always been saved at the last minute by public outcry.

The train had steam engines until 1972, when sparks from an engine set off a huge fire that devastated a large area. After that diesel engines were substituted. The railway company will, however, organize an excursion using one of the old steam engines if a large group of tourists requests it – presumably it will also take precautions against fire.

Travelling along at a leisurely pace of 20 to 25 km an hour, just as it did when it first took to the tracks in 1908, the train leaves Aveiro on the coast and travels through rural countryside where you see tile-roofed houses and people working in the fields and vineyards to Sernada de Vouga, where it meets the River Vouga. From there, it climbs through pine and eucalyptus forests to Poço de Santiago, where it crosses a high bridge with a breathtaking view of little wooden river boats below.

There are many more bridges, many tunnels and many curves, but the views are spectacular, each like a painted landscape: granite hills, deep valleys and old houses with wooden *espigueiros* (small granite houses on stilts) for storing grain.

At Vouzela the trains are substituted by buses belonging to the train company. They follow the same route through the spa at Termas de São Pedro and across the green plateau to the ancient town of Viseu with its many monuments, churches and modern restaurants, hotels and other tourist accommodation.

Aveiro, where the Vouga Line begins, can be easily reached from

Oporto by a southbound train along the coast, or from Lisbon by a

The Minho northbound train.
Line

The Minho Line (*Linha do Minho*) goes from Oporto up the coast through Viana do Castelo to Caminha, where it turns east up the River Minho to Valença on the Spanish border. After it leaves Oporto it has the sea on the left, and it passes through little fishing villages with brightly painted boats and modern towns with many new hotels. There are some forts and small castles along the shore. On the right all the way there are fields of corn, vineyards and wooded hills.

After Caminha, you can see Spain on the other side of the river, on which are many little boats. Finally you come to the twelfth-century walled town of Valença, surrounded by a new town. There is an interesting railway museum in Valença.

The Tâmega The Tâmega Line (*Linha do Tâmega*) runs on a single track along
Line the River Tâmega from Livração on the Douro through the mountains to the beautiful city of Amarante, up through a landscape of pine forests, vineyards and old houses. Much of the countryside is green farming land. You will see many imposing, white-painted manor houses and neat towns with their churches and gardens. Amarante, on the River Tâmega, is an unspoiled oasis.

The Corgo The Corgo Line (*Linha do Corgo*) runs from the port wine town of
Line Régua on the River Douro north to Vila Real, the home of Mateus Rosé wine. It borders the deep gorge of the River Corgo where vineyards cover the mountainsides, and large mansions and old farmhouses can be seen in the distance. The beautiful city of Vila Real with its ancient monuments, churches, Roman ruins and the Solar de Mateus also has many modern hotels and restaurants.

The Tua Line The Tua Line (*Linha da Tua*) is without doubt the most picturesque of all the lines in Portugal. It has Wild West style wooden carriages with wooden seats and coal-fuelled engines – the only ones still running in the country. Needless to say, the train goes very slowly.

The line begins at Tua on the River Douro, and ends at Bragança, in the remote north-east corner of the country. The train passes through two mountain ranges on its four-hour journey. There is an
The Sabor excellent *pousada* in Bragança, and there are also several hotels.
Line

Private bus lines have replaced the trains on the Sabor Line, but the scenery through the unspoilt and remote mountains is still unforgettable, especially in the spring when the almond trees are in bloom. In Miranda on the River Douro overlooking Spain there is an excellent *pousada*.

Where to Stay

There is a wide variety of accommodation for the tourist in Portugal, but the number of beds available in some areas is very limited. You should book ahead whenever possible – especially in popular areas such as the Algarve, Lisbon and Cascais.

Hotels

Hotel prices are not controlled by the government. Each hotel is free to charge whatever the owner wishes, but competition means that prices in each area tend to be more or less the same for each category. A four star hotel in Lisbon will cost you a lot more than a similar hotel in the mountains in the north of the country.

Categories Hotels are classified by stars. The luxury hotel is five star and will have every comfort imaginable, with decanters of port in your room, fresh fruit and flowers, and other special details. The four star hotel is quite luxurious, but considerably cheaper. The three star hotel lacks many of the amenities of the four star type but isn't very much cheaper. My advice is to pay the slightly higher rate for the additional comforts offered by the four star hotels. Two stars indicate that the hotel is very simple, but usually clean and adequate; one star indicates spartan, but usually clean.

Pensions Pensions are usually comfortable, clean and cheap. They are ranked with one, two, three or four stars, but there can be a considerable difference between two pensions within the same category. It is also true that a three star pension can sometimes be better than a hotel with the same number of stars. It is a matter of luck. If you start looking early in the day, you can usually find a pension in the town of your choice without making a reservation in advance.

Prices At Easter, Christmas and New Year, prices for rooms in hotels, pensions and other accommodation are the same as in the high season. Prices away from Lisbon, Oporto and the Algarve tend to be less, and prices vary within each category. Rooms with private bathroom are more expensive than those without. Based on 1990 prices, accommodation can be roughly categorized as follows for a double room per night:

Luxury – between 45,000 esc. and 60,000 esc.
Expensive – between 30,000 esc. and 45,000 esc.
Medium – between 10,000 esc. and 30,000 esc.
Inexpensive – below 10,000 esc.

Pousadas   These are government-owned inns located in beauty spots all around the country. They are to be found in restored fortresses, old palaces and in modern purpose-built structures. Each reflects the character of its surrounding region, so you get a better feeling of the country than you would in a hotel. Many pousadas have limited room, so make reservations well in advance, either directly with the pousada or through ENATUR, Avenida Santa Joana Princesa 10, 1700 Lisbon. Tel. (01) 881221/889078; telex 13609 or 63475.

Apartment-hotels and villas

Apartment-hotels and villa complexes have become very popular in Portugal. They are built like big, modern hotels, but they offer accommodation on an apartment basis, including a kitchenette, instead of simply a bedroom in a hotel. All of the large resort areas, such as Tróia, Cascais, Viana do Castelo and towns in the Algarve have these tourist developments. Supermarkets, bars, discos, television rooms, restaurants, swimming pools and many other facilities are to be found within the complex, and the cost is about the same as for a room in a hotel offering similar facilities. It is best to book in advance, but sometimes you can find a place on the spur of the moment.

These tourist developments are ideal for people who prefer to organize mealtimes to suit themselves and lounge around on their own balcony rather than dress up and eat at a certain time in a communal dining room. They are also cheaper than hotels because you can do some of your own cooking, and food bought in the markets is incredibly cheap. Some of the apartments accommodate as many as ten people and have four or five bedrooms, baths, living rooms, terraces and kitchen, so they are excellent for families. Prices go down drastically in the low season.

Rural Tourism

For those who have always wanted to stay in a palace where a king has slept, or in a rustic farmhouse on a remote mountain, or work on a farm among nature, Rural Tourism is the thing. Under an ambitious government plan which provides funds to restore palaces and farmhouses and turn them into residences for tourists, much of the country's cultural heritage is being saved while, from the point of view of the tourist, providing interesting accommodation, often in areas where it might otherwise be difficult to find it. Staying in a manor house or on a farm will also give you the chance really to get to know Portuguese people. The owners provide breakfast and will usually provide meals if given sufficient advance notice – they are required to do so if there are no adequate restaurants nearby.

There are three types of Rural Tourism: *Turismo de Habitação* – elegant manor houses of great architectural or historical value; *Turismo Rural* – rustic houses in a town or out in the countryside; and farms where tourists can take part in the work of the farm.

There are three categories of manor house: *Paços*, a place where a king has slept; *Casa Antiga*, a house owned by the same family for at least 300 years; and *Quinta*, a country estate.

There are now more than 200 Rural Tourism accommodations around the country, predominantly in the north. Authorized houses display a metal plaque with the symbol TER. Prices range between 4,000 esc. for a double room in a rustic house and 20,000 esc. in the more prestigious manor houses, including breakfast. Many of the manor houses and others are listed in the 'Where to stay' sections of the Gazeteer.

It is advisable to book in advance, either directly through the owners, or through the three authorized Rural Tourism associations or through travel agencies. Payment for your stay might be requested in advance. It is a good idea to consult the Regional Tourist Office in whatever town the residence is located to obtain maps and directions as some of the houses are sometimes in out-of-the-way places and difficult to find. The Direcção-Geral do Turismo (National Tourism Office) published a 1990 edition of an official guide to the Rural Tourism houses in four languages, including English, with colour photos of some of the houses, maps, addresses and phone numbers and a description of facilities available – tennis, horse riding, hunting, fishing, swimming, etc.

Addresses TURIHAB – Associação de Turismo de Habitação, Praça da República, 4990 Ponte de Lima. Tel. (058) 942729; telex 32618 PTPL; fax (058) 941864.

ACT – Associação das Casas em Turismo, Alto da Pampilheira Torre D-2, 3°A, 2750 Cascais. Tel. (01) 2842901/2844464.

PRIVATUR – Associação Portuguesa de Turismo de Habitação, Rua Castilho, 209 1°Ft., 1000 Lisbon. Tel. (01) 654953 or 2868232.

Camping

Portugal has some of the best camp sites in Europe. There are more than 175 around the country, located near large cities, by the beaches, on the shores of lakes and lagoons, and in the mountains. The ones beside the beaches near Lisbon and on the Algarve can become crowded in the summer.

Most of the camp sites have restaurants, supermarkets, banks, swimming pools, bars and newspaper shops, and some have discos, saunas, indoor sports facilities and travel agencies which will organize local tours and transportation for you.

The Lisbon Municipal Camp Site in Monsanto Park (Tel. [01] 704413) is large, hilly and covered with trees. It is a four star site open throughout the year and situated just ten minutes from Lisbon. It has swimming pools, tennis courts, football pitches, a restaurant, bank, post office, automatic washing machines, hot showers and other amenities. It covers several hectares so it is never very crowded.

Prices vary according to the category of camp site, and you can obtain a discount if you have an International Camping Card. Prices in a four-star site in high season will be about 250 esc. per adult; 165 esc. for a car; between 250 and 650 esc. for a caravan, depending on the size; and 200 esc. for electricity and water, plus eight per cent value added tax. In the low season, prices are reduced by two-thirds.

You must leave your passport or some form of identification at the camp site office. Be advised that you should never leave valuables in your tent, even though the camp sites are fenced in and often patrolled by security men with two-way radios.

A complete list of camp sites with a map is available from the Tourist Office.

Spas

Portugal has more than forty-five spas all over the north of the country and in the Algarve mountains, and many of these feature turn-of-the-century hotels dripping with chandeliers, statuary and marble staircases. Others, like that at Chaves, have modern hotels with all kinds of facilities for taking water cures, and doctors and nurses in attendance. The spas are in restful surroundings, with trees and lakes, and some offer facilities such as golf, tennis and riding. Their advertisements claim that they will cure problems associated with the liver, circulation, respiration and other assorted ailments.

There are spas in: Fonte de Monfortinho, Termas de Monte Real, Vimeiro, Caldas da Rainha, Caldas de Gerês, Chaves, Luso, Piedade, São Pedro do Sul, Vizela, Caldas de Monchique, Cúria, Caldelas, Felgueira, Pedras Salgadas, Caldas de São Jorge, Vidago, Termas dos Cucos, Termas de São Vicente. For a complete list of spas and a detailed description of each, ask the Tourist Office for a brochure.

Eating and Drinking

Portugal has not just one national dish – like *paella* in Spain or *mousaka* in Greece – but each region has its own specialities. You will find mountain trout in the Serra da Estrela, lobster on the seacoast, steamed clams in the Algarve, pork and clams in the Alentejo, grilled steaks and cured ham in Trás-os-Montes, and *caldo verde* (shredded cabbage soup) in the Minho, for example. In the cities there are also a great number of Chinese, African, French, Italian and Brazilian restaurants.

The Portuguese love their food. To them a good table (*boa mesa*) is very important, and the majority of housewives still have time to spend hours each day buying and preparing food for their families. Portuguese restaurants have not yet succumbed to serving only what they consider to be universal tourist fare (the inevitable veal chop and french fries, or some kind of pasta), as has happened in so many different countries. They still have a large variety of typical Portuguese dishes on the menu along with international ones. And you can still find so many different dishes that you will have difficulty choosing.

The Portuguese are better at preparing the fish with which the country abounds than they are at preparing meat, though now some of the cheaper – and not so cheap – restaurants serve fish that has been frozen. Dried cod is the basis of many famous Portuguese dishes – *bacalhau Gomes de Sá* , for example. This is a baked dish of sliced potatoes, shredded cod, onions, olives and hard-boiled eggs and a bit of olive oil.

Restaurants

Restaurants range from the very luxurious to the spartan. Service is usually very good except at overcrowded beach resorts where harassed waiters will tend to ignore you. Some waiters at the outdoor restaurants and cafés in Lisbon tend to do the same. Don't worry that you have become invisible – the waiter simply doesn't want to see you.

Most menus are translated into several languages – apparently by the owner's cousin who has spent only two weeks abroad.

By law, each restaurant must offer a tourist menu of good quality at a fixed price.

Opening hours

Restaurants are normally open from 12 noon to 3 p.m. for lunch and from 7 p.m. to 10 p.m. for dinner, though some stay open much later. There is really no fixed rule. You can always get a meal in a restaurant in one of the shopping centres, but don't expect the restaurants along the roads in the hinterlands to be very good.

Afternoon snacks

The Portuguese usually have a snack at about 4 p.m., sometimes sitting down in the pastry shops (*pastelarias*) or standing up at coffee counters. The snack may consist of meat or cod croquettes, savoury pastries filled with meat, shrimp or chicken, cold fried fish, cold breaded pork, or sweet pastries.

Prices

Prices tend to be much higher in restaurants in the Algarve than in Lisbon. Oporto restaurants charge somewhat less than those in Lisbon, and prices in the small towns in the north are lower still. You may find that the food served in the *fado* houses which cater to tourists is not very good, but is very expensive.

Average prices for a Lisbon restaurant would be approximately the following, providing you stay away from seafood and pricey wines. However, prices go up constantly so it is difficult to give an exact price for a meal in any restaurant.

Expensive

A meal in one of the best restaurants will cost around 5,500 esc. or more with entree, main course, dessert, wine and coffee.

Medium price

A good, but not so luxurious restaurant will charge you about 3,000 esc. or more. This is the category into which most restaurants fall. The food is very good, the waiters are pleasant, but you will not find elaborately decorated dishes.

Inexpensive

You can eat well in the less elaborate restaurants for about 1,500 esc. or more. Most of these have a menu of the day (*ementa do dia*) with a fixed price.

Your bill will go up to astronomical proportions if you order lobster in any of the restaurants and quite high if you choose some of the best vintage wines. A bottle of red or white table wine will cost between 1,000 and 4,000 esc. depending on quality. Always try the wines and food of the region you are visiting: this is what the local people do best, so it's a good way to get the real flavour of the country. The waiter will always be glad to explain what each dish on the menu is.

Food and drink

Regional dishes

Dishes differ very much from region to region. In the mountain areas in the north, the typical dishes tend to be rather heavy, as they depend mainly on pork, sausages, cured ham and beans. Portions are so generous in restaurants in the north that it may be wise to order two portions for three people. In the south and near the coast, dishes depend more on fish, beef and vegetables and the portions are smaller.

Regional dishes and their descriptions can be found in the Gazetteer under the 'What to eat' heading.

Cheeses

Portugal has a number of good cheeses, though virtually no blue cheeses of the Roquefort or Stilton type. Their best-known cheese, *queijo da Serra*, comes from the mountain farms of the Serra da Estrela in the Beira region. It is a round cheese with a soft, creamy centre, but is also sometimes left to dry and cure. It is commonly among the cheeses offered after dinner in restaurants.

The Serpa cheese from the Alentejo is similar to the Serra, with a soft, creamy centre, but it is smaller in size and not as widely available. Probably the finest cheese of this type comes from Azeitão on the Arrábida Peninsula south of Lisbon, but Azeitão cheese is produced in such small quantities that it is not always available and, when you can get it, it is very expensive.

The Alentejo has many different small cheeses that are served as appetizers. Some are fresh, white cheeses eaten before meals with a dash of pepper, and bread. Some of these cheeses are cured and served in little slices; others are preserved in brine, so they are very salty. They are good to eat with drinks. Most of these small cheeses were in the past made with goat's milk, but now most are made with pasteurized sheep's milk.

The only good native cow's milk cheese comes from the Azores in the mid-Atlantic. It is a Cheddar-like cheese called Ilha São Jorge, and is excellent when properly matured. Do not buy Ilha in a plastic wrap: demand it be sliced from the enormous round cheese.

Wine

Portuguese table wines are one of the best kept secrets in Europe. All the world has heard of port and madeira, but very few know of the good red and white wines. The Portuguese do not as a rule drink their own rosés which are so popular in other countries. These wines are almost exclusively for export and for visiting tourists. However, there are many demarcated areas for the red and white table wines such as Bucelas, Dão, Bairrada, Colares, Algarve, Carravelos, Douro and Setúbal. There are other non-demarcated areas which also have good wines.

The *vinho verde* wines are coming into their own. Individual growers are producing their own estate wines with individual characteristics, the best of which are arguably Palácio da Brejoeira and Casa da Bouça. *Vinho verde* is produced in both white and red varieties, but the whites are better and they are best drunk within the first two years after they are bottled. *Vinho verde* is good when drunk cold with fish or shellfish in the summertime. (See also pages 68–9.)

The port wines are produced by the established companies that have been making them on the Douro and shipping them from Oporto for centuries. The white, dry ports are now being promoted as aperitifs, while the tawnies are usually drunk after dinner and the rubies perhaps in the afternoon. Again, it is mainly foreigners who drink port wines (see pages 111–13). You can taste and buy them at the Port Wine Institute at the top of the Gloria Elevator which goes from the Praça dos Restauradores in Lisbon, and the Port Wine Institute bar in Oporto.

The Portuguese also produce sparkling wines (*vinhos espumantes*), the best known of which is Raposeira. They range from sweet to very dry, and in some parts of the country take the place of champagne at weddings, baptisms and other celebrations.

Portuguese brandies are not especially distinguished, but there are some fine *aguardentes* which, when matured long enough, are similar to cognac style brandies. They are called *aguardentes velhas*. The most popular spirit, however, is the humble *bagaço*, a clear spirit distilled from the lees of wine, which is drunk new.

The Moscatels from the Setúbal Peninsula are made from muscatel grapes. There is a very good one produced by the old company of José Maria de Fonseca in Azeitão. Liqueurs such as Medronho, made from small red berries grown in the Algarve, and Amêndoa Amarga, made from bitter almonds, must be well chilled.

Most of the wineries welcome visits by tourists who come to see the barrels and bottles, taste the different wines, and perhaps buy some to take home.

Entertainment

Bullfights The Portuguese bullfight is very different from the Spanish one. First of all, they don't kill the bull. Secondly, most of the fighting is done on horseback. Thirdly, the most popular part of the fight is when the *forcados* come out and wrestle the bull to the ground with their bare hands. The bull then leaves the ring alive, escorted by a herd of oxen. Sometimes he is reluctant to go, as though he had enjoyed his skirmishes with men and other beasts. That brings great cheering and whistles from the crowd. By the time the oxen finally get the bull out of the ring, you may have forgotten what the fighters and *forcados* did as they come back to take their turn around the ring to receive acclaim and tossed hats or flowers.

Bullfights began in the 1600s. It was a pastime of the aristocracy, who fought by ancient rules of honour and chivalry. The fighting was done from horseback and, with a few exceptions, this has continued in Portugal. Most bullfighters in Portugal wear eighteenth century style costume. The horsemen are called *cavaleiros* and are mounted on magnificent horses that perform intricate steps as they evade the bull and run enticingly before it. The *cavaleiro* makes a daring swoop and places a dart from which a little flag unfurls in the neck of the bull. This is done several times.

The men who fight on foot are called *toureiros*. They engage the bull first of all with a cape, with which they make many complicated passes. Then they pretend to fight and kill it with a sword, but only in very rare cases has any killing taken place – and then the bullfighter would be heavily fined.

When the *cavaleiro* or *toureiro* has finished with the bull, the *forcados* jump over the barrier into the ring. There are eight of them dressed in brown pants, white leggings, cumberbunds, white shirts, brown vests and tasselled stocking caps. They originated with the servants of the aristocrats who were usually allowed a bit of sport with the bull after the nobles had finished. They stand confronting the bull from across the ring in a line of eight, one behind the other. The head man shouts taunts at the bull until it charges, then he jumps over its horns and grabs it around its neck, often being twirled around in the air. The others jump on the bull and one grabs it by the tail. They wrestle it to the ground and then with a flourish allow it to get up before they disperse and jump back over the barrier. Some *forcados* get very battered and end up with broken bones.

In Portugal the men rather than the bull get the worst of the fight. These men are amateurs who belong to *forcado* clubs and are not paid for their performance, but do it for glory and the sport of it. One of the most famous groups is that which was founded in Lisbon by Nuno Salvação Barretta, once a famous *forcado* himself. (Sadly, Sr. Barretta died this year.) Other famous groups are from Santarém and Vila Franca de Xira.

Famous *cavaleiros* such as João Moura, Paulo Caetano and Ribeiro Telles have large stables of valuable well trained thoroughbred horses and large herds of fighting bulls on their estates in the Alentejo.

Fairs and festivals

There are fairs and festivals going on all over Portugal throughout the year. In the summer you can hardly drive 10 km without coming across a village decked out in flowers, streamers and lights with music blaring and people in costume dancing in the streets.

For more details, see page 58 and also the Calendar of Festivals on pages 58-61.

Nightlife

Even though each little village has its pub and disco, there is not a great deal of entertainment outside the cities and the beach resorts. Nightlife is centred in Lisbon, Cascais and the Algarve. Lisbon is alive with all sorts of new entertainment: discos have opened with exotic names such as Bananas, Coconuts and Afrodite, there are African nightclubs where you can dance to drums all night, and restaurants including Timorese, Chinese, Mexican, Italian, Spanish and French among many other nationalities. Brazilian music blares everywhere.

The Bairro Alto district in Lisbon, with its old, winding streets, is full of tascas, taverns, pubs and restaurants where you can find some form of entertainment almost any night of the week. Don't expect the centre of Lisbon around Rossio and Praça dos Restauradores to be alive and full of people at night: it isn't. It is virtually deserted after the shops and offices close, and you must go to the Bairro Alto or to Cascais for a lively atmosphere.

In the summer the Algarve is jumping. There are people in the pubs and open air cafés almost all night long.

Casinos

There are casinos in Alvor, Monte Gordo and Vilamoura in the Algarve; Figueira da Foz near Coimbra; Póvoa de Varzim north of Oporto, and the one in Estoril near Lisbon which was recently redecorated and has an excellent luxury restaurant and floor show. Visitors must present their passports to enter. The casinos are controlled by the government and are well run, often with modern art and other exhibits in their lobbies.

Fado

Fado is the traditional music of Portugal, although each region has its own particular folk music. *Fado* is a wailing lament sung to the accompaniment of special guitars. Its theme is usually unrequited love, but the songs often extol the virtues of their region, or tell of experiences in life.

There are two kinds of *fado*: Lisbon and Coimbra. The Coimbra *fado* is somewhat lighter and more melodic than its Lisbon counterpart and is sung only by men and on special occasions. Authentic Coimbra *fado* is not sung by professionals in public. It originated with the Coimbra University students who for centuries serenaded their girls under their verandas or who gathered on the steps of the Old Cathedral under the university to sing at special ceremonies. The *Balada da Despedida* (Farewell Ballad), sung at graduation, and the *Balada de Coimbra* (Coimbra Ballad), which closes all ceremonies, have become classics. Lisbon *fado* is sung by both men and women, usually in black and draped in shawls. The most famous woman *fado* singer of all time is the internationally known Amalia Rodrigues, who celebrated her fiftieth year as an entertainer in 1990.

Fado has its aficionados who take it very seriously indeed and frequent the *fado* houses every night to hear their favourite singers. There are even some judges, lawyers, doctors and others who take their own *fado* singing almost as seriously as they take their professions. Listeners sit in rapt attention to absorb every word and throb of the music. If you want to hear authentic *fado*, go to one of the good, serious *fado* houses such as Senhor Vinho in Lisbon. But be warned: do not utter a sound while the singing is going on, or you can expect serious fans to get very angry. Many of the fans also fancy themselves as *fado* singers and will join in the performance. In many *fado* bars it is only the customers who do the singing. You won't understand a word, but it is interesting to watch.

If you are a person who likes to talk while you eat or just want music as a background, you will be happier at one of the *fado* houses that cater to tourists, where there is also folk dancing which you may be invited to join. Adega de Machado would be a good place for that kind of evening.

The singing does not start until about 11 p.m. so, unless you are having dinner there too, don't go before then. You can have dinner in the *fado* houses, but some of them are more famous for their music than their food. Senhor Vinho is an exception.

Cultural events

There are many cultural events you might like to attend. The Gulbenkian Foundation in Lisbon offers concerts, ballet, and performances by individual artists. For more details, obtain a programme at the Gulbenkian (see page 259).

In the summer, there is a festival of classical music in the palaces and gardens in Sintra at which internationally famous musicians and orchestras perform. Inquire for dates and the programme at the Sintra Tourist Office (see page 231).

There are rock concerts, international folk music festivals, handicraft fairs and art exhibitions throughout the country. Inquire at any Tourist Office for more details.

Sport

Portugal is a great country for sports because its year-round good climate makes it possible to play every day. Many international professional sports teams train in the winter in Portugal. There are golf

Golf   courses in the Algarve, Lisbon, Espinho and Cascais designed by such famous men as Frank Pennink, Henry Cotton and Robert Trent Jones, and international golf tournaments are held each year in the Algarve.

Fishing   There is line fishing on all the rivers and by the sea. You can rent boats on the Algarve and at Sesimbra near Lisbon for deep-sea fishing.

Tennis   All-year-round tennis is being sponsored on the Algarve, and there are dozens of tennis courts – many covered and climatized – for amateurs and professionals alike in the region and elsewhere.

Squash   Indoor squash has become popular at the tourist resorts and hotels, with many good courts.

Water sports   All the beaches offer excellent opportunities for all kinds of water sports – water-skiing, windsurfing, sailing and parascending – with equipment available for rental.

Walking   Walking tours have been mapped out in Sintra, the Algarve, Gerês Park, Serra da Estrela, the Arrábida Peninsula and other regions, with books and maps available at the Tourist Offices.

Hunting   Horse riding and hunting have become very popular. The Tourist Offices also have a publication describing the different zones available for hunting and describing the game to be found there, along with the rules of the hunt and the dates of the open seasons.

Spectator sports   For those who enjoy spectator sports, Portugal offers world-class motor car racing at the Formula I track in Cascais and several soccer teams – Benfica, Sporting and the Belenenses in Lisbon and the Futbol Clube de Porto – which have several times won the European Cup.

Shopping

Portugal represents a bargain for a number of items. Gold and silver ware and jewellery are particularly good buys because the fine craftsmanship that goes into them is cheaper in Portugal than elsewhere. The gold and silver content of the pieces is strictly controlled so one is assured of buying the real thing. You will find reputable jewellers in hotels and even at the airports, but in Lisbon they are concentrated in the Rua do Ouro (Street of Gold) and Rua da Prata (Street of Silver).

Paintings by modern Portuguese artists and tapestries designed by Portugal's leading artists are a good investment. Sculpture, for centuries regarded simply as decoration for a church, monastery or garden and solidly traditional in material and design, has come into its own in Portugal in the late twentieth century. João Cutileiro has an *atelier* in Évora where he works with students. A graduate of the Slade in London, he is the best known sculptor in Portugal today. There are also some good surrealistic pieces around by Jorge Vieira.

The much-sought-after Arraiolos rugs are much, much cheaper in Portugal than elsewhere. Price for a genuine Arraiolos is about 25,000 esc. per sq. metre, or you can purchase the materials and a pattern and make one yourself.

Ceramics have been a Portuguese artistic forte for centuries. The most famous ceramics are, of course, the Vista Alegre, hand-painted porcelain from the Vista Alegre factory founded near Aveiro in 1824. The ceramics and pottery of Caldas da Rainha are also good buys.

Hand-embroidered linen from Madeira is beautiful and a good buy, but be sure to look for the little metal seal that shows it is the genuine article. Cheap copies are flooding the market from the Far East.

Fine crystal and glass are on display in shops in the big cities. The most famous factory is that formerly belonging to the Stephens brothers.

Basketwork, fishermen's sweaters, rag-rugs, clothes, shoes, purses and other leather goods are excellent buys. Copper bowls and kettles and the *cataplanas* (seashell-shaped steamers) are both lovely and practical.

If you want something really different, you can always buy hand-carved toothpicks, or a marvellous marble fireplace or even a brightly painted yoke for oxen that makes an amusing headboard for a bed.

General Basics

Clothing

Bear in mind that it can get very chilly in Portugal after the sun goes down, so it is wise to pack a sweater. Late autumn to spring are usually quite cool and wet, so pack heavy clothes, raincoat and an umbrella.

The Portuguese are very tolerant about what you wear. Shorts and other holiday clothes are acceptable even in city streets, but the countryside in the far north might be a bit more conservative. Bikinis are worn at all the beaches and pools and topless sunbathing is quite common, even in some parts of the conservative north. Nude bathing is technically illegal in Portugal, but there are a few beaches where nudism is tacitly accepted.

Cultural organizations

The American Cultural Centre, Avenida Duque de Loulé 22-B, Lisbon. Tel. (01) 570102. This has a library with 7,000 volumes, 130 periodicals and 1,000 pamphlets. It is open every day from 2 p.m. to 6 p.m. except at weekends.

The British Institute Library, Rua Luis Fernandes 3, Lisbon. Tel. (01) 369208. This has an excellent library and reading room. It is open daily, except Wednesday mornings.

Currency and currency regulations

The unit of currency is the escudo (esc.). There are coins in circulation of 1, 2.5, 5, 10, 20, 50 and 100 escudos, and banknotes of 500, 1,000, 5,000 and 10,000 escudos.

It is very difficult to change money outside banking hours (see page 63). If you change money at your hotel you will not get a good exchange rate such as you would at a bank. It is such a problem to change money that you would think Portugal didn't need it.

If you make a declaration of the amount of money you are bringing into the country when you arrive, you are allowed to take the same amount of foreign currency out of the country. Small amounts of escudos and amounts up to that declared on arrival may be changed back when you leave.

Documents needed to enter Portugal

British, American, Australian, New Zealand and Canadian citizens need only a valid passport to enter Portugal. The passports of the British citizen must be clearly marked British Citizen. British Dependent Territories Citizens, British Overseas Citizens and British Nationals (Overseas) must have visas before arrival.

Americans, Britons and Canadians may stay in the country for sixty days. After that they must apply for an extension of a further sixty days at the Serviços de Estrangeiros in Rua Conselheiro José Silvestre Ribeiro, Lote 22, Estrada da Luz, Lisbon (not far from the Zoo and American Embassy). Tel. (01) 7141179/7141027. A further extension of sixty days may be applied for, but after this 180-day period you must leave the country. No tourist is allowed to work in Portugal. Portugal is not yet a full member of the EEC. If you plan to remain in the country for more than sixty days, be sure to have your passport stamped when you enter the country, or you will have no way to prove how long you have been there.

Australians and New Zealanders may stay in Portugal for ninety days before applying for a renewal of their visa. There is no New Zealand Embassy in Portugal, but subjects of New Zealand can apply to the British Embassy if necessary.

Electrical current

The electrical current in Portugal is 220 volts, 50 cycles. Plugs are standard two-prong European, so you will need a plug adaptor.

Embassies and consulates

• **British Consulate**, Rua São Domingos à Lapa 37, 1200 Lisbon. Tel. (01) 3961191.

British Consulate, Avenida de Boa Vista 3072, 4100 Oporto. Tel. (02) 684789.

• **American Embassy and Consulate**, Avenida das Forças Armadas, 1200 Lisbon. Tel. (01) 7266600/7268880.

American Consulate, Rua Julio Dinis 826-3°, 1000 Oporto. Tel. (02) 63094/690008.

• **Australian Embassy**, Avenida da Liberdade 244, 4°, Lisbon. Tel. (01) 5233150.

• **Canadian Embassy**, Rua Rosa Araújo 2-6°, Lisbon. Tel. (01) 3474892.

• **South African Embassy**, Avenida Luis Bivar 10, Lisbon. Tel. (01) 535041/535713.

Etiquette

The Portuguese are formal people and put great store by good manners. Gentlemen may still kiss a lady's hand, so don't be surprised. All men shake hands on meeting. They may even hug each other if they are friends. It is polite to shake hands with your hairdresser or anyone who has done you a special favour. Whenever you meet someone you know, you exchange kisses on both cheeks. Young people exchange kisses on both cheeks when first introduced too.

The Portuguese almost never use the familiar *tu* (you) when addressing anyone. The person is addressed by his title using the third person: for example, you would ask '*O Senhor Gomes vai tomar café?*' ('Is Mr Gomes going to have coffee?' rather than 'Do you want coffee?') Similarly, you would address Ministers, doctors, civil servants and so on by their titles.

I have had the same good neighbour for over twenty years and we still address each other as Dona Martha and Dona Filipa; her children, whom I have watched grow up, continue to address me by my title, 'Mrs Martha'. That's the way things are done in Portugal.

Cards are exchanged almost immediately upon being introduced. If the card you are given has the last name struck out, it is a sign of friendliness. If the card has a corner turned down, this is a mark of respect.

Fires

Every summer the north of Portugal burns. Forest fires – most of them set alight intentionally by unscrupulous lumber dealers who want to buy the scorched wood cheap – devastate thousands of hectares of forests, threaten villages and kill wild and domestic animals. Many voluntary firemen have lost their lives fighting the fires.

At night you can often see several fires burning on distant – and not so distant – mountainsides; and, during the day, the smoke often blocks out what should be spectacular panoramic views.

So far, no tourists have been caught up in these fires. Roads in proximity to the fires are controlled by police and firemen and warnings are given by radio. However, it is well to be prudent and not venture into any threatened area.

Health

You do not need any special inoculations to enter Portugal and there is no need to present any vaccination certificates at the border. The water is safe to drink unless marked otherwise with a crossed-out P.

The chemist or pharmacy (*farmácia*) is open during shopping hours from 9 a.m. to 1 p.m. and from 3 p.m. to 7 p.m. There are none open permanently in shopping centres, but there is always a *Farmácia de Serviço* (duty chemist) open somewhere. On the door of every pharmacy that is closed, a list with the names and addresses of those that are on duty is on display. You will need a prescription to obtain certain medicines, just as in other countries.

All cities and most towns have emergency medical facilities. Telephone 115 for an ambulance. If you need some quick first aid, you can go to the nearest Centro de Enfermagem for assistance.

Many doctors in Portugal speak English and many were trained in Britain or the United States, so you should not have too much difficulty in finding one who can understand you. At the British Hospital in Lisbon, Rua Saraiva de Carvalho 49, tel. (01) 602020, there is a staff of English-speaking doctors and nurses.

Some of the hospitals in Portugal are new and well staffed even in cities as remote as Vila Real and Bragança in Trás-os-Montes. There is a large, well-staffed hospital in Faro in the Algarve accustomed to assisting tourists. In Lisbon there are several hospitals that deal with emergency cases: the British Hospital, the Santa Maria and the São José. Most accident cases are taken to the São José. It is a very old building much in need of repair. But don't worry if the rain leaks through the roof; the doctors and the equipment are very good.

There have been outbreaks of gastro-enteritis at the crowded beach resorts that have overburdened the local medical facilities, but the health authorities have installed new waste treatment plants to clean up the water. However, most of the beaches near Cascais and Estoril remain polluted. Don't go into the water at any beach near the towns unless you see the blue flag flying that signifies 'clean beach'.

There are other precautions you can take to avoid getting sick in Portugal: don't stay out in direct sun for more than a few minutes per day, especially without a hat; don't consume too much cheap wine; avoid all cakes and dishes with cream fillings or mayonnaise that are displayed in the open; and don't get run over by a Portuguese driver.

Holidays, fairs and festivals

There are public holidays that are celebrated nationally and holidays that are celebrated locally, so as you travel around the country you are bound to come across towns where everything is shut while the local people enjoy the celebrations.

Public holidays

1 January	New Year's Day
February/March (moveable)	Shrove Tuesday
March/April (moveable)	Good Friday
25 April	Anniversary of the 1974 Revolution
1 May	Labour Day
10 June	Day of Camões
June/July (moveable)	Corpus Christi
15 August	The Assumption
5 October	Anniversary of the First Republic
1 November	All Saints' Day
1 December	Restoration
8 December	Immaculate Conception
25 December	Christmas Day

Fairs and festivals

There are festivals and market fairs everywhere in Portugal, where you will find street stalls selling everything from hand-embroidered linen and lace, food and live cows to cassette tapes, clothes and household goods. Lists of festivals and fairs are available from local Tourist Offices and in most hotels. Some of the most interesting are listed below, and in the Gazetteer section under the appropriate town.

Calendar of Festivals and Fairs
(The exact dates change each year. Inquire at the Tourist Office.)

January

Fair of Saint Amaro in Castelo de Vide: see page 290.
Pilgrimage of Saint Anthony in Óbidos: see page 220.
Feast of Saint Gonçalo and Saint Cristovão in Vila Nova de Gaia: see page 127.

February

Feast of Saint Brás in Régua: see page 134.
Fair of Saint Mathias in Abrantes: see page 280.
Carnival in Ovar on the Ria de Aveiro. A colourful, noisy carnival with masquerades, parades of floats and battles with flowers.
Carnival in Nazaré. There are masquerades, dances and contests, and on Ash Wednesday the ceremonial burying of Saint Entrudo, an ancient rite.
Carnival in Loulé: see page 334.
Festivals in **Vinhais:** see page 169.

March

Procession of Our Lord of the Passos da Graça in Lisbon. A perfumed procession with statues of saints and religious objects entirely covered with violets wends its way through the old Graça quarter.

Procession of Monks in Mafra. As the procession files solemnly out of the convent with sumptuous religious images, the carillon peel from the towers.

April **Feasts of Holy Week** in Braga: see page 101.

Holy Week: festivals throughout the country.

Pilgrimage of Bom Jesus in Fão-Esposende honours the appearance in the sixteenth century of a statue of Jesus on the beach at nearby Ofir. There is singing, dancing and fireworks. On Monday of Holy Week, there is the moving Procession of Our Lord of the Cripples, during which Holy Communion is carried to the sick over carpets of flowers.

Passion Procession in Óbidos: see page 220.

Pilgrimage of Our Lady of Piety in Loulé is based on the belief that Our Lady descends to the town on Easter Sunday. On Sunday her image is carried up a mountain by the devout.

May **Festivals in Bragança**: see page 167.

Feast of Our Lady of the Ascension in Alcobaça: see page 216.

Pilgrimage to Santa Cruz in Óbidos: see page 220.

Pilgrimage to Our Lady of Penha in Portalegre: see page 293.

Feast of the Crosses in Barcelos: see page 97.

Feast of the Crosses in Serzedelo near Guimarães. Sixteen giant crosses totally covered in flowers are paraded through the streets over carpets of flowers.

Festival of the Castle in Monsanto: see page 191.

Feast of Our Lady of the Roses in Vila Franca do Lima: see page 78.

Pilgrimage to Fátima: see page 211.

Feast of Our Lord of Chagas (wounds) in Sesimbra commemorates the washing up on shore 400 years ago of an image of Christ. Each year on 4th May, fishermen carry the image from the seaside to the top of the mountain behind the town.

May Fair in Vila Viçosa: see page 301.

June **Pilgrimage to the Shrine of Saint Gonçalo** in Amarante: see page 131.

National Agricultural Fair in Santarém: see page 282.

Feast of Saint George in Ponte de Lima: see page 94.

Feast of Our Lord of Matosinhos in Matosinhos honours the image of Christ, believed to have been sculpted in Palestine by Nicodemus and washed on shore near the town in the tenth century.

Festivals of the Popular Saints in Lisbon: see page 261.

Feast of Corpus Christi in Penafiel: see page 124.

Feast of Corpus Christi in Monção: see page 86.

Feast of Saint John in Vila do Conde: see page 71.

Feasts of Saint Isabela in Coimbra: see page 203.

Feast of Corpo de Deus in Alcobaça: see page 216.

Fairs in **Torres Vedras**: see page 224.

Festivals of Saint Peter in Abrantes: see page 280.

Fairs of Saint Anthony and Saint Pedro in Vila Real: see page 141.

Feast of Saint John in Braga: see page 101.

Feast of Saint John in Oporto: see page 124.

Feast of Saint John in Sobrado near Valongo, east of Oporto, has its origins in remote times. More than 700 people dressed as Moors and Christians take part in ritual war dances and a battle in which the Christians are, naturally, victorious.

Feast of Saint Peter the Fisherman in Póvoa de Varzim. The typical quarters are brightly decorated and on the 28th the people dance around bonfires until midnight when there is a huge sardine fry. A large procession in honour of Saint Peter takes place on the 29th and end in a giant fireworks display.

Feast of Saint John on Figueira da Foz beach. The people dance around bonfires until dawn, when they throw themselves into the sea for a *banho santo* (holy bath).

Pilgrimage of Our Lady of Lapa: see page 176.

Vila de Moinhos Cavalcade near Viseu: see page 177.

Feasts of Saint Peter and Saint John in Castelo de Vide: see page 290.

Fairs of Saint Peter in Fronteira: see page 295.

Feast of Saint Peter in Montijo: see page 261.

San Pedro Fair in Sintra: see page 230.

Feast of Saint Peter in Regúa: see page 134.

Fair of Saint John in Évora: see page 308.

July

Pilgrimage to Saint Torquatus in Guimarães: see page 107.
Pilgrimage to Our Lady of Prayer in Vale de Maceira: see page 185.
National Ceramics Fair in Caldas da Rainha: see page 219.
Feasts of Tabuleiros in Tomar: see page 276.
Feast of Our Lord of Sufferers in Lousada begins on the last Saturday of the month with a big fair, and on Sunday there is an illuminated procession to the mountain. The festival is animated with monstrous 'giants of wood', 'cows of fire' and bands of music.
Feast of the Saintly Queen in Coimbra: see page 203.
Fair of Santiago in Mirandela: see page 155.
Handicraft Fair in Estoril and Cascais: see page 234.
Festival of the Red Ribbons (*Colete Encarnado*) in Vila Franca de Xira: see page 285.
Fair and Festival of Our Lady of Carmo in Faro on the 16th has a procession and a fair.
National Handicraft Fair in Vila do Conde: see page 71.

August

Festival of Meadela in Honour of Saint Cristina in Meadela near Viana do Castelo: see page 78.
Feast of Our Lady of Mercy in Régua: see page 134.
Gualterianas Festival in Guimarães: see page 107.
Feast of Our Lady of Bom Voyage in Peniche: see page 222.
Festivals in **Alijó**: see page 143.
Festivals in **Bragança**: see page 167.
Festivals in **Vimioso**: see page 164.
Festivals in **Abrantes**: see page 280.
Festival in **Gouveia**: see page 183.
Auto da Floripes in Neves: see page 78.
Feast of Saint Rita of Cassia in Caminha: see page 84.
Pilgrimage to Saint Benito of the Open Door in the Peneda-Gerês National Park: see page 88.
Feasts of Our Lady of the Assumption in Vinhais: see page 169.
Feast of Our Lady of Health and Solitude in Esposende: see page 76.
Feast of Our Lady of the Assumption in Póvoa de Varzim: see page 73.
The Feast of Saint Martha of Portuzelo in Neves: see page 79.
Feast of Our Lady of Agony in Viana: see page 79.
Feast of Our Lady of Fresta in Trancoso: see page 176.
Feast of Saint Bartholomew in Ponte da Barca: see page 92.
Pilgrimage of Saint Bartholomew of the Sea in Mar near Esposende: see page 76.
Feast of Saint Bartholomew in Oporto: see page 124.
Festivals in honour of Our Lady of Victory in Batalha, where a great monastery was erected in honour of the victory of the Portuguese over the Spaniards in 1385, are very animated with folk dancing, a fair and other diversions.
Fair of Saint Bernard in Alcobaça: see page 216.
Fair of Saint Bartholomew in Trancoso has been held under the walls of the impressive Trancoso castle since 1273. It is essentially a cattle fair, but many other articles are sold, especially on the 21st and 22nd.
Feast of Saint Bárbara in Miranda do Douro: see page 163.
Fair of Saint Matthew in Viseu goes on for a month – from the last week in August until the end of September with exhibits of agricultural products, wines, handicrafts and other products, and folklore festivals.
Festivals of the Green Caps and the Salt Gatherers in Alcochete are in honour of the men of the 'green caps', who herd the bulls, and of those who gather the salt. There are processions, sardine roasts, bull running and bull fights accompanied by music, folk dancing and fireworks.
Pilgrimage of Saint Mamede in Janas near Sintra takes place on the mountainside at a chapel reminiscent of a Roman temple. Farmers bring their animals there where they are led three times around the chapel to fulfill promises. There is an animal fair, a procession and a blessing of the cattle among other attractions.
Feast of Our Lady of Pilar in Vila Nova de Gaia: see page 127.
Feast of Our Lady of Vila Velha in Fronteira: see page 295.
August Fair in Beja is a big agricultural fair with handicrafts and bull fights.

Feast and Fair of Our Lady of the Martyrs in Castro Marim is a combination fair and religious festival.

September

Feast of Our Lady of Abundance in Vila Praia de Âncora: see page 83.

Feasts of Our Lady of the Rosary in Abrantes: see page 280.

Pilgrimage of Saint Paio da Torreira in Torreira near Murtosa on the Ria de Aveiro is a celebration during which the colourful seaweed gathering boats (*moliceiros*) bring pilgrims to the Saint Paio chapel. The religious festivities are followed by animated dancing, singing and by fireworks.

Pilgrimage of Our Lady of Nazo in Monte de Nazo near Miranda do Douro: see page 163.

Pilgrimage of Our Lady of Nazaré: see pages 163 and 218.

Festival of Our Lady of Victory in commemoration of the Battle of Buçaco in Mealhada re-enacts the British/Portuguese victory over Napoleon's forces in the Peninsula Wars, with participants wearing uniforms of those times.

Pilgrimage of Our Lady of the Remedies in Lamego: see page 137.

Harvest Festival in Palmela celebrates the grape. Grapes are crushed in giant vats by foot and the first wine is carried in procession to the centre of town to be blessed. Wine tasting, folk music and dancing are the main attractions.

Feast of Our Lady of Sorrows in Póvoa de Varzim: see page 73.

Feast of Saint Sebastião in Mirandela: see page 155.

Feasts of Our Lady of the Mountains in Bragança: see page 167.

Feasts of Saint António in Vinhais: see page 169.

Festival of Saints Luzia and Eufémia in Castelejo: see page 190.

Festivals in **Elvas**: see page 300.

Runa Fair in Torres Vedras: see page 224.

Festival of Our Lady of Bom Voyage is in the river town of Moita south of Lisbon. The fishermen carry the image of their patron saint down to the river to bless the boats. Later there are bull fights, bull running and other festivities.

National Onion Fair in Rio Maior features giant mountains of onions and contests for the best onion. The festival is animated by folk dancing and other diversions.

Fair of Saint Matthew and the Festival of Our Lord of Piety in Elvas: see page 300.

Algarve Folklore Festival on the first Friday and Saturday of the month takes place simultaneously in all major towns on the Algarve coast, bringing together folklore groups from all over Portugal.

Feast of Our Lady of Succour in Espinho: see page 128.

New Fair and Feast of Our Lady of Sorrows in Ponte de Lima: see page 94.

Feast of Saint Michael in Cabeçeiras de Basto: see page 142.

Pilgrimage to Our Lord of Bom Fim Sanctuary in Portalegre: see page 293.

October

Pilgrimage of Our Lady of Rosario and the Nut Fair in Gondomar near Oporto originated in the sixteenth century. There are processions and folk dancing and on Sunday the traditional fair.

Autumn Pilgrimage to Fátima: see page 211.

Pilgrimage of Our Lady of the Remedies in Peniche: see page 222.

Fair of Saint Simão in Alcobaça: see page 216.

Santa Iria Fair in Tomar: see page 277.

National Gastronomy Fair in Santarém at the end of October and the beginning of November brings together all the best cooks in the country to present their regional dishes to the thousands of visitors, who are also treated to the finest wines, folk dancing and examples of handicrafts from every corner of Portugal.

Santa Iria Fair in Óbidos: see page 220.

Santa Iria Fair in Faro is a traditional festival which goes on for several days.

October Fair in Monchique in the mountains of the Algarve sells everything from cattle to pottery of the region.

Saints Fair in Chaves: see page 152.

November

National Horse Fair in Golegã: see page 281.

Insurance

You should obtain travel insurance before you leave your own country to cover car accidents, health and the cost of transport home. If you have not done so, you can get it at the Automóvel Clube de Portugal, Rua Araújo 49a, Lisbon. Tel. (01) 524073/553858.

Lost property

If you lose something on a bus or tram in Lisbon, go to the Carris Bus Company office at the top of the Santa Justa Elevator between 3 p.m. and 7 p.m. Tel. (01) 3466141. Ask at the Anjos Police Station at Rua dos Anjos 56 between 9 a.m. and 12 noon or between 2 p.m. and 6 p.m. Other cities have similar lost and found departments; enquire at the Tourist Office for more details.

Laundry and dry-cleaning

There are laundry and dry-cleaning services in every town, but they are slow. There are almost no automatic ones except the automatic washing machines at camp sites. All hotels have cleaning and laundry services, but they are very expensive: you may find that your cleaning bill is as much as your hotel bill! Bags of detergent and a travelling iron are therefore a good idea.

Newspapers, radio, television and cinemas

English language newspapers and magazines

You can find English language newspapers in the big cities and large resort areas. These include *The Times*, *The Guardian*, *The Financial Times*, *The Sun* and others from Britain, and *The International Herald Tribune* published in Paris by the New York Times and the Washington Post. In Lisbon, these papers arrive the same day they are published, but they are later in other parts of the country.

You can also buy the American weekly news magazines such as *Time* and *Newsweek* on the stands in the big cities, but you will get the European edition of *Time* – which is somewhat different to the American one. These arrive about two days after they are published in the USA.

There are also local publications in English that provide national and international news and report on what is happening in the English community. *The Anglo-Portuguese News* is published every two weeks and is distributed on news-stands in Lisbon and the Algarve. *What's*

On in Lisbon is distributed by the Tourist Office. *The Algarve Magazine*, published in the Algarve, has local colour articles and descriptions of where to go and what to see.

Radio   There are news broadcasts in English, French and German during the summer on Channel One at times listed in the newspapers. There is an English language radio station broadcasting in the Algarve. There are stations owned by the state, the Catholic Church and private interests.

Television   All shows on Portuguese television, which is state-owned, are in their original language; none are dubbed. Portugal has two channels: Channel One, which goes on the air at 9 a.m., and Channel Two, which begins at 3 p.m. If you are near the Spanish border, you can get Spanish programmes. Brazilian soap operas are the favourite fare. American, British, Australian and other foreign serials and films are also shown.

Cinemas   All films are shown with their original soundtrack, and the same films will be showing in Portugal that are running in London or New York. In the cities, cinemas open around 2 p.m. and have five consecutive showings of the film. In the middle of the film there is an interval of ten minutes during which you can rush out and try to get to the bar. There are many small cinemas in the cities, and shopping centres usually have one or two. Since censorship lifted in Portugal, there are a few cinemas showing pornographic films. You should buy your tickets in advance for new films as they sell out fast. You can buy them at the cinema or in kiosks that advertise. Tickets cost between 350 and 400 esc. Tip the usherette 10 or 20 esc.

Opening hours

Shops are generally open from 9 a.m. to 1 p.m. and from 3 p.m. to 7 p.m., but shopping centres are usually open all day until midnight.

Banks are open from 8.30 a.m. to 3 p.m. every day except at weekends. There are banks open at the Airport and the Santa Apolónia Station in Lisbon for permanent service. Automatic money dispensers are numerous all over the country, but often run out of money.

Government offices are open from 9 a.m. to 12 noon and from 2.30 p.m. to 5.30 p.m.

Museums are open mornings and afternoons every day except Monday, apart from those with special opening and closing times, and these are noted in the Gazetteer under the relevant museum listing.

The siesta is not a habit in Portugal, but long lunches and teabreaks are.

Religion

Portugal is predominantly Catholic. The north of the country is very devout, Lisbon and the south less so. There are regular masses at the churches and some lovely ones are sung in the Cathedral and in the Jerónimos Monastery church in Lisbon at 11 a.m. on Sunday. There are masses in English in Lisbon and Oporto. Proper dress is expected.

Religion in Portugal over the years has been a matter of swinging from one extreme to another. Years ago the Inquisition was followed by the abolition of all religious orders and the confiscation of their property. Lately there has been a swing from the exclusive domination by the Catholic church during the Dictatorship to the absolute freedom of today, when there are followers of the Moonies, the Church of Christ, the Blue Army, Mormons, Jehovah's Witnesses, Children of God and other assorted sects in Portugal – much to the disgust of the Patriarch of Lisbon, who complained on television about their proliferation.

Telephoning home

To telephone home, dial the access code, followed by the country code, then the number. In case of difficulty, telephone the international operator on 099 for calls in Europe, 098 outside Europe.

Country	Access code	Country code	Cost (esc.) per minute
Australia	097	61	340
Britain	00	44	153
Eire	00	353	153
New Zealand	097	64	510
South Africa	097	27	464
United States and Canada	097	1	340

Urgent messages and shipments

Most good hotels and main Post Offices have telex machines and the hotel operators will send messages for you. There are telefax machines in all the better hotels in Lisbon and other towns around the country. Main Post Offices in the large towns – even in Bragança and Braga – also have telefax machines.

There are several courier services in Lisbon that will arrange delivery of urgent packages, including Sado Cargo, tel. (01) 805021/2, DHL, tel. (01) 807381/808670, Federal Express, tel. (01) 809174.

Time differences

There is no time difference between Portugal and Great Britain or Eire.

To calculate the time in the United States and Canada, subtract five to eight hours (Eastern Standard to Pacific time).

South Africa, Australia and New Zealand are ahead of the Portuguese clock, by two, nine and twelve hours respectively.

Tipping

Hotels and restaurants usually include taxes and service charges in their bills, but a small 5 to 10 per cent tip is in order if you are pleased with the service. Leave a tip for the hotel maid. At train and bus stations and at airports, the porter will charge 75 esc. per bag. Tip the hotel porter between 100 and 200 esc. for carrying them. At cinemas give the usherette 10 or 20 esc.

Toilets

It is impossible to make a generalized statement about toilets in Portugal. There are those in smart hotels and restaurants that are in marble and gold and there are those beside the roads in the hinterlands that are cowsheds. Apart from in good restaurants and bars there will usually be no toilet paper, so you had best carry a supply of tissues around with you. There is seldom a rubbish disposal unit, so you should supply yourself with an ample number of plastic bags if you are travelling with a baby.

Wildlife

The viper is the only poisonous snake in Portugal, but these are very rare. In the extremely unlikely event that you are bitten, you can telephone the emergency number for cases of poison in Lisbon – (01) 761176 – or rush to the nearest hospital.

There are mosquitoes and numerous other flying insects that bite and make a nuisance of themselves. You can buy mosquito repellents in local chemists and in tourist shops.

Gazetteer

The Minho

Introduction

The Minho occupies the north-west corner of Portugal, between the River Douro on the south, the River Minho on the north bordering Spain, the Atlantic Ocean on the west, and to the east the mountain ranges that divide it from Trás-os-Montes.

It is often called *Verde Minho* (Green Minho), because of its green forests and cultivated valleys. Parts of its coast are industrial and densely populated, but it does have some beautiful beaches – if you don't mind cold, rather rough sea. It abounds in spas; prehistoric fortified hill-towns; historic monuments; and national parks. It is famous for its festivals and pilgrimages, with their origins lost in time. The wine of the region is also called 'green': *vinho verde*. Some say it is named for the 'greenness' of the region; others say it is called 'green' because the wine is drunk when very young – one or two years at the most.

History The Minho was inhabited as far back as 4000 BC. Many signs of palaeolithic, neolithic and megalithic civilizations have been found, the most spectacular being colossal carved blocks of granite weighing more than 15 tons.

After the Roman conquests of the second century AD, the hill people of the *castros* and *citânias* (see page 17) became converted to Christianity. Early churches remain in several places (the eighth-century church in Bravães is particularly well preserved). The Moorish conquests between 764 and 840 brought destruction to the Minho. Some historians believe that whole populations moved out of the region and destroyed crops and houses to deter the Moors, who were finally driven out in the twelfth century.

In 1139 Dom Afonso Henriques of Guimarães, after he had won the Battle of São Mamede, declared himself King of Portugal, and for three centuries after that the north, particularly the Minho, dominated the country. This changed with the beginning of the Age of Discoveries in the fifteenth century, when commerce and finance became centred in Lisbon.

Matriarchy The society of the Minho has always been a matriarchal one. The women are the staunch defenders of the home, family, land, village and Church. In the past they have led revolts against authority to protect them. Land and family are very important to these northeners. Even as emigrants in other countries they tend to congregate by families, regions and villages.

Religion The people of the Minho are very religious, and they have an incredible number of churches, religious festivals and pilgrimages. The route that pilgrims on their way to the shrine at Santiago de Compostela have taken since the Middle Ages passes through Oporto, Viana do Castelo, Âncora, Caminha and Valença on the Spanish border. Old hostels and hospitals used by the pilgrims remain.

Vinho verde *Vinho verde* is so much a part of life in the Minho and parts of the other northern regions that you are considered rather eccentric if you prefer something else. In the Vinho Verde region, which includes all of the Minho, most of the Douro coast and some parts of Trás-os-Montes and the Beira coast, there are more than 100,000 growers producing 230 million litres per year. Most of these producers have small holdings that yield only sufficient wine for local use.

Wine has been grown in the region since the time of the Romans. Vinho Verde people claim it was the first Portuguese wine known on European markets. There is a record from 1295 showing that a pipe of *vinho verde* was sold to England for five pounds for the ceremonies surrounding the enthronement of a new bishop. The fine *vinho verdes* made from Alvarinho grapes have been exported to England since the sixteenth century, when they were traded for cod. The English called them 'eager wines'.

The grapes are grown in granite soils rich in potassium. The vines are allowed to climb up trees and twist around the branches; they are trained along wires to form tunnels over roadways or borders along farms; or they are supported by granite posts in the shape of crosses (*cruzetas*). The grapes are picked in October. Contrary to what is customary elsewhere in Portugal, the men pick the grapes and the women tend the ox-carts that transport them. The wine is bottled in March, for immediate drinking.

If you like a light, very dry, slightly effervescent, young wine that has bubbles that prickle your nose, then *vinho verde* is for you. But be sure to drink it within a year or two after it is bottled. It does not age. Its alcohol content is only 8° or 9°, except for the very fine Alvarinhos and Loureiros, that may reach 11° or 12° and can be kept a bit longer.

And, beware of *vinho verde* in fanciful bottles or with cute labels. Odd-shaped bottles such as flagons with handles have become popular for certain cheap *vinho verdes*, but good-quality *vinho verdes* – of which there are red and white varieties – almost invariably come in classical, hock-type bottles (tall and narrow-shouldered).

The reds tend to be rough and strongly grape-flavoured and make up seventy per cent of the production, most of which is consumed locally.

The best wines are the estate bottled whites made in small quantities by individual growers. You will notice that some of the *vinho verde* labels bear the names of manor houses – this is because many of the manor houses bottle their own wines. The finest of all is Palácio da Brejoeira, an Alvarinho, from the vineyards of the eighteenth-century neoclassical Brejoeira palace in Monção.

The more common *vinho verdes* come from large producers and co-operatives that buy grapes from many growers and market the wine under a brand-name such as 'Casal Garcia' or 'Gaitão'.

The Vinho Verde region also produces *aguardente*, a rough brandy in which the grapes' stalks, pips and skins are used when it is made, and deserving of its nickname of 'firewater', and *bagaceira*, distilled from lees. A dark *bagaceira* is made by ageing it in wooden casks. The alcohol content is between 45° and 60°. These spirits are unknown outside Portugal.

Vila do Conde

Vila do Conde is a picturesque and ancient fishing town; the older parts of the town remain more or less as they have been for centuries.

Getting there
Located 27 km north of Oporto on the N13 – only 17 km from Oporto's international airport – it is easily reached by train, bus or car. But if you are travelling by car, try to avoid rush hour traffic! As you drive in from Oporto, there is a splendid view of the old town with its rows of low seventeenth- and eighteenth-century houses on the slope of the hill dominated by the Santa Clara Convent.

History
Vila do Conde began as an Iron Age *castro* (fortified hill-town), probably on what is now the site of the Santa Clara Convent. There is evidence that it was occupied by the Romans, the Swabians, the Visigoths and the Moors. The town was granted a charter in 870.

During the Age of Discoveries in the fifteenth and sixteenth centuries, Vila do Conde became rich and prominent through its shipbuilding, commerce and fishing. But after the river mouth silted up the town began to decline.

Vila do Conde today
Today, as well as being a fishing town, Vila do Conde is a tourist centre and a centre of the textile industry and other industries. It has

many attractions for the tourist: interesting buildings, good restaurants, fine white sand beaches, swimming pools, tennis, fishing, a weekly fair on Friday and a huge annual craft fair.

What to see

The **Santa Clara Convent** was founded in 1318 by Dom Afonso Sanches, bastard son of King Dinis. The last nun died in 1893. The present convent building dates from the eighteenth century, as does the **aqueduct**, of which a great part is still standing. It originally had 999 arches – the builders did not want to build 1,000, as they were afraid of offending God if they made it too grandiose. The church is Gothic in style and has richly carved ceilings. The tombs of the founder and his wife and two children lie in a side-chapel.

The **Parish Church**, on which work was begun in 1496, was opened for worship in 1518. It has a fine Manueline portico attributed to João de Castilho; three large naves; gilt-carved work of the seventeenth and eighteenth centuries; glazed tiles; and a stone image of Saint John, the patron of the town.

The **Misericórdia Church**, built in the sixteenth century, has glazed polychrome tiles and a beautiful organ.

Other places of interest are the **Socorro Chapel**, with its Moorish appearance and glazed tiles; the seventeenth-century **Saint John the Baptist Castle** near the mouth of the River Ave; and the **Town Hall** in front of the Parish Church.

There are some interesting museums: the **Ethnological Museum**, Praça da República; the **Naval Industry Museum**, Rua da Lapa 14; and the **Casa de José Regio**, Avenida Campos Henriques.

Boatyards

Vila do Conde's boatyards – the oldest in Europe – make wooden hulls for local fishing boats and for boats bound for the Newfoundland cod banks, still using tools that have been used for hundreds of years. You can visit the boatyards down by the river to see the boat-builders at work.

In 1987 the boatyards completed an exact replica of the caravel in which Bartolomeu Dias sailed on the historic voyage that took him around the southern tip of Africa and opened the route to India. The replica caravel set sail from Portugal in October 1987, and reached the tip of Africa exactly 500 years after Bartolomeu Dias as part of the celebrations to commemorate the Discoveries!

Lacemaking

Lacemaking is another traditional craft that has been preserved. Lace has been made in Vila do Conde since the seventeenth century. The laces, called *Rendas de Bilros*, originally had only designs related to the sea, but today they also have other designs, many of them very complicated. You can visit the Lacemaking School, founded in 1909, in Largo do Carmo and watch the women at work. They also have lace for sale there.

Festivals

During Holy Week there is a procession through the streets of Vila do Conde over a carpet of fresh flowers laid in intricate designs.

The *Festas de São João* takes place during the days preceding the feast of Saint John the Baptist, on 24 June. The celebrations include a fair, fireworks, and folk costume parades. There is music and dancing round bonfires, and the lacemakers lead a floodlit procession down to the sea.

Craft fair

The biggest craft fair in Portugal is held in Vila do Conde during the last week in July and the first week in August. The fairground covers a large part of the town and each region of the country has its own pavilion, many of them with craftworkers demonstrating their craft. There are ceramics, jewellery, hand-painted wooden toys, leather goods, hand-embroidered linen, rugs, furniture, pottery, copper, of course the famous lace of Vila do Conde – and practically anything else you could think of. Constant entertainment is also provided, in the shape of folk singers, dancers and bands.

Excursions

Within a few kilometres of Vila do Conde there are some very old churches that are worth seeing. The **Church of São Cristovão de Rio Mau** on the road north to Vila Nova de Famalicão dates from 1151, and is an excellent example of Romanesque. The **Parish Church** of Azurara, just 1 km south of Vila do Conde on the N13, has a sixteenth-century Manueline doorway and gilt carved work; there is also a seventeenth-century monastery.

Where to stay
Inexpensive

Motel de Sant'Ana, Monte de Sant'Ana, Azurara. Tel. (052) 631994, telex 27695. A very modern, beautifully situated motel, overlooking the River Ave just 500 m from the old bridge at the entrance to Azurara. It has one- and two-bedroomed suites with bath, small kitchen, balcony, telephone, radio and TV. Its restaurant offers traditional Portuguese cooking and piano music during dinner. Or if you prefer you can eat on the terrace, where there is a grill. There is also a heated indoor swimming pool and a sauna.

Estalagem do Brasão, Avenida Conde Alberto Graça. Tel. (052) 632016. A four star inn, very comfortable and conveniently located, with bar, restaurant and snack bar.

Camp sites

Parque de Campismo de Azurara, Azurara. Just south of Vila do Conde.

Parque de Campismo de Vila do Conde, Árvore. On a lovely beach, 700 m from the N13.

Where to eat

The restaurants in the **Motel de Sant'Ana** and the **Estalagem do Brasão** are both good, and there are several other reasonable restaurants in Vila do Conde.

What to eat

Caldo verde (green cabbage soup), seafood, fish and *doçe de ovos* (egg-yolk and sugar sweets). There used to be many salmon in the rivers, but a combination of pollution and new dams has made them very scarce and expensive. However, there are very many good freshwater river fish, such as sável (shad) from the River Minho and trout from almost everywhere. Meals are traditionally accompanied with *vinho verde*.

Póvoa de Varzim

Póvoa de Varzim, on the coast, 30 km north of Oporto and only 3 km from Vila do Conde on the N13, is a town of high-rise hotels and tourist attractions. It has a wide avenue and promenade all along the beach front, with a 6 km stretch of fine sandy beach. There are water slides, beach shops, restaurants, discos, an enclosed boat marina, public swimming pools and tennis courts, and you can hire yourself a striped beach tent. You can also hire a rowing boat for inshore fishing or a motor boat for offshore (there are huge bass, sea mullet and sea bream), or you can go sailing on the lagoon. The coast with its many rocky formations offshore is good for skin-diving. Póvoa de Varzim also has colourful bullfights in season.

History

Póvoa de Varzim is at least 1,000 years old. A document dated in 953 shows land being given for a town. In 1308 King Dinis issued a royal charter granting land to fifty-four families, for them to build on. Descendants of some of those families still live in the town. In the eighteenth century Póvoa de Varzim became a popular bathing place. And in the latter half of the nineteenth century it grew to be the most important fishing centre north of Oporto.

Fishing community

The fishing community of Póvoa de Varzim is extremely interesting. It is a rather closed community, with its own customs and beliefs. For centuries the fishing families practised endogamy, marrying only within their own and related communities, and they maintained a class system in which the 'men of respect' more or less governed. And to some extent these traditions still persist. Each family still has its own sign for its boats and other fishing equipment, and this is passed down from father to son, from generation to generation. The sign may be a design of a sea object, or an animal, or a plant, or some object of religious or supernatural significance. The youngest son inherits, on the principle that he will be in the best condition to take over when his father is old and no longer able to work. The other sons must add numbers to the sign corresponding to their rank in the family – first son, second son, and so on. Many of these customs are similar to those practised in Brittany, Scandinavia and Galicia, attesting to the peaceful 'invasion' of the coast by those fishermen over the ages.

Many of the fishermen of Póvoa de Varzim still use the traditional boats known as *barcos poveiros*, which are large open sailing boats, very strong and seaworthy. Boats of this type can be seen all along the coast from Oporto to the Spanish border. However, they are now gradually being replaced by more modern motor boats.

The fishermen bring in their catch every day, and their women auction the fish off on the beach. This is very lively and colourful, and well worth seeing.

The fishermen are very religious. Most carry images of Our Lady of the Assumption in the prows of their boats, and Our Lady of Lapa was customarily given part of the profits from a catch for a fishermen's fund. They pray to Santo André for a safe voyage and a big catch. And throughout the spring and summer there is a succession of religious festivals (see below).

What to see

The **Municipal Museum of Ethnography**, Solar dos Carneiros, has permanent and temporary exhibits of archaeological finds; glazed tiles and ceramics; and objects related to the town's fishing history, to rural life and to religious practices.

In the Praça do Almada you will see a statue to Eça de Queirós, the great Portuguese novelist of the nineteenth century. The statue was paid for by emigrants from Póvoa de Varzim living in Brazil. The statue of Francisco Sá Carneiro in the Praça Luis de Camões was erected by the admirers of Francisco Sá Carneiro, who was one of Portugal's first prime ministers after the 1974 Revolution, and was killed in a plane crash while in office.

Crafts

Chunky hand knitted and embroidered fishermen's sweaters are a very good buy. The gold and silver work done by the goldsmiths and silversmiths of Póvoa de Varzim is beautiful. At the famous Gomes shop (Rua da Junqueira, tel. [052] 64638) you can watch the smiths at work. The smiths of nearby Terroso and Beiriz also make beautiful handbeaten silver. Rugs and carpets from Beiriz and blankets from Terroso are worth buying too. Póvoa de Varzim is also known for its lace, basketwork, carved wood pieces and miniature boats.

Festivals

The Lenten and Holy Week processions of Póvoa de Varzim are particularly splendid but the most famous local festival is held on 15 August, the Feast of Our Lady of the Assumption. The fishermen walk to the quay carrying life-size images of the saints, to bless those who go down to the sea. There is dancing, bull fights and fireworks.

On the Saturday before the Sunday of São Lazaro there is a lantern procession led by children carrying long poles with lanterns made in the form of boats, castles, religious symbols, fishing equipment or other objects related to the sea, while on the third Sunday of September there is a festival in honour of Our Lady of Sorrows, with processions of barefoot penitents, fishermen in costume and thousands of other people.

Excursions

Póvoa de Varzim makes an ideal base for excursions to other towns of historic or tourist interest in the north. It is only 20 km from Barcelos, about 28 km from Santo Tirso, Vila Nova de Famalicão and Matosinhos, 40 km from Viana do Castelo, Braga and Guimarães, and there are many interesting places to visit in the surrounding area.

At **A-Ver-o-Mar**, 3 km north of Póvoa, you will see the strange huts that have been built on the beach by the seaweed harvesters. They resemble African mud huts, with conical roofs, but are made entirely of seaweed.

At **Laundos**, 6 km from Póvoa, the chapel and windmills on top of the São Felix Hill are worth a visit.

In **Terroso** you can see the local people making rag blankets, and in **Beiriz** you can see rugs and carpets being made by local weavers, who pass on the art from mother to daughter.

At **Rates**, 15 km along the Póvoa-Guimarães road, is the Romanesque Church of São Pedro of Rates, built in the twelfth century. It has three naves, carved pillars and a colourful stained glass window.

Fão on the River Cávado, just 1 km from the sea, is a pleasant little town, a peaceful place where cows graze contentedly on the river bank. Near the bridge there is a good little restaurant shaped like an African hut. You can hire boats to go down to **Barro do Lago**, another pretty little town which is an especially good spot for bird watching.

There is an interesting legend attached to the town of **Ofir**, on the coast 17 km north of Póvoa. As you look out to sea, you will see a line of rocks topped by white sea foam. These are the famous *Cavalos de Ofir* (Horses of Ofir). According to the legend, in remote times the ships of King Solomon came here to the shore to collect gold from the mines inland to adorn his temple. In gratitude for the gold, King Solomon sent back ships loaded with horses, the finest that could be found. The ships were wrecked off the coast in a tempest, and as the horses struggled in the waves they were turned to stone where they can be seen today. The rocks are a favourite place for underwater explorers.

Everywhere along the coast you will see *Masseiras*, deep, rectangular excavations in the sand that are used for farming. The farmers dig deep until they reach fertile soil suitable for raising vegetables. They plant the sandy sides of the excavations with grape vines to prevent their collapsing. Because the climate is moist, and the pits are protected from wind, the farmers are able to harvest three crops a year.

Entertainment

One of the main attractions of Póvoa de Varzim is the **Casino**, a monumental building opened in 1934 and completely redecorated in 1984. It offers baccarat and roulette, and there are separate rooms with slot machines and bingo. But it has also become a cultural centre. Its salons are decorated with works by well known contemporary Portuguese artists, and art and craft exhibitions are held there. It also has an excellent restaurant and a night club with an international show. So even if you don't want to risk your fortune gambling it is still worth visiting the Casino, to have dinner, see the show and browse through the exhibition rooms.

There is a well known folk dance group known as *Rancho Poveiro*, which performs at hotels and other places of entertainment. The dancers wear pilgrimage costumes, the styles of which date from more than a hundred years ago.

Where to stay

During the summer hotel prices in the Póvoa de Varzim area range from 10,000 to 14,000 esc. for a double room with bath in a four star hotel and from 6,000 to 10,000 esc. in a three star hotel. In the low season, the prices are about half this.

Medium price **Hotel Vermar Dom Pedro**, Rua Alto de Martim Vaz. Tel. (052) 683401. A modern four star hotel on the beach, with 208 rooms, two heated swimming pools, two tennis courts, restaurant, grill room, bar, sauna and disco. English language newspapers and books are on sale at the tobacconist's. The service is very good: as an added touch, in the evening you are served with herbal tea to ensure you sleep well; and in the suites you are kept supplied with vintage port and fruit.

Grande Hotel, Passeio Alegre. Tel. (052) 622061. A three star hotel with 104 rooms which was recently renovated on the esplanade near the Casino. It caters mostly to businessmen.

Inexpensive **Hotel Costa Verde**, Avenida Vasco da Gama 56. Tel. (052) 681531. A four star inn with fifty rooms, bar and restaurant.

Pensão Gett, Avenida Mouzinho de Albuquerque 54. Tel. (052) 60026. A two star pension with bar.

There are also several good hotels in the vicinity of Póvoa.

Medium price **Estalagem Santo André**, A-Ver-o-Mar. Tel. (052) 681881/2/3. A four star inn that is actually built on the beach, so you can go from your room to the sea or the swimming pool. It has fifty rooms with bath, radio, balcony and TV. The restaurant is excellent.

Estalagem São Felix, Laundos. Tel. (052) 682176. A lovely four star inn on top of the hill, in the midst of pine trees. It has eight rooms, a restaurant with a wonderful view, a bar and a swimming pool.

Hotel de Ofir, Ofir. Tel. (053) 961383, telex 32492. A four star hotel that is really a wonderful self-contained tourist complex. It has 220 rooms with bath and provides facilities for tennis, boating, riding, water ski-ing, bowling, golf and mini-golf, a health club, a gym, a sauna and a jacuzzi, as well as a long stretch of white sand backed by pine woods. It is a marvellous place for families with children.

Inexpensive **Estalagem Parque do Rio**, P.O. Box 1, Ofir, 4740 Esposende. Tel. (053) 961521, telex 32066 RIOTUR. A five star inn just a short walk from the beach, in a pine wood overlooking the River Cávado. It has thirty-six rooms with bath, balcony and central heating, a good bar and a restaurant.

Hotel do Pinhal, Ofir. Tel. (053) 961473, telex 32857. A charming three star hotel with eighty-nine rooms, bar, restaurant and swimming pool.

Camp site **Parque de Campismo Rio Alto**, near Ofir. This camp site is on the beach. It has excellent facilities: supermarket, restaurant/snack bar, swimming pool and tennis.

Where to eat **Restaurante O Marinheiro**, Estrada Nacional Povoa-Porto. Tel. (052) 682151. Built in the shape of a boat, it serves mostly seafood and fish.

Restaurante Taurygalo, Estrada Nacional Povoa-Porto. Tel. (052) 681867. A modern restaurant specializing in grills.

The **Casino** has an excellent restaurant (tel. [052] 622112). The restaurant in the **Hotel Vermar Dom Pedro** (tel. [052] 61041) is also good. In the Póvoa area, I would recommend the **Estalagem Santo André** at A-Ver-o-Mar, or the **Estalagem São Felix** at Laundos.

What to eat

As you might expect, Póvoa specializes in seafood: *lagosta suada* (lobster); *açorda de marisco* (a sort of shellfish and bread kedgeree); *pescada à poveiro* (hake); *caldeirada de peixe* (rather like *bouillabaisse* with a difference); and sardines with rice.

What to drink

Some of the good white wines to be found around Póvoa de Varzim are CRF, Carvalho, Ribeiro, Fereira and Sogrape. Some good reds are CRF, Dão and Sogrape. In a restaurant these wines will cost around 900–1,000 esc. a bottle.

Warnings

A warning about the beaches: a wind usually comes up after four o'clock in the afternoon, so it is best to bathe in the morning. And a warning about traffic: it is very difficult to park on the Esplanade, the roads along the coast are crowded, and the roads between towns are not very good and not very well marked. However, a new highway linking Póvoa de Varzim with Oporto opened in 1988.

The Tourist Office is in the Avenida Mouzinho de Albuquerque 166. Tel. (052) 624609.

Esposende

Esposende is an old fishing village on the bank of the River Cávado, 46 km north of Oporto and 16 km from Póvoa de Varzim, on the N13.

What to see

Esposende has the ruins of a Roman town, and some interesting early buildings. The Parish Church, the Church of Bom Jesus and the Council Palace are all worth seeing.

Festivals

On 13 to 15 August a festival is held in honour of Our Lady of Health and Solitude. There are water sports on the river, processions, and folk singing and dancing.

On 24 August there is a pilgrimage to the shrine of Saint Bartholomew, where the help of the saint is evoked against the afflictions of madness, epilepsy, stammering and excessive fearfulness. Children who suffer from any of these things are brought to the seaside and dunked in the sea by women in white playing the role of priestesses. The connection between religion and superstition is even more evident in the subsequent ritual of offering black chickens to Saint Bartholomew – the sick person has to carry the black chicken several times around the chapel.

Esposende also has a market fair every two weeks.

Where to stay, and eat
Medium price

Estalagem Zende, Estrada Nacional. Tel. (053) 961855. A four star inn on the Viana do Castelo road. It has thirteen rooms with bath, telephone, TV, balcony and central heating. There is a good restaurant.

Inexpensive

Hotel Suave-Mar, 4740 Esposende, Avenida Eng. Arantes e Oliveira. Tel. (053) 961145/961902, telex 32362 SUAVEMAR. A three star hotel on the beach, overlooking the river. It has sixty-two rooms with bath, telephone and radio, central heating and air conditioning, a restaurant, a bar, a swimming pool and tennis courts.

Hotel Nélia, Avenida Valentim Ribeiro. Tel. (053) 961394, telex NELIOTEL-ESPOSENDE. A three star hotel with forty-two rooms, central heating, restaurant and bar.

Viana do Castelo

Viana do Castelo is at the mouth of the River Lima, 59 km north of Oporto by the N13.

History

There is evidence of habitation of the area since ancient times. Prehistoric stone fist-axes have been found at Viana's sea-port of Vila Praia de Âncora. And on the Monte Santa Luzia, which towers over the city, there is a *citânia* that has traces of Bronze Age, Iron Age and Roman occupation. The town received its first charter (under the name of Viana da Foz da Lima) in 1262, by which time it was an important maritime trade centre. The castle was built between 1263 and 1374, to defend the town from pirates.

Sailors and discoverers set out from Viana do Castelo to colonize Africa and the Azores. The Azores were settled by Gonçalo Velho from Viana; João Velho was one of the discoverers of the Congo; and in 1512 João Álvares Fernandes arrived in Newfoundland and tried to found a colony there.

In the fifteenth century many Jews came in from Aragon to escape persecution. When the Inquisition spread to Portugal they were segregated in what is still called the Judiaria in Rua Sequeiros and Rua Seteais.

In the fifteenth and sixteenth centuries Viana started to trade with England, Russia and other European countries, and with Brazil. This trade brought great prosperity to the town. The people tore down their defensive walls and built palaces (much of the wood in the buildings comes from Brazil). By the seventeenth and eighteenth centuries Brazilian gold had turned Viana into a bustling commercial city.

Viana today

Today Viana do Castelo is a tourist centre, with splendid beaches, many colourful festivals, good hotels and an abundance of entertainment. Its outskirts have been spoiled by ugly, uncontrolled building, but the old part of the town is beautiful, and very well preserved.

What to see

The triangular **Praça da República** makes a lovely town centre. In the middle is the **Chafariz Fountain**, constructed in 1553 by João Lopes the Elder. On one side of the Praça is the **Misericórdia Hospice**, designed in 1598 by João Lopes the Younger. This is an impressive example of Renaissance architecture, with balconies and arches supported by carved granite figures. The seventeenth-century church attached to it is decorated with fine tiles depicting stories from the Old

Testament. On the other side of the Misericórdia is the sixteenth-century **Town Hall**.

The **Parish Church**, which is said to have been built by the Bishop of Ceuta in 1483, has two square towers, a lovely portal with carved figures representing the Passion, and painted tiles.

The Rococo **Chapel of Nossa Senhora da Agonia** is to the west of the town. It has gold altars and the waxed-over body of Saint Severino dressed in gold garments and a turban.

Other buildings worth visiting are the Old Hospital, the Roqueta Tower, the Barra Castle, the Melos Alvins Palace, the House of João Velho, the House of the Arches (Casa dos Arcos), the Gothic Cathedral and the Church of São Domingos. The bridge over the River Lima was designed by Eiffel at the end of the last century.

You should also walk through the Rua São Pedro and the Rua Cândido dos Reis and see some of the houses that were built in the times when Viana was a maritime and commercial power.

The guided walking tours provided by the Tourist Office are a good way to see the old part of the town.

The **Municipal Museum** is in the eighteenth-century Barbosa Macieis Palace, Largo de São Domingos, tel. (058) 24223. It has good collections of faience, Coimbra pottery, and seventeenth- and eighteenth-century furniture, and some prehistoric pieces, including stone fist-axes found on the beach at Vila Praia de Âncora, and a famous statue of a Lusitanian warrior holding a shield.

Crafts

Viana is a centre for many crafts. Embroidered table linen (with white or red or blue embroidery on white linen) is an excellent buy. Ceramics, copper work, carved wooden figures, gold and silver filigree, regional costumes, dolls and *palmitos* (sprays of artificial flowers) are also made, and sold, in Viana and the surrounding area.

Festivals

In the month of May there are some charming flower festivals in the neighbourhood of Viana. Two particularly are worthy of note. The *Festas da Senhora das Rosas* held in Vila Franca do Lima in early May is a lovely procession: richly costumed young women with constructions of rose petals on their heads pass through a series of rose-covered arches. At the end of the month there is the *Festas dos Andores Floridos* in Alvarães, which is also a mass of flowers. A procession of floats totally covered with flower petals passes over a carpet of flowers.

In Viana itself the *Festas de Santa Cristina* at the beginning of August is a time of great gaiety. There are funfairs, folk music and dancing, a procession, and a parade with floats displaying the crafts and industries of the region. The festival is much enhanced by the beautiful costumes worn by the women – the black dresses covered with glass beads and spangles which are worn by the *mordomas*, the leaders of the festival, and the bright colours of the festival costumes of the country women.

Also at the beginning of August the *Auto da Floripes* or *Comedies of the*

Emperor Charlemagne and the Twelve Lords of France is performed in Neves, 10 km inland from Viana, as part of the *Festa da Senhora das Neves*. The *Auto da Floripes* is a medieval tragi-comic melodrama about a young Moorish princess who falls in love with a Christian king. It has been performed by the men of Neves since the twelfth or thirteenth century, and was passed down by word of mouth for generations, until it was written down by historian Mauricio Teixeira just a few years ago. This play is emphatically not a spectacle that has been rigged up for tourists. It is presented for the villagers, just as it has always been.

A little later in the month there is the *Festas de Santa Marta de Portuzelo*, which includes a procession with decorated vehicles full of 'choirs of virgins'. There is a procession of animals too, as the local farmers bring their livestock to the chapel to have them blessed by their protector Saint Martha. Of course, there is also a fair, and folk singing and dancing.

Back in Viana, the *Festas da Senhora da Agonia* towards the end of August is probably the most spectacular festival in the north of the country. It may be in honour of our Lady of Suffering, but there is no suffering about it. The tragic Virgin is carried in procession to the Chapel of Nossa Senhora da Agonia, over great carpets of flowers shaped into intricate designs; the Bishop leads a procession of fishermen to the sea to bless the boats; there is a parade of girls in traditional costumes, weighed down with kilos of gold jewellery, and another parade with floats displaying the products of the region. There are stalls selling *vinho verde* and all kinds of snacks. The festivities go on day and night for the three days and culminate in a blaze of fireworks over the river and the town.

Excursions

It is well worth making a trip up the Monte de Santa Luzia, for the panoramic view and to visit the Iron Age *citânia* and the Santa Luzia Sanctuary. You can drive up, or take the funicular that leaves from the Avenida 25 de Abril.

The *citânia* was in prehistoric times the site of the first town in the area, and was later occupied by the Romans. The remains of more than seventy round houses can be seen.

The Sanctuary is a grey, domed building built at the beginning of this century in a Byzantine style. It was built on the site of a small chapel that existed there in the Middle Ages. The story goes that when plague struck the city the people prayed to Santa Luzia for relief, and the plague was lifted. Every year there is a pilgrimage to the sanctuary in thanksgiving.

Twice a week there are half-day river trips up the River Lima on the *Translima*, which cruises under the bridge built by Eiffel, around the docks, the river mouth and the beaches. For information contact the *A Tenda* shop in Rua do Hospital Velho near the Tourist Office. Tel. (052) 22813.

There are also tours of the local *vinho verde* cellars and of the wine cellars in Oporto, and at the end of September and the beginning of October there are tours to take part in the grape harvests. You can make reservations through the travel agencies.

The local travel agencies offer other trips: to Oporto, to tour the city – and taste the port; to Braga, the ancient city of churches; to Barcelos for the fair; to the Peneda-Gerês National Park; and to Spain, along the coast.

Fishing

There is excellent fishing to be had in and around Viana. On the River Lima and its tributaries there are fishing reserves with trout, savel and some salmon; a map with the reserves marked is available at the Tourist Office. In addition, there is trout fishing on the River Âncora; on the River Minho you can fish for trout, salmon and scallops; at the Cais do Bugio (Bugio Wharf) and the Cabedelo for bass and grey mullet; and along the sea coast, from Castelo do Neiva to Caminha, for bass, grey mullet and sea bream.

Nightlife

Go to the central Praça da República at night and sit around in the open air cafés and restaurants. It is very animated, with music and sometimes folk dancing.

Or, for a really lively nightlife, go to the *Santoinho*. This is a huge *arraial* (a Minho party) held every Tuesday, Thursday and Saturday during August; on Thursdays and Saturdays in June, July and September; and on Saturdays in May and October. It takes place in a set of decorated pavilions in Darque, just across the river from Viana, starting at 8 p.m. and going on into the night.

The 1,975 esc. entrance fee covers all the red and white wine you can drink (you serve yourself from huge barrels) and all the food you can eat. Chickens, pork steaks and sardines are roasted over open spits. There is the inevitable *caldo verde* (green cabbage soup), and salads.

The entertainment is constant and animated, including lively processions with coloured lanterns and *gigantones* (giants of the forests); fireworks; and, of course, dancing – tangos, paso dobles, fox trots, rhumbas, rock, folk dancing, disco dancing, and anything else you can think of. Everyone dances, including old people and small children.

It is all great fun and a good laugh, and you will enjoy yourself if you join in; and if you are still on your feet in the early morning there is *champorreão* (champagne punch), made of champagne, beer, white *vinho verde*, lemon, sugar and ice.

Where to stay

In Viana a double room with bath and breakfast in a three or four star hotel costs around 10,000–15,000 esc. a night. Three star pensions and two star hotels charge between 4,000–8,000 esc.

Medium price

Hotel do Parque, Praça da Galiza. Tel. (058) 828605, telex 32511. A four star hotel with 120 rooms with bath. It has a roof-top restaurant with a splendid view, a bar, a swimming pool, disco and winter garden.

Hotel Afonso III, Avenida Dom Afonso III 494. Tel. (058) 829001, telex 32599. A new four star hotel with eighty-nine double rooms with bath. This hotel also has a panoramic roof-top restaurant, a bar, disco and swimming pool.

Viana Sol Hotel, Largo Vasco da Gama. Tel. (058) 828995, telex 32790 VERTUR P. A new three star hotel in the old part of the city. It has seventy-two double rooms with bath, a restaurant, bar, cinema, disco/pub, a sauna, squash courts and a pool.

Inexpensive

Albergaria Calatrava, Rua Manuel Fiuza Juniór 157. Tel. (058) 828911. A comfortable new four star inn, with a pleasant bar.

Pensão Terra Linda, Rua Luís Jacome 11. Tel. (058) 23541. A three star pension with a good restaurant. It has thirteen rooms with bath.

Pensão Laranjeira, Rua General Luís Rego 45. Tel. (058) 22261. A three star pension.

Pensão Magalhães, Rua Manuel Espregueira 62. Tel. (058) 23293. A two star pension.

Manor houses
Medium price

Paço d'Anha, Anha, 4900 Viana do Castelo Tel. (058) 322459. A house with interesting historical associations: Dom António Prior do Crato was staying at Paço d'Anha when he was proclaimed King of Portugal in 1580. The excellent Paço d'Anha *vinho verde* is produced here, and the vineyards and wine cellars can be visited by guests. Three separate farmhouses have been converted into apartments for tourists. Each apartment has a living room, two bedrooms, a bathroom and kitchen.

Inexpensive

Casa do Ameal, Meadela, Viana do Castelo. Tel. (058) 22403. A charming house just 1 km from the centre of Viana do Castelo in the Meadela suburb. It offers three double bedrooms in the main house and four large independent apartments, all with bath.

Casa de Cortegaça, Subportela, 4900 Viana do Castelo. Tel. (058) 971639. A sixteenth-century manor house in Subportela, 5 km from Viana do Castelo. In 1528 the property belonged to the daughter of João Álvares Fernandes, and it is still in the same family. It offers four double rooms with bath.

Casa Grande da Bandeira, Largo das Carmelitas, 4900 Viana do Castelo. Tel. (058) 23169. A typical eighteenth-century manor house, offering two double rooms with bath.

Pousada
Medium price

Hotel de Santa Luzia, Monte de Santa Luzia. Tel. (058) 828889, telex 32420. A recently redecorated turn-of-the-century four star hotel on the Monte de Santa Luzia, overlooking the Sanctuary. It has forty-four rooms and three suites, a restaurant, bar and swimming pool. There are wonderful views from the rooms.

Camp sites

Parque do Cabedelo, Cabedelo, Viana do Castelo. Tel. (058) 322167.

Parque do Inatel, Cabedelo, Viana do Castelo. Tel. (058) 23242.

Where to eat

Viana is full of restaurants. I would recommend the following, in particular.

O Espigueiro, Lugar do Santoinho, Darque. Tel. (058) 322156.

This restaurant, in Darque, just across the bridge from Viana do Castelo, is decorated in regional style and the waiters wear regional costumes. It serves good regional food.

Cozinha das Malheiras, Palácio das Malheiras, Rua Gago Coutinho. Tel. (058) 23680. An elegant, little restaurant on the ground floor of the Malheiras Palace. The service is excellent. One speciality is rice with seafood.

Restaurante Verde Viana is a good, modern restaurant in the new shopping centre with a varied menu. Tel. (058) 829932/828203.

Casa das Armas, Largo 5 de Outubro 30 r/c. Tel. (058) 24999. A modern restaurant in an old, traditional house.

Os Três Potes, Beco dos Fornos. Tel. (058) 829928. A restaurant in the wall of the old castle, just off the Praça da República. The owner is English. The waiters dress in regional costume, there is regional food, and on Friday and Saturday nights from June to September there is folk dancing.

Coffee shops

Natário, Rua Manuel Espregueira 37. This tiny coffee house and pastry shop is well worth a visit. The owner, Manuel Natário, makes delicious croquettes, almond cakes and all kinds of sweets. Everything is fresh and hot, especially in the morning. As a further attraction, you might spot here the famous Brazilian writer Jorge Amado, who is a frequent visitor. Natário stays open till 1 a.m.

Caravela, Praça da República. Also has good coffee and cakes.

What to eat and drink

To get the flavour of Viana, try some of these: *caldo verde* (green cabbage soup), lobster with rice, dried cod, stuffed spider crab, octopus with rice, fish cakes, *cozido à portuguesa* (beef, pork, sausages and chickens boiled with vegetables), roast kid, *meias luas* (fried pastry stuffed with almonds), Viana tart (pastry stuffed with egg yolks and sugar). And of course drink *vinho verde*.

The Tourist Office is in the Rua do Hospital Velho. Tel. (058) 22620. It is in an old, beautifully restored building that used to be a hostel for pilgrims on their way to Santiago de Compostela. It has a beautiful display of regional costumes and all of the regional crafts, with items for sale. The Office has brochures in English describing the region, and will also provide guides, and make hotel reservations.

There are several travel agencies in Viana.

Avic, Avenida dos Combatentes da Grande Guerra. Tel. (058) 829705.

Mincur, Praça da República. Tel. (058) 22689.

Jumbo, Praça da República. Tel. (058) 24811/2.

Atlas, Avenida dos Combatentes da Grande Guerra. Tel. (058) 24821.

Afife

Afife, 11 km north of Viana do Castelo, was an old fort town guarding the coast. In the old days the men here were excused from military service because they had to guard the coast from pirates. It is now a resort, with marvellous beaches.

Where to stay
Inexpensive
Vila Praia de Âncora

Pensão Residencial Compostela, Afife. Tel. (058) 66534. A three star inn with fifty rooms with bath, a restaurant and a bar.

Vila Praia de Âncora, 17 km north of Viana, is a port on the estuary of the River Âncora, with a small castle in the middle where boats tie up. The town is on the site of a very ancient fishing village. Prehistoric stone fist-axes (now in the Municipal Museum in Viana do Castelo) were found here. According to legend, Âncora got its present name when the wife of one Dom Ramiro ran away with the Emir of Gaia. She was retrieved, brought back, tied to an anchor and dropped in the river, which became the River Âncora (Anchor).

Âncora has good, sandy beaches, excellent seafood restaurants (most of them very cheap), hotels, pensions and self-catering apartments. You can always find a deserted beach, and there are pine woods for picnics.

Festival

In September there is the *Festas da Senhora da Bonança*. Fishermen carry the image of their patron saint, the Lady of Calm Weather, out to sea in their boats. There is also a ceremony in which the boats are blessed.

Where to stay
Inexpensive

Hotel Meira, Rua 5 de Outubro 56. Tel. (058) 911111, telex 32619. A modern two star hotel on the beach, with forty-five rooms with bath, telephone and radio, a good restaurant that serves regional food, a bar, roof-top terrace and snack bar, and a swimming pool.

Serraia da Gelfa, near Vila Praia de Âncora. Tel. (058) 911630. An inn with a good restaurant, swimming pool and tennis courts.

Caminha

Caminha is 24 km north of Viana do Castelo at the mouth of the River Minho on the Spanish border. It is surrounded by water on three sides. The town had its orgins in Celtic and Roman times, and later became an important fishing centre. In the fifteenth and sixteenth centuries it played an important part in Portuguese overseas expansion. Many of the fine old buildings date from that time.

What to see

The **Parish Church** was constructed like a fortress in late Gothic style, in 1480. It has three naves separated by round arches, and the ceiling is elaborately carved. The adjoining **Mareantes Chapel** was built, so the story goes, because in 1539 a fisherman found on the beach a strongbox containing an image of Christ, two silver chalices and some embroidered vestments. The chapel was built to house them. It is believed that the strongbox may have been thrown into the sea by some English Catholic in the reign of Henry VIII, to save the sacred objects from being destroyed; it could have been washed up on the Portuguese shore by chance. The image of Christ can be seen in the chapel. The **Misericórdia Church**, built in 1551, has a beautiful Renaissance portal.

The fourteenth-century **Clock Tower** was part of the fortifications of the town.

The **Pitta Palace** is a lovely fifteenth-century Gothic palace with seven windows in the Manueline style.

The **Town Hall** was built in the seventeenth century. It has a lovely loggia held up by pillars. The granite interior staircase is also interesting.

Festival

In August Caminha celebrates the *Festas de Santa Rita de Cassia*, with folk dancing, fireworks and processions.

Where
to stay
Inexpensive

Pensão Restaurante Santa Rita, Rua de São João 28 r/c. Tel. (058) 92436. A three star pension.

Pensão Restaurante Galo de Ouro, Rua da Corredoura 15. Tel. (058) 921160. A three star pension with eleven rooms – three with bath – and central heating, and a restaurant.

Residencial São Pedro, Seixas do Minho. Tel. (058) 921475. A three star pension in Seixas do Minho, on the road to the border. It has modern rooms with bath, heating and radio, a bar, a swimming pool and a beautiful view of the river.

Manor houses
Inexpensive

Quinta da Graça, 4190 Caminha. Tel. (052) 921157. A seventeenth-century manor house with a view of the river and the Coura valley. It offers six very pleasant rooms with bath.

Casa da Anta, Lanhelas, 4910 Caminha. Tel. (058) 921434. A farmhouse offering four double rooms with bath. They rent bicycles.

Casa do Esteiro, Lanhelas, 4910 Caminha. Tel. (058) 921356. A house at the edge of a little wood in Caminha. It has an apartment with two double bedrooms, bath, kitchen and sitting room.

Camp site
Where to eat

Mata do Camarido, Orbitur, Caminha. Tel. (058) 921294.

Restaurante Remo, Avenida Dr Dantas Carneiro. Tel. (058) 921459. A restaurant that serves good Portuguese and Spanish food. It has a view of the river, and Spain.

Foz do Minho, Avenida Marginal. Tel. (058) 921301. This restaurant specializes in eel, kid, cod dishes and shellfish.

What to eat

As you would expect, Caminha has some interesting fish and shellfish dishes. Try cold savel, pickled savel, and eel Minho fashion.

**Vilar dos
Mouros**

Vilar dos Mouros is a picturesque little town in a rural setting, just 7 km inland from Caminha on the N301. It has windmills, watermills and a medieval bridge.

**Vila Nova
de Cerveira**

Vila Nova de Cerveira, 12 km from Caminha on the N13, has wooded granite hills on one side and the River Minho on the other. There are many shops selling copper ware, carved granite statues, iron furniture, woven rag rugs and blankets and lots of other locally made objects. Spaniards come across the river here to shop.

Where
to stay
Inexpensive
Pousada
Medium price

Estalagem da Boega, Vila Nova de Cerveira. Tel. (051) 95231. A four star inn with forty rooms with bath, a restaurant, bar, swimming pool, tennis courts, and beautiful views of the River Minho and Spain.

Pousada Dom Dinis, Vila Nova de Cerveira. Tel. (051) 95601, telex 32821. A luxury class pousada in a castle built by King Afonso III. It has twenty-six rooms and two suites, bars, lounges and recreation rooms.

Where to eat

Restaurante Quinta do Outeiral, Gondarém. Tel. (051) 95231.

What to eat	Try *arroz de debulho* (rice with shad), lampreys, fried grey mullet.
Valença do Minho	The frontier town of Valença do Minho, 52 km north of Viana do Castelo, is a total fortress, surrounded by two sets of walls and a moat, constructed to protect Valença against the Spaniards. To enter the town you pass over a drawbridge and through arched doorways, and at night the city is still closed off with big, thick doors.
	Today the Spaniards invade with pesetas instead of lances. Over six million tourists a year, mostly Spaniards, cross the bridge over the River Minho from Spain. The shops are full of goods intended for the tourist market – linens, shoes, cutlery, every kind of craft product, and knick-knacks in quantity.
What to see	The double defence walls of Valença are held up by twelve bulwarks and four towers. The walls are very thick indeed – they now have shops between them.
	The Praça da República is full of interesting old houses.
	For train enthusiasts, the Vintage Train Museum has a steam locomotive built in 1875 by the English Beyer Peacock.
Excursion	It is worth the short trip to **Ganfei** on the N101 to see the imposing Ganfei Monastery, which was one of the most important Benedictine monasteries in the north of Portugal. It owes its name to Ganfredo, a Norman priest and saint who reconstructed the monastery in 1018. It was remodelled in the eighteenth century, but maintains most of its original interior. It has three naves, with zoomorphic figures and traces of medieval frescoes.
Where to stay *Inexpensive*	**Pensão Monte do Faro**, Monte do Faro. Tel. (051) 22411. A three star pension with a restaurant, and beautiful views.
Pousada *Medium price*	**Pousada de São Teotónio**, Valença do Minho. Tel. (051) 22242/52, telex 32837. A first class pousada, within the fortress walls, overlooking the River Minho and Spain. It is a modern structure, opened in 1962, but is decorated in keeping with its medieval setting. It has sixteen rooms with bath, a restaurant and a bar.
Where to eat	The restaurant in the **Pensão Monte do Faro** is good. It serves regional dishes.
	Restaurante Stop, São Pedro da Torre. A roadside restaurant 5 km from Valença on the Viana–Valença road. It serves good food, and also has some rooms with bath.
What to eat	Try river fish, eels and salted cod. Another cod dish is *bacalhau zé de pipo*, cooked *au gratin* in the oven.
Monção	Monção is a picturesque frontier town with some of its old walls still standing. The twelfth-century Lapela Tower still seems to stand guard against the Spaniards. There is no bridge across the Minho here: cars have to cross to Spain by boat.
	To get from Valença to Monção you drive along the bank of the river, but the road leaves a good deal to be desired. It is narrow, and full of curves. There are old granite block houses with gardens where hydrangeas bloom, emigrant houses (looking very out of place), and

lots of *espigueiros* and haystacks. There are many vineyards and grape arbours – this is the country of the famous Alpedrinha grapes.

It was at Ponte do Mouro (Bridge of the Moor), just 7 km from Monção, that in the fourteenth century King João I and the English John of Gaunt, Duke of Lancaster formed an alliance against the Castilians, and the marriage of João to John of Gaunt's daughter, Philippa, was arranged.

The women of Monção have figured prominently in its history. There is a story that in 1368 when the town was besieged by Castilians, it was saved by a young noblewoman, Deu-la-Deu Martins. To make the besiegers believe that the town could hold out indefinitely, Deu-la-Deu baked bread with the last bit of grain and threw it over the wall, crying that there was plenty more where that came from. Discouraged, the Castilians returned to Spain. You can still eat 'Deu-la-Deu' rolls baked there today.

The Romanesque Parish Church dates from the thirteenth century. It has a funeral monument in honour of Deu-la-Deu Martins, and a bas-relief showing a wolf that the local people associate with the devil. The fourteenth-century castle has some parts of its walls and two portals still standing. The Misericórdia Chapel and the São Francisco Chapel both date from the seventeenth century.

Quilts, pottery, wickerwork, ox-yokes and straw raincoats are made, and can be bought, in Monção.

On 18 June Monção celebrates the *Festas do Corpus Christi*. There is a picturesque combat between a 'Saint George' on a white horse brandishing a sword and a huge, brightly coloured 'dragon' which is vanquished after a great number of comic antics. There is also a procession led, as in the Middle Ages, by a 'blessed ox' with varnished horns decorated with flowers and ribbons.

Just 5 km from Monção is the beautiful nineteenth-century Palácio da Brejoeira, which produces, and gives its name to, the best and most expensive *vinho verde* in Portugal. You can see the palace from the road, but it is not open to visitors.

At Barbeita, 8 km east of Monção, is a prehistoric hill town, the Castro da Nossa Senhora da Assunção. Also at Barbeita you can see the Rio Mouro Bridge, which has a stone commemorating the meeting between King João I and John of Gaunt.

The Caldas de Monção, Parque das Termas, is a spa where rheumatism is treated.

Albergaria Atlântico, Rua General Pimenta de Castro 13. Tel. (051) 52355/6. A good four star inn with a bar and restaurant.

Pensão Mané, Rua General Pimenta de Castro 5. Tel. (051) 52376. A three star pension with a bar and restaurant.

Casa de Rodas, 4950 Monção. Tel. (051) 52105. A manor house just 2 km from Monção, on an estate that produces *vinho verde*. It has four bedrooms and three bathrooms for tourists.

Quinta de Montes, not far from Monção in Troviscoso. Tel. (051) 52771. An old house of historic interest with three rooms with bath.

Quinta de Santo António is a large rustic house in Albergaria de Sá near Monção. Tel. (051) 54206. It has three apartments for guests, all with bath, a games room, billiards, TV and a swimming pool.

Where to eat The restaurant in the **Pensão Mané** (address above) is good.

What to eat The specialities of Monção are lampreys, salmon, chicken with rice, and (of course) Deu-la-Deu buns. Above all, do try the Palácio da Brejoeira *vinho verde*.

The Tourist Office is in the Largo do Loreto. Tel. (051) 52757.

Melgaço Melgaço is a tiny ancient town, 23 km from Monção by the N202. Along the road – which is not too good – you will see beautiful eight-eenth-century manor houses overlooking the River Minho, old stone villages, and grape arbours.

History Just 9 km from the Spanish border, Melgaço has repeatedly been invaded over the centuries. Melgaço too has a tale of rescue by a woman. During their war against the Castilians, so the story goes, King João I and John of Gaunt kept Melgaço's castle (which was then occupied by the Castilians) under siege for fifty-two days. Finally a woman known as *A Renagada* (the Renegade), who was fighting on the side of the Castilians, heard that there was also a woman, Inês Negra, fighting for the Portuguese. *A Renegada* challenged Inês Negra to single combat to decide which forces should have the castle. Inês Negra came out victorious, and the Castilians surrendered the castle.

What to see The twelfth-century castle and the Church of Nossa Senhora da Orada, of the same period, are worth seeing.

Where to stay The best places to stay are in the Peso spa, 4 km from Melgaço on the N202.

Inexpensive **Hotel Rocha**, Peso. Tel. (051) 42356. A one star hotel.

Pensão Boa Vista, Peso. Tel. (051) 22464. A three star pension.

In Melgaço itself is **Pensão Pemba**, Largo da Calçada. Tel. (051) 42555. A two star pension that offers five rooms, three with bath.

Where to eat The **Hotel Rocha** and the **Pensão Boa Vista** both have quite good food.

What to eat Smoked ham, kid, lamprey cakes, suckling pig are specialities. And be sure to try the Alvarinho wines.

The Tourist Office is in the Town Hall in the Peso spa.

The Peneda-Gerês National Park

The National Park of Peneda-Gerês is one of the least explored natural reserves in Europe. The Park covers 70,000 hectares in the shape of a horseshoe bordered on the north by Spain and on the south by the River Cávado. It is divided in two by the River Lima. The Peneda Mountains are in the north of the region and the Gerês Mountains in the south.

Getting there
Melgaço is one of the gateways to the Park; the other entrances are reached from Arcos de Valdevez on the N101 or from Ponte da Barca on the N101/N203 and lead to Soajo and Lindoso; from Caniçada on the N308-1 off the Braga to Chaves road to Caldas do Gerês; or from Outeiro on the N308 to Parada. There are no roads across the park. Park areas are signposted with a deer's head and the letters PN in a circle with a green background.

Plants and animals
In the Peneda-Gerês Park there are plants and animals not to be seen anywhere else in the world. There are eighteen species of plants, including a wild Geres iris, a Geres fern and a Geres juniper, which are found only in the Park. One hundred and forty-two different types of birds have been recorded (so bring your binoculars). Roe deer, wolves, wildcats and wild horses all run free, and among the horses are Luso-Galician wild ponies which are special to the Park.

History
The Park has a long history. The dolmens in Castro Laboreiro, Mezio, Paradela, Cambeses, Pitões and Tourém are thought to be more than 5,000 years old. There are many Celtic markings on the granite outcroppings in the Park, especially at Calcedónia. At São João do Campo there is a granite monolith known as the Cross of São João: this has a Latin inscription. There are also more Roman milestones here than anywhere else on the Iberian Peninsula – a hundred of them mark the Roman military road built by the Emperor Vespasian that linked Bracara Augusta (Braga) to Astorga in Spain, and to Rome.

Pilgrimage
In August one of the biggest pilgrimages in Portugal takes place to the shrine of São Bento da Porta Aberta, in the Park. São Bento, who was called 'the saint of the open door' because he lived in a cave which even the wolves did not enter, cures people's warts – in case you are interested.

Crafts
Most of the crafts are based on coarse linen or wool.

Sightseeing
After you leave Melgaço for the Park, you climb for 18 km up a very steep, winding road through high granite mountains with terraced farms on their sides. From here you will look far down into the valley of the River Minho. The country becomes more wild and arid as you climb, until you come to a boulder-strewn landscape, dotted with herds of goats and oxen, and the straw or stone huts that are shelters for the shepherds.

Phantom villages

Among the most curious sights of this region are the 'phantom villages' – villages of empty granite houses. In April the villagers go into the high mountains with their flocks and they stay there till December, living in *brando* (soft) houses which are little more than improvized shelters, and raising potatoes and barley. In the winter they move back down to their *inverneiras* (winter houses), that are made of granite blocks with straw or slate roofs. The cattle live on the ground floor and the families above. While the people are snowed in during the winter they weave their flax and wool. They practise communal life, holding their flocks, pastures, mills and ovens in common.

Castro Laboreiro

The strange old town of Castro Laboreiro is 950 m up in the clouds where it is cool even in summer. Castro Laboreiro is dominated by the ruins of a castle which was built by Portugal's first king, Afonso Henriques, and destroyed, much later, when lightning struck its powder magazine.

At Castro Laboreiro there are many ancient dolmens, and some strange geological formations that look like giant stone turtles. In the square there are stone crosses and an old stone church.

Look out for the Castro Laboreiro sheep dog, a big dog rather like a mastiff, kept for herding sheep and warding off wolves. It is not a friendly dog. The village priest raises Castro Laboreiros.

Where to stay, and eat Inexpensive

Pensão Abrigo in the village square at Castro Laboreiro. Tel. (051) 45126. Has six rooms and a very good restaurant. It makes an excellent base for walking expeditions in the mountains.

Entering the park from Arcos de Valdevez to go to Soajo and Lindoso, you climb a very narrow winding road with deep valleys and stone villages.

Soajo

Soajo seems quite cut off from the outside world. Its inhabitants, *monteiros* (huntsmen) who hunted bears, wild boar, wild goats, wolves, roebuck and foxes, were long ago granted by the king special privileges that made the town almost autonomous. The people are still very independent and remote.

The *espigueiros* (small granaries on stilts) of Soajo stand in a large group on a wide open threshing floor high above the valleys; they make an impressive sight. In the town square there is a stone pillory that is a national monument.

The way from Soajo to Lindoso is up an almost perpendicular winding granite road. You will see many old stone houses and a man-made waterfall tumbling hundreds of metres down the mountain.

Lindoso

At Lindoso there is another impressive concentration of *espigueiros*, best viewed from the castle walls. The castle was built in the thirteenth century and is quite well preserved, with its walls and several watchtowers still standing. One old house inside has been restored. The mountain road back via Ponte da Barca is tortuous, so drive carefully.

Caldas do Gerês

From the Caniçada entrance, you have a 7 km drive into the park to Caldas do Gerês, a spa first used by the Romans, and a fashionable watering place in the eighteenth century. It has swimming pools, tennis and boating, and there are several turn-of-the-century hotels. You can get guides here to tour the park, or take sightseeing trips on the special local buses. You can go up to the waterfalls at Ponte do Arado, to swim in their pools and see the old bridge. Or to the Barca da Mó, to see the old Roman military road, and the Miradouro da Junceda, for the spectacular view of the Park.

What to do

Sport

The Peneda-Gerês Park is a wonderful place for mountaineering enthusiasts. It's good for fishermen, too. There is trout fishing in all of the rivers, and on the lakes at Caniçada, Vilarinho das Furnas and Paradela there are water sports and boating.

Tours

Organized tours on horseback through the Park are available. For example, there is a seven-day tour, with a guide, which includes stops at comfortable hotels and sightseeing in the mountains and in Braga and the Citânia de Briteiros. A two-day tour takes you through typical villages, to the rivers and waterfall, and provides lodging in good inns. For real nature-lovers, there is a seven-day tour with stops for camping. To make a reservation, contact one of the agencies listed below.

The Tourist Delegation in the Peneda-Gerês Park, Vilar da Vega, Terras de Boura. Tel. (053) 39181.

Vasco H. Pires, Cooperativa Trote-Gerês, Cavalos, Cabril 5495, Borralha. Tel. (053) 659292.

There are also planned walking tours through the Park. Maps are available at the Tourist Offices.

Where to stay

Inexpensive

Hotel do Parque, Avenida Manuel Francisco da Costa, Caldas do Gerês. Tel. (053) 65112. A two star hotel of the *belle époque*. It has hardly changed since the turn of the century – very atmospheric.

Hotel das Termas is another old, Victorian-style hotel in the centre of town. Tel. (053) 39143.

There are three pensions in the Avenida Manuel Francisco da Costa in Caldas do Gerês: **Pensão Baltazar**, tel. (053) 65131; **Pensão Geresiana**, tel. (053) 65130 and **Pensão Casa da Ponte**, tel. (053) 39125. They are all three star.

Estalagem de São Bento, near the shrine of São Bento. Tel. (053) 65106. An excellent four star inn.

Pousada
Medium price

Pousada de São Bento, Caniçada. Tel. (053) 647190. A first class pousada built to resemble a Swiss chalet. It has eighteen rooms, a good restaurant and a swimming pool, and spectacular views over the River Cávado.

Manor house
Medium price

Casa de Requeixo, Frades (EN 103 Braga/Chaves), 4300 Povoa de Lanhoso. Tel. (053) 631112. A sixteenth-century country manor, 10 km from Peneda-Gerês Park, it has four bedrooms with bath, river swimming and horse-riding nearby. It has central heating, so is open all year.

Inexpensive **Casa do Adro**, Soajo, 4970 Arcos de Valdevez. Tel. (058) 47327 or (053) 78487. A typical Minho house, high in the mountains. It has five double bedrooms for guests.

What to eat Try the trout, lampreys, game, chicken with rice, and, to drink, the fine Alvarinho wines.

There are several Tourist Offices which deal with the Park. In Braga, Rua de São Geraldo 29, tel. (053) 76924; in Caldas do Gerês, tel. (062) 39133; in Arcos de Valdevez, tel. (058) 66001, and in Montealegre, tel. (076) 52254/6.

Arcos de Valdevez Arcos de Valdevez, on the River Vez, is one of the access points to the Peneda-Gerês National Park. The town dates from the tenth century, and has many interesting buildings.

What to see The **Church of Nossa Senhora da Conceição da Praça** is an enchanting Romanesque chapel, recently restored. The **Parish Church**, built at the end of the seventeenth century, has extensive tilework, and an interesting bas-relief of the Last Supper. The Baroque **Church of Nossa Senhora da Lapa**, built in 1767, is octagonal in shape. It is rich in carved stone and gilt decoration.

There is also a Manueline **pillory**, with the coat of arms of King Manuel I carved by João Lopes.

Where to stay Inexpensive **Pensão Sol do Vale (residencial)**, Rua Dr Germano de Amorim. Tel. (058) 66534. A three star pension with thirty-five rooms with bath.

Pensão Tavares, Rua Padre Manuel José da Cunha Brito. Tel. (058) 66253. A three star pension with thirteen rooms with bath.

Manor houses Medium price **Paço da Glória**, Lugar da Portela. Tel. (058) 42117. An imposing eighteenth-century house with an ancient three-storey crenellated tower, overlooking the countryside in solitary splendour. For guests it has four double rooms in the main house and five in annexes. There are charming gardens, and a swimming pool.

Casa do Requeijo, Lugar do Requeijo.Tel. (058) 631112. A large, seventeenth-century house with gardens that slope down to the River Vez. It has two fully equipped apartments, eight bedrooms with bath, a swimming pool, tennis court, ping-pong, barbecue, boating and fishing.

Where to eat What to eat **Restaurante Alameda**, Avenida Marginal. Tel. (058) 65476. Rice with lampreys is a speciality.

The Tourist Office is in the Avenida Marginal. Tel. (058) 66100.

Ponte da Barca Ponte da Barca is on the River Lima, at the junction of the N203 and the N101, and just 8 km from an entrance to the Peneda-Gerês National Park. In the old days the nobles of Ponte da Barca and Ponte de Lima disputed which was the more important of the two towns. In time Ponte de Lima outstripped Ponte da Barca economically, but Ponte da Barca still has many buildings that are reminders of its age of prominence.

What to see The present **Bridge** is a seventeenth-century structure. Before that there was a pontoon bridge on which houses were built for boatmen, but it became inadequate as traffic increased. It used to be the custom to baptize unborn babies under the bridge at midnight, with the first passer-by acting as godparent – the mother was sprinkled with water from an olive branch dipped in the river water, which was reputed to be miraculous.

The **Parish Church** was built between 1717 and 1738. It has an impressive stairway, and the interior of the building is covered with glazed figurative tiles.

Festival

The *Festas de São Bartolomeu* takes place in Ponte da Barca in late August: there are displays of cork and linen work and decorative work in a naïve style – and also a funfair and music.

Where to stay
Inexpensive

Pensão Freitas, Rua Conselheiro Rosa Paixoto. Tel. (058) 42113. A two star pension, it has fourteen rooms without bath.

Manor house
Medium price

Paço Vedro, 4980 Ponte da Barca. Tel. (058) 42117. An eighteenth-century manor house located 2 km from Ponte da Barca, in the centre of an estate with many trees. Its baronial halls and antique furniture provide an elegant setting. For guests there are three double rooms and two suites with bath and central heating. There are also billiard and music rooms and a private bar.

Casa da Agrela, São Pedro de Vade. Tel. (058) 42313. Offers three bedrooms with bath, chapel, bar, TV, library, games room, swimming pool, bicycles and farming activities.

Inexpensive

Quinta da Prova, Ponte da Barca. Tel. (058) 42163. A big farmhouse with three apartments for guests, who can take part in the activities of the farm.

Casa de Calvos, Tavora Santa Maria. Tel. (058) 65465. A historic house with one apartment and two double rooms with bath for guests.

Where to eat

Bar do Rio, on the river edge, near the bridge. A restaurant run by the Town Hall. You can leave your car near the bridge and walk to the restaurant along a path paved with granite stones and bordered by green lawns and weeping willow trees. The restaurant itself is a reconstructed stone house, and it has a lovely lawn and terrace with tables shaded by bright umbrellas. The food is very good – I would especially recommend the steaks and the freshwater fish. You can also hire a boat and go swimming in the river from a float, which is one of the main attractions of a visit here.

What to eat

Lampreys, croquettes of cod, and rice with giblets are specialities of Ponte da Barca.

Ponte de Lima

Ponte de Lima is 25 km east of Viana do Castelo by the N202 and 32 km north of Braga by the N201. As its name suggests, it is on the bank of the River Lima – the river the Roman soldiers identified with the Lethe, the 'River of Forgetfulness': during their wars with the Lusitanians their leaders had great difficulty in persuading them to cross it, because they were afraid it would make them forget their own country, and they would never go home.

History

There was an ancient Celtic settlement at Ponte de Lima. After the Romans captured the town they developed it into a trade centre and built a bridge – which is still used – and thick walls to protect it. Forum Limicorum, as the Romans called it, was on the Roman road that linked Braga with Astorga in Spain. You can still see many of the Roman milestones.

Ponte de Lima was granted its first charter by Dona Teresa, Countess of Burgundy, in 1125. In the fourteenth century massive walls, with six entranceways and ten watchtowers, were built round the town, to replace ruined Roman walls, and in 1355 the old Roman bridge was extended for the visit of King Pedro.

Over the centuries, the town and its surroundings have produced famous generals, poets and explorers. Ferdinand Magellan, one of the first explorers to circumnavigate the globe, was born here. Many noble families with titles older than the nation itself have their palaces and manor houses in the town or nearby. A large number of them have been turned into guest houses for tourists.

Ponte de Lima today

With its medieval towers and whitewashed houses, Ponte de Lima makes a lovely picture. Every other Monday there is a colourful market by the banks of the river; and most mornings women of the town go down to the river to wash their clothes and spread them out to dry.

What to see

The main city walls were torn down in the nineteenth century to allow the town to expand, but two towers, São Paulo and Cadeia, linked by an extension of wall, are still standing. The Cadeia Tower has an interesting door.

The Roman-medieval bridge has twenty-four arches, of which the four on the right bank are the original Roman ones.

The **Chapel of São Miguel**, or **Anjo da Guarda** (Guardian Angel), a Gothic chapel near the bridge, is said to have been built to commemorate a miracle in which an innocent person was saved from death. The **Church of Santo António dos Capuchos** dates from the fourteenth century: it has Hispano-Arab glazed tiles. The fifteenth-century **Parish Church** has richly ornate chapels.

There is an eighteenth-century Baroque town fountain, with the Ponte de Lima arms, in the Praça de Camões.

The old prison contains historical archives, including the original 1125 town charter.

There are many Gothic, Manueline and Baroque houses from the sixteenth, seventeenth and eighteenth centuries. The eighteenth-century mansion of the Counts of Aurora is particularly interesting.

Crafts

Embroidered linen, tin lamps, carved wooden furniture, blankets, rugs and wickerwork are all made in and around Ponte de Lima.

Festivals

In early June the *Festas do São Jorge* takes place. There is a procession in which Saint George is represented on horseback, followed by a peculiar pantomime cow-fight.

The New Fairs, which take place in late September, have been held since the twelfth century. Anything and everything that is connected with farming is sold at the fairs. There is a procession dedicated to Our Lady of Sorrows, and, of course, there is folk dancing and singing.

Sport

There is good fishing on the river, and there is also small-game shooting. The Tourist Office and the manor house owners often organize shoots.

Where to stay
Inexpensive

Pensão São João, Rua do Rosário 6. Tel. (058) 941288. A two star pension with eleven rooms, three with bath.

Manor houses

The Ponte de Lima area has twenty-seven manor houses that take guests. There is only room here to mention a few of the most interesting, but if you inquire at the Tourist Office or contact Turihab (tel. [058] 942335 or 942729) they will let you have details of many more. They will also make reservations for you.

Medium price

Paço de Calheiros, Calheiros, 4990 Ponte de Lima. Tel. (058) 947164. One of the most imposing of the manor houses. A long two-storeyed house built in the eighteenth century using stones from a much earlier manor, it stands on a high hill above Ponte de Lima and dominates the valley. The Counts of Calheiros, who have held the land on which the house is built since 1336, claim their name is older than Portugal. Totally restored and modernized, the Paço de Calheiros has for guests seven double bedrooms and one single bedroom, all with bath.

Inexpensive

Casa do Outeiro, Arcozelo, 4990 Ponte de Lima. Tel. (058) 941206. One of the most impressive and best preserved houses in the area, Casa do Outeiro dates from the sixteenth century and has been owned by the same family for four hundred years. It offers two double bedrooms with bath.

Moinho de Estorãos, Estorãos, 4990 Ponte de Lima. Tel. (058) 941546. An old watermill by a Roman bridge over the little River Estorãos near Ponte de Lima. It was built in the middle of the seventeenth century and in the beginning of the nineteenth it was renovated and enlarged by the sister of the village priest. It was on land belonging to the Count of Bertiandos. In the beginning, the owners had to pay a chicken a year as rent; later they paid 10 esc., then 100, and finally 200. The mill has modern appliances and a double bedroom, sitting room with fireplace, bathroom and kitchen.

Where to eat

Solar do Taberneiro, Centro Comercial Rio Lima. Tel. (058) 942169.

Monte da Madalena, Monte de Santa Madalena. Tel. (058) 941239.

Restaurante Encanada, Praça Municipal. Tel. (058) 941189.

What to eat **Restaurante Gaio**, Rua Agostinho Taveira. Tel. (058) 941251.
Try *arroz de sarrabulho* (meats cooked with rice and pig's blood),
rojões de porco (little bits of pork, marinated and deep-fried), lampreys.

The Tourist Office is in the Praça da República. Tel. (058) 942335,
telex 32618. The Office has a display of the crafts of the region on sale.

Vila Verde Vila Verde, 21 km south of Ponte de Lima on the N101, is an old
town (dating from the tenth century), set in very pretty countryside.

What to see Have a look at the Roman bridge, the Romanesque Parish Church
and the São António Chapel.

Vila Verde is the seat of government for several parishes, one of
which, **Gondomar**, is a little town that is very well worth seeing.
With its stone streets and thatch-roofed granite houses, it seems to
have stopped in time.

Manor house **Quinta das Tongas**, 4730 Vila Verde. Tel. (053) 32143. Quinta
Inexpensive das Tongas is situated 1 km out of town, in a wood. For guests there is
a small rustic house near the main manor, with three double bed-
rooms, bathroom, living room and kitchen.

Barcelos

Barcelos is on the River Cávado just 11 km from the coast and 15 km
from Braga. It is the craft centre of the country. Its weekly fair, held
every Thursday in the Campo da República in the centre of the town,
covers a huge area and sells crafts, clothing, dishes, ox-carts, fruit,
vegetables, and just about everything else imaginable. There is a
permanent exhibition of crafts, with items for sale, in the Torre da
Porta Nova near the Largo do Município.

History Archaeological finds have revealed that the Barcelos area was
inhabited in the late Stone Age. There are several Iron Age *castros*, for
example Castro Faria and Castro Boriz, and the Romans built around
the medicinal springs at Santa Eulália de Aguas Santas. Barcelos was
granted its charter in 1140.

Legend of Everywhere you go in Portugal you will see painted pottery
the cockerel cockerels, ceramic cockerels, carved wooden cockerels, and assorted
other cockerels, and it was in Barcelos that the legend of the cockerel
originated. This legend dates back to the fourteenth century. It comes
in various versions, but according to a fairly standard one, a Galician
pilgrim on his way to Santiago was wrongly accused of theft and
sentenced to death. Protesting his innocence, the pilgrim found his
way to the judge who had sentenced him, who was just sitting down to
dinner to eat a roast cockerel. Pointing to the cockerel, the pilgrim
cried, 'If I am innocent, may that cockerel get up and crow!' The cockerel got up and crowed lustily, and the pilgrim was released.

What to see The fifteenth-century **Ducal Palace** collapsed in 1800, but still has some walls and a tall chimney standing, and its ruins have been turned into an archaeological museum. There is here an elaborately carved stone monument dating from the fourteenth century that shows Christ on the cross with a cockerel at his feet, and other figures that could be pilgrims. This figure, which was brought to the museum from Força Velha, just across the River Cávado is called the *Cruzeiro do Senhor do Galo*.

The fifteenth-century bridge which you have to cross to get into the town is well preserved, but it is very narrow, and this causes terrible traffic jams, especially on market days. It is probably better to park your car on the other side and walk over.

The **Parish Church**, in the Largo do Município, was built in the thirteenth century and restored in the sixteenth. It has a carved pillory from the sixteenth century, and eighteenth-century figurative glazed tiles. The **Regional Ceramic Museum**, which has examples of all the crafts of the region, is in part of the church.

The eighteenth-century **Terço Church** has figurative glazed tiles, a panelled ceiling and a Baroque altar. The **Church of the Beneditas Convent** has eighteenth-century figurative glazed tiles. The **Senhor da Cruz** is an eighteenth-century Baroque church with a large cupola and a profusion of Baroque carved work. It is the focus of a yearly procession in honour of the Miracle of the Cross (see facing page).

There are many fifteenth-century mansions in Barcelos, but the **Solar dos Pinheiros** is one of the most beautiful. It was built in 1448 for Pedro Esteves, a magistrate for the house of Bragança, the former royal house of Portugal. In the south tower there is a statue of *Barbadão* (The Bearded One), the Jewish grandfather of the first Duke of Bragança, pulling out his beard. (For the story of how he came to grow the beard, see page 173.)

The **Hospital of the Misericórdia** was an old Capuchin monastery. Its gardens are now the city park.

Crafts
Barcelos has a profusion of folk art. In particular, the immense quantities of clay in the area made it a great centre for pottery making, and this tradition continues today. There are painted cockerels in all sizes and all colours. There are colourful figurative sculptures of chickens, oxen, fanciful devils, animals playing musical instruments, and grotesque combinations of all of these. One attractive group, which is much reproduced, is made up of musicians playing all of the local musical instruments.

You will also see lace and embroidered linen, ceramics, straw hats, baskets, hand-loomed rugs and bedspreads and wooden carvings.

The most famous potter of the region was Rosa Ramalho. Among the best-known of her glazed pottery images are one of Christ on the Cross, and others of a pregnant goat, a noble on horseback, and various creatures playing guitars. She died a few years ago, and her original work is now quite scarce and expensive, but it is sometimes possible to find examples in good shops. Her family is carrying on, reproducing many of her favourite pieces and inventing new ones.

Festival

The *Festas das Cruzes* takes place at the beginning of May. It has been celebrated in Barcelos since 1504, when, it is said, a peasant who insisted on working on the Day of the Holy Cross saw a luminous, perfumed cross appear on the ground where he was digging. Now the 'Miracle of the Cross' is celebrated every year, by a procession which crosses a carpet made of millions of flower petals leading into the Church of Senhor da Cruz. During the festival the women of the region get out their colourful regional dresses and load themselves with massive gold chains that represent the wealth of the family. The celebrations end with a giant firework display on the river.

Where to stay
Inexpensive

Albergaria Condes de Barcelos, Avenida Alcaides de Faria. Tel. (053) 811061, telex 32532. An attractive four star inn with thirty rooms and a bar.

Albergaria Dom Nuno, Avenida Dom Nuno A. Pereira. Tel. (053) 815084. A three star inn with twenty-seven rooms and a bar.

Pensão Arantes, Avenida Liberdade 32-36. Tel. (053) 82326. A two star pension.

Manor houses
Inexpensive

Casa do Monte, Abade do Neiva, 4750 Barcelos. Tel. (053) 811519. A large two-storey house surrounded by colourful gardens and trees. There are three double bedrooms for guests, and it has a swimming pool.

Casa dos Assentos, Quintiães, 4700 Barcelos. Tel. (053) 88160. Casa dos Assentos is part of a large ivy-covered manor house built in the seventeenth century – the part where the records (*assentos*) were kept. The house has spacious lawns and gardens and a swimming pool. There are two independent apartments in the main house, each with two double rooms, bathroom, living room and kitchen.

Where to eat

Restaurante Bagoeira, Avenida Sidónio Pais 57. Tel. (053) 82236.

What to eat

Try *arroz de frango* (rice with chicken), *arroz de sarrabulho* (stewed meats with pig's blood and rice), *rojões de porco* (fried pieces of pork), lampreys, cod, oranges stuffed with sweet pumpkin.

The Tourist Office is in the Rua Duques de Bragança. Tel. (053) 812135.

Braga

Braga lies in the middle of the Minho, just 52 km from Oporto. It is the religious centre of the country, and has over 300 churches.

History

When, in the second century BC, the settlement on this spot was conquered by the Romans, they named it Bracara Augusta. At the hub of five roads leading to Rome, it was a very important crossroads.

In the fifth century AD, after the Romans had been driven out by the Swabians, Braga became the capital of the Swabian kingdom of Galicia. During the sixth and seventh centuries it developed into an important religious centre, and the Bishops of Braga became immensely powerful. Then about 730 Braga was conquered, and almost destroyed, by the Moors.

Braga's influence in affairs of Church and of State was restored after the town was taken by the Castilians in the eleventh century. The Bishops, who soon became Archbishops, were referred to as the 'Senhores de Braga'. They wielded more power than the monarchy. This situation persisted well into this century – in fact till the 1974 Revolution. This did prompt them to be a bit less autocratic, but even so they still exert great influence. For a very long time all of the industry of Braga was devoted to the needs of the Church – vestments, sacred ornaments, sculpture, carvings, furniture, and so on. In recent

Braga today

years the need to diversify has finally been recognized, and Braga is now attempting to modernize and industrialize – with an unfortunate lack of control as far as its historic monuments are concerned.

What to see

There are Roman ruins being excavated in the city. You have to get special permission to see them, from the University of the Minho in Braga, in the Avenida Central.

The twelfth-century **Cathedral** was a Romanesque structure. Its beginnings were financed by Henry of Burgundy and his wife Dona Teresa, and the work was continued by their son Dom Afonso Henriques, the first King of Portugal. In the sixteenth century Archbishop Diogo de Sousa completed the porch, modified the Romanesque portico, put up his coat of arms and rebuilt the apse in flamboyant ogival style. At the end of the eighteenth century Archbishop Rodrigo de Moura Teles had the doors made, constructed the bell towers, opened the enormous windows in the nave, and gave the façade its present Baroque style. The marble pulpits, the brass balustrades, the magnificent organs and the Bishop's chair, in black wood, were also added at this period, as were lots of the carvings.

There are many chapels inside the Cathedral.

The Gothic **Chapel of the Kings** contains the tombs of Dom Henry of Burgundy and Dona Teresa. It also contains the embalmed body of Archbishop Lourenço Vicente.

The **Chapel of Glória** in the cloister was built in 1330 by Archbishop Gonçalo Pereira. Its walls are covered in *mudéjar*-style frescoes, and there is a lovely eighteenth-century ceiling.

The **Chapel of São Pedro de Rates** is covered with tiles by António Oliveira Bernardes.

The **Chapel of Nossa Senhora da Piedade** has the tomb of Archbishop Diogo de Sousa. The figure of the Archbishop is believed to have been executed by Nicolau de Chanterene. This chapel also has a Renaissance altar, and a beautifully worked ceiling.

The **Chapel of São Geraldo** is a fine example of pure Gothic. It has an interesting fresco of the virgin with angels.

A statue of Nossa Senhora da Piedade, believed to be the work of Nicolau de Chanterene, stands outside the apse of the Cathedral.

It is worth dedicating quite a lot of time and attention to the **Cathedral Museum**: it contains an extraordinarily diversified collection of religious objects, each one with its own history. There is no particular order or logic in their presentation, so be sure to go with the Cathedral guide.

It has most of the pieces removed from the Cathedral between the twelfth and the eighteenth centuries to make way for objects in other styles. There are gold and silver embroidered vestments from the fifteenth to eighteenth centuries. There is a pair of adorned shoes with high platform soles, which belonged to Archbishop Rodrigo de Moura Teles, who was so short that he could not reach the altar without them. People in Braga say 'He was a very little man who did very great things' – among the many churches he had built was the great Church of Bom Jesus that dominates the city. There is a Hispano-Arab casket in ivory from the tenth century. There is a large collection of embroidered mitres (only the Bishops of Braga were allowed to wear three-pointed mitres). There is the iron cross which Frei Henrique de Coimbra used for saying Mass in Brazil in 1500, after Pedro Alvares Cabral had landed there for the first time, and taken possession of the country for the Crown of Portugal. There is an enormous treasury of gold and silver objects, including an 8.5 kg receptacle of pure silver encrusted with 450 precious stones that belonged to Dom Gaspar de Bragança. A seventeenth-century organ that is still in working order is in the collection. There are rings, keys to the city, scissors to cut altar candles, Chinese jars, wooden images, valuable paintings, trunks with secret locks and drawers for guarding the church treasure, a saddle that supposedly belonged to Saint George, music boxes, a thirteenth-century Christ on the Cross, books with hand-written Gregorian chants, a thirteenth-century painting of the Madonna and Child and an endless collection of other objects.

The **Misericórdia Church**, next to the Cathedral, is Renaissance in style, with a portico built in 1562. The carved work in the church is among the best in the country, and includes a sculptured composition of the Visitation done by the Coimbra School. The decorated panel behind the altar is the work of Marceliano de Araujo.

The sixteenth-century **Chapel of Nossa Senhora da Conceição** has a sculptured group depicting the burial of Christ, from the seventeenth century, and eighteenth-century glazed tiles.

The **Chapel and Casa dos Coimbras** were built in 1525 by Archbishop João Coimbra. The chapel has a square crenellated tower, a Gothic porch protecting the main doorway, and interesting tiles showing the story of Adam and Eve. All that remains of the house are some fine Manueline windows.

The **Church of Santa Cruz** is seventeenth-century Baroque with Rococo ornamentation. It has some impressive gilt carved work.

The **São Marcos Hospital and Church** is a Baroque rebuilding of the fifteenth-century São Marcos Chapel. Along the roof you can see eight life-size statues of apostles and martyrs.

The **Fonte do Ídolo** (Fountain of the Idol) is in the Rua do Raio in the centre of the town. Some historians believe it was an altar for offerings to the Lusitanian idol Tongenabiago. Everyone agrees it dates from pre-Roman times, despite its inscriptions: 'Celsius fecit' and 'Ambrosius fecit'. It is a kind of immersion fountain, with a high-relief human bust over the water spout and another life-size figure holding a child on its lap at the side. There is a sculptured bird and a half-circle over the bust.

The **Populo Church** was built in the sixteenth century as a tomb for Archbishop Agostinho de Jesus. It was reconstructed in the eighteenth century by architect Carlos Amarante, who also added the imposing façade to the adjoining convent. The interior has tiles by António de Oliveira Bernardes and many attractive panels.

The **Chapel of São Sebastião das Carvalheiras** was begun in the fifteenth century and remodelled in 1715 by Archbishop Rodrigo de Moura Teles. Its glazed tiles are by António de Oliveira Bernardes.

The **Church of São Vicente** is rich in carvings and figurative glazed tiles. The present church dates from the sixteenth and seventeenth centuries, but it was built on the site of a seventh-century Visigoth church. There is a stone in the sacristy with a funeral inscription dated May 618 that is the oldest Christian monument in Braga.

The **Torre de Menagem** (Keep) behind the Arcades was built in 1738 as part of the defence walls for the town.

The **Town Hall**, built in the eighteenth century, is an outstanding example of the Baroque. It has a stairway with tiles depicting the arrival of Archbishop José de Bragança (bastard brother of King João V).

The **Archbishop's Palace**, which is now part of the Public Library, comprises buildings from the fourteenth, fifteenth and sixteenth centuries. Its fourteenth-century Gothic wing is the remains of the old palace erected by Archbishop Gonçalo Pereira.

The **Santa Bárbara Gardens** behind the Public Library have parts of the old wall built in 1378, and a lovely fountain.

The **Arca da Porta Nova** was built in the eighteenth century, as the main entrance to the city, by Archbishop José de Bragança. His coat of arms is displayed, along with the figure of a woman who historically has represented Braga.

The **Salvador Chapel**, dating from the seventeenth century, is now part of the Conde de Agrolongo Asilo. It has a lovely façade, carvings, glazed tiles, painted box ceiling and gilt work.

The **Congregados Church** was built in the early sixteenth century by André Soares. With its Baroque façade, added in the seventeenth century, and its two bell towers, it is a majestic building.

The **Church of São Vitor** was built in the seventeenth century by Archbishop Luis de Sousa, on the site of a former Romanesque church. It has a wonderful collection of carvings and glazed tiles.

The **City Museum** is in the **Biscainhos Palace**, in the centre of the town. The palace, which was built in the sixteenth century, has a lovely carved wood ceiling, figurative glazed tiles and a superb atrium with a staircase adorned by granite sculptured figures. The museum has an interesting collection of Indo-Portuguese furniture.

The **Diogo de Sousa Museum** has a rather cluttered collection of Roman remains, utensils and ancient pottery.

Crafts   Braga specializes in the making of ornate devotive candles. The other crafts of the town include: wooden articles, such as rustic furniture and painted ox-yokes; simple earthenware and decorative pottery; copper, iron and tin ware; wicker and straw articles such as hats, furniture, lampshades and straw raincoats; hand-loomed quilts, bedspreads, rugs and mats; poultry feather mats and rugs; lacework; dried flowers; and paper fans.

Festivals   The Holy Week Festival (*Semana Santa*) in Braga is naturally the most sumptuous in the country. The streets are decorated with flowers and bright lights. There are many solemn and colourful processions, the most famous being the *Ecce Homo*, in which hundreds of barefoot penitents march carrying torches, and the *Enterro do Senhor* (Burying of Christ), in which thousands participate.

Towards the end of June there is another big festival, the *Festas de São João*. There are parades, processions, bands, singing and dancing. Many of the ancient rites of the Summer Solstice persist, in spite of the Church's efforts to turn the event into a Christian festival. There is a procession for Saint John, in which the little shepherd is shown as about four years old, but there are also bonfires on which herbs are thrown to make divinations. One curious note is the custom of passing round leeks to smell.

On festival days many women of the area wear a costume that includes a long cape and a little hat with ribbons and mirrors. As in all of the Minho, bright kerchiefs and gold jewellery are also very much in evidence.

Excursions   The **Tibães Monastery** is 6 km from Braga on the N101. It dates from the eleventh century, but was rebuilt in the eighteenth. It is now privately owned, except for its church cloister which has interesting panels, polychrome mouldings and blue tiles, but is in rather a poor state of repair.

The **Church of São Frutoso** is 3 km from Braga on the N205. It is believed to have been built for the Bishop of Frutoso of Dume in the seventh century, destroyed by the Moors and rebuilt in the eleventh century. Some experts say it was built in the Byzantine style in the form of a Greek cross, with four naves and a cupola in the centre (only the cupola and one brick vault remain).

Bom Jesus
Sanctuary

The Bom Jesus Sanctuary is one of the most spectacular monuments in Portugal. It stands on a densely wooded hill above Braga, just 3 km from the city on the N203, and commands a view of the foothills of the Gerês and Soajo mountains in the Peneda-Gerês Park, and of the distant Atlantic beaches. The entire area is full of the sound of running water from the many fountains and natural springs, and is shaded by enormous trees.

The main feature of the Sanctuary is the monumental Baroque staircase leading up to it. No one was able to tell me how many steps there were, and I soon lost count, but there must be hundreds. Unless you are really feeling athletic, you would be well advised to take the lift up, and walk down the stairs.

The lift is a feature in itself. Built in the nineteenth century, it operates by water, of which there is such an abundance at Bom Jesus. There are two carriages – one up, one down. A tank in one is filled with water from an underground spring at the measure of 100 litres per person, and the weight pulls the second carriage up as the first one goes down. The used water is donated to the farmers in the area. This old lift travels 285 m on a 40 per cent incline in three minutes.

The Bom Jesus Church, designed by Carlos Amarante and completed in 1811, has a neoclassical main door with four heavy columns on either side supporting a balcony with statues of the Four Evangelists. The interior is in the shape of a Latin cross. Near the church is the Chapel of Miracles, where pilgrims light candles and pray for miracles.

In the grounds at the top of the stairs there are three famous old hotels which were built at the same time as the Sanctuary: the Hotel do Parque, the Hotel do Elevador and the Hotel Sul Americano. In the circular patio in front of the hotels there are chapels representing the Apparition to Mary Magdalen, the Meeting at Emmaus and the Ascension, separated by fountains with statues of Matthew, Mark, Luke and John. On up the hill through grottoes, paths and fountains you will come to a lake with boats for hire, tennis courts and other sports facilities.

Now for your journey down the staircase. At the top of the stairway there are enormous statues of the men who condemned Jesus: Annas, Caiaphas, Herod and Pontius Pilate. Going down you will see a terrace with the Pelican fountain, which has biblical figures and is set in a lovely garden. The equestrian statue of Longuinhos there is the object of a superstition. It is believed that if a girl goes round the statue three times she will be married.

The next section of the stairway is the Stairway of Virtues, with Faith, Hope and Charity represented by fountains and surrounded by allegorical figures. The next two flights of stairs represent the five senses, by means of biblical figures. The first is the Fountain of Touch (with images of Solomon, Isaiah and Isaac). Then come the Fountains of Taste, Smell, Hearing and Sight. Finally there are the steps that lead to five chapels representing the Passion of Christ – the Sacred Way. Each chapel has naïve figures representing scenes of the Passion. At the bottom of the staircase is a dilapidated arch with the coat of arms of Archbishop Rodrigo de Moura Teles, who built Bom Jesus.

From Bom Jesus you can make a circular trip to visit two other important sanctuaries nearby: Sameiro and Santa Marta da Falperra.

The **Sanctuary of Sameiro** on the N309 is, after Fátima, the most important centre for Marian devotion in Portugal. It is visited by hundreds of thousands of pilgrims every year. The church is not particularly interesting, but the surrounding woods and paths are pleasant.

The **Santa Marta da Falperra Sanctuary** is farther along the road, in woods which in the old days were a hiding place for robbers. There was a local Robin Hood called Zé de Telhado who used to steal from the rich and give to the poor – according to legend. Santa Marta da Falperra was considered the protector of thieves. The woods are now calm and peaceful and free of robbers.

The **Church of Santa Maria Madalena**, part of the Santa Marta da Falperra Sanctuary, has a strange Rococo exterior with a whitewashed façade and a profusion of granite ornament all around. It has a high octagonal interior with a blue and gold retable.

A short trip from Braga on N209 will take you to **Póvoa de Lanhoso**. Afonso Henriques, first King of Portugal, shut up his mother, Dona Teresa, in the castle here, after he had defeated her and her supporters at the battle of São Mamede (1128). The castle has an even more unhappy legend connected with it. The story goes that a Mayor of Póvoa returned home to find his wife in flagrant adultery with her father confessor; enraged, he had everyone who was in the castle shut up there, and burned alive.

The Iron Age **Citânia de Lanhoso**, with the remains of many round houses, is nearby.

Fishing

Braga is near many of the Minho rivers and the reservoirs in the Peneda-Gerês National Park. If you would like to do some fishing, the Braga Amateur Fishermen's Club, Rua dos Chãos 112, will be able to help you with information.

Where to stay
Medium price

Hotel do Parque, Bom Jesus do Monte. Tel. (053) 767548. This four star hotel dates from the building of the Sanctuary, but has lately been restored and refurbished. It has original paintings and some antique furniture from noble houses, as well as reproduction antiques. There is a bar, but meals are taken in its twin hotel, the Hotel do Elevador, just in front.

Hotel do Elevador, Bom Jesus do Monte. Tel. (053) 676611. An elegant four star hotel, positioned just beside the famous lift, and much favoured by Lisbon society. It has a lovely restaurant with a view of Braga, and the distant mountains.

Hotel Turismo, Avenida João XXI. Tel. (053) 612200. A four star hotel with comfortable rooms and a nice bar, restaurant and swimming pool. There are 132 rooms.

Inexpensive

Hotel Carandá, Avenida da Liberdade 96. Tel. (053) 77016. A three star hotel with 100 rooms with bath and TV, and bar and restaurant.

Residencial dos Terceiros, Rua dos Capelistas 85. Tel. (053) 70466. A three star pension with simple modern rooms and a bar.

Pensão Dom Vilas, Rua Conselheiro Lobato 434. Tel. (053) 25104. A three star pension with thirty-two rooms with bath and TV, and a bar.

Manor houses
Inexpensive

There are many manor houses in the Braga area – the Tourist Office will be able to supply you with a list. There is only room here to mention a couple of the most interesting.

Casa dos Lagos, Bom Jesus do Monte, 4750 Braga. Tel. (053) 676738. A green, terraced mansion in the lush gardens of Bom Jesus, on the high hill that overlooks the city of Braga. The house has an apartment with two double bedrooms, bathroom, sitting room and kitchen.

Casa da Pedro Cavalgada, Lugar do Assente-Palmeira, 4700 Braga. Tel. (053) 24596 or 22309. A large nineteenth-century granite stone building, it is 2 km from Braga. It was here that the well known authority on Minho folklore, Professor Mota Leite, lived and wrote. The house has an apartment with two double bedrooms, bathroom, two sitting rooms, and a swimming pool.

Where to eat

In Braga itself there are lots of restaurants, in every price range – you should have no great difficulty in finding one you like. I can personally recommend the restaurant in the **Hotel do Elevador** at Bom Jesus, and the following are also good:

Restaurante Portico at Bom Jesus. Tel. (053) 676672. A small, new restaurant serving typical Portuguese dishes.

In downtown Braga the **Restaurante Abade de Prescas**, Praça Mouzinho de Albuquerque 7-1°, also serves typical Portuguese dishes. Tel. (053) 76750.

What to eat

The specialities of Braga are dried cod, *arroz de sarrabulho* (meats with pig's blood and rice), roast kid, pastries. And to accompany them all, *vinho verde*.

There are Tourist Offices in the Rua Justino Cruz 90, 6th floor, tel. (053) 76924, and in the Avenida da Liberdade 1, tel. (053) 614565 or 22550.

Guimarães

The ancient town of Guimarães is 51 km from Oporto by the N14 and 22 km from Braga by the N101, on a plain surrounded by mountains.

History The town grew up around the Monastery of Salvador do Mundo, which was built in 949, by the order of the pious Countess Mumadona, wife of Count Hermegildo Mendes of the Senhores da Quintana de Vimaranes. It is the place which saw the establishment of Portugal as an independent nation. In 1097 Alfonso VI, King of Galicia, Castile, León and Portugal, granted Portugal (which then consisted of the land between the Minho and the Douro) to his son-in-law Henry of Burgundy, as a feudal holding. After Henry's death in about 1112, his wife Dona Teresa (the illegitimate daughter of Alfonso VI) ruled as regent for their young son, Afonso Henriques. To the displeasure of the Portuguese barons Teresa became closely allied with the Spanish overlords, and eventually the Portuguese united against her, under the leadership of Afonso Henriques. In 1128, at the battle of São Mamede, near his capital of Guimarães, Afonso Henriques defeated Dona Teresa and her supporters. Subsequently Afonso Henriques became recognized as King of Portugal, though complete independence did not come until the break-up of the kingdom of León-Castile on the death of Afonso VII. The independence of Portugal was formally recognized by Pope Alexander III in 1179. Afonso Henriques died in 1185 at around eighty years of age, having reigned for fifty-seven years. Tradition says he was of enormous height, tremendous strength, and had a long, flowing beard.

Guimarães today Today, the city of Guimarães has been industrialized without much thought for the aesthetic. It has textile and shoe factories and ugly apartment buildings among the beautiful monuments. But the old part of the city is being restored.

What to see The tenth-century **Castle** on the hill which dominates the centre of Guimarães may have been built for the Countess Mumadona. It was the birthplace of Afonso Henriques.

The twelfth-century **Church of São Miguel do Castelo** is just down the hill in the woods near the Castle. It is a Romanesque church which has fortunately escaped restoration. It contains a baptismal font said to be the one used for the christening of Afonso Henriques.

The fifteenth-century **Palace of the Dukes of Bragança**, built by the first Duke of Bragança, the bastard son of King João I, is on the same hill. The second Duke, Fernando II, was beheaded by order of King João II, and the Palace was confiscated by the Crown. It was allowed to fall into ruin, until in this century the dictator António Salazar had it completely restored, for use as an official residence of the Head of State during visits to northern Portugal, and as a museum. It has collections of tapestries, furniture, tiles and portraits, and some ancient documents.

The **Capuchos Convent**, also known as the Misericórdia Hospital, is what is left of a monastery which was built in the seventeenth century by Capuchin monks using stones taken from the Bragança Palace. There remains a magnificent sacristy with rich carvings and a lovely colonnaded cloister round a fountain.

The seventeenth-century **Chapel of Santa Cruz**, nearby, is in the Mannerist style. There are tiles all round the chapel.

The **Largo do Carmo** and the **Rua da Santa Maria** have lovely eighteenth-century houses, with wooden balustrades and verandas, ornate doors and ceramic statuettes. Most of them are painted in a pleasant ochre colour. The **Church and Convent of Carmo**, in the square, are seventeenth-century Baroque. The inside of the church is rich in gilt carvings.

The seventeenth-century **Santa Clara Convent** has a Baroque façade and a lovely eighteenth-century two-storey cloister. It now houses the municipal archives.

The fourteenth-century **Church of Nossa Senhora da Oliveira** in the centre of the town has a beautiful façade with a tower on the left. It has suffered many modifications in style over the centuries – Gothic now predominates. The church had its origins in the primitive temple Countess Mumadona had erected in the tenth century to celebrate the 'Miracle of the Olive Tree'. According to the legend, in the sixth century the Visigoth warrior Wamba said that he would become king if his staff would sprout olive leaves when he stuck it in the ground. It did. He did. In the fourteenth century King João I built additions to the church in gratitude for his victory over the Castilians at Aljubarrota in 1385.

In front of the church the **Padrão do Salado**, a porch with four pointed Moorish arches, was built in 1340 by King Afonso IV to commemorate the victory over the Moors at Salado.

The **Alberto Sampaio Regional Museum**, which is also in part of the Nossa Senhora da Oliveira complex, has a priceless collection of tiles, including Hispano-Arabic tiles from the fifteenth and sixteenth centuries and 'rug' tiles from the seventeenth and eighteenth centuries. It also contains paintings, tapestries, ceramics, sculpture and gold work.

The fourteenth-century **Antigos Paços do Concelho** (Old Town Hall) was added to in the seventeenth century and is now the municipal library.

The **Church of São Francisco** dates from the fifteenth century, but was added to over the centuries and lavishly decorated in the eighteenth. It is rich in gilt carved work, and in historical tiles.

The seventeenth-century **Imaculada Conceição Chapel** has gilt carvings and glazed tiles.

The fourteenth-century **Church of São Domingos** was ordered built by Dom Lourenço Vicente, an Archbishop of Braga and a hero of the battle of Aljubarrota. It has a superb Gothic cloister.

The **Martins Sarmento Museum**, in the Rua Paio Galvão, contains the finds of the great nineteenth-century archaeologist Dr Francisco Martins Sarmento, who dedicated his life to excavating the Iron Age *castros* of Briteiros and Sabroso (see page 108). As well as the usual ancient coins, votive ornaments, pots and jewellery left by the Celts, Visigoths and Romans, it contains some pieces of outstanding interest. There is the *Pedra Formosa*, a granite slab with decorative carvings which was found at Briteiros. There are two granite statues of Lusitanian warriors. Most extraordinary of all, there is the Colossus of Pedralva, a seated granite idol 3 m high which was found at Briteiros in 1930. This figure is so heavy it took twenty-four pairs of oxen to drag it to the museum.

Crafts

Guimarães produces linen made from home-grown flax, embroidery, gold and silver filigree, cutlery, brasswork and pottery. Look out for the little earthenware pots covered with shiny mica which are called *Cantarinhas das Prendas*. When a girl becomes engaged she collects valuables like gold and jewellery, which she keeps in one of these pots to present to the groom before they are married.

Festivals

In early July thousands of pilgrims throng into Guimarães for the *Romaria de São Torcato*, a pilgrimage to the Sanctuary of the Iberian martyr Saint Torquatus, 7 km to the north-east of Guimarães.

The *Festas Gualterianas* is a festival in honour of Saint Walter, which has been celebrated in Guimarães since 1452. It includes a procession based on medieval tradition, with satirical allegories, and a funfair with folk bands and dancing.

Excursions
Santa Marinha
da Costa

The Santa Marinha da Costa Monastery, 4 km up the Penha Mountain overlooking Guimarães, is one of the most impressive monuments in Portugal. It has a fascinating history, and traces of every period of that history are still to be seen. It has been turned into a luxurious pousada, and if you possibly can you should treat yourself to at least one night there.

Archaeological finds that were made during its recent restoration indicate that there were pre-Roman and Roman temples on the site. There is also a small Visigoth temple. Tradition says that the site was acquired by Countess Mumadona and the temple reconstructed around 950. At one time it may have been used as a fortification against the Moors.

There is an arch which is probably the finest example of Mozarabic architecture in Portugal.

In 1154 Dona Mafalda, the wife of King Afonso Henriques, gave the monastery to the Augustinian Order to honour a vow to Santa Marinha, the protector of pregnant women. The Augustinians made additions to it.

In the sixteenth century it passed to the Jeronimite Fathers, who replaced much of the old building. The cloister, which was rebuilt at the end of the sixteenth century, is almost intact.

In the seventeenth and eighteenth centuries the walls of the Monastery were covered with tiles. Those in the church, vestry and cloister date from 1643. Those in the Staircases, chapter house and the Saint Jerome Veranda were placed in 1747 and are believed to be the work of Policarpo de Oliveira Bernardes. The tiles depict life in Portugal in the eighteenth century – there are pictorial representations of shepherds, banquets, wild boar hunts, the theatre, and much more.

When the religious orders were abolished in Portugal in the nineteenth century the monastery became private property. It was bought by the State in 1972, and restored under the supervision of the architect Fernando Távora.

Penha Mountain

At the summit of the Penha Mountain there are grottoes, monuments, taverns, restaurants, and a view. The twentieth-century Sanctuary of Nossa Senhora da Penha is dedicated to travellers. Near it there is a monument to Gago Coutinho and Sacudura Cabral, the first people to fly across the South Atlantic.

Citânia de Briteiros

About 15 km north of Guimarães is the Citânia de Briteiros, the most famous and most interesting of the Iron Age hill-towns which have so far been investigated (see page 17). It was excavated almost singlehandedly by Dr Martins Sarmento, beginning in 1875.

Briteiros sits on a steep-sided hill 336 m high. There are the remains of two hundred houses here – round, elliptical and rectangular. One house had a surprisingly large diameter of 11 m, another was rectangular with two circular houses attached, and another had stone benches around the inside. The houses had conical thatched roofs.

The most interesting and controversial structure found at Briteiros has an uncovered rectangular atrium paved with stones through which two conduits run into a water tank; a covered square antechamber; and a covered tiled gallery with what appears to be a furnace attached. Entrance to the tiled gallery was through an arched opening only 50 cm high. Over this there was the granite slab known as the *Pedra Formosa* (see page 107). The structure and the *Pedra Formosa* have been the object of controversy since they were discovered. There are seventeen known structures of this kind in other *castros*, and they have generally been believed to have to do with funeral rites. Recent opinion, however, inclines to the view that they may have been hot baths or saunas for the towns. As for the *Pedra Formosa*, Dr Sarmento believed that it was a sacrificial stone. Others have thought that it was the door closing the entrance to a tomb.

Castro de Sabroso

Dr Martins Sarmento also excavated the Castro de Sabroso, which can be seen from the hill top at Briteiros. From Taipas, take the Santa Cristina de Longos road as far as Cancela, where a road to the right leads to the Castro de Sabroso at the top of its hill.

The Castro de Sabroso is smaller and probably older than the Citânia de Briteiros. It has only one defence wall and there are no signs of Romanization. There are traces of thirty-five round houses and a few rectangular ones. One interesting feature is that the walls are thicker and better joined than at Briteiros.

Where to stay
Medium price

Hotel Fundador Dom Pedro, Avenida Dom Afonso Henriques. Tel. (053) 413781. A modern three star hotel with fifty-four rooms, nine suites, bars, restaurant, sauna and gym.

Inexpensive

Albergaria das Palmeiras, Rua Gil Vicente. Tel. (053) 410324. A four star inn with twenty-three rooms, bar, restaurant and swimming pool.

Manor houses
Medium price

Paço de São Cipriano, Taboadelo, 4800 Guimarães. Tel. (053) 481337. A centuries-old pale stone mansion with a crenellated tower and a red tile roof. At one time it had a lodging house for pilgrims on their way to Santiago. The house offers five double bedrooms with bath, and a swimming pool.

Casa Conde Paco Vieira, Mesão Frio, 5 km from Guimarães. Tel. (053) 441227. A renovated seventeenth-century house set within a lovely farm. It has four rooms with bath.

Inexpensive

Casa do Ribeiro, São Cristovão de Selho, 4800 Guimarães. Tel. (053) 432881. A sprawling Minho mansion, in an estate which covers more than 6,000 hectares of woods and streams. The house has two twin bedrooms and one single bedroom, with baths.

Casa dos Pombais, Avenida de Londres. Tel. (053) 412917. An eighteenth-century mansion in the city centre surrounded by a beautiful garden, offers two rooms with bath.

Pousadas
Medium price

Pousada da Santa Marinha da Costa. Tel. (053) 418453, telex 32686. A luxury pousada in the old monastery of Santa Marinha da Costa (see page 107). It is a fascinating, as well as very comfortable, place to stay. There is an excellent restaurant, too.

Pousada da Nossa Senhora da Oliveira, Rua da Oliveira. Tel. (053) 412157, telex 32875. A first class pousada near the beautiful Church of Nossa Senhora da Oliveira in the centre of Guimarães.

Where to eat

The **Pousada da Santa Marinha**, the **Pousada da Nossa Senhora da Oliveira** and the **Hotel Fundador Dom Pedro** all have good restaurants, with a wide selection of regional and international dishes. In a lower price bracket, the following restaurants are worth trying.

Restaurante Jordão, Avenida Dom Afonso Henriques 55. Tel. (053) 40198.

Restaurante Arbelo, Belos Ares, Mesão Frio. Tel. (053) 411675.

Tourist Offices for Guimarães are the Penha-Guimarães Tourist Board, Avenida Resistência ão Fascismo 83. Tel. (053) 412450; or Largo Conego José Maria Gomes. Tel. (053) 416123.

The Taipas Tourist Office is the Caldas das Taipas Tourist Board, Taipas. Tel. (053) 471156.

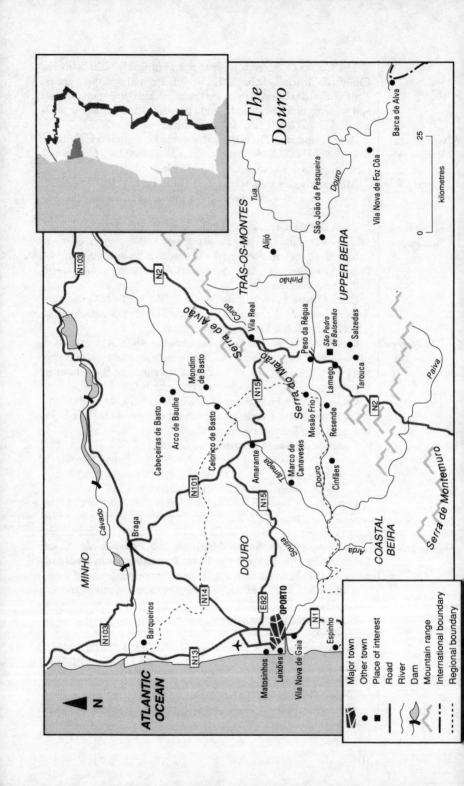

The Douro

Introduction

The Lower Douro (Douro Litoral)

The Lower Douro includes Oporto and its immediate surroundings, and extends eastwards as far as the Marão mountain range. This small area is the most densely populated region of Portugal. Its people are engaged in fishing, fish-canning, textile manufacture, leather work, furniture-making and wine export. The famous port wine is not produced in the Lower Douro, but it is brought down there from the Upper Douro and stored in wine cellars in Vila Nova de Gaia, at Oporto, for shipping.

The Marão mountains trap the moisture that blows in from the Atlantic, and the region has a very mild, rainy climate. Four important tributaries of the River Douro flow through the region: the rivers Paiva, Arda, Tâmega and Sousa. Because so much water pours down the tributaries from the mountains, there is often severe flooding – sometimes engulfing the port wine cellars in Vila Nova de Gaia.

The biggest city in the Lower Douro is Oporto, the original Portucale, that gave its name to the nation, and the birthplace of the nation's hero, Henry the Navigator.

The Upper Douro (Alto Douro)

The Upper Douro extends eastwards from Barqueiros, where the mountains begin to climb westward, to Mazouco near the Spanish border in Trás-os-Montes, and covers an area of 250,000 hectares. It is a land of high, rugged hillsides covered with schist and outcroppings of granite, and it is surrounded by granite mountains that shelter it from the moist Atlantic winds. It has scorching summers where temperatures can reach 40°C/104°F and the winters are warm, with light rainfall. There are small areas with Mediterranean microclimates, where olive, almond, fig, cork and citrus fruit trees flourish. Most importantly, so do vines. The terrain and climate of the Upper Douro provide the ideal combination needed to produce the particular grapes that make the very special wine known as port. And the Upper Douro is where the grapes used for making port have been grown for centuries.

Port

The port wine area was the first wine-producing area in the world to be demarcated. In 1756 the Prime Minister of Portugal, the future Marquês de Pombal, set official limits to the port wine area as part of an attempt to break the monopoly held by English wine shippers in Oporto. He established the demarcated region, around the Douro, by placing 335 granite marking posts on which were carved the word *Feitoria* (factory) and the date. About a hundred of these *Pombalino* posts are still around – some being used as doorposts or other supports or simply lying in the underbrush, but a few still standing proudly erect on the hillsides.

Today the demarcated port wine area is many times the size of the eighteenth-century zone. It now begins at Barqueiros and extends into Trás-os-Montes to Barca de Alva on the frontier with Spain. Twenty-five thousand hectares of land are planted in vineyards culti-vated by about 25,000 growers. Forty per cent of the grapes go to make port, and the rest are used for red and white table wines, rosés and sparkling wines. Most port still comes from around the Douro, but much of the best port is now produced up its tributaries, the Rivers Corgo, Torto, Tua, Pinhão and others.

Harvest   The *vindima* (grape harvest) that takes place in the Douro at the end of September or in early October is a joyful, colourful event. There are organized tours to the *vindimas* during the season – for details, consult your travel agent, or the Tourist Office in Oporto. The grape pickers come from all the villages around, and there is much singing and revelry. When the grapes have been picked they are placed in big baskets that the men carry on their backs over mountainsides that are often too steep for any other form of transport. Traditionally the grapes are then trodden in stone tanks by the barefoot men, but many of the growers now use modern machine crushers (though some people say this robs the wine of taste). The wine is then allowed to ferment, beginning the long process that will turn it into port.

The wine   There are various legends about the origins of port. I am rather inclined to the theory of the well-known cellar master at Ferreira, Fernando Nicolau d'Almeida, who believes that port as we know it today was discovered by mistake, when a vintage that contained an exceptional amount of sugar created so much alcohol that fermenta-tion (which converts sugar into alcohol) was arrested very early. The wine produced was remarkably strong and sweet. Today, the same effect is produced by fortifying the wine with brandy after about thirty-six hours of fermentation. The proportions are about one part of brandy to four of wine. The high alcohol level causes the natural fermentation to slow down, and after about forty-eight hours it stops altogether, leaving a great deal of unfermented sugar in the wine. The wine stays sweet, and the brandy keeps alcoholic strength high.

The wine is then stored in huge wooden barrels called pipes, each containing 522 litres. After about six months the new wine (except for a little which is kept up the Douro) is taken to Vila Nova de Gaia, and the maturation of the wine is completed in the wine lodges there. Until the late nineteenth century, when a double-track railway 207 km long was built between Oporto and the Spanish border, the River Douro was the only route for bringing the wine down from the Upper Douro.

For hundreds of years the barrels of wine were stacked on to boats known as *barcos rabelos* which then descended dangerous swirling rapids and deep gorges to Vila Nova de Gaia.

In the 1970s, with the building of dams which have turned most of the River Douro into a series of placid lakes, the *rabelos* disappeared from the river. But you can still see them in front of the wine warehouses in Vila Nova de Gaia, advertising the different brands of port.

The wine is kept in pipes for about three years, during which, at intervals, it is cleared by being drawn off its lees. After this the wines are tasted and categorized.

Types of port

When one year produces a wine of outstanding quality, much of it is bottled, unblended, at this relatively early point, and will need to be kept for at least fifteen to twenty years before being ready to drink: this is vintage port, the king of ports. Then there is what is known as late-bottled vintage port – port made exclusively from the grapes of one good but not exceptional year, matured in a wooden cask for about eight years, and bottled only then, when it is ready for drinking. Most port, however, is a blend of wines from several years. Blended port is matured in a cask, for varying lengths of time. Tawny port is aged in barrels sometimes for as long as twenty years, or even more: it is burnt topaz in colour and has a smooth, delicate flavour. Ruby port, aged for a much shorter time, sometimes only two or three years, is sweet and fruity. *Tinto* is young, red and sweet. *Branco* (white) port, made from white grapes, is lighter, with less body. It may be either sweet or dry – dry white port makes a good aperitif. All ports are high in alcohol: reds vary between 19° and 22°, whites between 16.5° and 20°.

Oporto

Getting there

Oporto is Portugal's second largest city, with a population of 450,000. It is very easy to get to. As well as the large port, it has an international airport at Pedras Rubras and two main railway stations, the São Bento station in the centre of the town and Campanhã on the outskirts. If you are driving you can reach Oporto by the A1 or N1 from the south, the N15 from the east or the N13 or N14 from the north. Oporto is also the gateway to most of northern Portugal.

History

At Oporto there are traces of civilizations going back three or four thousand years. There was an old *castro* (see page 17) on the hill by the river here, and Phoenicians came to the river mouth to trade. The site was occupied by Romans, Visigoths, Swabians, Moors, and later, for a short time, by Napoleon's troops.

The Middle Ages

The town was granted a charter in 1120 by Dona Teresa, mother of Afonso Henriques, Portugal's first king. In the Middle Ages the Bishops of Oporto became very powerful. In 1147 Bishop Pedro

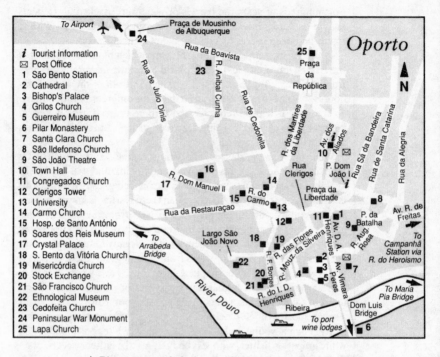

i Tourist information
✉ Post Office
1 São Bento Station
2 Cathedral
3 Bishop's Palace
4 Grilos Church
5 Guerreiro Museum
6 Pilar Monastery
7 Santa Clara Church
8 São Ildefonso Church
9 São João Theatre
10 Town Hall
11 Congregados Church
12 Clerigos Tower
13 University
14 Carmo Church
15 Hosp. de Santo António
16 Soares dos Reis Museum
17 Crystal Palace
18 S. Bento da Vitória Church
19 Misericórdia Church
20 Stock Exchange
21 São Francisco Church
22 Ethnological Museum
23 Cedofeita Church
24 Peninsular War Monument
25 Lapa Church

Pitões persuaded the English and Norman Crusaders, who had stopped to replenish their stores on the way to the Holy Land, to help the Christian King of Portugal expel the Moors from Lisbon. They succeeded in doing this, but later there was conflict between the Crusaders, who pillaged, and the Portuguese. Disputes of various kinds between the Portuguese, foreign Crusaders, pirates and Moors continued off and on for several centuries. There were also struggles between the clergy, the monarchy and the powerful merchant class, who had become rich thanks to trade with northern Europe.

The walled city

In the fourteenth century King Afonso V ordered the city enclosed by walls. These were finished during the reign of King Fernando, and were known as the *Fernandino* walls. The city was contained within them until the end of the eighteenth century, when it expanded outside.

Henry the Navigator

During the fifteenth century, in the time of Prince Henry the Navigator, Oporto and the Douro region became very involved in the Portuguese explorations for a route around Africa and in the conquest of North Africa. During that period the Oporto shipyards built six major armadas in sixty-six years. In 1415 Henry gathered a fleet there to join his father the King to sail to Ceuta in North Africa to capture it from the Moors. The people of the Douro were so enthusiastic that they slaughtered all of their cattle for food for the fleet. They kept only tripe for themselves, earning the name of *tripeiros* – tripe-eaters. After the

Discoverers pushed their way round Africa to India and sailed to Brazil, the people of the Douro became very rich through trade, and erected many magnificent churches, palaces and houses.

Spanish domination

In the sixteenth century Portugal was annexed by Spain and was ruled by Philip I and Philip II. When the Spaniards were finally driven out, King João IV was crowned in Oporto in 1640.

British factors

By the seventeenth century British wine merchants (or 'factors', as they were called) were well established in Oporto, and they continued to flourish throughout the succeeding centuries.

War with the French

In 1808, during the Peninsular War, the French captured Oporto; but the people rose against the occupying power, the French governor of Oporto was arrested and a provincial government was set up under the Bishop of Oporto. And, in response to an appeal from the provisional government, British troops commanded by Sir Arthur Wellesley landed south of Oporto and routed the French. The following year Napoleon made another attempt to take Portugal. In Oporto Captain Robert Wilson had raised the Loyal Lusitanian Legion, but French troops under Marshal Soult took the city while the defenders retreated south across the River Douro, over a bridge of boats that collapsed under them, drowning many. However, the French occupation was again brief. Wellesley (now Viscount Wellington) returned, with 17,000 British and 7,000 Portuguese troops, and drove the French out of Oporto. The French were finally defeated in Portugal in 1811. But there was more trouble to come.

Liberalism

During the war with France, King João VI and his court had fled to Brazil. They lingered there too long, enjoying the adulation of Brazilian-Portuguese society, while at home movements demanding a liberal constitution were growing in strength.

In 1820, in Oporto, liberal army officers and civilians with Masonic connections formed an alliance with the aims of curbing the powers of the monarchy and introducing universal suffrage. A representative *Cortes* (parliament) met in Lisbon in 1821 and wrote a constitution with provisions which included the suppression of feudal rights and of the Inquisition and the institution of a single-chamber parliament, to be elected every two years.

When, shortly after this, King João finally returned to Portugal he was presented with this constitution, which he reluctantly signed.

Back in Brazil João's son Pedro was also proving himself a liberal. He proclaimed Brazil independent and was named constitutional Emperor of Brazil.

But in Portugal, in 1823, a reaction against the liberal constitution began, led by Pedro's younger brother Miguel and their mother Carlota-Joaquina (sister of the Spanish King Fernando VII). The constitution was suspended, but Miguel was sent into exile.

War of Succession

When João died in 1826 Pedro was proclaimed king. From Brazil, he swiftly promulgated a new constitutional charter, this time instituting a two-chamber parliament, with a house of deputies, partly elected and partly nominated, and an upper house of hereditary peers. He also said that if his seven-year-old daughter Maria were betrothed to his brother Miguel, he would abdicate in favour of Maria and appoint Miguel regent. Miguel agreed, but as soon as he returned to Portugal he immediately dissolved the *Cortes*, rescinded the constitution and had himself crowned king. A reign of terror began. The liberals and moderates fled – mostly to England. All of this caused dissent in England, with the Tories supporting Miguel, and the Whigs Pedro.

In 1831 Pedro abdicated from the throne of Brazil and sailed to the Portuguese Azores to prepare an expedition to invade Portugal and put Maria on the throne. His hopes of raising a volunteer army in England were thwarted by the Tories, but four hundred Englishmen did sign up to go to Portugal, for the cause or for adventure and glory. They sailed for the Azores, where they trained and drank wine. They were a motley crew, and Pedro was not too enthusiastic about them.

But finally they sailed to Portugal, with forty-two ships. They landed at Mindelo, and advanced on Oporto. Miguel's army and his Oporto collaborators escaped across the Douro, and the people of Oporto let political prisoners out of prison, and burned the gallows.

For a year, the supporters of Miguel besieged Oporto. During this time, a British gunboat under the command of Captain Glascock sat in the river to protect British interests. The ship was to remain strictly neutral, and the Captain gave dinners for officers from both the *Miguelista* forces and those of Pedro, where the officers picked each other's brains for military secrets. Meanwhile, the poor of the city and the common soldiers were reduced to eating the cats and dogs.

The siege ended when Admiral Charles Napier came out from England to take over Pedro's forces, gathered the army together in Oporto and set off to attack Lisbon. Miguel hastened to defend Lisbon. Napier with his English and Portuguese forces won the war for Pedro, and Miguel surrendered at Évoramonte, in the south of Portugal, and went into exile. Pedro died only four months later, but before that he had returned to Oporto, to thank the people for the support they had given him – and he literally left his heart (encased in gold) to the city. Until recently, it was kept in a special museum in the Lapa Church.

The war had left Portugal terribly in debt. To raise money, the Government dissolved the monasteries and convents and confiscated their properties, which were then sold off.

Baron de Forrester

In 1831 – the same year Pedro left Brazil for Portugal – a most remarkable young Englishman arrived in Oporto to take up a post in his family's wine company. He was Joseph James Forrester, and he was then twenty-two years old. Unlike most of his countrymen, he learned Portuguese and took an active role in everything Portuguese. He explored and mapped all of the Douro region, from the Atlantic to the Spanish frontier. He also studied and wrote about the diseases that attacked the grape vines. And he wrote many papers exhorting the wine merchants to stop adulterating port with sugar, elderberries and brandy, and to produce a pure, natural wine. As if this were not enough, he also excelled as a painter of landscapes and portraits.

Forrester was publicly praised by bishops, intellectuals and nobles, and the King of Portugal named him Baron de Forrester for his services to Portugal. Sadly, in 1861 he was drowned in the Douro, when the boat he was sailing in with the Portuguese wine grower Adelaida Ferreira and her daughter capsized. Both ladies got to shore, apparently because they were buoyed up by their voluminous petticoats.

Adelaida Ferreira

Dona Adelaida Ferreira was a remarkable person herself. Born in 1811, she built up the land holdings first established by her great-grandfather from three *quintas* to thirty, and became the richest woman in Portugal. While acquiring her great estates that stretched along the Douro all the way to the Spanish border, she opened roads, created production centres, built schools, nurseries and hospitals – all at her own expense. A tiny little woman adored by everyone, she was given the affectionate nickname of *Ferreirinha* (Little Ferreira). Her company's wine is still referred to as *Ferreirinha* today. The Ferreira company is now headed by the eighth generation of the family, and occupies first place in sales of port. Like nearly all the great port companies, they have warehouses and cellars in Vila Nova de Gaia.

Oporto today

Port and the other Douro wines still dominate the region, but other industries have grown to importance. Oporto and its environs have a large fishing fleet, an oil refinery, textile, chemical, shoemaking, ceramics, metalworking, fish-canning, furniture-making and other industries. Oporto's large port is the outlet for most of the northern trade. Its people are hardworking and proud of it. Once the cradle of liberalism, Oporto today is a bastion of conservatism.

A great part of Oporto looks as if it is falling down – and it is. Its houses and public buildings are in a dilapidated state. However, recently there have been efforts to restore some of them, particularly those on the historic, picturesque riverfront.

Traffic is horrendous, and the streets are confusing and badly marked. Don't drive unless you have endless patience and super-fast reflexes. Oporto is built on a series of hills that slope down to the River Douro, which is spanned by three bridges. This means that you have splendid views; but if you decide to walk you will find that most of the streets are perpendicular and most of the places you want to go are uphill. However, it is worth putting up with these discomforts to see the beautiful historic buildings and imbibe the famous wines.

What to see

Most of Oporto's monuments are clustered in an area of the old part of town that fans out in all directions from the Praça da República and the Avenida da Liberdade and stretches down to the river. Distances between them are not very far, but the streets are confusing and there are few places to park. My advice is to put on your tennis shoes and walk, or hire a taxi with an English-speaking driver, or go on a city tour organized by a travel agency. There are double-decker Cityrama buses with English-speaking hostesses: you can make reservations at Cityrama, Rua Entreparedes 17, tel. (02) 317155, telex 25344P, or at Claras Turismo (Porto and Minho), Praça Dom João I.

I have tried to arrange the monuments in some kind of order, so that if you are walking you can find them without too much trouble; but the maze-like nature of the streets being what it is, you may get lost anyway. Don't worry, just ask for directions from a Portuguese – they are always helpful – or grab a taxi.

The **Cathedral** is on a hill just above the river, in its own square near the Rua Mouzinho da Silveira; the smaller streets of Rua Comércio Porto and Rua Fernando Borges lead into it. The original structure, dating from the twelfth and thirteenth centuries, was a Romanesque building constructed like a fortress, with towers and battlements. It has been much added to over the ages. It has a splendid rose window over its Baroque doorway; stained glass windows; a seventeenth-century silver altar in the chapel (this was painted over during the French occupation to hide it from marauding Napoleonic troops); a fourteenth-century cloister decorated with tiles depicting scenes from the life of the Virgin and from Ovid's *Metamorphoses*; carved choir stalls; an eighteenth-century chapel attributed to Nicolau Nasoni, and a sacristy with an image of Our Lady of Vandoma. King João I and Philippa of Lancaster were married here in 1387, and their son Prince Henry the Navigator (Infante Dom Henrique) was christened here. There is a Baroque carved golden retable dating from 1610 over the altar, and a crypt where the Bishops of Oporto are buried. Open 9 a.m. to 12.30 p.m. and 3 p.m. to 5 p.m.

The **Bishop's Palace** near the Cathedral has an interesting, long Baroque façade. It is now used for municipal offices.

The **Grilos Church**, just around the corner near Rua Mouzinho da Silveira, was built in the sixteenth century for the Jesuits. It is laid out in the form of a cross with a vaulted dome. The carved wooden altarpiece represents the Presentation of Jesus in the Temple. Get permission to visit from the Seminary in the Cathedral.

The **Museum of Sacred Art** in the Cathedral Square near the Grilos Church has religious objects from the twelfth to nineteenth centuries, old glass and coin collections and fifteenth- to nineteenth-century liturgical musical instruments.

Open Tuesday to Friday 2 p.m. to 4 p.m.

The **Guerreiro Junqueira Museum** is near the Cathedral in Rua de Dom Hugo. It is an eighteenth-century Baroque house that was the home of the poet Guerreiro Junqueira. It has a valuable collection of ornamental art, furniture, tapestries, silver and alabaster figures.

Open Tuesday to Saturday 11.30 a.m. to 12.30 p.m. and 2.30 p.m. to 6 p.m.

The **Dom Luis Bridge** is the middle one of the three bridges over the River Douro. It has an upper and lower span leading to the port wine lodges in Vila Nova de Gaia. It is an iron bridge designed by Seyrig, a collaborator of Eiffel, and was opened in 1886.

The **Pilar Monastery**, across the Dom Luis Bridge on the south side of the river, is an octagonal church founded in the sixteenth century by the Order of Saint Augustine. It has a beautiful dome and a circular cloister supported by Ionic columns and a highly decorated pediment. The view of Oporto from its terrace is spectacular. It was here that Wellington gathered his troops to drive out the French.

The remains of the **Fernandina Wall** can be seen on your right as you come back across the Dom Luis Bridge. The walls, which were 3 km long and 11 m high, were begun in 1336 and finished in 1376, in the reign of King Fernando. They were later systematically demolished as the city expanded. There are other stretches of the wall still standing next to the Santa Clara Church and some bits near the São João Novo Church at Miragaia.

The **Santa Clara Church** is on Rua Saraiva de Carvalho, on the other side of the main road that leads up to the Cathedral. Originally a Romanesque church, built in the fifteenth century, it has had many additions over the centuries. The church doors are a mixture of Gothic, Manueline and Renaissance. The inside was decorated in the sixteenth century, when gold was pouring in from Portugal's overseas colonies. It is completely covered in richly carved, Baroque polychrome gilded woodwork from ceiling to floor. There are golden angels, leaves, designs, cherubs and statues. Everything is gold. The choirs have beautifully painted ceilings and carved choir stalls.

Open Monday to Friday 9.30 a.m. to 11.30 a.m. and 3 p.m. to 6 p.m., and Saturdays 9 a.m. to 12 noon. Closed Sunday.

The **São Ildefonso Church** is near the Praça da Batalha, going up Rua Augusta Rosa by the São João Theatre. It is an eighteenth-century church with a glazed tile façade added in 1932.

The **Chapel of Souls** is up Rua de Santa Catarina, on the corner of Rua de Fernandes Tomás. It is a nineteenth-century chapel with a glazed tile façade added in 1944.

The **Town Hall** is at the top of the double avenue Avenida dos Aliados. It was built in this century and has tapestries and panels depicting scenes from Oporto.

Open 9.30 a.m. to 12 noon and 2.30 p.m. to 5 p.m. Closed Saturday and Sunday.

The **São Bento Station** is down the Avenida Dom Afonso Henriques, in the Praça de Almeida Garrett. It was built at the beginning of this century on the site of the old Ave Maria Convent. The walls of its waiting room are covered with glazed tiles by Jorge Colaço depicting the evolution of transport, the first trains and other historical events. It is from this station that trains depart for the scenic route up the length of the River Douro to the Spanish border (see page 38).

The **Congregados Church** is in the same square. It dates from the seventeenth century and has a façade of glazed tiles added in 1861.

The **Clerigos Church and Tower**, behind the Rua da Assunção, is so tall you can't miss it – it dominates the Oporto skyline. This church, which was built in the eighteenth century by Italian architect Nicolau Nasoni, was the first church in Portugal built on an oval plan. The tower is 76 m high, and if you can climb the 225 steps to the top, you will have spectacular views.

Open Monday to Friday 7.30 a.m. to 9.30 a.m., 10.30 a.m. to 12 noon and 3.30 p.m. to 8 p.m., and Sunday 10.30 a.m. to 3 p.m. and 8.30 p.m. to 11.30 p.m.

The eighteenth-century **University** is in its own square on Rua Dom Manuel II.

The **Carmo Church**, nearby in the Rua do Carmo, is eighteenth-century Rococo with a *rocaille* façade and walls covered with twentieth-century glazed tiles.

Open 9 a.m. to 12 noon and 2 p.m. to 5 p.m.

The **Hospital de Santo António** in the same area was built in the eighteenth century. This enormous hospital was the first neo-Palladian building in Portugal.

The **Soares dos Reis Museum** is in the eighteenth-century royal Carrancas Palace, behind the Hospital on Rua Dom Manuel II. Soares dos Reis was the most famous Portuguese sculptor of the last century, and many of his works are exhibited here. The museum also has French, Italian, Flemish and Portuguese paintings, early gold and silver jewellery, and an excellent ceramics collection. A sword that belonged to Dom Afonso Henriques, first King of Portugal, is here too.

Open 10 a.m. to 12 noon and 2.30 p.m. to 5 p.m. Closed Monday.

The **Casa de Serralves** (Museum of Modern Art), Rua de Serralves 977, holds temporary expositions of paintings, jewellery, photography and sculpture.

The **Palácio de Cristal** (The Crystal Palace) is a landmark in Oporto and is used for conferences, banquets, etc.

The **Romantic Museum** nearby in the Quinta da Maceirinha, Rua de Entre Quineros 220. It has a collection of objects and furnishings from the wealthy, mid-nineteenth-century period in Oporto. In the **Solar do Vinho do Oporto**, in the basement of the Quinta da Maceirinha, you can taste port from all of the Oporto firms.

Museum open 10 a.m. to 5 p.m. Closed Sunday and Monday.

The **São Bento da Vitória Church**, in the same area, is a seventeenth-century Baroque church belonging to the Benedictine monastery. It has extensive gilt carvings and many panels depicting the life of Saint Benedict.

The **Misericórdia Church**, behind the São Bento da Vitória Church on Rua das Flores, was designed in the eighteenth century by

Nicolau Nasoni and Manuel Alvaler. The many glazed tiles and carvings are interesting.

Open 8 a.m. to 12 noon and 3 p.m. to 5 p.m.

The adjoining **Casa da Misericórdia** houses the sixteenth-century canvas *Fons Vitae*, which has an extraordinary combination of Christ on the Cross and the Portuguese royal family in brightly coloured dress.

The **Palácio da Bolsa** (Stock Exchange) is down towards the river on Rua Ferreira Borges. It has an incredible room called the Moorish Hall, which is decorated all in gold with brilliant chandeliers in imitation of the Moorish Alhambra.

Open 10 a.m. to 5 p.m. Closed Saturday and Sunday.

The **Market of Ferreira Borges** is just in front of the Stock Exchange.

The **Church of São Francisco** is at the place where Rua Ferreira Borges and Rua do Infante Dom Henriques join. It dates from the fourteenth and fifteenth centuries and is basically Gothic in style, but with later additions. It has a lovely rose window and a rich, opulent Baroque interior with an excessive amount of gilt wood carvings, painted polychrome sculptures and glazed tiles. There are gold birds, vines, angels, bunches of grapes and flowers as decorations. Its adjoining convent was destroyed by fire in 1832.

Open 10 a.m. to 12 noon and 2.30 p.m. to 5 p.m. Closed Sunday and Monday.

The **Ethnological Museum** is in Largo São João Novo in the Miragaia area, in an eighteenth-century mansion designed by Nicolau Nasoni. It exhibits the life and customs of the Douro region, showing old looms, a reconstructed wine cellar, ceramics, ox-yokes, religious artifacts, fishing equipment, toys and many other things.

The **São João Novo Church** is nearby. It has carved work and glazed tiles from the seventeenth century.

The **Church of São Pedro de Miragaia** in Miragaia is an eighteenth-century church with glazed tiles and gilt carved work. It has a lovely choir. In the adjoining sixteenth-century Chapel of the Holy Ghost, you will see the famous Pentecostal triptych of the Flemish school. The Friars' Hall has an interesting plastered ceiling.

Open Monday to Saturday 4 p.m. to 7 p.m. and Sunday 9 a.m. to 12 noon.

The **Church of São Nicolau**, down by the river in Ribeira, is a classical eighteenth-century Baroque church.

Open Monday to Friday 9 a.m. to 12 noon and 4 p.m. to 8 p.m., and Saturday and Sunday 9 a.m. to 12.30 p.m. Closed Tuesday.

The **Casa do Infante** (House of Prince Henry the Navigator) is by the river near the São Nicolau Church. Tradition rather shakily says that Henry the Navigator was born here in the fourteenth century. From the fourteenth to the nineteenth centuries, it was used as the

Customs Hall. It was restored in the twentieth century, and is now the Historical Museum.

Open Monday to Friday 9 a.m. to 12 noon and 2 p.m. to 5 p.m.

The Romanesque **Cedofeita Church** is up the hill and to the west, near the Praça de Mousinho de Albuquerque on Rua da Boavista. It is the oldest church in Oporto, dating from the twelfth century. It has a single nave covered by a vault resting on three arches.

The **Bom Sucesso Market** is in the Praça de Mousinho de Albuquerque.

There is a **Monument to the Peninsular War** in the Praça de Mousinho de Albuquerque in Rua de Bom Sucesso. It is a 45 m high statue planned by sculptor Alves de Souza and architect Marques da Silva. At the top it has a lion subjugating an eagle, signifying the Portuguese/English victory over Napoleon's forces in Oporto.

The **Queijo Palace** or the São Francisco Javier Fort is on the Atlantic at the west end of Avenida da Boavista near Gonçalves Zarco Square and the Esplanade do Rio de Janeiro. In its foundations is a boulder which was sacred to the Celts six centuries BC and which was used by the Druids to make sacrifices. In 1643, King João IV ordered a fort there to be paid for by the people of Oporto, to protect them from English, French, Dutch and Turkish pirates. The fort is on the beach among the rocks, with the sea coming in, and its heavy, sloping walls, watchtowers, drawbridge and old weapons are well preserved. The fort was used during the expulsion of the French in 1809. It was held by Miguelista forces in the War of Succession and badly damaged, but it has been completely restored.

The **Fortress of São João da Foz** is off the Avenida de Dom Carlos I in the Passeio Alegre Gardens, where the River Douro meets the Atlantic. There was originally a thirteenth-century Benedictine monastery and church on the site, but in 1560 the Queen Regent Dona Catarina ordered the fort built. Work continued during the reign of King João IV, amid disputes with the Benedictines and protests from the people of Oporto at the taxes raised to build it. The fort kept the chancel of the monastery as a military chapel and the rest of the monastery was demolished. There are still houses inhabited inside the fort.

The **São Miguel Lighthouse** is on a promontory on Rua do Passeio Alegre, near the Passeio Alegre Gardens. It was built in 1527 by the Bishop of Viseu for the nearby Benedictine Monastery.

The **Ponte de Arrabeda** is a remarkably long reinforced concrete bridge designed by Edgar Cardoso and opened at the mouth of the river in this century.

The **Freixo Palace** is an eighteenth-century building designed by Nicolau Nasoni.

The **Military Museum** is on the east side of the city, located appropriately between Rua do Heroismo (Heroism Street) and the cemetery, Prado do Repouso.

The **Lapa Church** is also on the east side of the city, in the Praça da República. It is an eighteenth-century church with a mausoleum containing the heart of King Pedro IV, donated by him to the city in 1837 in gratitude for Oporto's support in the War of Succession.

The Maria Pia Bridge is the bridge furthest up river. An iron bridge which is the work of Alexandre Gustave Eiffel, it was opened in 1877 for the railroad.

The **Factory House** in Rua do Infante Dom Henriques (formerly Rua dos Ingleses) is an austere Georgian building that was built by the British wine merchants of Oporto in 1786. It was planned and designed by John Whitehead, then British Consul in Oporto. The merchants did business there by day, and by night they entertained royally in its spacious ballroom, dining rooms and drawing rooms. It is still a gathering place for the British port men; but, with the pressure of modern business, they do not linger over their port as they once did.

After Wellington and his troops relieved Oporto in 1809, the British officers were wined and dined royally in the Factory House, and showered with cases of fine port. You can see the names of these officers in the Factory House register.

There is an equestrian statue of Pedro IV by French artist Calmels (1866) in the wide Praça da Liberdade in the centre of Oporto. A stone effigy of the Portuguese poet Almeida Garrett stands in front of it.

The streets of Rua das Flores, Rua Clerigos, Rua do Almada and Rua da Santa Catarina have many old Baroque palaces, houses and shops selling gold and silver filigree, antique porcelain, and the **Bairro do Barredo** has many picturesque old houses with balconies (with washing hanging out) and narrow stone stairs with arches. The neighbourhood is being refurbished and its bright colours restored.

The **Ribeira** is the part of the old town down by the river. It has a colourful market with flowers, fish and regional crafts, and some very good, picturesque old restaurants in the houses that line the river. Many of the old houses are being restored, in a belated attempt to save the historic riverside. Just walk down from the top part of the town and you will come to this charming old neighbourhood.

Crafts

While you are in Oporto, look out for *palmitos* (sprays of flowers made out of shiny paper), gold work and gold and silver filigree, embroidery, lace, regional kerchiefs, aprons and tablecloths, leather jackets, shoes, wallets and belts, straw and wickerwork wallets, baskets and hats, glass and crystal, ceramics and tapestry.

Markets

Bolhão Market, Rua Sá da Bandeira. Open Monday to Friday 7 a.m. to 5 p.m., Saturday 7 a.m. to 1 p.m.

Bom Sucesso Market, Praça do Bom Sucesso. Open Monday to Friday 7 a.m. to 5 p.m., Saturday 7 a.m. to 1 p.m.

Vandoma Fair, next to the Cathedral. Open Saturday 7 a.m. to 1 p.m. Antiques are sold at this market.

Festivals

If you are in Oporto in June, you might find it interesting to visit

Penafiel, 35 km along the N15, for the Corpo de Deus Festival on 18 June. Corpus Christi festivals began in the thirteenth century, and they had close links with the medieval craftsmen's guilds. The Penafiel Festival is one of the very few remaining festivals of this type. It is a curious mixture of Masses, blessing of cattle, sword dances, battles between Moors and Christians, fireworks, girls in traditional dress and laden with gold, and angels in white.

In Oporto itself, on 23 and 24 June the *Festas de São João* are celebrated. People sing and dance, eat roast kid, and drink *vinho verde* all night long around bonfires. They also maintain the curious custom of striking each other with leeks.

In August the *Festas de São Bartolomeu* are celebrated in Oporto. Originally this was a folk pilgrimage to the shrine of Saint Bartholomew that ended with all the people throwing themselves in the sea to bathe. This has developed into a strange parade known as the *Cortejo de Papel*, in which people dress in paper costumes that satirize figures in the news – mostly politicians – and follow a carriage containing a Neptune surrounded by sirens to a beach where a symbolic battle takes place between 'pirates' from the sea and 'land people', with Neptune acting as arbitrator. Finally everyone rushes into the sea for a 'holy bath'. This may be connected with the old superstition that a bath in the sea can cast out the devil or take away the evil eye – it is said that on the feast day of Saint Bartholomew 'the devil runs loose'.

Cruises

Various cruises along the port wine route are available. There is a 25-km cruise to Crestuma with lunch on board; weekend cruises through the port wine valley up to Pocinho with lunch and dinner on board, an overnight in Regua followed by a visit and lunch to a wine estate; and mini-cruises under Oporto's three bridges, which leave every hour. The boats leave from the quay at Praça da Ribeira and the quay in front of the Ferreira Wine Lodge at Vila Nova de Gaia. For the trips upriver, the schedules are fixed each month and are available at the Tourist Office or directly through Endouro, Muro dos Bacalhoeiros 104. Tel. (02) 324236.

Where to stay

Oporto is full of hotels in all price ranges, but it is often difficult to find a place to stay. Try to book in advance. The following list is just a small selection.

Expensive

Hotel Infante de Sagres, Praça Dona Filipa de Lencastre 62. Tel. (02) 28101/8. I can recommend this five star hotel with its old-world elegance. It has a nice bar and restaurant.

Hotel Sheraton Porto, Avenida da Boavista 1269. Tel. (02) 668822. A luxurious five star hotel. It has 253 air-conditioned rooms and suites with mini-bars and TV. There is a restaurant, swimming pool, a squash court and a health club.

Hotel Meridien, Avenida da Boavista 1466. Tel. (02) 668863. A five star hotel with 227 rooms, bar, restaurant, two pools, sauna, shops, horse riding and many other amenities.

Medium price **Grande Hotel da Batalha**, Praça da Batalha 116. Tel. (02) 20571. A four star hotel with 144 rooms.

Inexpensive **Hotel Peninsular**, Rua Sá da Bandeira 21. Tel. (02) 23012. A two star hotel in the centre of Oporto. It has a restaurant with Portuguese and Indian cooking.

Albergaria Miradouro, Rua da Alegria 598. Tel. (02) 570717. A four star inn with thirty rooms, TV, bar and restaurant.

Pensão Aviz, Avenida Rodrigues de Freitas 451. Tel. (02) 320722. A three star pension with bar and restaurant.

Camp site **Prelada**, Rua Monte dos Burgos. Tel. (02) 62616. Open all year.

Where to eat Oporto and the surrounding towns – Matosinhos, Espinho, Leixões – have so many different kinds of restaurants, with such a wide variety of dishes, that you can choose whatever you like, from French *haute cuisine* to sardines grilled over charcoal by the riverfront. Naturally, the best seafood is found in restaurants by the sea. The *tascas* (taverns) by the riverside have all of the dishes typical of the region. You should make at least one visit to a *tasca* while you are in Oporto – they have the real atmosphere of the centuries-old city.

The following list is a selection of recommended restaurants.

Les Terrasses, Hotel Meridien Porto, Avenida da Boavista 1466. Tel. (02) 668863. A luxurious restaurant that serves excellent food.

Portucale, 598 Rua da Alegria. Tel. (02) 570717. Has a sweeping view of the city from its oak panelled rooms. Probably the best restaurant in town, it serves a varied menu of continental and Portuguese dishes.

Escondidinho, Rua Passos Manuel 144. Tel. (02) 2001079. Serves excellent regional food. Decorated in tiles and examples of local handicrafts, it is in what looks like a typical country house.

O Brasil, Alameda Eça de Queiroz 40. Tel. (02) 499203. A restaurant with an agreeable atmosphere and a varied menu.

Taverna Bebobos, Cais da Ribeira 24. Tel. (02) 313565. A century-old waterfront tavern serving regional food. It is not open on Sundays. Closed the first half of September.

Girasol, Rua Sá da Bandeira 131. Tel. (02) 27393. A big, popular restaurant that serves regional dishes.

Mal Cozinhado, Rua do Outeirinho 13. Tel. (02) 3881319. A restaurant near the Campanhã train station that serves a combination of international and regional dishes and has *fado* singing in the late evening.

Casa Aleixo, Rua da Estação 216. Tel. (02) 570462. A moderately priced restaurant with excellent traditional dishes.

What to eat *Caldo verde* (a soup of green cabbage and puréed potatoes, with spicy sausage added) is the favourite soup of Oporto. *Caldeirada* (a stew with nine or ten different kinds of fish cooked with tomatoes and onions and herbs) is good in almost all of the restaurants. Cod is also done in a variety of ways – one of them is *gomes da sá* (layers of shredded, boiled cod, sliced, hard-boiled eggs, fried onions and chopped parsley, with olive oil poured over it, baked in the oven). You can also get lamprey in season. The cured hams and cheeses are very good. Desserts are mainly made of eggs, sugar and almonds and have droll religious names like *Barriga de Freira* (Nun's Belly), because they were originally made in convents.

Of course, the best-known Oporto dish is *tripas à moda do Oporto*, which is said to have been invented in the fifteenth century after the population had slaughtered all of their cattle for meat for Prince Henry the Navigator's troops. It is made of veal tripe, leg of veal, pig's ear, pig's head, streaky bacon, spicy sausage, chicken, carrots, onions, white beans, parsley, bayleaves, salt and pepper and cumin seeds. They are all boiled together and served with white rice. Believe it or not, it is delicious. Try it.

All of these dishes are eaten with *vinho verde* or the white and red table wines of the Douro region.

Tourist Office, Rua Clube Fenianos 25, 4000 Oporto. Tel. (02) 31274.

Nightlife   Oporto has a varied nightlife with many discos, pubs and *fado* houses.

Swing, 766 Rua Julio Dinis. Tel. (02) 690019. Has an upstairs pub and a downstairs disco, attracting Oporto's smart set.

Twins, 1000 Rua do Passeio Alegre. Tel. (02) 685740. Also a pub-cum-disco-dining room in the Foz suburb near the mouth of the Douro.

Green's, 1086 Rua Padre Luis Cabral. Tel. (02) 685704. Another pub-cum-disco-cum-restaurant.

The Olympia is a smart disco in the Meridien hotel, Avenida da Boavista 1466. Tel. (02) 668863.

Amnesia, at Praia Francelo beach, 10 km south of Oporto, is a crazy new disco where the waiters sing and dance with the guests.

Fado is not very popular north of Coimbra, but there are a few places in Oporto where you can hear it.

Casa das Mariquinhas, Rua São Sebastião 25. Tel. (02) 316083. Offers a fair representation of the *fado* singing so popular in Coimbra and Lisbon.

Many pubs, like **Postigo do Carvão** by the Ribeira riverfront, have live music and some like the **Aniki-Bobo** next door offer jazz.

Vila Nova de Gaia   Vila Nova de Gaia, just across the river from Oporto, is where the port wine lodges for ageing and bottling the wine are located. It is built on the site of a pre-Roman settlement. In the Middle Ages, it was made a separate town from Oporto, in an attempt to take away some of the power from the powerful Bishops of Oporto. It has suffered greatly through the centuries from invasions, wars and devastating floods that periodically inundated it. One of the worst was registered in 1727, but there were many others until the dams were built on the Douro –

you can see the watermarks from the floods when you visit the lodges. Vila Nova de Gaia's narrow, twisted streets contain many different shops, warehouses and the famous cellars of the port wine shippers.

Wine lodges   You should not leave Oporto without a visit to one of the lodges. The lodges are open till 6 p.m. each day, and you can arrange a tour through the Tourist Office or your hotel. There is the Ferreira lodge, which has cellars with wine dating back as far as 1811. Sandeman, with its famous symbol of the black silhouette of a Portuguese student in black cape and hat, has its lodge right by the river, where a *rabelo* boat is anchored with the Sandeman name and symbol on its sail. Sandeman was established in 1790 by Scotsman George Sandeman with a loan of £300; the company now exports to 112 countries and has its own vineyards up the river. The Calem lodge on Avenida Diogo Leite has ports from its own farms up the Douro in Pinhão. The Borges lodge, founded in 1884, has excellent vintage port. Other well-known companies such as Croft, Taylor, Cintra, Barros, Cockburn and Fonseca also have lodges in Vila Nova de Gaia.

You will be shown how the wine is mixed and aged in the barrels and how it is bottled. Many of the wooden barrels used for ageing the wine are still carved and shaped by hand, as they have been for centuries. Finally you will be able to taste the wines in the tasting rooms, and buy bottles to take home.

What to see   The Serra do Pilar Monastery has a Renaissance cloister, a seventeenth-century barrel vault roof, eighteenth-century carved gilt work and painted wood sculptures. On a hill facing Oporto, it has a lovely view of the city.

The Parish Church dates from the sixteenth century. It was restored and added to in 1745 by Nicolau Nasoni.

Festivals   The celebrations for the *Festa de São Gonçalo e São Cristovão* at the beginning of January have much of the fertility rite about them. (São Gonçalo is revered all over the north of Portugal as the saint who provides husbands.) An image of São Gonçalo found in the River Douro centuries ago is paraded through the streets followed by the whole town beating drums. Douro boatmen carry three strange figures: a figure of São Cristovão with a gigantic head, a small, pretty image of São Gonçalo – curiously, both dressed in eighteenth-century clothes – and a third figure dressed as a priest. The right to carry the images is passed down from father to son. Much port is drunk, accompanied by cakes in phallic shapes.

The *Festa da Nossa Senhora do Pilar* takes place in August.

Where   **Hotel Novotel Porto**, Chas – Afurada. Tel. (02) 7814242. A three
to stay   star hotel with ninety-three rooms with bath and TV, covered pool,
Medium price   bar, and gardens.

Pensão Davilina, Avenida da República 157. Tel. (02) 307596. A three star pension with twenty-seven rooms with bath and TV, and restaurant.

Manor house | **Vila Mar**, Avenida da República 1894, in Praia da Granja Beach,
Inexpensive | Valadares. Tel. (02) 7620108. Offers two rooms to guests.

Camp site | **Parque de Campismo Marisol**, Rua Alto das Chaquedas 82, Canidelo, Vila Nova de Gaia. Tel. (02) 715942.

Where to eat | **Sebastião Alfaiate**, Rua Machado dos Santos 647–651. Tel. (02) 302886. A restaurant that has good food at reasonable prices.

Matosinhos

Matosinhos used to be a fishing port. Stretching round the busy sea port of Leixões with its artificial harbour, it has been overcome by industry, but it still retains many of its old customs and beliefs. Its excellent seafood restaurants and its position conveniently close to Oporto have made it a popular place to go to eat, and it also has a small beach and several churches worth visiting. Gonçalves Zarco, the discoverer of Madeira and the Azores, was born in Matosinhos.

What to see

The Church of Bom Jesus is an eighteenth-century Baroque church with a façade by Nicolau Nasoni. It houses a statue of Christ that was found on the beach several hundred years ago, and, according to legend, was carved by the disciple Nicodemus. There is a great pilgrimage to the statue every June.

The Quinta do Viso is an imposing eighteenth-century mansion.

Where to stay | **Hotel Porto-Mar**, Rua Brito Capelo 167. Tel. (02) 932104. A two
Inexpensive | star hotel with thirty-two rooms, twenty-six with bath, a bar and restaurant.

Pensão Senhora de Matosinhos, Rua do Godinho 634. Tel. (02) 930548/932436. A three star pension with sixteen rooms with bath and TV.

Where to eat | **Esplanada Marisqueira**, Rua Roberto Ivens 628–638. Tel. (02) 930660. A seafood restaurant that serves specialities like *arroz de marisco* (seafood with rice) and different types of fresh fish. It also has a private vivarium.

Garrafão, Leça da Palmeira. Tel. (02) 9951735/9951660. A restaurant that serves excellent seafood and has a pleasant atmosphere.

O Chanquinhas, Rua Santana 243. Tel. (02) 9951884. A restaurant that has first-class food.

Convés, Rua do Godinho 283. Tel. (02) 930172. A good snack bar.

What to eat

Matosinhos has excellent seafood. It is well worth trying *arroz de marisco* (shellfish with rice), *açorda* (a sort of kedgeree made with bread), *caldeirada de peixe* (fish stew), *sardinhas assadas* (charcoal-grilled sardines), and *mexilhãos à moda de Leça* (mussels with parsley). For a sweet, try *broinhas de Leixões* (honey cakes).

The Tourist Office is in the Market Building. Tel. (02) 934414.

Espinho

Espinho is just 16 km south of Oporto. In a hundred years it has grown from a group of fishing huts on the beach to a glittering resort with palm-lined esplanades, excellent hotels and restaurants, and a casino with an international show. It even has its own small airport.

What to see

A curious form of offshore trawling, where the fishermen use oxen on the beaches to help pull in the nets is still to be seen at Espinho.

Crafts

The local artisans carve miniatures of boats and other articles in wood. These and other craft objects can be bought at the weekly fair, held on Mondays.

Festival

In September the *Festas da Senhora da Ajuda* are celebrated. The statue of the town's patron saint, Our Lady of Succour, is taken to the sea, to give a blessing. This is followed by music, fireworks and a fair.

Sport

Espinho also offers riding, tennis, sailing – and the oldest golf course on the Peninsula, Oporto Golf Club, which was opened by British port shippers in 1890. Just south of Espinho there is the Lagoa de Parâmos, for windsurfing and other water sports.

Where to stay
Medium price

Hotel Praia Golf, Rua 6. Tel. (02) 720630. A four star hotel with 139 rooms with bath and TV, three swimming pools, tennis, golf, bar, restaurant, snack bar and many other facilities.

Inexpensive

Hotel Mar Azul, Avenida 8, 676. Tel. (02) 720824. A two star hotel with twenty-four bedrooms with bath. It has a disco.

Where to eat

América, Rua 31, 693. Tel. (02) 722279. A two star restaurant that specializes in fresh seafood.

Aquário Marisqueira, Rua 19, 28. Tel. (02) 720377. A restaurant that serves fresh seafood and regional dishes.

Café Moderno, Rua 19, 175. Tel. (02) 720963. A snack bar and café that serves homemade pastries.

Espinho has marvellous seafood.

Upper Douro

Amarante

Amarante, on the banks of the River Tâmega, is one of the loveliest towns in Portugal. Its mansion and restaurants with their verandas and wooden balustrades lean over the water amidst luxuriant vegetation. In the early morning mist it has a fairy tale atmosphere.

Getting there
History

Amarante is 70 km from Oporto by the N15. It is also on the Tâmega scenic train route.

The origins of the town are unknown; but the numerous remains of Iron Age *castros* (see page 17), dolmens and Luso-Roman ruins indicate that it was occupied in very ancient times.

Some historians claim that Amarante was founded in 360 BC by an invading tribe. Others say it was founded by the Roman governor Amarantus. Those of more religious bent claim it was founded by the priest from Guimarães who later became Saint Gonçalo.

In 1809 the people of the town under the Count of Amarante heroically defended it against attacking French troops. They swarmed over the bridge and attacked the French, who retaliated by sacking and burning many of the principal buildings and houses. You can still see on the buildings the black marks from the fire.

Amarante today

Fortunately for the beauty of the town, Amarante has not been invaded by ugly factories and modern, characterless buildings. It has kept its charming restaurants and tea-houses with their verandas over the river and its narrow, cobbled streets. At the same time, new hotels have been built outside the centre of the town.

What to see

The **São Gonçalo Bridge** was built between 1740 and 1815. It is a three-span granite bridge with four semicircular platforms along its roadway.

The **Church and Monastery of São Gonçalo** stands impressively by the bridge. It was ordered built in 1540 by King João III and was finished in 1620. There are stone statues of Saint Francis of Assisi and Saint Dominic in its lovely portico. Its façade has two large windows and a rose window. Its doors are in the Mannerist style. Its famous and much-photographed loggia has five arches with statues of King João III, King Sebastião, King Henrique and King Filipe I. Inside there are glazed tiles, carvings, a gilt retable and the tomb of São Gonçalo. The tower was added in the eighteenth century.

The **Church of São Domingos** is a small eighteenth-century Baroque church with beautiful carving in its interior.

The **Church of São Pedro** also dates from the eighteenth century. It has a two-storey bell tower and a Baroque façade. Inside, it has one nave decorated in glazed tiles. There is a lovely decorated ceiling in the sacristy.

The **Town Fountain** is sixteenth century.

The **Albano Sardoeira Museum** has paintings, including some interesting ones by contemporary Portuguese artists, sculpture, archaeological finds and rugs from Arraiolos.

But the most fascinating things in the museum are the 'devils': two black statues, one of a male and one of a female devil, each seated on a block of stone. These statues were carved by António Ferreira de Carvalho in the nineteenth century – the Friars of the Monastery had them made to replace the original 'devils', which were destroyed in fires set by invading French troops – and a very interesting thing about them is that they are negroes, with typical negroid features. The sculptor must have been impressed by Africans he had seen from Portugal's African territories, but why he associated them with devils remains a mystery.

They were venerated every 24 August, the feast day of Saint Bartholomew, when, according to superstition, 'the devil runs loose'. The people ornamented the statues and made offerings to them to appease the devil. In 1870 the Archbishop of Braga, who took a dim view of this, decided to put a stop to it on the pretext that the statues were indecent because they displayed their sexual organs. He gave orders that they should be burnt; but the Friars limited themselves to cutting off the male devil's offending phallus. Later the devils were sold to England, but this caused such consternation among the people of Amarante that they had to be brought back.

The **Forest Park** is a wooded hillside by the river with many paths for walking, and a mini-zoo.

The town and countryside abound in manors (*solares*), many of them former homes of important artists, writers, poets and politicians. Some of the most interesting are Casa de Manhufe, Casa de Souto Verde, Casa de Tardinhade and the ruins of the Solar de Magalhães, destroyed by the French.

Crafts

The women in many of the villages around Amarante do beautiful embroidery. They make linen bedspreads, place mats, towels, sheets and many other embroidered things in linen and cotton. It is an art that is dying out as women go to work in factories or at less time-consuming jobs. A 3 m × 1.80 m tablecloth, for example, takes more than a year to embroider. You can buy from the women in their homes or at shops – many along the roadsides. Rag rugs and woollen rugs, knitted articles, basketwork, ironwork, copper utensils and black, earthenware pots and jugs are also made around Amarante.

Festivals

Every Thursday and Saturday evening from the beginning of June to the end of October, a public party known as the *Arraiais de São Gonçalo* is held in the gardens of the Casa da Calçada on top of a hill over the river. It goes on from 7 p.m. to 1 a.m., and for about 1,800 esc. you can eat and drink as much as you want, dance to the local bands and watch folk dancing. You will also be treated to firework displays, a parade of *Gigantes* (people dressed up as giants with enormous, ugly heads in bright colours), and a *Marcha Popular* in which everyone marches around singing and carrying torches. The *Arraiais* is organized by the Hotel Navarras, tel. (055) 424036/424657.

The *Festa e Romaria de São Gonçalo*, which takes place early in June, is very colourful. São Gonçalo is said to have reconstructed the Roman bridge at Amarante in the thirteenth century. But this is not what made him famous. He achieved his celebrity as the saint who helped old maids get married. There are several legends as to how this came about. Some say he was a frolicsome, waggish hermit who was much criticized for his impious ways: he organized dances for ladies of doubtful repute, where he played the guitar, sang and danced in an effort to find them husbands and keep them out of temptation. In another version, it is said that the people of Aboadela forced couples 'living in sin' to go to the priest, Gonçalo, to be married. The name Aboadela was in time corrupted to *as velhas* (old women), so Gonçalo became the priest who 'married old women'.

The pilgrimage brings people from all of the outlying districts. Women take bouquets of red carnations to the Church of São Gonçalo, and pull the red cord of the saint's habit and kiss his statue, while praying for a husband. I met an old woman in Amarante who said she had got a good one this way.

There is also a big fair with crafts, folk dancing and singing in the streets and a spectacular display of fireworks.

The Amarante market fair takes place twice a month, on the first Saturday and the 17th of the month.

The market fair at Marco de Canaveses, nearby, is twice a week, on Monday and Thursday.

Excursions

There are many dolmens in the vicinity, which the local people refer to as 'little houses of the Moors'. There are also many 'balancing rocks' about.

The **Lugar do Castelo** and **Meninas** are ancient *castros* (see page 17).

For people who like Romanesque churches, the villages around Amarante are a treasure-trove.

In **Freixo de Baixo**, 5 km to the north-west, the Parish Church dates from the twelfth century. Inside is an interesting fresco.

In **Travanca**, 14 km to the west, there is a tenth-century monastery made of large granite blocks. Its doorway has four archivolts with sculptured capitals.

In **Mancelos** (Vila Meã), 14 km to the west, the Parish Church, dedicated to Saint Martin, is twelfth-century Romanesque.

In **Lufrei**, 3 km to the east, the Parish Church is twelfth-century Romanesque.

In **Jazente**, 5 km to the south-east, the Parish Church is thirteenth-century Romanesque.

In **Gatão**, 4 km to the north-east, the São João Church is twelfth-century Romanesque. It was restored in the eighteenth century.

In **Gondar**, 6 km to the south-east, there is a twelfth-century Parish Church and a ruined monastery.

Sport

You can fish for trout in the River Tâmega, or rent a small boat to explore the river and its many little tree-covered islands. There is a small sandy beach, which you can swim from, on the river bank.

There is also hunting in the region.

Where to stay

Inexpensive

Hotel Residencial Navarras, Rua António Carneiro, 4600 Amarante. Tel. (055) 424036. A three star hotel with sixty-one rooms. It is completely air-conditioned and has a bar, a large dining room with an esplanade, and an indoor swimming pool.

Hotel Silva, Rua Cândido dos Reis. Tel. (055) 423110. An old one star hotel in the centre of town.

Hotel Amaranto, Rua Madalena, 4600 Amarante. Tel. (055) 422106/7. A three star hotel with thirty-five rooms with bath and TV. It has a lovely view of the town, bars and an excellent restaurant.

Pensão Restaurante Príncipe, Largo Conselheiro António Cândido. Tel. (055) 43009. A three star pension with nine rooms, three of them with bath.

Manor house

Inexpensive

Casa Zé da Calçada, Rua 31 de Janeiro, Cepelos-4600 Amarante. Tel. (055) 422023. In front of the famous Zé da Calçada restaurant that overlooks the river. It has three double bedrooms with bath.

Pousada
Inexpensive

Pousada de São Gonçalo, Serra do Marão. Tel. (055) 461113, telex 26231. A medium range pousada with fifteen rooms, in the Marão mountains about 25 km from Amarante. It has wonderful views, and a good restaurant with local hams, fruits and desserts.

Tourist
village

Torre de Nevões, Marco de Canaveses. Tel. (055) 52806/52334. A tourist village in a pine wood in the mountains near the town of Marco de Canaveses, 24 km from Amarante. It is a peculiar conglomeration of prefabricated cabins, a twelfth-century restored farmhouse, an inn and a disco with flashing lights among ancient pillars. It has ten double bedrooms, fifteen apartments, five bungalows, a rather dubious swimming pool, tennis court, soccer field, a small lake, restaurant, tavern and disco. It is all right for those who want something far out in the woods and a bit different.

Camp site

Parque de Campismo de Amarante, Quinta dos Frades. Tel. (055) 42133. In a lovely spot by the River Tâmega. It has a good restaurant and a mini-market.

Where to eat

Zé de Calçada, Rua 31 de Janeiro 83. Tel. (055) 422023. A restaurant known all over Portugal. It has good regional cooking, and a lovely terrace overlooking the River Tâmega.

Grelha, Murtas Madalena. Tel. (055) 423272. A restaurant, café and nightclub with *fado* singing. It serves excellent regional food and international cuisine.

Restaurante do Parque de Campismo, Quinta dos Frades. Tel. (055) 42454. A good restaurant, on the camp site.

Above all, don't miss a visit to the **Adega Regional**, a typical *tasca* (tavern), in a cave cut out of the granite hillside in the narrow main street behind the restaurants that face the river. The owner, Senhor Cardoso, has been there for thirty years, dispensing cups of *vinho verde* and plates of delicious, locally cured ham and spicy sausages from those he has hanging from the roof. It is a custom to pass the wine cup around among friends. Try the *salpicão* (a sausage marinated in red wine and then smoke-cured).

What to eat

Rice and kid done in the oven; shad; lamprey; trout; *feijoada* (meats and sausages boiled with beans); *cozido à Portuguesa* (meats and chicken boiled with vegetables); *rojões* (deep-fried titbits of pork); and cod *zé da calçada*. The sweet desserts are made with eggs, sugar and almonds and have names like *foguetes* (rockets) and *brisas do Tâmega* (breezes of Tâmega).

The most famous of these sweets are made by the owner of the veranda'd tea-house and pastry shop next to the Zé da Calçada Restaurant. She has been baking Amarante sweets for forty years.

What to drink

The local *vinho verde*. Some of the local labels are Quinta do Outeiro, Caves Manuel Pinheiro, Caves Moura Basto and Caves de Arca.

The Tourist Office is in the Cândido dos Reis, 4600 Amarante. Tel. (055) 422980. The Tourist Office is one of the few places (apart from hotels) where you can change money outside banking hours. They will change for you from 10 a.m. to 7 p.m.

Peso da Régua

Getting there

Peso da Régua sits at the junction of the Douro and Corgo rivers, where the Upper Douro, with the best grapes, really begins. It is 160 km up the River Douro from Oporto if you come by the main road, N15, through Amarante. But the best way to get to Régua is to take the Douro scenic train from Oporto.

History

The highest part of the town, Peso, was granted by Count Henrique to the Bishop of Oporto in the eleventh century, and it got its first charter in 1513. However, it was the Marquês de Pombal who, in the eighteenth century, gave Régua the role it has today of trade and shipping centre of the Douro, the link between the growers who produce the wine and the traders in Oporto. From here the river boats, the *rabelos*, used to set off on their perilous journey down the river with the wine barrels. In July 1959 the railway reached Régua, and changed its life profoundly.

In this century the wine producers formed the Casa do Douro, an association to protect their interests and assure the quality of the wine. Their headquarters are in the Casa do Douro building.

Régua today

As a town Régua is not very interesting, but it is surrounded by countryside of imposing beauty. It is a bustling place, especially at harvest time, when people come in from all over the place to pick and crush the grapes. There is a frantic race against weather and other possible calamities until the wine is safely stored away in barrels.

What to see

The Casa do Douro is a solid, no-nonsense building, but it has three beautiful stained glass windows by painter Lino António which depict the history of port and how it is made.

The Parish Church dates from the eighteenth century. It has a religious painting by Pedro Alexandrino.

O Cruzeiro Church has an altar with elaborate gilt work.

Crafts

Look out for leather work, basketwork and regional dolls.

Festivals

The *Festa de São Brás* is celebrated at the beginning of February, the *Festa de São Pedro* on 29 June, the *Festa da Nossa Senhora das Graças* at the beginning of August and the *Festa da Nossa Senhora do Socorro* on 15 August.

Excursion

Mesão Frio, 12 km west of Régua on the N108, is an ancient town set over the River Douro. The Casa da Rede there is a magnificent eighteenth-century building with a Baroque entrance, beautiful windows and a garden that overlooks the river. There are also two interesting churches, the Gothic Parish Church and the Santa Cristina Church, which was once part of a Franciscan monastery. There are also facilities for water sports on the reservoir of the dam that tames the river below the town.

Where to stay
Inexpensive

Residencial Império, Rua José Vasques Osório 8. Tel. (054) 22399. A very good new inn near the station with twenty-eight rooms with bath, and a bar.

Pensão Columbiano, Avenida Sacadura Cabral. Tel. (054) 23704. A three star pension with seventy rooms, fifty-six with bath, TV in the rooms, and a bar.

Manor house

Casa dos Varais, Cambres, 5050 Peso da Régua. Tel. (054) 23251 or (02) 674442. A large eighteenth-century house with a beautiful view of the Douro. It offers two double bedrooms, a private living room for guests, terraces and pleasant gardens.

Where to eat What to eat

There are several reasonable restaurants and snack bars in Régua.

Try freshwater fish from the river, *cabrito assado* (roast lamb), *vitela assada* (roast veal), *cozido à Portuguesa* (a boiled dish of meat, vegetables and sausages), *arroz de forno* (rice baked in the oven), *sopa de vindimas* (harvest soup).

The Tourist Offices for the area are the *Posto de Turismo*, Largo da Estação, 5050 Peso da Régua, tel. (054) 22846; and the *Junta de Turismo das Caldas de Moledo*, Caldas de Moledo, 5050 Peso da Régua, tel. (054) 23846.

Lamego

Getting there

Lamego is 10 km south of Peso da Régua and about 170 km from Oporto – a two and a half hour drive by way of Amarante or one of the scenic roads beside the river. The scenic Douro train passes through Régua, from where it is only a short distance to Lamego.

Lamego sits in a valley among vineyards and orchards, totally surrounded by mountains. It is at the crossroads that connects the remote lands in the north of Portugal with the south. In the past, it was also the place where traders from Córdoba and Granada in Spain met those coming inland from ports on the Atlantic. It has been destroyed many times, during invasions by Swabians, Visigoths, Moors and Spaniards.

History

The Castle at Lamego is built on the site of what must have been an ancient *castro* (see page 17). A Roman town charter was granted to Lamego in the fourth century AD, and it is one of the oldest and most famous episcopal cities in the Peninsula – its diocese is mentioned as far back as 569. It was also the place where, in 1143, the first Portuguese parliament met – an assembly of the king's military men called the *Cortes de Lamego*.

Lamego was much favoured by the first Portuguese kings, and during the twelfth century it became a a powerful diocese. It was King

Afonso III who, in the thirteenth century, built the present walls with their imposing towers and entrances, two of which remain: the Porta dos Figos and the Porta do Sol.

The town outgrew its walls when it became a thriving commercial centre exporting to Granada, Lisbon and the Algarve. The people produced grain, fruits, vegetables and wine and raised cattle. The silk and leather industries flourished. There was also in the town a large community of Jews who dedicated themselves to commerce, medicine and metalwork. The old *Judiaria* was by the Porta do Sol.

During the fourteenth century the favour of the kings was withdrawn: many of the privileges Lamego had enjoyed were revoked, and heavy taxes were imposed. The town declined until the sixteenth century, when the whole of Portugal benefited from the riches brought in from its overseas empire. In Lamego, as in many other Portuguese towns, much of the new-found wealth was used to build sumptuous mansions. Lamego became a Baroque town.

The people of Lamego claim that the fragrant, raisin-sweet wine of Lamego was the original port. Certainly, in the seventeenth century Lamego wine was discovered by Englishmen visiting the region. They bought it and shipped it to England, where it became very popular. The Marquês de Pombal later had a good road built from Lamego to Régua, so that the wine could be shipped down the Douro to Oporto.

Lamego suffered during the French invasions and the War of Succession, and once more slipped back into obscurity.

Lamego today

Most of Lamego's historic buildings are concentrated around the flowery park and Largo da Sé. These buildings are well preserved, and the gardens and square are lovely. However, the old parts of the town by the river and near the Castle are very dilapidated. There are also many tasteless, ugly buildings around the town.

What to see

The **Cathedral**, in the square, is a mixture of Romanesque, Gothic and Renaissance. The lower part of the tower was built in the second half of the twelfth century, but the top part is sixteenth century. The Gothic west front dates from the sixteenth century. The cloister, also built in the sixteenth century, is a combination of Renaissance and Gothic. The interior of the church dates from the eighteenth century, and is decorated with Nasoni frescoes.

The **Museum**, also in the square, is housed in what was formerly the Bishop's Palace, which was restored in the second half of the eighteenth century. Its collections include four complete chapels from the demolished Chagas Monastery, as well as many gold and silver chalices, candlesticks, platters and other valuable objects of church furnishing. It also has collections of archaeological finds; Roman monuments; Portuguese paintings from the sixteenth, seventeenth and eighteenth centuries, including paintings by Grão Vasco; some wonderful sixteenth-century Flemish tapestries; and sculpture, furniture and ceramics.

The **Church of Santa Cruz** was founded in 1596 and dedicated to Saint John the Baptist. Its interior is decorated with tiles and carvings.

The **Desterro Chapel** was reconstructed in 1640 by the Bailiff of Leça, Friar Luis Álvares de Távora; he transformed the primitive chapel that already existed on the site. Inside it has seventeenth- and eighteenth-century gilt carvings and tiles.

The **Almacave Church** was built in the twelfth century. It was here that the first *Cortes* (parliament) of Portugal met in 1143.

Lamego also has several impressive palaces from the seventeenth and eighteenth centuries, exhibiting the coats of arms of some of the noble families of the region: Castro, Fonseca, Coutinho, Vilhenas, Carvalhos, Leitões and Manuéis.

The **Castle** was built on the site of a *castro* at the base of Mount Penedine across a small river from what is now Lamego. To get there, you have to go along a street that is possibly the narrowest and most rocky on the Iberian Peninsula – it is probably best to go on foot. The Castle is Romanesque. Its defence walls are well delineated and the twelfth-century keep is very well preserved. There is a vaulted cistern that may be of Moorish origin in the courtyard. Until recently the villagers were using the Castle as a rubbish dump, but it has been rescued and is now being taken care of by the local boy scouts.

The **Bairro da Fonte** is the old, dilapidated quarter of Lamego under the bridge and on the banks of the river near the Castle. The people there are almost self-sufficient. They grow food on the terraced banks of the river, grind their grain in the watermills and bake their own bread in old-fashioned ovens. There are even two blacksmiths who work in open forges.

The **Sanctuary of Nossa Senhora dos Remédios** is at the top of a steep, winding road through a lovely wooded park. The church sits at the head of a double flight of stairs with over seven hundred steps. The upper terrace is surrounded by statues of kings in Moorish dress, and there are also arches, pillars, obelisks, dolphins and ornate fountains in profusion. The church is like a cameo in blue and gold, with tiles on the walls. The church was finished in 1761, but the staircase was not completed until this century.

Festivals

The *Festas da Nossa Senhora dos Remédios*, which lasts from the end of August to the middle of September, is one of the largest fairs in Portugal. During all this time there are folk dances, fireworks, battles of flowers, exhibitions and sports contests. People come from all the villages and stay throughout the festivities, singing and dancing in the streets and sleeping in the parks or countryside. Some of the more serious pilgrims also crawl on their knees all the way up the hundreds of steps that lead to the church. The main procession has large floats with images representing the Life of Christ, pulled by yoked oxen.

There is a market fair in Lamego on Wednesdays.

Crafts

Look out for black pottery made about 30 km from Lamego in a small place called Fazamões, near São Martinho de Mouros in the district of Resende. This is made by a very ancient method – fired in a hole in the ground, where the smoke produced in the kiln is allowed to penetrate the clay for eight days until it achieves an even black colour. The pottery is unglazed. If you are interested in this craft, it is possible to visit the primitive kilns.

Excursions

In the **Meadas Mountains** high above the town you feel you are on top of the world. On the highest peak, surrounded by pine trees and flowering shrubs, is the tiny Chapel of Our Lady of the Mountain.

Also in the mountains is the Turiserra tourist complex, with motel, restaurant, mini-golf, tennis, and small apartments and nice cabins in native stone, with verandas with marvellous views.

The **Church of São Pedro de Balsemão**, 15 km east of Lamego, is well worth a visit. To get there you go through the Bairro da Fonte area below the bridge and follow the small unmarked road on the bank of the River Balsemão, passing many watermills and little waterfalls. The church was originally a seventh-century Visigoth temple, which was remodelled in the fourteenth century by the Bishop of Oporto, Dom Afonso Pires, whose carved marble tomb guarded by a lion is in the church. The church also has a fourteenth-century stone sculpture of *Nossa Senhora do Ó* (Our Lady of O – thus called because of the totally round shape of the pregnant Virgin's stomach).

The **Church of the Monastery of São Francisco** is on the Ferreirim estate, 7 km south of Lamego off the N226. It was built in 1425. It has several sixteenth-century paintings, and eighteenth-century tiles in its *Senhora das Dores* (Our Lady of Pain) chapel.

The **São João de Tarouca Monastery** is 12 km south of Lamego by the N226. This famous Cistercian monastery, the first in Portugal, was built in the twelfth century. The structure is basically Romanesque, but the portal is Renaissance and the altars are Baroque. The retable is tremendously rich in gold carvings. The mosaics on the wall date from the seventeenth century. The blue tiles in the main chapel are eighteenth-century: they tell the story of the opening of the church, which was attended by Portugal's first king, Afonso Henriques, and four bishops, in 1152. The sacristy has a lovely painted ceiling and 4,709 tiles – no two of which are alike. There is a fourteenth-century granite statue of the Virgin and Child, 2 m high and weighing over 1,000 kg. And notice too the primitive paintings, including a picture of an enthroned Saint Peter. The tomb of Dom Pedro, Count of Barcelos, the bastard son of King Dinis, is also in the church: he was a keen hunter, and his tomb has carved images of a javelin hunt.

The fortified **Bridge of Ucanha** is over the River Varoso in the little town of Ucanha near Tarouca. The only fortified bridge in Portugal, it was built in the thirteenth to fourteenth centuries, probably as a frontier post. Go under the bridge and look at the old watermills that are still in use.

Resende, 30 km west of Lamego along the south bank of the River Douro by the N226–N222, has some interesting churches. The **Parish Church of Barro** is Romanesque in shape, but has a curious façade divided into four different parts in four different styles. One part has a rose window, another has a door with an archivolt. The **Church of Nossa Senhora de Carquere** has a thirteenth-century Gothic chapel. The tower also dates from the thirteenth century, but the aisle of the church is sixteenth-century Manueline. The **Church of São Martinho de Mouros** is an excellent example of a rural Romanesque church. It has a rather military look. Inside there are primitive paintings of *Saint Martin and the Pauper* and *The Vision of Saint Martin*.

The town of **Cinfães**, 33 km on down the road from Resende and 63 km west of Lamego, is also interesting. It has been inhabited since prehistoric times, and the first King of Portugal, Afonso Henriques, was partly brought up here. The convent of **Santa Maria de Tarouquela** in Cinfães was first written about in 1162. It belonged then to nuns of the Augustinian Order, but it was later transferred to the Brothers of São Bento. The convent no longer exists, but its twelfth-century church is still standing.

Where to stay
Inexpensive

Hotel Parque, Nossa Senhora dos Remédios, 5100 Lamego. Tel. (054) 62105/6, telex 27723 PARTEL P. A lovely nineteenth-century hotel in the gardens next to the Sanctuary of Nossa Senhora dos Remédios. It was totally renovated recently. All rooms have bath, and some rooms and suites have telephone and TV. It has wonderful views of the Sanctuary gardens and the city.

Residencial Solar, Largo da Sé, 5100 Lamego. Tel. (054) 62060. A three star pension in the centre of town. It is small and comfortable, with twenty-five big rooms with bath. It has a bar but no restaurant.

Albergaria do Cerrado, Lugar do Cerrado. Tel. (054) 63154. A four star inn with thirty rooms with bath and TV, gardens and a bar.

Pensão Imperio, Travessa dos Loureiros 6. Tel. (054) 62742. Has twelve rooms with bath, a bar and restaurant.

Manor house
Inexpensive

Vila Hostilina, 5100 Lamego. Tel. (054) 62394. A restored farmhouse set in gardens and vineyards at the top of the town, with splendid views of the mountains and the valley. The manor has seven lovely rooms with bath, telephone, radio and central heating. Excellent meals are served in the dining room on request. There is a rustic bar in the wine cellar where the owners store their own wine, for which the grapes are still crushed by foot. Guests who want to participate, at harvest time, are welcome to do so. There is a tennis court, outdoor swimming pool and health club, with gym, sauna, exercise machines and karate lessons. Altogether a very special place to stay! In the high season, reserve in advance.

Where to eat

The **Restaurante Hotel Parque** has excellent regional cooking, good service and a lovely view, but is a bit pricey. The **Restaurante Turiserra** is a modern restaurant in the tourist complex in the Meadas Mountains – to find it just follow the 'Turiserra' signs. Here again there is a fantastic view. There are also several reasonable restaurants, with moderate prices, in the town.

What to eat
Try stuffed baked kid; trout baked with cured ham; roast lamb; smoked ham and spicy sausages; *Queijo Paiva* cheese; goat's milk cheese; *bacalhau desfiado* (flaked dried cod with onions and olive oil); *bolo de Lamego* (ham baked in a pastry crust); *chilas* (pumpkin sweets with sugar and eggs).

What to drink
Lamego is famous not only for its port but also for its excellent sparkling wines made by the champagne method. The ports come from the Real Companhia Velha and Sandeman, the sparkling wines from the Caves de Raposeira and the smaller Caves de Murganheira 12 km away in Salzedas. You can visit the cellars of any of these companies to taste the wines in any month but August. It is not necessary to make an appointment unless you are a large party.

It is the custom in Lamego to have dry white port as an aperitif. With your meal you can have a white or red table wine or even a *bruto* sparkling wine, and then sparkling wine with dessert.

The Tourist Office is near the Cathedral square, on the Avenida Visconde Guedes Teixeira, 5100 Lamego. Tel. (054) 422980.

Vila Real

Vila Real is located just where the Douro region meets Trás-os-Montes, north of Lamego and Peso da Régua on the N2, and 120 km east of Oporto. You can reach it from Régua on the scenic Corgo line train (see page 40).

History
There are many traces of Roman and Visigoth occupation in the area. The town was founded by King Dinis in the eleventh century and granted a charter in 1272. Because of the wine trade and its favourable position between the two regions of the Douro and Trás-os-Montes, Vila Real has been a prosperous trading centre since the fifteenth century.

Vila Real today
Vila Real has grown into a modern town without losing too much of its ancient charm. It has wide new boulevards entering the town; and there are excellent new facilities being built for tourists: a camp site, swimming pools, tennis courts, a lake in the river for swimming, and more hotels. There is a new road to Oporto, and by 1992 it will extend all the way to the Spanish border at Bragança.

Rosé wine
Rosé wine is produced in many parts of Portugal, so it is not really exclusive to any one region, but it began in the area around Vila Real. Portuguese rosés (made from red grapes) are light, fruity wines, sweet

or just on the dry side, with an alcohol level of around 11° or 12°.

What to see

The **Solar de Mateus**, in the village of Mateus on the outskirts of Vila Real, has what is probably the most widely known façade in Portugal, as its picture graces the label of the Mateus Rosé wine bottles that are shipped all over the world. Designed in the eighteenth century by Nicolau Nasoni, it is a very impressive building. It is built in the shape of a horseshoe, and its two wings are approached by a double staircase. The façade is adorned by a huge carved granite coat of arms, and statues of classical figures. The building – now a little bit dishevelled – is surrounded by lovely gardens and pools.

In the part of the palace open to the public, you can see the collection of paintings, and letters from Frederick the Great, Wellington, Talleyrand and others.

The **Cathedral** was part of the Dominican Monastery ordered built by King João I in 1427. It is Gothic in style, with three interior naves and an impressive apse.

The **Misericórdia Church** is predominantly Romanesque. The **São Dinis Church** was built in the fourteenth century. It has six sixteenth-century gilt retables in its side chapels, and a granite statue of Our Lady of Desterro. The **Church of São Pedro** has an altar of carved gilt woodwork. Its façade and doorway are by Nicolau Nasoni.

The **Piscais Bridge** is Roman.

Crafts

The black pottery produced in the tiny village of Bisalhães, 6 km from Vila Real, is still made by ancient methods. The designs (usually flower patterns or geometric designs) are passed down from mother to daughter, and are scratched on the pottery with a stone. The kiln is a hole in the ground: a pine fire is lit, the pots are put in and the hole is covered so that air cannot get in.

They make a traditional joke ewer called a *segredo* (secret), which pours water or wine down the front of anyone who tries to drink from it. There is a trick to this – but I will let you discover it for yourself.

Festivals

The *Feira de Santo António* in mid-June is a cattle fair. The *Feira de São Pedro* a couple of weeks later is a craft fair. It is sometimes called the *Feira dos Pucarinhos* (the Fair of the Little Mugs) because so much of it is given over to the sale of the traditional black pottery.

Excursions

The **Sanctuary of Panóias** is 5 km from Vila Real, easily reachable by car. It is an open place surrounded by several granite peaks close together. It is thought to have been used in Roman times as a place of sacrifice to Oriental or Hellenic deities.

You should also take a drive into the high **Alvão Mountains**, where there are spectacular views and you can drink fresh mountain water out of roadside fountains. Above the tree-line there are vast stretches of open space, and it is very cool here, even in August. The Alvão Natural Park is an excellent place for walking.

At the foot of the mountains, near Vila Real, are a Roman bridge and the Quintela Tower.

Where to stay
Inexpensive

Hotel Miracorgo, Avenida 1° de Maio 76–78. Tel. (059) 25001/6. A three star hotel in the centre of town overlooking the gorge of the River Corgo. It has seventy-six air-conditioned rooms, a bar, health club and swimming pool.

Hotel Cabanelas, Rua Dom Pedro de Castro. Tel. (059) 23153/4. A two star hotel with twenty-four rooms with bath, and a bar.

Hotel Tocaio, Avenida Carvalho Araujo 45. Tel. (054) 23106. A two star hotel with fifty-two rooms with bath, a bar and restaurant.

Where to eat

Restaurante Espadeiro, Avenida Almeida Lucena. Tel. (059) 22302. A restaurant that serves good regional food.

The Tourist Office, the Região de Turismo da Serra do Marão, is at the Avenida 1° de Maio 70–1. Tel. (059) 22819.

District of Vila Real

Mondim de Basto

Mondim de Basto, Celorico de Basto and Cabeçeiras de Basto on the River Tâmega are sister towns north of Vila Real, on the border with the Trás-os-Montes region.

Mondim de Basto is a small town noted for its seventeenth- and eighteenth-century houses. The nearby Monte Farinha has one of the most breathtaking views in the whole of Portugal. There is a lovely waterfall at Figas do Ermelo. Castro dos Palhaços is an ancient fortified hill-town.

Celorico de Basto
Cabeçeiras de Basto
What to see

Celorico de Basto is a small town with several interesting buildings. Arnoia Castle, 3 km south-west, is twelfth-century Romanesque.

Cabeçeiras de Basto is a village with many seventeenth- and eighteenth-century houses.

Here also you can see the Church of the Refojos Convent. This was a very old church, but no traces left of what it was before it was completely renovated in the seventeenth century. Its proportions are impressive. Inside it has a life-size figure of Christ, and a green and gilt organ sustained by fauns and surrounded by a large collection of comic masks. The entire church is rich in gilt.

The Statue of Basto is a decapitated statue of a Lusitanian warrior, which must date from Celtic times, to which a new head was added in 1612. The head has a moustache and a very tall military headdress.

Festival

The *Festas de São Miguel* in September is a wine harvest fair that began in the thirteenth century and was later combined with devotions to the town's patron, Saint Michael. It includes a livestock fair, a regional craft fair and an ancient sport known as a 'quarter staff contest'.

Alijó

Alijó is 27 km east of Vila Real and 11 km north of the Tua railway station, from which the scenic train departs up the River Tua on the Tua line (see page 40).

History

The many dolmens, Celtic carvings on the rocks and old *castros* in the area indicate that the town had very ancient beginnings. It was also occupied by the Romans. It was granted a charter in 1226.

What to see

The Town Hall dates from the seventeenth century. Its coat of arms was damaged during the Peninsular War. The Parish Church is eighteenth-century. There is a plane tree which was planted in 1856, and has grown to a tremendous size.

Festivals

Several festivals and pilgrimages take place in or near Alijó in August: the *Festa de São Jesus do Outeiro*, the *Festa de Santa Maria Maior*, the *Festa da Nossa Senhora da Piedade* (in Sanfins do Douro), and the *Romaria de Nossa Senhora dos Aflitos* (in Pegarinhos).

Where to stay
Pousada
Inexpensive

Pousada de Barão de Forrester, Rua José Rufino, Alijó. Tel. (059) 62215, telex 26364. Medium range with eleven rooms, lounge, bar and a restaurant that serves good regional food and wines.

There are also various inns and pensions. For information, contact the Tourist Office in Vila Real (see page 141).

São João da Pesqueira

São João da Pesqueira is a very old town which was granted its charter by Portugal's first king. It sits high above the river with views of the mountains in all directions. Below is the railway and the Valeira Dam which finally tamed the dreaded Cachão de Valeira with its rapids and waterfalls that in past centuries made transporting the wine down the river to Oporto such a dangerous business.

What to see

The Casa do Cabo is an eighteenth-century palace with thirteen beautiful, ornately carved granite windows. It is now a law court.

The hermitage of São Salvador do Mundo (The Saviour of the World) is a series of a dozen little chapels running up the side of the mountain and ending on Fraga peak.

Where to stay, and eat
Inexpensive
Vila Nova de Foz Côa

Pensão do Marquês, São João da Pesqueira. Tel. (054) 44158. A two star pension with a restaurant.

Vila Nova de Foz Côa lies in the wild upper reaches of the River Douro, near the Pocinho dam. The easiest way to get there is by train, although you can reach it by road, taking the N220 from Moncorvo.

What to see

The Parish Church is a Gothic/Manueline church built in the sixteenth century and remodelled in the eighteenth. It has a lovely doorway and a beautiful tower with three bells.

The pillory in front of the Town Hall is elaborately carved in granite.

The Numão Castle, situated on top of the highest peak, was built in 1130. It is now mostly in ruins, but the large fortified tower, the inner and outer walls and parts of the chapel can still be seen.

Where to stay

There are several hotels and restaurants in the town.

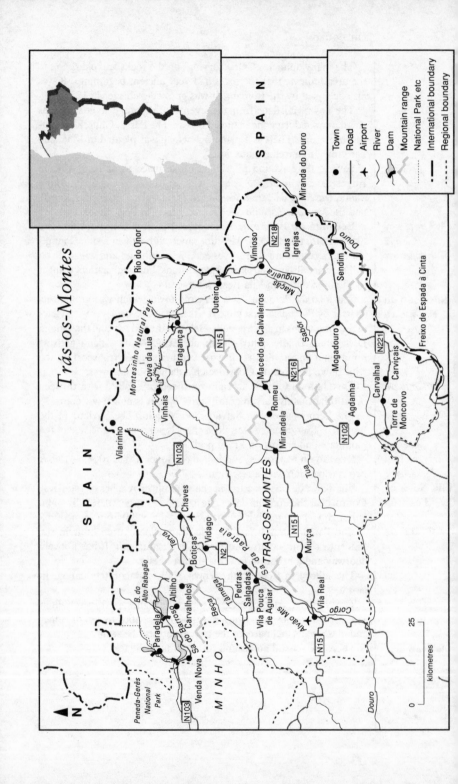

Trás-os-Montes

Introduction

If you want to go back in time – to the Middle Ages, perhaps, or even to an era as remote as the Old Testament – visit Trás-os-Montes (Behind the Mountains) in the remote north-east corner of Portugal, bordered on the north and east by Spain.

Terrain and climate

It has three ranges of high mountains that run roughly north to south, with deep, wide valleys in between the vast plateaux on their summits. There is little rain, and there are great differences of temperature: it is often below freezing for long periods in winter, and in summer temperatures can soar above 40°C/104°F. However, Trás-os-Montes also has protected valleys with Mediterranean-type microclimates where almond, olive and citrus fruit trees grow. And all over the region there are vineyards producing the local wines that are so different from area to area. Vast stretches of Trás-os-Montes are in the upper reaches of the port wine demarcated area (shown on the map of The Douro on page 110).

Economy

Trás-os-Montes depends on agriculture and commerce; it has almost no industry.

Dialect

The only really discernibly separate dialect in Portugal is the Mirandês spoken in Trás-os-Montes. It is a mixture of Gallego/Spanish, Portuguese and some Hebrew. It was dying out, but is now being taught in some schools in Bragança and Miranda do Douro.

History

Because Trás-os-Montes has been so remote and undisturbed, the evidence of past civilizations is still very visible. The bulldozers of modernization have not buried them under factories, or swept them away to make room for some vast housing projects. Many of the stones and pillars of *castros* and castles have gone, though, to pave village squares or to make houses, so you may find a carved Celtic pillar or a Roman column holding up part of a farmer's house.

Villages

The typical Trás-os-Montes village is a group of large granite or schist block houses clustered together against a hillside, with narrow streets paved with stones or not paved at all. The farm animals live in the village with the people. The villagers are to a great extent self-sufficient, getting the grains for their bread from their own fields and the grapes for their wine from their own vineyards. They make their own cheeses, cured hams and sausages and honey. They have chestnuts, dried fruits and vegetables. Many of the women still card and spin wool into cloth and make flax into rough linen. And they do these things using the same tools and instruments as were being used in the time of the Old Testament. Most people still beat the grain with the ancient threshing stick bent at the end, even though some villages have bought modern threshing machines (they complain that these machines make so much noise that they can no longer sing the ancient songs they always sang together as they worked).

Houses

The typical Trás-os-Montes house has been very well described by A. Pinelo Tiza. He says that its chief characteristic is that it is really part of its surroundings: it is made of the stone of the region, granite and schist (the granite in Trás-os-Montes is lighter and more golden in colour than that of the Minho), and roofed with slate from the mountainsides or straw from the fields. The beams, floors, doors, balconies and windows are all made of solid oak or chestnut. The house fits perfectly into its environment.

The houses are well adapted to the very hot summers and the very cold winters. The house usually has two floors. The animals live in the ground floor where the warmth of their bodies heats the house in winter. In summer the animals are in the pasture or working in the fields, so the empty ground floor cools the upper level. The ground floor is also used for storing cereals, fodder, chestnuts and potatoes. There is, of course, a wine cellar. There is a balcony facing the autumn sun where seeds, vegetables and fruits (figs and apples, for example) are laid out to dry. A winter's supply of wood is piled outside the house.

The family lives on the upper floor, which is reached by an outside staircase. The rooms are usually very big, with walls plastered with clay and painted with white lime. The huge kitchen with an open fireplace is where they spend most of their time in winter. It is where they take their meals, prepare food for their animals, card the wool, cure the hams and sausages hung from the beams, and entertain their friends, who sit around the fire on long wooden benches.

If the house is built on the side of a hill so that the kitchen can be on the ground, there is often a well inside the kitchen. Most of the cooking is done in a black iron pot over an open wood fire.

The house has a *sobrado* – an entrance courtyard with stairs leading to the upper balcony that gives access to the kitchen and other rooms. The family and their workers eat in the courtyard in the summer.

Communal life

Communal life still exists in many villages of Trás-os-Montes. It is a heritage of a prehistoric time when land boundaries were vague and people felt the necessity to work together in order to survive – and when land belonged to the gods rather than to people. In communal villages, such as Rio do Onor and Vilarinho das Furnas, all of the pastures, woods, planted crops, water, animals, mills, ovens, forges, public buildings and agricultural machinery are the common property of the village. After harvest, all of the grain is put away and handed out as needed (in ancient times, anyone who kept part back for himself was put to death).

In order to deal with their common problems and mete out the work, it was necessary to have rules, and for someone to be in charge, so they devised a sort of representative democracy. They have a *conselho* (governing body) made up of one representative of each family. The *conselho* each year elect two chiefs (*mordomos*) from among themselves. They vote by whispering a name into the ear of the teller, who carves a nick in a stick. (They used to keep all their accounts on similar sticks, and the *mordomos* carry sticks (*talas*) as their sign of office.) The *mordomos* mete out the daily work, like taking care of the mill or pasturing the cattle.

The people in the communal villages used to be very self-enclosed. They married only within the village and the young men forcefully drove off any other young men from different villages who might come around. That has changed to some extent through emigration to the cities and other countries and through television. However, I have come across villages where everyone has the same family name.

Bread

Bread is so important to the people of Trás-os-Montes that they make a cult of it. It symbolizes the fertility of Mother Earth, because the bread comes from the earth through the grain. So the villagers give the bread shapes that represent fertility: the star, representing the sun (the greatest star) that gives light and warmth; the human form, representing the people who, by working with their hands, 'make the earth fertile'; zoomorphic forms representing fecundity, wisdom and immortality.

During the winter festivals bread is the centre of rites and ceremonies representing abundance, fertility, power, social order and strength. On the feast days of São Estevão, São Gonçalo, São Sebastião, New Year and Epiphany, the villagers make tall pyramids of dozens of loaves of bread, with other foods like dried fruit and hard-boiled eggs, strung from poles (*charolos*) to signify harvest plenty. The *charolo* is brought in procession into the church, where it is blessed by the priest and then taken into the churchyard and auctioned off, loaf by loaf and egg by egg. The bread is all then ceremoniously eaten. The blessing is supposed to ward off sickness in people, animals and crops and to keep away the plague, the evil eye and evil spirits.

Bread is also important on other occasions. When races are run in the village or there are contests of hand-to-hand combat, bread is given as prizes. Folk dancers eat bread while dancing, and later share the loaves with all the other people.

Wine

Wine is almost as important to the people as bread. They firmly believe that it makes their blood stronger and generally gives them strength. During planting and harvesting and most other times of the year, you will see men, women and children drink great numbers of *garafões* (5-litre jugs) of wine to keep them going. If you tentatively suggest that so much wine might not be good for children, you are met by derisive laughter.

The Trás-os-Montes wine-producing region borders the *vinho verde* region on the west and Douro on the south. The region is a plateau for the most part, with granite and schist outcroppings and surrounded by high mountains. The vines grow on the hillsides of the valleys of rivers that are tributaries of the Douro.

Superstitions

In the past the people of Trás-os-Montes were always very superstitious, and some of the superstitions persist. Many people still believe in witches, wolfmen, the evil eye, golden-haired fairies living down wells, and the cult of the dead. There are rites for birth, puberty, marriage and death.

Cult of the dead

There is still a strong belief that the dead come back at certain times of the year to take vengeance on those who have betrayed them. The most common dates for the return of the dead are 26 December (the feast of São Estevão), 6 January (the feast of the Epiphany), New Year's Eve and the pre-Lenten carnival. During these dates, the unmarried men in the village dress up in devil masks to frighten off the evil spirits. The masks are very elaborate and frightening. They are the common property of the village and when they are not being used they are kept in the church. The masked men run through the village and into houses, frightening the women and children and demanding food and wine and tributes for the church. Then they make a feast in a barn, and invite the whole village to eat and dance. The next day they go to Mass with bread and cakes to be blessed; after the blessing these are put on a table and eaten, with wine (the men sit at the table; the women stand behind). Next there is a *colóquio* or *loas* (a public declamation) in which the young men recite an account in verse of all of the events of the past year in the village. Then there is more eating and drinking and dancing.

Songs and romances

Songs in a direct line of descent from those sung and recited in the Middle Ages are still very much a part of life in Trás-os-Montes. Some of these songs go back to before the fourteenth century, when they were first recorded. The subject may be biblical, epic, or to do with tragic love. There are many references to Galicia in Spain, the Romans and the Moors.

There are also traditional plays put on each year during religious festivals. The men practise their parts during the long winter evenings, while the women weave.

Modern inroads

But, of course, even Trás-os-Montes has been affected by modern times. There are whole villages that are totally deserted because the people have emigrated to northern Europe to seek more money and an easier life. Others are inhabited solely by old men, women and children. Evidence of the emigration glares out at you in the hideous additions in bright colours and garish styles that returning emigrants have added to the old granite houses.

You may be quite surprised at the inroads of modernity you do find in the villages. I was invited into the home of a very old lady, dressed from head to toe in the traditional black, whom I met in a field by her village where she was helping thresh wheat with a hand-carved wooden pitchfork. Inside her stone house, she had colour television and a modern tiled bathroom. We sat eating the delicious ham she had cured over the fireplace during the winter and drinking the wine her family had raised from grape to glass, while her cows munched hay contentedly in the room below and we watched a television programme beamed out of Lisbon.

Getting there

There are several ways to get to Trás-os-Montes and to travel within the region.

By car   From Oporto, take the N15 to Vila Real, Mirandela and Bragança and the N218 to Miranda do Douro. From Viano do Castelo, take the N103 to Braga, Chaves and Bragança and the N218 to Miranda do Douro. From Vila Real, take the N2 to Chaves, the N103 to Bragança and the N218 to Miranda do Douro. From Guarda, take the N221 to Freixo de Espada à Cinta, Mogadouro and Miranda do Douro and the N218 to Bragança.

By air   Fly to Bragança and get Avis in Oporto (tel. [02] 315947/311235, telex 22373) to meet you with a car.

By sea   From England, take a car ferry to northern Spain and drive down into northern Portugal.

By train   Take advantage of the scenic trains that run up the valleys of the River Douro and its tributaries.

If you leave the trip on the Tua line to Bragança last, you can fly back to Oporto or Lisbon from Bragança – in case you are tired of trains by that time. There are hotels, pensions and restaurants in the town on the scenic train lines, if you want to make stopovers.

By bus   There are buses linking nearly all the towns.

If you travel by the N103 to Bragança via Braga and Chaves, you will skirt the southern edge of the Peneda-Gerês National Park and go by the beautiful lakes formed by the *barragems* (dams) of Venda Nova and Alto Rabagão.

eneda-Gerês National Park   About 30 km from Barragem do Alto Rabagão you will come to the Peneda-Gerês National Park, near the beautiful Paradela Lake.

If you then retrace your route and rejoin the N103, going towards Chaves, you will come to Sapiãos, where there is a turn-off on N312 to Boticas, 4 km away. The road is winding and not very good, but the scenery is beautiful.

Boticas
Buried wine   The people of Boticas have a strange custom: they bury their wine for a year before drinking it. This started during the French invasions in the Peninsular War. To save their wine from being taken by the

French troops, they buried the bottles in cellars, under floors, and anywhere else they could think of. When the French departed and the villagers dug up the bottles, they found the wine tasted better. So to this day they still bury the bottles of wine, which they call *mortos* (dead men). When inviting a friend for a glass of wine, they will say, 'Let's go and dig up a dead fellow.'

What to see There is a Roman bridge over the River Beça.

The Parish Church is a simple granite building with a carved pillory at the side.

The Covas de Barroso Church in the mountains is twelfth-century Romanesque.

Fairs There are market fairs on the 10th and 20th of every month. They sell everything from cattle to black iron cooking pots to modern cassette tapes.

Surrounding area Boticas is the gateway to some of the most interesting and primitive regions in Trás-os-Montes, with medieval stone villages, *castros*, stones carved with prehistoric signs, and old mines. It is very interesting to drive up into the Barroso mountains to see the stone villages, the long-horned cattle, the thatched houses and the forests of great oaks, some of the trees hundreds of years old. Visit **Vilharinho Seco**, where there are many granite *espigueiros* (small houses on stilts for storing grain); and granite block houses where the well for water is in the kitchen and the women cook over open fires. Drive through **Altilho**, where until just recently the villagers lived by begging round the rest of the country. Drive on up the mountain to **Alturas de Barroso**, where the villagers tie a red flag to the highest tree to tell everyone around that the town is having a festival. Perhaps you will find the red flag flying, and be able to join the festivities. Along the roads you will see small altars with images of saints. These mark the place where someone has died. People leave offerings to buy holy oil, paint for the altar, flowers, and so on.

In this region, farmers often use cows rather then oxen for pulling their ploughs and carts, because they cannot afford the luxury of keeping animals with only one function.

On the other hand, the *Chegas de Bois* (ox fights) have long been a favourite entertainment. Originally there was a 'village ox' that belonged to everybody. When the ox was five or six he was ready to compete, and the villagers would challenge the ox from another village to a fight. The contest was held half-way between the two villages. The ox fight is still a popular sport today, but most of the animals are now owned by individuals rather than villages. It is not a fight to the death, but rather a test of strength between the two animals. They are put face to face and they lock horns and push and jostle each other until one feels he has been defeated, and runs away pursued by the other. The fight never lasts more than fifteen or twenty minutes. Sometimes the ox who was defeated will feel so ashamed of losing that he sulks for days. Unfortunately, it has also happened that the owner of the defeated ox has been so disappointed that he has dispatched his ox forthwith to the butcher's.

Fishing Boticas is near three rivers, the Tâmega, Terva and Beça, all of them good for trout fishing.

Where to eat **Restaurante Santa Cruz**, Boticas. A restaurant by the river with a glass-enclosed veranda overlooking gardens between two rivers. It serves enormous helpings of simple food.

What to eat The specialities of the area are trout, kid, veal, smoked ham and sausages.

Carvalhelhos Carvalhelhos, 8 km from Boticas on the N311, bottles water famous all over Portugal. It is also a nice spa, with gardens and springs and an excellent hotel.

Castro The Carvalhelhos Castro is one of the most interesting Iron Age hill-top towns in the region. It is only a short distance from the spa, and it is possible to drive there. It has three rows of walls; deep defence ditches; round stone houses and fields of pointed granite defence stones.

Where to stay Inexpensive **Estalagem de Carvalhelhos**, Carvalhelhos. Tel. (091) 42116. A new, modern four star inn open from June to the end of September. It has twenty double rooms with bath, a restaurant, sitting rooms and veranda. It is an excellent, quiet place for resting and exploring the countryside, and is reasonably priced.

Chaves

Getting there From Carvalhelhos return to Boticas and take the N103 to Chaves. The road is good.

Chaves is just 9 km from the Spanish border, on the River Tâmega and on what used to be the old Roman road from Braga to Astorga in Asturias. This road was used to transport gold from the mines that were abundant in the region.

History There are traces of occupation in the area since Palaeolithic and Neolithic times: Iron Age *castros*; dolmens; prehistoric stone monuments; rock tombs; necropolises; Celtic and pre-Celtic stone carvings.

The town of Chaves was founded in 78 BC by the Roman emperor Flavius Vespasian, who named it Aquae Flaviae. The Romans exploited its mines for gold and other minerals. They also built baths to take advantage of its hot mineral waters.

The Swabians invaded in 456, followed by the Visigoths and the Moors. The town was liberated from the Moors in 1160, and granted a charter. A fort was built to defend the Tâmega valley. Chaves was further fortified in the fourteenth century by King Dinis, and ramparts were added in the sixteenth century.

Chaves today

The town is an important agricultural centre. But undoubtedly it is best known as a thermal spa, where water gushes out of natural springs at an amazing temperature of 73°C/163°F. It contains mainly bicarbonate of soda, and is thought to cure rheumatism, stomach and liver disorders and hypertension.

What to see

The **Trajan Bridge** was ordered to be built by the Roman Emperor Trajan, and was completed in AD 104. There is a Roman inscription on the milestone at the southern end.

The **Castle**, in the Praça de Camões, was built in the twelfth century; its crenellated battlements were added by King Dinis in the four-teenth century.

The Palace of the Dukes of Bragança, also in the Praça de Camões, is now the **Regional Museum**.

The **Misericórdia Church**, in the same square, dates from the sixteenth century. The blue and white glazed tiles in the interior depict scenes from the New Testament. The altar is Baroque.

The nearby **Parish Church** is Romanesque in origin, but was remodelled in the sixteenth century.

Chaves is often called the **City of Verandas**, because of the many lovely verandas in the Praça de Camões and Rua Direita.

The **Fort of São Francisco** and the **Fort of São Neutal** are both from the seventeenth century.

Crafts

Look out for black pottery; rough wool capes; baskets, rugs and blankets.

Festivals

There are during the year many festivals and fairs that attract both Portuguese and Spaniards.

The *Feira dos Santos* is a great annual fair held on 31 October and 1 November. Livestock, farm equipment, household utensils, regional crafts, gold filigree and pottery are all sold there.

Excursions

There are several Romanesque churches and old forts nearby, as well as archaeological sites with stone carvings and tombs.

The **Church of Santa Maria Maior** is the oldest in the region.

The **Church of Our Lady of Azinheira** is outside Chaves on the road to Outeiro Seco. It is a lovely Romanesque church, with the addi-tion of excellent sixteenth-century frescoes.

The **Monforte Castle** is on a hill dominating the Chaves valley. It was probably a Lusitanian hill-top town that was later fortified by the Romans to guard their road to Astorga. It was taken by many different invaders including the Moors. King Dinis added the keep, three other towers and extended the walls. He is quoted as saying, 'Eu Diniz, sete Castelos fiz; mas, de todos o mas forte é o de Monforte' ('I Dinis made seven castles, but the strongest was Monforte'). During the reign of King João I, the mayor of the castle obtained a royal declaration allow-ing Monforte to be a sanctuary for fugitives so long as they were not wanted for treason or fraud. The castle is still impressive, but totally abandoned.

The **Roman Church** in the village of Granjinha outside Chaves dates from the eighth or ninth century. In the midst of old, stone houses with chickens running loose, the church has been much dismantled by the villagers, who have used its pillars and stones to build their houses. But it still stands, with its altar covered by Roman inscriptions, its baptismal font where babies were totally submerged rather than sprinkled, its arches looking rather Arabic, and its underground tombs. Legend says that there is a statue of Venus buried in front of it: local Catholics, in far distant times, decided the semi-nude statue was indecent, and buried it. It waits to be dug up.

Rock carvings can be seen at Outeiro Machado in the valley of d'Anta, on the Salto and Moeda hills, on the Cruzes' cliff in Almeijoadas and in many other places. One of the most interesting is the 50 m long granite boulder in a field near Outeiro Machado (signs saying '*Arte Rupestre*' will lead you to it), which is covered with symbols dating from prehistory – probably from the time of the Celts. There are drawings of axes, swastikas, lined squares, and astral symbols. At one end, there is a carved-out space with a drainage tunnel that could have been for sacrifice. There is a legend that a treasure in gold is buried beneath it (there were many gold mines nearby in the ancient past), so some of the local villagers tried to dynamite it – fortunately they did not do too much damage.

There is a beach on the River Tâmega at Açude da Veiga.

Where to stay

Inexpensive

Estalagem Santiago, Rua do Olival. Tel. (076) 22545/6. A four star inn with thirty rooms with bath, a bar and restaurant.

Hotel Trajano, Travessa Cândido Reis. Tel. (076) 22415/6. A two star hotel with thirty-nine rooms with bath, a bar and restaurant.

Pensão Brites, Avenida Duarte Pacheco. Tel. (076) 21226. A three star inn with nineteen rooms with bath and TV.

Pensão 4 Estações, Avenida Duarte Pacheco. Tel. (076) 23986. A three star inn with fourteen rooms with bath and TV, and a bar.

Camp site

Camping Chaves, São Roque. Tel. (076) 22733.

Where to eat

Restaurante Arado, Ribeira do Pinheiro. Tel. (076) 21996.

Restaurante Ponte Romana, Rua da Ponte. Tel. (076) 22712.

What to eat

The cured ham of Chaves has the reputation of being the best in the country. Trout, veal steaks and roast kid are also good.

The Tourist Office is in the Rua de Santo António 213. Tel. (076) 21029. There are also two Tourist Posts, at Terreiro de Cavalaria, tel. (076) 21029, and at the thermal spa, tel. (076) 21445. They will help you with hotel reservations.

South of Chaves on the N2 going towards Vila Real, you will find the turn-of-the-century watering places of Vidago and Pedras Salgadas. They are in a charming setting of trees and flowers, and are sheltered from winds by the surrounding mountains.

Vidago

Vidago is only 12 km from Chaves airport.

Vidago's medicinal waters are famous, and it was a favourite watering place for the Portuguese kings. It has a nine-hole golf course, a swimming pool, tennis courts, a riding ring, and a small lake for boating. The trails through the woods are good for either riding or walking. Three km away on the shore of the River Tâmega there is a river beach with a tea-house and restaurant.

Where to stay, and eat Medium price

Vidago Palace Hotel, Vidago. Tel. (076) 97356/7/8. A pink, sprawling *belle époque* structure, surrounded by parks. It has an elegant, red-carpeted double staircase with many statues and marble columns. Its dining room is very large, with a white and gold ceiling, and there is piano music while you eat. The hotel also has a lovely swimming pool and, surprisingly, a very modern disco, with flashing lights and the latest music. The Palace does look a bit dishevelled nowadays, like an ageing beauty, but it is still elegant, and a nice place to stay.

There are also several other hotels and pensions, and various restaurants.

The Tourist Office is in Largo Miguel Carvalho. Tel. (076) 97470.

Pedras Salgadas

Pedras Salgadas, 25 km from Chaves airport, is a spa that dates from the beginning of the century. It has tennis courts, a swimming pool, mini-golf, a lake for boats, a casino and a disco, and it is surrounded by a vast, wooded park.

Where to stay Inexpensive

Pensão das Pedras Salgadas, Parque. Tel. (076) 44156. A two star pension with 106 rooms, 41 with bath, a bar, restaurant, tennis court and golf.

Pensão São Martinho, Rua Henrique Maia. Tel. (076) 44278. A three star pension with eighteen rooms with bath, a restaurant and snack bar.

Vila Pouca de Aguiar

Vila Pouca de Aguiar, just south of Pedras Salgadas on the N2, is situated at the head of the River Corgo, surrounded by the Alvão and Padrela mountains. There are several scenic look-out points more than 1,000 m above the valley.

There are many traces of ancient habitation of the area: important dolmens, rock designs, the Grande Necropole in Povoação, old *castros* in Cidadelhe de Aguiar and Trandeiras, and stretches of Roman roads. The Pena de Aguiar Castle dates from the ninth and tenth centuries. There is an interesting Gothic church in nearby Três Minas.

The town has several restaurants serving simple food.

Murça

If you drive south of Vila Pouca de Aguiar on N212, you will come to the main Bragança road, N15. Drive east along it for 8 km and you will come to Murça.

History

The first recorded settlement on the site of Murça was Roman. There was a *castro* on a nearby hill top, and you can still see a stretch of the old Roman way that led up from the Tinhela Bridge to the *castro*. Murça was later dominated by the Moors. It was retaken by the Christians and granted a charter in 1224.

What to see

Murça is a not very attractive town out in the middle of nowhere, but it does have the famous *Porca de Murça* standing in the town square. This is an Iron Age carved granite boar, 1.85 m long and 1.1 m high. It is by far the most famous of the ancient zoomorphic images which are to be found throughout Trás-os-Montes. No one has been able to discover the origin of these figures, but it has been suggested that they may have been worshipped in some prehistoric cult, or, possibly, that they were put in the fields to protect the crops from evil spirits.

The Parish Church has a Gothic figure of Saint Vincent. The Misericórdia Church has a very early Baroque façade with granite columns and carved grapes and vine leaves on vases at each corner. There are also carvings of large granite birds.

Where to stay

There is a motel with cabins on the outskirts of Murça.

Mirandela

If you travel 26 km north-east of Murça on the N15 towards Bragança, you will come to Mirandela. The road is full of trucks, and there is not much to see.

Mirandela is a pretty town in the middle of a rolling plateau by the River Tua on the Tua scenic train route to Bragança. This is an agricultural area where barley is grown and cattle are raised.

What to see

Mirandela was granted its first charter in 1250.

The seventeenth-century Palácio dos Távoras has a triple façade with decorated pediments with coats of arms. It is now the Town Hall.

The Roman Bridge over the River Tua has twenty arches of unequal sizes.

The Castle dates from the eleventh century.

Crafts

Bedspreads, woollen blankets, tin work and wrought iron are produced in Mirandela.

Festivals

The *Festa da Senhora do Amparo e Feira de São Tiago*, at the end of July and beginning of August, is a very animated festival, with a big procession, traditional Trás-os-Montes games, a funfair and fireworks.

The *Festas de São Sebastião* takes place in mid-September.

Where to stay Inexpensive

Pensão Globo, Rua Dr Trigo Negreiros. Tel. (078) 22711/2. A three star modern pension with thirty rooms with bath, a bar and restaurant.

Hotel Mira Tua, Rua de República 20. Tel. (078) 22403. A two star hotel with thirty-one rooms with bath.

Where to eat

Restaurante Snack Bar Selecto, Bairro da Preguiça 81. Tel. (078) 23262.

O Grés, Avenida Nossa Senhora do Amparo. Tel. (078) 22670. A restaurant and ice cream shop with a very nice atmosphere and good service.

What to eat

The specialities of Mirandela are *alheiras* (a kind of garlic sausage), cured ham, freshwater fish and *posta Mirandês* (a large, thick steak braised over a wood fire).

Travelling 13 km towards Bragança on the N15, you will come to **Romeu**, a village which has a large park and a little zoo, but is best known for its restaurant, **Maria Rita**, which serves good regional food. Tel. (078) 93134.

Macedo de Cavaleiros

If you turn right on to the N216 after leaving Romeu you will come to Macedo de Cavaleiros, which is very near the Azibe dam with its lake 91 km long. According to legend, the town got its name (which means 'knight's club' – the club in question being of the weapon, not the establishment, variety!) in the time of the Moors, when two noblemen of the town used clubs to fight them. The Christian king, hearing this, named the town for the gentlemen.

What to see

Macedo is a neat farming town, with a nice square and garden. In the town and the towns nearby there are about twenty noble manor houses with impressive antique furnishings and art collections, though you cannot visit them. None of them takes in guests. Each town also has a carved pillory, some of them very elaborate.

Crafts

Woven fabrics, linen and wool work, crocheted bedspreads, baskets, woodwork and ironwork are all made in and around Macedo.

Sports

You can take part in windsurfing, fishing, swimming and boating in the Azibe reservoir. There is also hunting, in season.

Where to stay
Medium price

Estalagem do Caçedor, Largo Manuel Pinto de Azevedo. Tel. (078) 42354/6. A five star inn with twenty-five rooms. This is a really marvellous place to stay. The inn is in an elegant town house which has been beautifully adapted, with every modern convenience, including a lovely outdoor swimming pool, bar and restaurant. All the bedrooms are furnished with antique furniture and handmade bedspreads and linen. The dining room and drawing room are decorated with hunting motifs (the name means 'hunter's inn'). The owner has some amazing collections: Portuguese crafts; objects and prints connected with hunting; mugs; hundreds of silver and ceramic shoes; even a chair that was the carved mahogany lavatory seat of the King of Portugal!

The inn is open all the year round, but you should always reserve in advance, especially during the hunting season, in the winter. A double room with bath costs about 12,000 esc. Breakfast is included.

Inexpensive

Pensão Monte-Mel, Praça Agostinho Valente 26. Tel. (078) 42378. A three star pension with twelve rooms and a bar.

Where to eat

Restaurante Saldanha. A prize-winning restaurant that serves regional food.

Dom Mário, Rua do Mercado. Tel. (078) 42327. A restaurant that specializes in seafood, rabbit and pheasant. It has *fado* singing.

Torre de Moncorvo

If you return to Mirandela and then drive 50 km south along the N213–N215–N102–N325 you will come to Torre de Moncorvo. It is also on the Sabor scenic bus route.

History

Some say that the town was called after the nobleman Mendo Curvo, who built a fortress there in the eleventh century. Others say it was named for a man named Mendo who had a *corvo* (crow). The region has some of the largest iron deposits in Europe, and for a long time Moncorvo was an important mining centre. King Dinis had a castle and tower built, and gave the town the right to have a duty-free fair a month long.

What to see　　The eleventh-century **Castle** was torn down to pave the Praça do Município, so very little of it is left. But the medieval entrance to the old wall, with a tiny chapel dedicated to Nossa Senhora dos Remédios, is intact.

The **Parish Church** in the square dominates the town. The first stone was laid in 1544, and it took a century to build. The result is a rather grand basilica that never quite made it to cathedral. It has a square tower and an impressive front with, surprisingly, two fig trees growing out of it. The inside has huge vaulted Gothic ceilings, eight heavy pillars, and a fine chancel with faded wall paintings. There is a seventeenth-century triptych with scenes from the life of the Virgin.

The sixteenth-century **Misericórdia Church** is in the Rua dos Campos Monteiro, down the street from the square. Inside there is an unusual pulpit carved in marble in the form of a chalice.

The streets of the town have many interesting old houses. The eighteenth-century **Solar dos Pimenteis** in Praça General Claudino is particularly fine.

Crafts　　Red clay pottery, weaving, and basket work are produced in and around Moncorvo.

Excursions　　The Iron Museum in nearby **Carvalhal** is worth a visit.

In **Vila de Mós** you will see a Roman fountain, the traces of a Roman road, a ninth-century iron smelter and the ruins of a medieval castle.

In **Carviçais** you can see the *castro* of Cigadonha and the necropolis of São Cristovão.

In **Agdanha** there is a twelfth-century Romanesque church. The *castro* of Castelo Velho is nearby.

Where to stay
Inexpensive　　**Pensão-Restaurante Passarinho**, Rua Infante Dom Henrique 23. Tel. (079) 22319. A two star pension with restaurant. It has nine rooms, three of them with bath. It also has a quaint, old-fashioned dining room with a view of rooftops and church. The restaurant serves plain but good home cooking.

Pensão Brasilia, Estrada Nacional 220. Tel. (079) 22494. A three star pension with nine rooms with bath, a bar, restaurant and snack bar.

What to eat　　Specialities are *amêndoa coberta* (sugared almonds), and *canelões* (cinnamon sweets).

The Tourist Office is in Rua Manuel Seixas. Tel. (079) 22288/9.

Freixo de Espada à Cinta　　If you drive east along the N220 for 26 km and then turn south on to the N221 and continue for another 14 km you will come to Freixo de Espada à Cinta.

Freixo de Espada à Cinta (Ash Tree with a Sword Around It) is on a fertile plain with millions of almond trees, which in the spring make a dazzling display. It is 4 km from the River Douro and the Spanish border, and 14 km from the Sabor scenic bus route.

History

There are several versions of how the town got its name. One says it was called after a Visigoth nobleman named Espadacinta. A second says that King Dinis came here and lay down under the ash tree to rest, and hung his sword on a branch of the tree. Still another says it was named for a Spanish nobleman from León who had an ash tree and a sword in his coat of arms, and who fought nobly in the town.

Whatever the truth may be, the town is very ancient and in the past was extremely important. There are three *castros* nearby, and an old Roman road. Later there came the Visigoths and the Moors. It was taken from the Moors by the Christian kings in the eleventh century. In order to populate it and make it strong, they gave it the privilege of becoming a sanctuary for fugitives –except those accused of treason or fraud. It was given its first charter in 1140 by Count Henry, father of King Afonso Henriques, Portugal's first monarch. The old castle was reconstructed in the thirteenth century by the ever-busy King Dinis, who added the tower and enlarged the walls. Freixo suffered much during the long struggles with the Spaniards from León, but usually held out successfully.

Freixo de Espada à Cinta has sent out more missionaries than any other town in Portugal; many of them became martyrs. In the fifteenth century Jorge Álvares, a great ship's master from the town, was the first man to reach Japan and chronicle the event. The great Portuguese poet Guerra Junqueiro was born here. Statues of the two men can be seen in the town. Freixo was also once the centre of a flourishing silk industry, which is now being revived.

Freixo today

Today Freixo is a rather sleepy border town. It is an agricultural centre for growing almonds, olives, oranges and other citrus fruits, and it is part of the demarcated port wine area. It attracts many tourists – mostly Spaniards – when the almond trees are in bloom.

What to see

Of the four towers that were built by King Dinis in the thirteenth century, the **Castle** has only one left. This tower, the Torre do Galo (Cockerel's Tower), is seven-sided and stands behind the Parish Church beside the famous ash tree from which Freixo gets its name. It is 21 m high with a pyramidal roof added much later. There is a spectacular view from the top.

Some stretches of the original castle walls still survive.

The **Parish Church** was begun by King Dinis. In 1342 the people of Freixo were granted a concession to use church tithes to complete the castle walls. There was money left, and over the centuries they spent it on additions to the church, which took on a Manueline style and was finally completed in the seventeenth century. The church very much resembles the great Jerónimos Monastery church in Lisbon – which is not really surprising, as the architect João de Castilho, who worked on the Jerónimos, also did a lot of work on the Freixo church. (He was married to a lady from Freixo.) Inside there are fine paintings attributed to Grão Vasco. Have a look, too, at the carved image of Saint Matthew on the right-hand altar – he's wearing glasses!

The **Misericórdia Church** has a sixteenth-century front and a high, long, narrow nave. It is adorned with an abundance of gilt and rather gaudy retables.

Crafts

Silk and wool bedspreads, carpets, lace tablecloths and bedspreads are produced around Freixo de Espada à Cinta.

Excursion

The **Penedo Durão** look-out point is at the top of the mountain, with a fantastic view of the four million almond trees in bloom in the spring.

Where to stay, and eat Medium price

Quinta da Boavista, Freixo de Espada à Cinta. Tel. (079) 62145. A small tourist development consisting of four houses with three bedrooms each. All of the houses are fully furnished and they all have central heating. Two have air conditioning as well. The development also has a bar, a swimming pool and tennis courts. The houses are rented at 15,000 esc. a day, with discounts for long stays.

There are several restaurants in the town.

What to eat

Specialities include meat pies, sausages, fresh oranges and other fruits, regional sweets of eggs and almonds.

Mogadouro

Forty-five km north of Freixo de Espada à Cinta, up the N221 through dry, barren hills and valleys, you come to Mogadouro.

Mogadouro is in a valley surrounded by farmlands, at the foot of the mountains that lead to Miranda do Douro.

History

The name Mogadouro comes from the Arabic name Macaduron. There are vestiges here of Celtic, Visigoth and Roman civilizations. The town was granted its first charter in 1272, by King Afonso II. At one time the Knights Templar were here, and built a large fortress. After the military order of the Templars was suppressed King Dinis created the Order of Christ, and in 1311 he turned the town over to them. The Castle at Mogadouro, built on the site of a Neolithic fortress, was of strategic importance in the wars against the Spaniards of León and Castile. Much later it was given to the Tavora family, who made many restorations.

Mogadouro was once an important silk-making centre.

What to see

You can see the ruins of the twelfth-century Castle; the Parish Church and the Misericórdia Church, both dating from the sixteenth century; the seventeenth-century São Monastery; the pillory; and the Monoptero Sanctuary in honour of Saint Gonçalo, built by the Tavoras in the nineteenth century.

Crafts

Silk and wool articles, leather goods, baskets, pottery and rag rugs are made in Mogadouro.

Excursions

There are twelfth-century Romanesque churches in nearby Algosinho and Azinhoso.

Where to
stay, and eat
What to eat
Sendim

There are several pensions and restaurants in the town.

Try grilled veal steak, cured ham and sausages, sheep's-milk cheese, and honey.

Twenty-seven km east of Mogadouro on the N221 you will come to the small town of Sendim. The town is not much to look at, but it is prosperous and bustling. It is only 3 km from the River Douro and the Spanish border. And it is worth stopping there to eat at Alice's restaurant.

Alice's
restaurant

Did you know that Alice has a restaurant in the remote Trás-os-Montes? Well, she has: it is called Gabriela's, and it is at the Largo da Praça 28, in the square in front of the church at Sendim. The restaurant was started seventy years ago by Alice's mother Gabriela, who was a famous cook, as Alice is.

Alice (pronounced Aleesee) has cooked for the last two presidents of Portugal, she has done special banquets in the Ritz and the Estoril Casino in Lisbon, and she has done programmes for national television. She received the Coq d'Or golden award for her restaurant, marking it as one of the best in the world.

Try Alice's *posta Mirandesa à Gabriela*, a thick veal steak roasted over an open fire. In summer she makes her fire of grape vines, and in the winter of the wood of olive trees, to impart a special flavour to the meat. She also has a wonderful sauce for the veal, but that is a professional secret.

Alice also serves quail, *cozido à transmontana*, Cod *à bras* and other interesting dishes.

Duas
Igrejas

Twenty-seven km north of Sendim on the N221, and only 11 km south of Miranda do Douro, you come to the tiny town of Duas Igrejas, famous for its *Pauliteiros de Miranda* folk dancers. The men of Duas Igrejas have carried on the old tradition of the stick dances. Of very ancient origin, the dance is a ritual sword fight, with a group of eight men thrusting and retreating to the tune of drums, cymbals and bagpipes. The dance was originally performed with swords. The men still dance in costumes that are like those worn by sword dancers in the Balkans, or those worn in North Africa at the time of Saint Augustine - hats with flowers, and embroidered skirts, vests and aprons. You can see some of these costumes in the museum in Miranda do Douro, or, better still, attend one of the many local festivals where the dancers perform - for example, the *Festas da Nossa Senhora da Assunção*, held on 15 August in Duas Igrejas itself.

Miranda do Douro

Getting
there

Miranda do Douro is 8 km north of Duas Igrejas on the N221, by the deep, rocky gorge of the River Douro, on the other side of which is

Spain. It is at the northern end of the Sabor scenic bus route.

After a series of calamities in the eighteenth century, Miranda do Douro became the most isolated town in Portugal, and it remained that way for two hundred years. Then, in 1955, a dam was built with a road on top which opened up Miranda to the towns of Zamora and Salamanca in Spain. You can take a car ferry from England and drive down to Miranda through Spain.

History

Miranda's past is very obscure. It received its first town charter in 1136 from King Afonso Henriques. In the thirteenth century King Dinis walled the town, and built a castle. Between 1286 and 1292 the Archbishop of Braga had a church, Santa Maria, built on the site where the Cathedral now stands. The town grew and became prosperous through trade with Spanish towns. Its importance increased when it was made a diocese with a bishop, in 1545. Its Cathedral was built in 1552. During the Renaissance, it was the most important centre of culture and religion in Trás-os-Montes.

Miranda's bad times began early in the eighteenth century, during Spain's War of Succession, when it was occupied by a large Spanish army. The Spaniards were let into the city through the treachery of a Portuguese soldier who opened the gate to them: the gate he opened is now called Porta Falsa (Gate of Deceit). The Spaniards remained for a year and a half, till troops from the south liberated the city and took them prisoner.

In 1762 Trás-os-Montes was once again invaded. Miranda was besieged, and during the siege suffered a terrible calamity, when the powder magazine in the castle exploded. The castle was destroyed, along with two hundred other houses, and four hundred soldiers and civilians were buried in the ruins.

The final blow came when, in 1770, the Bishop moved to Bragança, so Miranda was no longer the centre of the Church in Trás-os-Montes. The town sank into oblivion until 1955, when the dam was built.

Dialect

Miranda do Douro has its own dialect, Mirandês, which is a mixture of Gallego/Spanish, Portuguese and a few Hebrew words. (There was a large colony of Jews in Miranda until they were driven underground or fled from the Inquisition.) This language was dying out, but now it is being taught in schools.

What to see

The **Cathedral**, which was built in the sixteenth century, has two towers. Inside, there is extensive gilt and polychrome carving, including a gilt carved retable on the *Senhora da Piedade* altar. If you look at the details on the capes of the four Evangelists (Matthew, Mark, Luke and John), you will notice that they depict objects from Brazil and Portugal's colonies in Africa.

On the high altar there is a retable by the Spanish Gregório Fernandes, with fifty-six images in high relief.

There is a filigree altar to São Pedro at the back of the Cathedral.

The most curious object is the clothed statue of the *Menino Jesus da*

Cartolinha (Baby Jesus in a Top Hat). With its top hat and its brightly painted egg-shaped head, it looks more like a slightly raffish gentleman of the last century. This statue is much revered, because of the legend attached to it. It is said that during the battle to expel the Spaniards in 1711, a little boy with a sword in his hand rushed out among the Portuguese, to lead them and to give them courage. They won, but after the battle they could not find the little boy. They decided that it must have been Jesus who helped them. The image was made to commemorate the miracle. I haven't been able to find out why he wears the top hat. His other clothes are changed frequently, as he has an extensive wardrobe, made for him over the centuries by his devoted followers.

The **Bishop's Palace** that stands by the Cathedral is in ruins. It was burned in 1706.

The **Castle** is also mostly in ruins, because of the explosion of the powder magazine during the 1762 siege. The keep is still standing, however. During the Peninsular War Wellington used it as his headquarters for a short time.

The eighteenth-century **Misericórdia Church** has a Baroque façade.

The **Church of the Frades Trinos**, which dates from the seventeenth century, has Corinthian columns.

The **Fountain** beside the medieval bridge was built in the seventeenth century.

The eighteenth-century **Santa Cruz Chapel** has a Neoclassical façade, with some Baroque touches.

In **Rua da Costanilha** there are fifteenth-century houses made of large granite blocks, with carved granite window frames.

The **Nossa Senhora do Amparo Arch** is behind Rua da Costanilha.

The **Terra de Miranda Museum** has a very interesting collection that tells the story of Miranda and its region. The Director is Dr António Maria Mourinho, who was formerly the parish priest of Duas Igrejas. Following in the footsteps of the famous Abbot of Baçal, Dr Mourinho is attempting to preserve the culture of the region and to revive many of the old crafts, dances and festivals. He organized and still directs the famous *Pauliteiros de Miranda* stick dancers in Duas Igrejas (see page 160).

Among the items in the museum's collection there are stones carved with astral symbols and what appear to be signs from pre-Latin languages; burned wheat and rye found in ancient *castros*; a carved granite head of Iberian origin found in the river; a pre-Roman two-headed axe and some pre-Roman lances; Celtic jewellery; Roman lapidaries and pottery; and stones from an old Jewish synagogue. There are Roman scales, Moorish daggers, spinning wheels, locks, coins, even a copper still used for making *aguardente* (firewater).

There is a collection of rustic furniture from the region, and a complete Mirandês kitchen, including the big bench in front of the fireplace where women had their babies, the family sat to card wool, and the last rites were administered to the dying. (The bench had a small chest at its head that held the Bible, and sometimes other books such as the *Tales of Charlemagne*. A crucifix hung at the back, to ward off the devil.)

There are also costumes for all occasions, including beautiful examples of the hooded *Capas de Honra* (Capes of Honour) which are worn by the important men of the town during ceremonies. They are made of coarse wool and hand embroidered. And, of course, there are many *Pauliteiros* costumes.

Crafts

Look out for capes and waistcoats made out of brown woollen cloth (the type used for making monks' robes); woollen bedspreads and rugs; wickerwork; wooden objects; wrought iron; and *facas de palacoulo* (knives with forks attached, used by shepherds).

Folk dances

The Miranda area is rich in colourful dances. As well as the stick dances, there is the *Pingacho* (a kind of ballet), the *Geribaila* (a round dance) and the *Mira-me Miguel* (danced to a song in dialect, sung by a shepherd and a shepherdess). All of these dances are accompanied by the music of bagpipes, flutes, castanets, triangles, tambourines and drums – most of the instruments made by the players themselves. You will see many of these dances if you can manage to visit one of the local festivals.

Festivals

The *Festas da Santa Bárbara* is celebrated in mid-August. The famous dance of the *Pauliteiros* is a highlight of the festival.

The *Romaria de Nossa Senhora do Nazaré*, in early September, is primarily a 'cook-out', where thick, tender veal steaks are prepared over open fires for the pilgrims and visitors. However, there are also many unusual folk dances and songs.

Where to stay

Inexpensive
Pousada
Pousada
Inexpensive

Pensão Planalto, Rua 1° de Maio. Tel. (073) 43262. A three star pension with forty-two rooms, and a bar.

Pousada Santa Catarina, Estrada da Barragem. Tel. (073) 42255. A modern, comfortable medium range pousada with twelve rooms, a good restaurant and a bar.

Where to eat

O Mirandês, Largo da Meagem. A restaurant that serves regional specialities such as melon with smoked ham, cod, veal steaks and spit-roasted pork.

Café Kivoli, Largo da Misericórdia. Tel. (073) 42417. Good for light meals and snacks.

What to eat

Try *posta à Mirandesa* (a thick veal steak), *fumeiro* (smoked sausage), *empadas* (pastries with meat filling), *folares da Páscoa* (Easter cakes, with eggs inside them).

Vimioso

Vimioso is 28 km north of Miranda do Douro on the N218, between the Angueira and Maçãs rivers. Its strategic position made it important in the defence of Portugal against Spain.

History	Vimioso probably began as an Iron Age *castro*, and later developed into a settlement with a castle. However, there is nothing left now of either *castro* or castle. The town was granted a charter by King Manuel in 1516.
What to see	The Parish Church was built in 1570. It has two towers, linked by a balustrade, and many gargoyles.
Crafts	Copper work, marble items, leatherwork, weaving, baskets and bedspreads are produced in and around Vimioso.
Festivals	The *Festas de São Lourenço*, the *Festas da Santa Bárbara e Nossa Senhora da Saúde*, and the *Festas de São Bartolomeu* all take place in August.
Excursion	Algoso Castle is 15 km south of Vimioso on the N219. It sits on the Cabeço da Penedia promontory 500 m above the River Angueira. It may have been built by the Moors. There was an old settlement of granite houses built under the castle walls in the twelfth century. Later, King Dinis carried out improvements to the castle and the walls. The keep and part of the walls still stand.

A legend says that a mayor of the castle, Dom Soeiro, was in love with a betrothed girl, and refused to authorize her marriage to the man she loved unless the bridegroom wore a shirt of nettles on the wedding day. This put the bridegroom in a prickly situation. But he went to a witch named Aldosa, who lived in a marsh under a bridge, and she gave him a shirt of soft nettles to fool the mayor.

Where to stay, and eat Inexpensive	**Pensão Charneca**, Rua do Hospital. Tel. (073) 52109. A two star pension with ten rooms, four of them with bath. It has a restaurant.
	Cruzeiro, Largo do Cruzeiro. Tel. (073) 52417. A restaurant and snack bar that serves a thick steak it calls *posta à Cruzeiro*.
	Cervejaria Morais, Rua Dr Trigo Negreiros 56. Tel. (073) 52264. A restaurant that serves specialities such as cod baked in the oven, and a mixed grill.
What to eat	Vimioso is famous for the freshwater lobsters that come from its rivers. It also has smoked sausages, smoked ham, veal, and the Easter buns known as *folares da Páscoa*.
Outeiro	Outeiro is 23 km north of Vimioso on the N218-2, and 28 km south of Bragança. The town had a castle at one time, but there are now only a few stones of it left. It does have the large Santo Cristo Church, with two towers, a Manueline doorway and a nice Gothic rose window. The sacristy has a coffered ceiling with primitive paintings of the life of Christ.

Bragança

Getting there	Bragança is 29 km north of Outeiro on the N218, and 253 km from Oporto on the N15 via Vila Real. The roads are kept free of snow in

winter. Air-conditioned buses with television bring you from Oporto in six hours and Lisbon in thirteen, with stops for meals. Bragança is eight hours from Oporto by train on the scenic railway (taking the Douro line from Oporto and changing at Tua to the Tua line for Bragança). There is also an airport with regional airline flights to and from Oporto (forty-five minutes), Lisbon (one and a half hours), Vila Real, Viseu and Covilhã.

By 1992 a new, wide motorway will be completed between Bragança and Oporto and Zamora in Spain.

History

The history of Bragança is the story of its old citadel with its imposing castle – the best preserved in Portugal. It is an exceptional castle that has been the scene of many battles, tragic loves and the comings and goings of many invaders of different nationalities and religions.

The original settlement was probably a Neolithic one on a nearby hill called Brigantia. When the Romans took it, it became the centre of Roman military roads. Julius Caesar made Brigantia a Roman municipality and turned it into a powerful military garrison. Later the Romans were driven out by the Visigoths. They in their turn were routed by the Moors. There followed four centuries of struggle with the Christians, during which the castle was destroyed and rebuilt many times.

Finally, the first King of Portugal, Dom Afonso Henriques, had his brother-in-law Fernão Mendes build another castle on another hill with the stones from the ruins of Brigantia. The Moors destroyed that one, too, but the Christian King Sancho I retook this second hill, built high walls around it and named it Bragança. It was granted a charter in 1187. King Dinis –that tireless builder – put up a second set of walls.

The castle was also damaged in the wars with the King of León. Later the Castilians laid siege to it and occupied it. The Spaniards invaded again in 1762, and caused terrible destruction before being dislodged. Napoleon's forces invaded during the Peninsular War, destroying and pillaging.

Bragança was made a dukedom in 1442, and the illegitimate son of King Dom João I and his mistress, the daughter of a Jewish merchant (see page 173), was named Duke. The Braganças later became the kings of Portugal.

The city was greatly developed by the Jews, who came there from Spain and North Africa, and it became a very important centre of the silk industry. In the sixteenth century, with the introduction of the Inquisition and the forced conversions of Jews to Catholicism, most of them fled or became 'New Christians' and 'secret Jews'.

In 1927 an army captain, Arthur Carlos de Barros Bastos from Oporto, made an attempt to revive Judaism in Bragança. A synagogue and a Jewish school teaching in Hebrew were set up. The movement soon died out, however, because of persecution by the Catholic Dictator António Salazar. Captain Barros Bastos was drummed out of the army and died in disgrace – a Portuguese Dreyfus.

Bragança today

Bragança today is a bustling agricultural city without industries. It is certainly worth a visit, for its many monuments and the Abade de Baçal Museum. Don't be put off by the ugly modern outskirts.

What to see

The **Castle Citadel** dominates the town from its high hill. The castle was last reconstructed at the end of the fourteenth century by King João I. Inside the walls you will see the keep, the Princess Tower, the pillory, the *Domus Municipalis* and the Church of Santa Maria. The wall has two gates: the Porto de Santo António in the outer wall with various towers, and the Porta da Vila. The second wall has towers, wide balconies, ramparts and many niches.

The **Keep** is a Gothic tower 33 m high and 17 m wide, with battlements, watchtowers, a drawbridge, dungeons, vaulted rooms and an amazing outside staircase. It is now used as a military museum. You can climb up the steep, narrow outside staircase if you wish, and if you don't suffer from vertigo.

The **Princess Tower** is the most famous of the towers, because of the romantic legends and true stories of princesses being locked up in it. One is the inevitable legend of a Moorish princess who loved a Christian warrior rather than the Moor her father had chosen for her. Her father locked her in the tower. One night, in an attempt to convince her that her lover was dead, he entered her room and pretended to be the lover's ghost. When the sun came up she saw it was her father and she jumped off the tower to her death. Another story – this one probably true – says that the Princess Sancha, sister of Portugal's first king, locked herself in the tower to pine over the infidelities of her husband, Fernão Mendes. There is also the true story of the beautiful Spanish noblewoman Dona Leonor, who was married to Dom Jaime, the fourth Duke of Bragança, a notoriously jealous man. He locked her up in the tower so that no other man could see her. Later, when he moved his court to Vila Viçosa, he murdered her.

The medieval **Pillory** by the Castle is a very odd construction. Its shaft has been driven through an ancient granite statue of a wild boar.

The twelfth-century **Domus Municipalis** (Town Hall) is one of the few Romanesque civic buildings still in existence in Portugal. It is a pentagonal stone building with many arched open windows and stone seats all around the walls where the *Homens Bons* (Good Men) sat when they met. There is a cistern under the structure.

The **Church of Santa Maria**, which was reconstructed in the eighteenth century, is a mixture of Romanesque and Baroque.

The **Cathedral**, dating from 1545, was originally a church belonging to the Jesuits. It became the Cathedral when the Bishop moved here from Miranda do Douro in 1770. It is basically in the Renaissance style. The sacristy has a coffered ceiling with scenes from the life of Saint Ignatius.

The **Misericórdia Church**, near the Cathedral, was founded in

1418, which makes it one of the oldest churches in Portugal. It has a heavily carved gilt retable from the seventeenth century.

The **Church of São Bento** has a splendid painted ceiling with geometric designs.

The **Church of São Vicente** was originally thirteenth-century Romanesque, but it was reconstructed in the seventeenth century and heavily decorated in gilt. The chapels are also rich in gilt work. There are seventeenth-century glazed tiles round the nave.

The **Santa Clara Church** was built in the sixteenth century. It has eighteenth-century paintings on the ceilings.

The **Abade de Baçal Museum** is in the old Bishop's Palace. It is dedicated to the most remarkable man Bragança has produced, Francisco Manuel Alves (1865–1947), the Abbot of Baçal, a tiny parish near Bragança. He was a man far ahead of his time. He criticized the Catholic Church for the Inquisition, declared that it should promote social justice, and set forth a doctrine of religious tolerance. He wrote a history several hundred pages long of the Jews in Bragança, and prepared a catalogue of the 1,705 people from the district of Bragança who were accused of being Jews and sentenced by the Inquisition. He even condemned the doctrine of clerical celibacy. But the work for which he is chiefly remembered is his great record in eleven volumes containing all the information he was able to gather on the region of Bragança: the fruit of years spent tirelessly scouring the region for archaeological remains, and taking notes of all the customs, history, beliefs and way of living of the people.

The Museum contains archaeological remains, ancient carved granite boars, utensils of various kinds, coins, vestments, paintings, sculpture and furniture.

Crafts   Baskets, pottery, copper objects, leather goods and woven fabrics are all produced in Bragança.

Festivals   The *Festas da Santa Cruz*, the *Feira das Cantarinhas* and the *Festas da Nossa Senhora da Ribeira* all take place in May. The *Festas da Nossa Senhora das Graças* and the *Festas de São Bartolomeu* are in August, and the *Festas da Nossa Senhora da Serra* are in September.

Sport   Rabbits, hares, partridges and wild boar are hunted in the area, and all of the rivers are rich in trout and barbel.

Where to stay
Inexpensive
Hotel Bragança, Rua Eng. Arantes Oliveira. Tel. (073) 22579. A three star hotel with forty-two rooms with baths, a bar and restaurant.

Albergaria Santa Isabel, Rua Alexandre Herculano 67. Tel. (073) 22427. A four star inn with fourteen rooms with bath, and a bar.

Pensão Nordeste Shalon, Avenida Abade de Baçal. Tel. (073) 24667. A three-star pension with thirty rooms with bath and TV, and a bar.

Pensão Planatório, Estrada das Cantarias. Tel. (073) 22425/6. A three star pension with thirty rooms with bath, and central heating. It has a very good, award-winning restaurant.

Pensão Cruzeiro, Travessa do Hospital. Tel. (073) 22634. A three star pension with twenty-five rooms, five with bath, and a bar.

Pousada
Inexpensive

Pousada de São Bartolomeu, Estrada do Turismo. Tel. (073) 22493. A medium range pousada with sixteen comfortable rooms and a restaurant with excellent regional cooking. From the balconies off the rooms and from the restaurant, there are wonderful views of the Castle, on a hill opposite, of the city and of the mountains and valleys of Trás-os-Montes.

Camp site

The Bragança camp site is on the River Sabor. It has a river beach.

Where to eat

The **Pensão Planatório** and the **Pousada de São Bartolomeu** both have very good restaurants.

The following are also good.

Café Restaurante Flórida, Rua Alexandre Herculano 1. Tel. (073) 22250. A four star restaurant and snack bar. It also has a café with delicious homemade cakes.

Lá em Casa, Rua Marquês de Pombal. Tel. (073) 22111. A two star restaurant with regional cooking. It has a nice, comfortable atmosphere.

Solar Bragançano in a palatial townhouse in the main square, Praça da Sé. Tel. (073) 23875. Serves excellent regional food in a pleasant atmosphere.

O António, Bairro da Cooperativa. Tel. (073) 24388. A restaurant that serves specialities like cod stuffed with bacon, fish with shellfish sauce, duck with rice, veal steak and roast lamb.

What to eat

The specialities of Bragança are spicy sausages, cured ham, kid, *cozido à transmontana* (a stew of different meats, sausages and vegetables), *posta à Mirandesa* (steak), and *folares de Páscoa* (Easter cakes).

The Tourist Office is in the Town Hall. Tel. (073) 22271/2/3, telex 22637.

Montesinho
Natural
Park

The Montesinho Natural Park is a 75,000 hectare natural park north of Bragança. The entrances to the park are at Bragança and Vinhais. This is a land of high plateaux and mountains where you can drive for many kilometres without seeing a single person, or a house. The park has quantities of rabbits, quail, hare, wild boar, wolves and foxes, and it is cut by many rivers full of fish.

The villages here are very primitive: in many of them, communal life is still practised. **Montesinho**, at an altitude of 1,025 m, has a shelter house in Lama Grande. **Santa Cruz**, in the Coroa mountains, has a sulphur spring nearby. **Cova de Lua** in the centre of the park has a little chapel where there is a picnic ground. **França** has an interesting working windmill and a trout farm nearby.

Rio do Onor

Rio do Onor is cut in half by a small stream, so that one half of it is in Portugal and the other is in Spain; the villagers pass freely from one side to the other. It is only 20 km north of Bragança by bus or car on a fairly good road.

The communal life of Rio do Onor has been the subject of study by sociologists. The villagers still own their land in common, and elect *mordomos* each year to govern them and distribute the daily work among them. It is fascinating to see all the cattle come home in the evening, each cow going to her own house. Rio do Onor has been such a closed community that nearly everyone in the village has the family name of Preto.

Vinhais

Vinhais is 34 km west of Bragança on the N103, at the southern edge of the Montesinho Natural Park. On the road, 5 km out of Bragança, you will see the curious **Castro de Avelãs Monastery**. It is totally abandoned, but interesting. A combination of Romanesque and Arabic, possibly from the tenth century, it is composed of three cylindrical joined towers. The one in the middle has three storeys, and those on the sides each have two. There are blind windows all over it. Once a flourishing centre of the Benedictine Order, it fell into ruin when the religious orders were suppressed in the nineteenth century.

What to see

Vinhais was probably originally a pre-Roman *castro*. The present town was founded by King Sancho II in the thirteenth century. There is little left of the old castle, but inside the walls there are houses where people live. The Parish Church and the pillory are also inside. There are many noble houses in the town.

It is not certain whether the São Facundo Church was originally Roman or Visigoth.

The São Francisco Monastery Church has a fine painted ceiling.

Baskets, weaving and woodwork are produced in the town.

Festivals

The *Festas da Senhora dos Remédios* and the *Feira do Fumeiro* take place in February, the *Festas da Nossa Senhora da Assunção* on 15 August and the *Festas de Santo António* in September.

Where to stay
Inexpensive

Pensão Ribeirinha, Rua Nova. Tel. (073) 72490. A one star pension with eighteen rooms. No private baths.

Where to eat

Rossio, Portela dos Frades. Tel. (073) 72441. A café and restaurant.

What to eat

Specialities are trout, smoked ham, *Requeijão de Coutim e Pinheiros* (cream cheese), and *Manteiga de Travanca* (a type of butter).

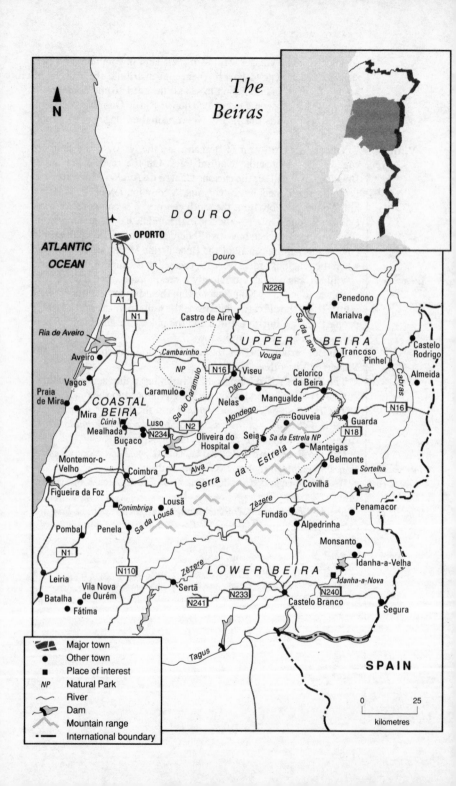

The Beiras

Introduction

The Beira region encompasses nearly all of the land between the Douro and the Tagus (Tejo) rivers. As its name, Beira (brink or edge), implies, it is an area of transition, between the north and the south of Portugal. It is usually divided into three regions: the Beira Alta (the Upper Beira), the Beira Baixa (the Lower Beira) and the Beira Litoral (the Coastal Beira). But the divisions tend to overlap.

The mountain scenery and the vast green forests of this largely agricultural region are very beautiful. Granite villages cling to the sides of the mountains and sheep and goats are to be seen everywhere.

The Upper and Lower Beiras have always been thinly populated, and in recent years a high rate of emigration to foreign countries and to the cities has left the region with empty houses everywhere, and an ageing population. The people of the Beiras are friendly towards tourists, and very helpful, but they tend to be more reticent than the people of the Minho, for example.

History From the sixth century BC the Beiras were inhabited by Lusitanians. When the Romans invaded central Portugal in about 193 BC they came up against the great stamina and ferocious fighting spirit of the Lusitanians, notably the shepherd warrior Viriato, who became known as 'the terror of Rome'. Viriato kept the Romans at bay for nine years, and at one time he drove their legions out of the Beiras and pursued them all the way to Madrid and Toledo, through Andalucia and over into North Africa. In the end he was defeated by the treachery of false friends, who killed him in his tent as he slept, in return for a promise of Roman gold. All over the country there are granite tombs with the name 'Viriato' carved on them – probably because many male babies were named after the famous hero. Several towns claim to be his birthplace, but the most likely is the village of Folgosinho in the Serra da Estrela. It has an ancient stone house with a stone on which is carved 'Hic Domus Viriati Fuit' – 'This was the house of Viriato.'

In spite of their mountains, the Beiras were always subject to invasions. In addition to the Romans, Vandals, Visigoths, Moors and Spaniards all came and settled and left their traces. Napoleon's troops under Junot invaded Portugal through the Beiras, and sacked the city of Castelo Branco. And during the nineteenth-century War of Succession the Beiras suffered political and military persecution.

171

Wines　　The Dão wines, cultivated at altitudes between 200 and 500 m, in the valleys of the River Mondego and its tributaries, particularly the River Dão, are considered the best table wines in Portugal. These wines have been known since the fourteenth century, perhaps even earlier. The region was demarcated in 1908. The vines grow on the granite and schist hillsides, where the summers are warm and dry. The red Dãos are aged for at least eighteen months before bottling. They are corpulent, velvety wines, ruby-coloured when young and a reddish-brown when aged. The white Dãos are matured in casks, or partly in casks, partly in bottles, for ten months. They are light, pale yellow, fruity in flavour and with a high alcohol content.

The Lafões wines have some characteristics of *vinho verde*, but they are smoother, more full-bodied and more alcoholic, and, unlike *vinho verdes*, they can be aged. These wines are bottled under the name Lafões-Adega Cooperativa. The region from which they come, between the Vinho Verde district in the Minho and the Dão region (see above), is not yet demarcated.

Differences in soil and amount of rainfall mean that the wines produced in the Lower Beira (around the towns of Covilhã, Belmonte, Fundão and Castelo Branco) are quite different from those of the Upper Beira. Most are full-bodied, smooth and high in alcohol content. They can be aged and matured. Those from Covilhã are rather less alcoholic and more acid. Fundão and Covilhã are two of the labels. People in the region seem to think Fundão is the best.

The Bairrada table wines produced in the demarcated region of the Coastal Beira, near Buçaco, are of a very high quality. Wine was being made here as early as the tenth and eleventh centuries – all the monasteries had extensive vineyards. But in 1760 the Prime Minister, the Marquês de Pombal, ordered that all of the vines should be pulled up, in order to protect the port wines of the nearby Douro. In 1790 Queen Maria I revoked this order, and after that production quickly reached high levels. Sparkling wines – whites, rosés and reds, and ranging from extra-dry to sweet – are also produced in this region.

The Upper Beira

The Upper Beira (Beira Alta) is a vast upland lying to the north of the central mountain ranges and encompassing more than half of the Serra da Estrela Natural Park.

Guarda　　The capital of the Upper Beira is Guarda, the highest city in Portugal. It is located at the north-eastern edge of the Serra da Estrela, just 47 km from the Spanish border on the road to Salamanca and Madrid.

Founded by the Romans, Guarda was destroyed and rebuilt many times in the wars between the Moors and the Christians.

Guarda has many associations with the kings of Portugal. In the thirteenth century King Dinis held his court there while he was negotiating with the Spaniards of Castile. In the fifteenth century the treaty of Tordesillas, dividing the world between Spain and Portugal, was signed in Guarda. King Sancho I felt inspired there to write a love poem that is carved on a marble tablet fixed to a wall. The Braganças, the ruling family of Portugal from 1640 to 1910, had their origins in Guarda. King João I fell in love with Inês Fernandes, the beautiful daughter of a Jewish shoemaker of Guarda. They had a son whom the king made the first Duke of Bragança. This honour was not sufficient compensation for Inês's father. He felt his daughter's disgrace so deeply that he swore never to cut his beard for the rest of his life. He became known as *Barbadão* (the Bearded One). The Fernandes family lived in what is now Rua de Dom Sancho.

The Jews played a great part in the history of Guarda. Spanish Jews fled to Guarda from Spain in the fifteenth century, when they were persecuted and expelled by Ferdinand and Isabella. They contributed much to the development of the region, particularly to the once-flourishing silk industry. The Jewish quarter ran along what is now Rua do Amparo – an inscription in Hebrew is still over one doorway.

Guarda was occupied many times by the Spaniards – sometimes after being betrayed to them by its own people. In 1383 the Bishop of Guarda opened the city's gates to the King of Castile.

Guarda's twelfth-century castle, built at a height of 1,056 m, has a splendid panoramic view. Three portals – *Ferreiros* (Iron Mongers), *Estrela* (Star) and *Rei Dom Dinis* (King Dom Dinis) – plus the keep and sections of the old twelfth-century walls still stand.

The **Cathedral** is built like a mammoth fortress, out of blocks of granite. Work was begun on it in 1390, but it was not completed until 1540. It has Manueline pillars and Renaissance and Baroque features that were added over the centuries. The carvings in the Cathedral are well worth looking at. There is a retable of decorated panels representing the life of Christ and including over a hundred carved figures, the work of the Frenchman Jean de Rouen. At a less elevated level, each seat in the choir stalls has a lifelike face carved under it. In the connecting **Pinas Chapel** you can see the tomb of the Cathedral's founder, who, according to legend, threw himself from the roof because the building was criticized by the people. Both closed on Mondays.

The seventeenth-century **Misericórdia Church**, with two tall towers, is an example of Baroque architecture. Its altars are Rococo in style. Worth a visit, too, are the eleventh-century **Mileu Chapel** and the sixteenth-century church of **Nossa Senhora dos Remédios**. Guarda also has many interesting old Gothic-style houses.

The **Municipal Museum**, which was once a seminary, houses

archaeological finds, primitive paintings, and a collection of fifteenth-century weights and measures.

Crafts Look out for hand-embroidered linen, woollen blankets, basketry, hand-decorated candles and ceramics.

Where to stay **Hotel de Turismo**, Avenida Coronel Orlando de Carvalho. Tel.
Medium price (071) 22206, telex 18760. Four star, and the best hotel in town. It has 105 rooms with bath and TV, a swimming pool, restaurant and bar.

Inexpensive **Pensão Residência Filipe**, Rua Vasco da Gama 9. Tel. (071) 22658/9. A four star inn, with a bar and restaurant.

Pensão Aliança, Rua Vasco da Gama 8. Tel. (071) 22135. Slightly more modest, but comfortable. A three star pension with thirty rooms, sixteen with bath. It has a bar and restaurant.

Pensão Gare, Avenida João de Ruão. Tel. (071) 29488. A two star pension with nineteen rooms, eleven with bath.

Manor house **Solar de Alarcão**, Rue Miguel de Alarcão. Tel. (071) 21275. A sev-
Medium price enteenth-century manor house with several rooms for guests.

Inexpensive **Quinta de São José**, Aldeia Viçosa, 6000 Guarda. Tel. (071) 96210. A granite and white-painted farmhouse in a small town 20 km from Guarda on N16. Offers one small flat big enough for two couples – two bedrooms, a living room and bath.

Camp site **Parque de Campismo Orbitur,** 6300 Guarda. Tel. (071) 21406.
Where to eat **O Telheiro**, in the city on Estrada Nacional 16. Tel. (071) 21356. Its speciality is *cabrito assado* (roast kid).

A Mexicana, Estrada Nacional 16 near the O Telheiro. Tel. (071) 21512. A small restaurant decorated Mexican style, but serving excellent Portuguese dishes.

What to eat Try roast lamb, *coelho à malcata* (rabbit in red wine), *murcelas* (blood sausages with greens), trout from Sabugal, game, almond cakes and Serra cheese.

The Tourist Office is in the Edificio da Câmara Praça Luis de Camões, 6300 Guarda. Tel. (071) 22251.

Pinhel Pinhel is 35 km north-east of Guarda on route N16–N221. This
What to see town has been over the centuries the scene of many battles. Until the twelfth century it was a frontier post belonging to the Spanish kingdom of León, and its primitive wall and castle date from that time. Much of the wall was torn down to provide stone to build houses, but two splendid square towers still stand, one with a pretty Manueline window. There are many churches: the fourteenth-century Santa Maria do Castelo; the ruined seventeenth-century Misericórdia, with a beautiful Manueline portal; the eighteenth-century Parish Church; and several others. The town has many fine eighteenth-century houses. The Casa Grande was, according to legend, built by imps: the builder was in league with the Devil.

In the area there are many Roman monuments, including the church of the Trinity, which has a four-arched portal, and the Roman bridge over the River Cabras, on the way to Castelo Rodrigo.

Just before you reach Pinhel, coming from Guarda, there is an ancient prehistoric dolmen. It is the Anta da Pêra do Moço, a huge block of granite with five granite supports.

Where to stay
Inexpensive
Pensão Falcão, Avenida Carneiro Gusmão. Tel. (071) 52361. A three star pension with twenty-four rooms with bath.

What to drink
The Pinhel region is known for its claret-type wines.

Castelo Rodrigo
What to see
Castelo Rodrigo, 20 km north of Pinhel by route N221, is a walled town with thirteen round towers, constructed in the reign of King Dinis. There is the ruined palace of Cristovão de Moura, the traitor who, in 1385, betrayed Portugal to the Spaniards: the castle was burned down by the villagers in 1640, when Portugal regained its independence. (Back in the fourteenth century, King João I had punished Castelo Rodrigo by decreeing that its coat of arms be displayed always upside-down.) There is a pillory, and many of the houses have Manueline windows. Nearby you can see the ruins of a Cistercian monastery, the Santa Maria de Aguiar, where, in the sixteenth century, the monks were greatly criticized for their immorality. At Figueira de Castelo Rodrigo, 3 km away, the Parish Church has an interesting arch with S-shaped stones, but no keystone.

In February, the land around Castelo Rodrigo is a mass of almond trees in bloom.

Where to stay
Inexpensive
There are two pensions with restaurants. **Pensão Restaurante Central**, Largo da Igreja, Escalhão. Tel. (071) 34126. **Pensão Restaurante Santos**, Rua Osório de Vasconcelos. Tel. (071) 32171.

What to eat
The region is known for its roast kid, sweets and red wine.

Almeida
Almeida is 23 km south of Figueira de Castelo Rodrigo by route N332. It was an important fortress from the twelfth to the nineteenth centuries – during the Peninsular War it was occupied by Wellington and Masséna in turn. You have to go over bridges and through tunnels to get into the town, which is contained within an enormous star-shaped fortification (completed by Vaubon in the eighteenth century), and surrounded by a ditch 15 m deep.

Celorico da Beira

What to see
Celorico da Beira is at the northern end of the Serra da Estrela mountains, 25 km from Guarda on route N16. In the Middle Ages it was very important in defending the country against the Castilian Spaniards, and its square castle and tower were built then. The Parish Church has an interesting painted ceiling. There are many prehistoric dolmens in the surrounding countryside.

Where to stay
Inexpensive
Hotel Mira Serra, Bairro de Santa Eufêmia, São Pedro. Tel. (071) 72604/5. An excellent hotel with forty-two rooms with bath and TV, a bar, restaurant and gardens.

Pensão Parque, Rua Andrade Corvo 48. Tel. (071) 721977. A three star pension with a bar.

Manor house
Medium price
Quinta da Ponte, Faia, 6360 Celorico da Beira. Tel. (071) 96126. Reservations (01) 691508 (Lisbon). An eighteenth-century manor house on a farm through which the River Mondego flows. Recently

restored and modernized, it offers ten apartments with bath, a pool, tennis courts and trout fishing.

Trancoso
What to see

Trancoso is a walled town 18 km north of Celorico da Beira on the N226. It was settled many years ago by the Jews, and the old Jewish quarter still exists. Each house has two doors, one wide and one narrow, for shop and home. Trancoso has several interesting monuments: a medieval castle and walls; a pillory; the Romanesque Santa Luzia Chapel; the white, six-sided São Bartolomeu Chapel; a fountain built in 1589 that looks like a Greek temple; and several seventeenth- and eighteenth-century churches.

Fair

Between 15 and 24 August Trancoso has a famous fair in honour of its patron saint, Our Lady of Fresta.

Marialva

Marialva lies 22 km north of Trancoso on the N102. Above the modern town there is a totally deserted medieval town, with ruined walls, castles, towers and churches that stand like ghosts.

Penedono

Penedono is 31 km north of Trancoso on route N226–N229. It has a beautiful small castle, very well preserved, set on a hill on top of boulders, with a pillory and a small Baroque church below. Legend says that the man who owned it was one of the 'Twelve Knights of Portugal' who were asked by John of Gaunt's son-in-law, King João I, to go to England to joust for the honour of twelve English ladies.

Lapa

Shrine

Lapa is a tiny town 8 km off route N323 between Moimenta da Beira and Vila Nova de Paiva, west of Penedono. It has a strange church with boulders inside that form an altar, with an image of the Virgin about which there is an old legend. It is said that Joana, a deaf and dumb child, found an image of the Virgin and put it in her workbasket. When her mother saw it she threw it in the fire, because she thought it would distract Joana from her work. By a miracle, Joana spoke, saying, 'Don't burn it, Mother. It is our Lady of Lapa.' The doll was pulled from the fire and it is now on the altar, where people go to

Pilgrimage

pray for miracles. There is a pilgrimage, the Romaria da Senhora da Lapa, every June.

Viseu

Viseu is often called the 'City of Green Pines', because it is surrounded by forests of tall pine trees. From its strategic position at the hub of seven roads that lead in from the interior, the mountains and the Atlantic coast, it dominates the western part of the Upper Beira.

Getting there

There are regular regional airline flights between Viseu and Lisbon (see page 33). And there are buses that follow the old scenic train route and between all of the towns in the Viseu region, with connections for Lisbon.

History

Viseu began as a pre-Roman *castro* (see page 17) in the midst of a wide plateau on a high hill – the position now occupied by the Cathedral which the first King of Portugal, Afonso Henriques, had built. It has been populated through the ages by different invaders: in turn the Romans, the Moors, and the rulers of León and Astúrias.

In the sixteenth century Viseu became a renowned art centre. The great painter Vasco Fernandes (Grão Vasco) lived and worked there and attracted many other artists.

What to see   Viseu has monuments from all of the periods of its history, including a granite statue of the Lusitanian warrior **Viriato** (see page 171) and the old Roman fortifications – known, misleadingly, as the **Cova de Viriato** but in fact built by Decimus Brutus after Viriato's death. There are two doors of the old city wall still standing – the **Porta do Soar** and the **Porta dos Cavaleiros**.

Many kings and noblemen made their homes in Viseu at various times. The **Rua Direita** and the tiny streets that lead off it are lined with fine old houses with lovely carved doors and windows. There are many interesting Baroque houses.

There are also several splendid churches with beautifully decorated altars and chapels. The **Cathedral** was largely rebuilt between the sixteenth and eighteenth centuries, and it has a Renaissance façade. The interior is richly decorated, with a golden altar screen and colourful painted ceilings. The Cathedral treasury has an enormous collection of gold and silver vessels, statues and vestments.

The **São Francisco Church**, near the central Rossio square, is faced with blue and white decorative tiles. The **Misericórdia Church** in the Praça da Sé, built in the sixteenth century by Dom Jorge de Ataíde as a small hermitage, was enlarged three centuries later in Neoclassical style. The **Carmo Church** and the **Nossa Senhora da Vitória Chapel**, on the south side of the Rossio hill, are also worth visiting.

Grão Vasco left a collection of his paintings to the town, and they are exhibited, together with those of other Portuguese painters, in the **Grão Vasco Museum** in the Praça da Sé.

The **Almeida Moreira Museum**, Largo Major Teles, shows a private collection of antiques, furniture, tiles, paintings and ceramics.

Crafts   Ironwork, tinwork, leather, basketwork, embroideries, tapestries.

Procession   On 24 June there is a procession in honour of Saint John the Baptist that is really worth seeing. It takes place in the picturesque Vila de Moinhos (Village of the Watermills), which straddles the River Pavia just outside Viseu. As its name implies, Vila de Moinhos has always been a town of millers. Back in the seventeenth century a great dispute arose between the millers and the nearby farmers over the use of the water from the river. (Disputes over water rights continue to be one of the main causes of murder in Portugal.) When the case was finally taken to court, the millers promised their patron saint, John the Baptist, that if the case was decided in their favour they would make an annual procession to his shrine. They won their case, and set about fulfilling their promise. Every year, on the feast day of Saint John the Baptist, the millers, dressed in costumes parodying the nobility, procede on horseback through Viseu to the saint's shrine. At the head of the procession are three men impeccably dressed in black, mounted on superb horses. Nowadays, in addition to the millers, there are many enormous, colourful floats, bands and folk dancing groups.

Where to stay
Inexpensive
Grão Vasco Hotel, Rua Gaspar Barreiros. Tel. (032) 23511/2/3, telex GRANVASCO VISEU. A four star hotel with a restaurant, bar and swimming pool. It offers eighty-eight rooms with bath.

Hotel Mana, Via Caçador. Tel. (032) 26143. A three star hotel with forty-six rooms with bath and TV, a bar, restaurant, shops, money exchange and gardens.

Hotel Avenida, Avenida 28 de Maio. Tel. (032) 23432/3, telex HOTELAVENIDA-VISEU. A two star hotel with bar and restaurant. Thirty-seven rooms, twenty-seven with private bath.

Pensão Bela Vista, Rua Alexandre Herculano 510. Tel. (032) 26026. A comfortable three star pension with bar and restaurant.

Manor houses
Medium price
Casa de Rebordinho, Rebordinho, 3500 Viseu. Tel. (032) 21258/ 21337 or (01) 9232448. A very large farmhouse, 5 km from Viseu on N231, with three double and one single bedrooms, baths and living room.

Inexpensive
Quinta do Vale do Chão, Santar, 3520 Nelas. Tel. (032) 944319 or (01) 765974. One of the noble houses for which the region is known. It offers one double bedroom with bath, one room with twin beds, and a large salon.

Camp site
Parque de Campismo da Orbitur, Parque Fontelo. Tel. (032) 25547.

Where to eat
Dom Duarte Restaurante-Snack, Estrada Nacional 2, Campo. Tel. (032) 29797.

Santa Eulália Café-Restaurante Churrasqueira, Bairro Santa Eulália Repeses. Tel. (032) 26283.

What to eat
Trout in vinegar, chicken stewed in an earthenware pot, roast kid or mutton, apple pudding, stuffed baked apples, chestnuts with eggs.

The Tourist Office is in the Avenida Gulbenkian. Tel. (032) 22294.

Castro de Aire
What to see
Castro de Aire, 37 km north of Viseu on the N2, sits in wild uplands on the site of an Iron Age hill-town. There is a lovely square with many grand old houses. The Romanesque Matriz da Erminda Church and the São Sebastião Chapel are also well worth seeing, and the ruins of the doors to the old town, the Portas de Montemuro, are interesting. At 6 km from the town there is the twelfth-century Romanesque Paiva Chapel. There are also many neolithic remains nearby. Near Vila Nova de Paiva, some 15 km east, is the Dolmen de Pendilhe, the most important necropolis in the Viseu district.

A strong community spirit still persists in the stone villages around Castro de Aire, with the people sharing land, threshing floors, watermills and their labour.

Crafts
Basketry, black pottery, wooden clogs and woven goods.

Where to stay
Inexpensive
Pensão Avenida, Avenida General Humberto Delgado 74. Tel. (032) 32101. A comfortable two star pension with bar.

São Pedro do Sul
São Pedro do Sul is 22 km north-west of Viseu on the N16. The town has some fine buildings. The Parish Church has a golden

What to see | retable, silver lamps, an eighteenth-century organ and an ornate ceiling in the sacristy. The façade of the Misericórdia Church is covered with pale blue and white tiles, and it has ornate granite-bordered windows. The town hall is an old Baroque friary.

Where to stay
Inexpensive

About 3 km out of the town on the N228 there is a spa with some good pensions.

Pensão Ultramarina, Estrada Nacional. Tel. (032) 72311. A good three star pension.

Pensão Lafões, Rua do Correio. Tel. (032) 71616. A good three star pension with restaurant and garage.

Pensão-Restaurante Pedro, Estrada Nacional. Tel. (032) 71244. A two star pension.

Where to eat

Miradouro Café-Restaurante, Pedreira. Tel. (032) 71529.

São Pedro Café-Restaurante, Praça República. Tel. (032) 71539.

Tourist Office, Estrada Nacional 16, Várzea. Tel. (032) 71320.

Cambarinho Natural Park

Oliveira de Frades and **Vouzela** are two towns in the Cambarinho Natural Park. This area in the Caramulo mountains 20 km west of Viseu was set aside as a reserve to protect a rare purple form of Iberian oleander.

The region has many vineyards and cattle, and is noted for its delicious veal steaks, its pastries and its fine linens. Vouzela has a thirteenth-century Romanesque church.

The Tourist Office is in the Praça Conselheiro Morais de Carvalho, Vouzela. Tel. (032) 77517.

Caramulo

What to see

Caramulo is at the south-western tip of the Cambarinho Natural Park, 43 km south-west of Viseu on route N2–N230. Its Abel Laçerda Museum is particularly famous for its vintage cars, but it also has an interesting collection of seventeenth- and eighteenth-century Portuguese primitive paintings, paintings by Picasso and Salvador Dali, and collections of sculpture, silver, furniture, tapestries, carpets and Chinese porcelain.

Where to stay
Inexpensive
Pousada
Inexpensive

Pensão Restaurante São Cristovão, Avenida Dr Jerónimo Lacerda. Tel. (032) 86323.

Pousada de São Jeronimo, Caramulo. Tel. (032) 86291, telex 53512. An excellent medium range pousada, with six rooms, in a modern building on a mountain slope.

The Tourist Office is on the main road. Tel. (032) 86437.

Mangualde

What to see

Mangualde is 16 km south-east of Viseu on the N16. There is an interesting prehistoric dolmen, the Anta da Cunha Baixa. Also worth visiting are the eighteenth-century Misericórdia Church, the Anadia Palace and the hermitage of Nossa Senhora do Castelo. There are many festivals in July and August.

Where to stay
Inexpensive

Hotel Senhora do Castelo, Monte Senhora do Castelo. Tel. (032) 98514, telex 43063 MONTE P. A three star hotel with eighty rooms with TV, a bar, restaurant and money exchange.

South-west of Mangualde at **Nelas** (celebrated for its needlepoint carpets), there are several good places to stay.

Albergaria São Pedro, Bairro das Toiças, Rua 4. Tel. (032) 94585/6/7. A four star inn with sixty-nine rooms with bath, a bar and money exchange.

Estalagem Cruz da Matá, Lugar da Cruz da Matá. Tel. (032) 62556. A four star inn with thirteen rooms with bath.

Pensão Maial, Canas de Senhorim, Caldas da Pouseira. Tel. (032) 94223. A three star pension with twenty-five rooms.

Manor houses
Inexpensive

Quinta da Alameda, Santas, 2520 Nelas. Tel. (032) 94882/94329. A large stone farmhouse just off the N231 between Nelas and Viseu. The inside of the house is very pretty. It offers two bedrooms with bath, and guests can use the tennis court and swimming pool.

Casa da Corredoura, Vilar Seco, 3520 Nelas (contact Maria Gilhermina Casanova Alves, Rua Artilaria 1, 4-3 Dto., 1200 Lisbon. Tel. (01) 683289.) A rustic house with modern comforts, set in the midst of vineyards in Vilar Seco, just 4 km from Nelas. It offers three double bedrooms with bath, a living room, a kitchen and maid service. Minimum stay ten days.

Another 7 km south of Nelas at **Canas de Senhorim** you will find a very good hotel and a lovely eighteenth-century manor house.

Where to stay
Medium price

Hotel de Urgeiriça, Canas de Senhorim. Tel. (032) 67267/8. A three star hotel which is like a beautiful country house set in beautiful surroundings, with a swimming pool and tennis courts. It has small chalets in the grounds.

Manor houses
Inexpensive

Casa Abreu Madeira, Largo Abreu Madeira 7, 3523 Canas de Senhorim. Tel. (032) 67183. An eighteenth-century manor house on a large farm that produces grapes from which Dão wines are made. Offers two double bedrooms with bath, and guests have the use of several salons, a games room with table tennis and billiards, and a swimming pool.

In **Penalva do Castelo**, 12 km north of Mangualde, there is another manor house.

Casa Magalhães Coutinho, 3550 Penalva do Castelo. Tel. (032) 64219 or (01) 545442. Offers two double bedrooms with bath, living rooms and a pretty garden.

Where to eat
Aguiar da Beira

Avis, Rua Grémio, Mangualde. Tel. (032) 62795.

Aguiar da Beira, 42 km north-east of Viseu on the N229, is a small granite medieval town, very out of the way. The first inhabitants of the region were cave-dwellers. Later a castle was built on a high point.

What to see

The town has an interesting square, a pillory, and a fifteenth-century church tower. Under the medieval council chamber there is a spring that is reached through a Gothic doorway.

The Serra da Estrela

The Serra da Estrela mountain range, which divides the Beiras and is shared by them, has the highest mountains in Portugal. It is the only place in Portugal where winter sports such as skiing are attempted –

not very successfully, because there isn't really enough snow. However, the Serra does offer excellent walking and hiking over mapped trails, and there is good fishing to be had in the mountain streams.

When to go

The best time to go to the Serra is in the summer or autumn. Surprisingly, prices are lower in the summer, because it is considered the low season. In winter, as soon as there is snow (any time between December and March), the local Portuguese pour in to show it to their children, and to sledge down the mountains on plastic bags.

Scenic routes

The Serra da Estrela was declared a Natural Park in 1976. The Park Service keeps the roads up well: they have many curves and are very steep, running along the tops of deep rocky valleys, but they are well surfaced and are kept free of snow even in the winter. Beside the roads there are many look-out points from which you get spectacular views. When you reach the top of the mountains, you feel as if you are on top of the world, with clouds below you and rocky expanses all around. Below in the valleys there are many lakes and great numbers of goats and sheep, with shepherds in black accompanied by their sheepdogs.

Coming up the main road from Covilhã, you will see an enormous Virgin carved in the rocky mountainside on the right. This is Our Lady of the Shepherds. The statue is cracked now because it was struck by lightning. Further along you will come to the Lagoa Comprida (Long Lagoon), at the very summit of the mountain.

The Torre, the highest peak in the Serra, is 2 km off the road to the left as you reach the highest pass. The Penhas Douradas near Sabugueiro are three peaks at 1,668 m: they are called 'golden peaks' because they turn gold when the sun strikes them at sunset.

There are also two other routes through the Serra da Estrela, each of them with totally different scenery. If you go into the mountains from Belmonte, which is north of Covilhã on the N18, you will follow the River Zêzere upwards through forests of pine, chestnut and oak trees. In the autumn, you can stop by the road and pick up bushels of chestnuts. As the road comes to the top of the pass above the river valley, the forests fall away. There are many waterfalls and springs, and on the right you will see a giant balancing rock.

The third road goes through the southern side of the mountains by way of beautiful little stone villages like Loriga and Esteves de Baixa. There are thousands of chestnut trees here too, and juniper bushes grow in the rocks.

Along the roads there are tourist shops and stalls selling Serra cheeses, sheepskin rugs, shepherds' coats and dark striped blankets, honey of the region, smoked hams, pillows, ceramics, pottery, nuts, and even Serra da Estrela dogs. You can buy regional crafts, and food, in the villages as well. There are also many pensions and restaurants.

Shepherds

There are enormous herds of goats and sheep in the Serra, just as there were in the time of the Lusitanians. The shepherds in black with wool blankets over their shoulders, accompanied by their sheepdogs, must look very much as they did then. When the pasturage is not good, the shepherds migrate with their flocks to other distant mountains. This movement of thousands of sheep is called *transumância*.

Cheese

The famous cheeses of the Serra da Estrela are made by shepherds' wives, following the method that has been used for hundreds of years.

The cheeses are made between December and March. The mountain towns of Seia, Gouveia and Celorico da Beira hold big cheese fairs in February and March. If you want to buy a Serra da Estrela cheese, get it from a shop that specializes in cheese, not from one of the tourist stalls along the mountain roads. The cheeses that are sold at the roadside sometimes have potatoes mixed in with the milk, and you don't want to pay a lot of money for a rather tasteless lump of potato.

Sheepdogs

The same message applies to buying Serra da Estrela sheepdogs: only buy where you can be sure of getting the genuine article. The Tourist Department recommends two places where you can get thoroughbreds: the Canil de Gouveia in Gouveia and the Caverna de Viriato, a small restaurant near the Pousada de São Lourenço (see facing page) in the Penhas Douradas mountains.

The real Serra da Estrela sheepdog looks very like a mastiff, thickset and powerful, with calm, bright eyes and an imposing demeanour. They are wolf-grey or yellow in colour, sometimes with white markings, and they are usually about 70 cm long and weigh 40 to 50 kg. There are short- and long-haired Serra da Estrelas, but both have abundant rough hair that grows unevenly over their bodies.

Ancient monuments

Throughout the Serra da Estrela you can see the remains of *castros* (see page 17), dolmens and ancient funeral monuments.

Fairs and festivals

Apart from the cheese fairs in February and March, there are honey fairs in September and there are many animal fairs: most of the dog fairs are in August. There are always various festivals and pilgrimages, and there is a good deal of folk dancing to be seen.

Walking tours

The Serra da Estrela Natural Park is a perfect place for walking tours, because of its beautiful mountain scenery, its emptiness, and its well-signed trails. Inquire at the Tourist Office for maps.

Sport

There are two small ski runs in the Serra da Estrela – one in Torres and another at Penhas da Saúde. You can hire skiing equipment.

The high plains of the Serra da Estrela, which have very little wind, are highly suitable for gliding, and this has become a popular sport.

Manteigas
What to see

Manteigas is a mountain town in a region full of weird rock formations left by glaciers. Its Church of Santa Maria and São Pedro is interesting. In the vicinity of Manteigas, things to see include the source of the River Zêzere, the Torre mountains, the Penhas Douradas and the Poço do Inferno (Well of Hell), a waterfall that freezes into a spectacular mass of ice in the winter.

Where to stay Inexpensive

Hotel de Manteigas, Manteigas. Tel. (075) 47114. A two star hotel on the mountainside with twenty-six double rooms with bath, a restaurant, bar, gym, sauna and tennis.

Pensão Serradalto, Rua 1° de Maio, Serradalto-Manteigas. Tel. (075) 98151. A three star pension recommended by the Tourist Office. All rooms have private bath, and there is a bar.

Pensão Estrela, Rua Dr Sobral 5, Manteigas. Tel. (075) 47288. A two star pension, also recommended. It has rooms with baths, heating in the winter, and a restaurant.

Manor house
Medium price

Casa de São Roque, Rua de Santo António 67, 6260 Manteigas. Tel. (075) 98125. An imposing three-storey town house. It has one suite and five double rooms for guests, in addition to several salons, a dining room and a terrace overlooking the valley.

Pousada
Medium price

Pousada de São Lourenço, Manteigas, Serra da Estrela. Tel. (075) 47150, telex 53992. A medium range pousada with fourteen rooms, on the slope of the Estrela mountain – a marvellous location if you enjoy walking, mountaineering or fishing.

Where to eat

There are some reasonable restaurants – you should have no problem finding somewhere to eat.

Gouveia

Gouveia, on the western side of the mountains, is on the N232 and dates from about the sixth century BC. It was badly damaged in battles between Moors and Christians. Things to see include the eighteenth-century Parish Church, the town hall, the Casa da Torre with its Renaissance windows, the pillory, the tile-faced church of São Pedro and the Misericórdia Church. There are also some lovely gardens and beautiful old manor houses.

What to see

Castro

Nearby is the ancient *castro* of Alfatima, which you must climb to reach. In remote times, it was abandoned by its inhabitants because the place was plagued by locusts each year. According to a stone tablet found on the site (now in the Santa Maria Church in Manteigas), Julius Caesar was here in the year 38 BC. The name Alfatima supposedly comes from Fátima, the beautiful daughter of the Moorish Emir of Manteigas, who fled to the top of the mountain with her jewels and gold during the Christian reconquest.

Festival

The *Festas do Senhor do Calvário* takes place in Gouveia from 6 to 10 August. There is a fair with crafts and amusements of various kinds, and a competition for Serra da Estrela sheepdogs. On the Saturday there is a folk song and dance festival, and on the Sunday a procession.

Where
to stay
Inexpensive

Estalagem Dom José, Cruzamento da Pulga, 6920 Gouveia. Tel. (032) 42219. An excellent four star inn 5 km along the road to Coimbra. It is very pretty and has a good restaurant.

Hotel do Gouveia, Avenida 1° de Maio. Tel. (032) 42890/3, telex HOTGVA 53789. A hotel with twenty-seven double rooms with bath, music, telephone and central heating, and four suites each with a living room and TV. It has a bar, a restaurant serving regional food, a swimming pool and tennis courts.

Pensão Estrela do Parque, Avenida República 36. Tel. (032) 42171. A good two star pension with nineteen rooms, four with bath.

Manor houses

Casa Rainha, Rua Direita 68, Toural, 6290 Gouveia. Tel. (032)

Medium price | 42132 or (01) 793174. A classical eighteenth-century manor house. It offers two double rooms with bath, living room and garden.

Inexpensive | **Casa Grande**, Rua do Fundo do Lagar, 6290 Gouveia. Tel. (038) 42204 or (02) 816587. An imposing manor house in the small mountain town of Paços da Serra, half-way between Gouveia and Seia on the N232. It has two flats for guests in adjoining buildings. Each flat has one bedroom, bathroom, living room and kitchen. Next to the main house is the newly converted **Casa da Oitão**, which has one double bedroom, a bathroom, a living room and a small kitchen.

Where to eat | There are several reasonable restaurants in Gouveia.

The Tourist Office is at the Avenida 1° de Maio. Tel. (032) 42185.

Seia
What to see | Seia, on the N339, is the western door to the Serra da Estrela. The town was taken from the Moors in 1136. It has the Casa dos Mouros dolmen, a Parish Church with traces of Romanesque, Gothic manor houses, the eighteenth-century Misericórdia Church, and the chapel of Nossa Senhora do Espinheiro, with a gilded altarpiece.

Where to stay
Inexpensive | **Estalagem de Seia**, Avenida Afonso Costa, Seia. Tel. (038) 22666 and 22682/3. A four star inn in a classical granite building, in the centre of town. It is furnished with antiques, and has a beautiful restaurant, two swimming pools and a bar.

Hotel Camelo, Rua 1° de Maio. Tel. (038) 22530. A three star hotel with forty-seven rooms with bath and TV, a bar, money exchange and an excellent restaurant.

Pensão Restaurante Serra da Estrela, Largo Marquês da Silva. Tel. (038) 22573. Very good – recommended by the Tourist Office. It offers twenty-one rooms with bath and TV, a bar and restaurant.

Abrigo da Montanha, Sabugueiro. Tel. (038) 22772. Just a few minutes from Seia, up the road into the mountains. It has twenty rooms, a restaurant and an excellent shop with regional crafts.

Manor houses
Medium price | **Casa da Ponte**, Alvoca da Serra, 2670 Seia. Tel. (038) 93351 or (01) 771175. A manor house at Alvoca da Serra in the green, forest-covered mountains in the southern part of the Natural Park – an excellent location for walking in the mountains. It offers seven double bedrooms with bath, and a swimming pool.

Casa do Sabugueiro, Sabugueiro, 6270 Seia. Tel. (038) 22825. A manor house at Sabugueiro, on the N339 between Seia and Covilhã. The house is in a narrow, stone-paved street in the town. On its lower floor you can still see the old cheese dairy, the bread oven, the room for smoking hams and sausages, and the special room for tasting all these things. It offers six apartments, each with two bedrooms, bathroom, living room and kitchen.

Where to eat | The restaurants in the **Estalagem de Seia**, **Pensão Restaurante Residência Camelo**, **Pensão Restaurante Serra da Estrela** all have good reputations.

Linhares | Linhares is a village 8 km off the N17, at the end of a winding road.

It has many large manor houses, some of them in ruins, and a two-towered castle. The Parish Church and the Misericórdia Church have Portuguese primitive paintings.

Oliveira do Hospital

Oliveira do Hospital is set in vineyards at the very edge of the Serra at its south-western tip, on the N17. The Parish Church has carved granite tombs and a painted ceiling.

Festival

On 5 July the *Romaria da Senhora das Preces* in the town of Vale de Maceira nearby attracts thousands to its shrine and fair.

Where to stay
Inexpensive

Hotel São Paulo, Rua Antunes Varela. Tel. (032) 52393/52361, telex 43140 MOSULO P. A three star hotel with forty-three rooms with bath, a bar and restaurant.

Manor house
Medium price

Casa do Beco, Lagares da Beira, 3400 Oliveira do Hospital. Tel. (032) 54118. A large granite block house in the traditional style of the region, in Meruge, a small town on the banks of the River Cobral 8 km from Oliveira do Hospital. It has two flats, each with a double bedroom with bath, a living room with a double sofa bed and a small kitchen.

Pousada
Medium price

Pousada de Santa Bárbara, Póvoa das Quartas. Tel. (032) 52252/3 or 52826, telex 53794. This first class pousada is a comfortable modern building set among pine trees, in Póvoa das Quartas, just 15 km south-west of Oliveira do Hospital on the River Alva. It has sixteen rooms, restaurant, swimming pool and tennis courts.

The Tourist Office is in the Edificio da Câmera. Tel. (032) 52522.

Avô

South of Oliveira do Hospital, just off the N17 along the N230–N342, is the picturesque town of Avô, which hangs over the River Alva. It has a charming reconstructed castle.

Where to stay

Pensão José Jerónimo, Avô. Tel. (038) 47224.

Lourosa

A little west of Avô along the N17, you will find Lourosa, which has a pre-Romanesque church dating from about 912. It is made of stone taken from older Visigoth and Moorish buildings, and it has a pillory and arch dedicated to Jupiter. It may have been partially destroyed when Almansor passed through the area in 987.

The Lower Beira

The Lower Beira lies to the south of the Serra da Estrela, bordering the Alentejo on the south and Spain on the east.

This part of the region was to a large extent cut off from the rest of the country until this century, and many old customs and beliefs, particularly those related to religion, still persist.

On Christmas Eve the villagers in many towns burn huge Yule logs in front of their churches. The idea is to prepare a warm place for Christ, who is about to be born, and to ensure that there will be no poor people cold that night. The log is supposed to be a stolen one, so men go out to get it at night with sacks thrown over their heads and their oxen covered in blankets. When the log is lit, everyone dances round the fire. Where it is not the custom to burn the log publicly, each family burns one at home.

For the past four hundred years, it has been the custom, on the Friday before the beginning of Lent, to have processions of penitents outside the churches. These processions always take place at night, and priests play no part in them. Fifteen unmarried men, barefoot, wearing sheets and with crowns of brambles on their heads, march in the dark, following the Stations of the Cross. They carry the symbols of the martyrdom of Christ – hammer and nails, soldiers' spears, a huge cross; one of them has a whip with which he lashes himself at each Station; another drags a ploughshare tied to his leg, representing the 'burden of their sins'; and the one who comes last carries a broom with which he brushes the backs of the others, to signify purification.

There are also many flower festivals during the month of May.

It is customary for the women to make straw or rag dolls to put in the windows of their houses as a protection against thunderstorms.

Covilhã

Covilhã is the eastern gateway to the Serra da Estrela. It is built on steep terraces on the mountainside, and each street has a panoramic view of the plains below and the distant mountains.

Getting there

Covilhã is between Guarda and Castelo Branco on the N18. There are trains from Lisbon, Oporto and Coimbra – or, if you like, you can fly from Lisbon: Covilhã has a small airport which will take planes with up to twenty passengers.

Industry

The town is the centre of the wool industry, but it also relies heavily on local tourism.

History and legend

Covilhã was probably founded by the Romans as a defence against the Lusitanians. However, there is an old legend according to which it was founded by a Count Julião about AD 690. Count Julião had a beautiful daughter called Florinda, who was supposedly to blame for the Moorish occupation of the Iberian Peninsula. In one version of the story, she was seduced by King Rodrigo. Her father, then Governor of Ceuta in North Africa, brought the Moors into Portugal and Spain to help him to avenge the affront to his daughter. In another version, the Count called in the Moors to help him fight King Rodrigo because Rodrigo had overthrown his brother-in-law, Visigoth King Witiza.

Pero de Covilhã

Covilhã was the birthplace of Pero de Covilhã, one of the most adventurous pioneers in the Age of Discoveries and one of the most curious figures of his time.

On 7 May 1487 Pero de Covilhã set off overland, accompanied by one Afonso Paiva, on a mission for the King of Portugal. The main purpose of the journey was to find out if a water-route to India was possible. But the Portuguese were anxious to keep this intention secret, especially from the Spaniards, so they pretended that their sole aim was to find the fabled land of Prester John.

They took off for India overland by way of Italy, Rhodes and Egypt. In Cairo they separated: Afonso Paiva headed for Ethiopia to look for Prester John, and Pero de Covilhã went to Calcutta, Goa and Ormuz. When he returned to Cairo he found that Afonso Paiva was dead, but two emissaries from the King of Portugal were waiting for him. One was to return to Portugal with all the information Pero de Covilhã had collected about trade and the water-route to India, and the other was to accompany him to look for Prester John.

The companion went only part way before returning to Portugal, but Pero de Covilhã continued. He visited Mecca, Medina and Mount Sinai, and his final stop was Abyssinia, where he was received by the Negus and took part in the wars of succession. He was made governor of a province, married a native woman and had many children.

At the beginning of the sixteenth century, a Portuguese ambassador on his way to India found Pero de Covilhã at the court of the Negus, wielding much power. The ambassador tried to persuade him to return to Portugal, but he preferred to stay where he was. He is said to have lived to a great old age.

What to see   You get wonderful views of the mountains from Covilhã. However, there is not a lot to be seen in the town itself. The Romanesque chapel of **São Martinho e Calvário**, in the lower town, is worth a visit, and the Manueline windows carved in stone in the old walls of the city are interesting. The large central square (which has a statue of Pero de Covilhã) is quite attractive, but unfortunately the town fathers tore down the historic old Jewish quarter to enlarge it.

Where   **Pensão Solneve**, Rua Visconde da Coriscada 126. Tel. (075)
to stay   23001/2. A three star pension in the centre of Covilhã. It has an excel-
Inexpensive   lent restaurant that specializes in regional cooking. During the summer it sponsors tours for visitors.

Residencial Santa Eufémia, Sítio da Palmatória. Tel. (075) 26081/2. A new hotel with clean, comfortable rooms. It has a bar, breakfast room, TV and central heating.

Residência Montalto, Praça da Município 1. Tel. (075) 25091. A small four star inn in the main square. It has a bar.

Pensão Restaurante Café Regional, Rua das Flores 4–5. Tel. (075) 22596. Very good for a modest pension. It has seventeen rooms, four with bath, serves good regional food, and is conveniently located in the centre.

Estalagem o Pastor, Penhas da Saúde. Tel. (075) 22810. A four star inn on the mountain, with ten rooms.

Manor houses   **Casa de Cima**, Castelo Novo, 6230 Fundão. Tel. (075) 57309. A
Inexpensive   large stone block house at Castelo Novo, near Covilhã. It offers three double bedrooms, several living rooms and a garden.

Where to eat   There are lots of restaurants in Covilhã, and you should have no difficulty in finding somewhere reasonable to eat.

Where to drink   The **Taverna del Rei** in Rua Vasco da Gama, not far from the

Residencial Santa Eufémia, is a nice pub.

What to eat Specialities of Covilhã include *panela do forno* (rice with sausage, and pig's ears and trotters) and *feijoada à Serrana* (many different types of meat and sausages cooked with white beans).

What to drink Among red wines, it is worth trying Cova da Beira and (if you can get it) red Fundão Reserve '81. White Covilhã and Vila Nova de Tazem are good white wines.

The Tourist Office is in the Praça do Município. Tel. (075) 22170/51. There are also information posts in the mountains.

Belmonte Belmonte sits on a high hill half-way between Covilhã and Guarda. It is dominated by its medieval castle and a huge granite cross.

Industry The town has a flourishing textile and clothing industry.

History and Belmonte was the birthplace of Pedro Álvares Cabral, who discov-
what to see ered Brazil in 1500, and there is a statue of him in the square. He was baptized in the Romanesque São Tiago Church that stands on the hill by the castle, and the tombs of the Cabral family are in a nearby chapel. The ornate Parish Church is worth a visit.

The Romans occupied Belmonte for more than four hundred years, and there are many Roman remains. The most noteworthy of these is the Centum Cellas, which stands in an open field 1.5 km north of Belmonte. It is a three-storey Roman building constructed of granite blocks, with large windows and doors – no one has discovered what the Romans used it for.

Belmonte is also the home of nearly a hundred families of *Marranos* (Hidden Jews), who are officially Catholics and are baptized, marry and bury their dead in the Catholic church, but carry on their old Jewish customs in secret.

Where **Hotel Belsol**, Estrada Nacional N18. Tel. (075) 91345/91322. A
to stay modern, comfortable, two star hotel on a hill on the highway leading
Inexpensive into Belmonte. It has a nice panelled bar with TV, and a large restaurant that serves regional dishes.

Pensão Restaurante Chavas da Beira, Trigais. Tel. (075) 45129. A three star pension with a good restaurant and a swimming pool, 7 km from Belmonte.

Manor houses **Sortelha**, 12 km east of Belmonte off the N345–1, is a forgotten
Inexpensive medieval village surrounded by walls and thick shrubs. Four typical granite block houses have been modernized for tourists while keeping their traditional structure and characteristics.

Casa do Cruzeiro and **Casa do Vento Que Soa**, Sortelha, 6320 Sabugal. Tel. (071) 68182.

Casa do Palheiro, Sortelha, 6320 Sabugal. Tel. (071) 68182.

Casa Árabe, Sortelha, 6320 Sabugal. Tel. (071) 68129 or (01) 2690149/2432179.

Casa do Pátio, Solar da Nossa Senhora da Conceição, Charters. Tel. (071) 68113. A typical granite block rural house which is in the grounds of the manor house. It has a double bedroom with bath, a living room with a sofa bed and a small kitchen.

Where to eat

The **Hotel Belsol** and the **Pensão Restaurante Chaves da Beira** both have good restaurants.

The Tourist Office is at the Castle. Tel. (075) 91101.

Castelo Branco

Castelo Branco, the capital and geographic centre of the Lower Beira, is spread out on a plain surrounded by mountains. It is an ancient city that dates from the time of the Romans, who called it Albi

History

Castrum. It was conquered from the Moors by Portugal's first king, Dom Afonso Henriques, and in 1165 it was given to the Order of the Knights Templar, who built their castle on top of its highest hill. Because of its exposed position, Castelo Branco was often attacked and sacked. During Portugal's War of Succession, its walls were torn down and the Santa Maria do Castelo Church was set on fire. In 1807 Napoleon's forces under Junot came in and occupied it; the next year it was 'liberated' by the English, who sacked it. In spite of these disasters, Castelo Branco still has some interesting buildings.

What to see

The elegant **Belver Castle** was built in 1390 by the order of the Knights of the Hospital of St John of Jerusalem. The fourteenth-century hermitage of **Nossa Senhora de Mércoles** has a magnificent Romano-Gothic portal. The **São Miguel Church** was built in the thirteenth and fourteenth centuries.

The **gardens of the Bishop's Palace**, laid out in 1725 by João V, are charming. An interesting feature is a staircase bordered by the statues of kings – the statues of the kings of Portugal being twice as big as those of the Spanish kings, Philip I and Philip II (they occupied Portugal between 1580 and 1640 – and were not very popular). Another staircase has saints. There are ornately decorated stone pools.

The **Francisco Tavares Proença Júnior Museum**, in the Bishop's Palace, has a collection of primitive Portuguese paintings, portraits of bishops, and English prints from the Peninsular War. There too is the tombstone of a young Englishman, apparently killed in that war. The Centre for Regional Industries is part of the museum.

Crafts

The silk-embroidered bedspreads of Castelo Branco are unique, embroidered with millions of stitches in many colours and patterns. They have been made by the women of the region since the eighth century. Some of the bedspreads are made by women in their homes, but most are now made in the Centre for Regional Industries in the Francisco Tavares Museum. They can be bought, or made to order, there. Needless to say, they are very expensive.

Where to stay

Inexpensive

Pensão Caravela, Rua do Saibreiro 24. Tel. (072) 23940. A three star pension with twenty-four rooms, ten with bath, and a bar.

Pensão Arraiana, Avenida 1° Maio 18. Tel. (072) 21634/7. A three star pension with eighteen rooms with bath and TV, bar and money exchange.

Camp site

Parque de Campismo de Castelo Branco, N18, Castelo Branco. Tel. (072) 21615.

Where to eat	**Califa**, Rua Oadetes de Toledo 10. Tel. (072) 24246. A large, well-appointed restaurant with a long and varied menu.
	O Piscina, a large, elegant restaurant in the town castle. Good food, and a swimming pool. Tel. (072) 25105.
What to eat	The specialities of Castelo Branco include *maranhos* (stuffed sheep's stomach), turkey liver and blood stew, rabbit with a special regional sauce, plums stuffed with walnuts, chestnut jam, *papos de anjo* (a dessert made of eggs and syrup with cinnamon and lemon).
	The Tourist Office is in the Alameda da Liberdade, tel. (072) 21002.
Alpedrinha	Alpedrinha lies 58 km north of Castelo Branco on the N18. It is a very old town, with splendid houses.
Where to stay	**Estalagem São Jorge**, in the main street. Tel. (075) 57154/57354.
Inexpensive	A four star inn. It has fifteen rooms with bath, a bar, and restaurant.
Manor house	**Casa do Barreiro**, Largo das Escolas, Alpedrinha. Tel. (075)
Inexpensive	57120. A large, turn-of-the-century manor set in an estate. It offers five rooms furnished with authentic antiques.
Fundão	Fundão is 5 km north of Alpedrinha on the N18. In the seventeenth and eighteenth centuries it was the residence of many noble families, and an important commercial centre.
What to see	Fundão has some interesting churches. The eighteenth-century Parish Church, the Misericórdia Church and the chapels of Santo António and Santa da Luz are all worth seeing.
Festival	On 15–16 September the *Romaria da Santa Luzia e Santa Eufémia*, a pilgrimage to the chapels of Santa Luzia and Santa Eufémia, takes place in the nearby town of Castelejo. There are processions and folk songs and dances.
Where to stay	**Estalagem da Neve**, Rua de São Sebastião. Tel. (075) 52215. A lovely four star inn set in a garden. It has a good restaurant with local cooking, and in the summer the tables are set under the trees. It also has a bar, a swimming pool and a car park.
Inexpensive	
	Hotel do Fundão, Rua Vasco da Gama. Tel. (075) 52051/2. A three star hotel with forty double rooms with bath, telephone and piped music and ten suites with TV and bar.
	Pensão Tarouca, Rua 25 de Abril 41. Tel. (075) 52168. A three star pension with twenty-two rooms, six with bath, and a bar.
Where to eat	The **Estalagem da Neve** has the best restaurant. Alternatively, you could try the **Pensão Central Amaral**, Rua José da Cunha Taborda 57, tel. (075) 52168.
	Tourist Office, Avenida da Liberdade. Tel. (075) 52770.
Idanha-a-Nova	Idanha-a-Nova is 31 km north-east of Castelo Branco on route N233–N353, on a slope overlooking rich grain fields. There are the ruins of a castle built by the Templars. Also interesting is the shrine of Nossa Senhora do Almoitão, to which there is an important pilgrimage (with lots of singing and dancing to ancient songs) on 24 April. Bull fights are very popular.
Idanha-a-Velha	Idanha-a-Velha is 47 km north-east of Castelo Branco on route

N233–N239–N332. It was originally a Celtic city. Then the Romans turned it into one of the biggest and most opulent of the Lusitanian cities, and called it Egitania. It was sacked and burned by the Swabians in 420 and rebuilt by the Visigoths in 534. When the Moors took it they gave it the name of Idanha. It was said to be a city of bad luck: after its bishopric was moved to Braga, it was attacked by a plague of ants, which lasted for a hundred years, during which most of the population moved away from Idanha-a-Velha (Old Idanha) to Idanha-a-Nova (New Idanha) or to Monsanto. There is an ancient Palaeo-Christian parish church containing many Roman inscriptions. It was built on an earlier Visigoth place of worship.

Monsanto

Monsanto, about 15 km from Idanha-a-Velha on the N239, is a strange, ancient village built among enormous boulders on a very high, steep hill. On the top of the hill there is a square fortress, rebuilt by King Dinis, and the ruins of a Visigoth fortress. The spaces between the boulders have been turned into houses and shops. Monsanto began as a Lusitanian hill town and was then occupied by the Romans, followed by the Templars.

Festival

On 3 May each year there is the festival known as the *Festa das Cruzes* or *Festa do Castelo*, held to commemorate a legendary siege that the inhabitants were able to withstand by subterfuge: they fattened a calf with the last of their grain and threw it over the parapet to convince their attackers that they had abundant food, and would be able to hold out. The attackers were fooled and withdrew. During the festival the women of Monsanto go up to the ruins of the castle, banging ancient drums and beating timbrels, and throw down from the walls a 'calf' made of flowers. The oldest of the women sing and dance with *marafonas* – dolls they believe give protection against thunderstorms.

Penamacor

Penamacor is 46 km north of Castelo Branco on the N233, on a high hill overlooking a barren plain. Within the walls of a very large castle there is a small village of ancient granite houses.

Segura

Segura is on the Spanish frontier, 58 km east of Castelo Branco on route N233–N240. It was through Segura that Junot's French forces invaded Portugal in 1807. There is a Roman bridge, and the town has a Roman gateway in what were the fortified walls. The Misericórdia Church is sixteenth-century Manueline.

Sertã

Sertã is west of Castelo Branco on the N233–N241. Sertã was a well-fortified Lusitanian town. Legend has it that in a battle with the Romans, a Lusitanian noble was killed. His wife then threatened the Romans with a frying pan (*sertã*) of hot oil and forced them to retreat. Sertã is famous for its *aguardente*.

Sertã has a medieval castle, and a pillory. Also worth seeing are the fourteenth-century Parish Church and the sixteenth-century Misericórdia Church.

Where to stay
Inexpensive

Pensão Residência Cristina, Rua Cândido dos Reis 32. Tel. (074) 61225. A three star pension with thirteen rooms with bath.

The Coastal Beira

The Coastal Beira stretches down the Atlantic coast from the Douro region to Estremadura. It is cut in two by the main Lisbon–Oporto road and railway line.

Aveiro

Aveiro, 56 km south of Oporto by the A1–N16, is near the Atlantic, on the estuary of the River Vouga. It is called the Venice of Portugal (the people of Aveiro, however, prefer to call Venice the Aveiro of Italy), because it sits on the vast Ria de Aveiro salt-water lagoon, and is crossed by canals. One canal down the middle is lined with colourful houses and crossed by charming bridges.

History

The first mention of Aveiro was made in a will left by the Countess Mumadona of Guimarães in 959. In the fourteenth century, after the Moors were driven out of the region, King Fernando gave Aveiro to his bride Leonor. It was a popular spot with Portuguese royalty. Pedro, the son of King João I, lived in Aveiro and built walls for the city. In 1485 King João II gave the town to his sister Dona Joana, known for her saintliness, who had entered the convent of Jesus there. However, in 1759 the last Duke of Aveiro became embroiled in a plot to assassinate King José. The king's Prime Minister, the Marquês de Pombal, had the duke executed and all of his property confiscated. In 1828 some of the nobility took the side of the liberal King Pedro IV in the War of Succession between Pedro and his absolutist brother Miguel – and got their heads chopped off and paraded around on poles by the supporters of Miguel. This has not been forgotten or forgiven even to the present day.

Until the sixteenth century Aveiro was an important port, thriving on trade in metals, salted fish (especially cod, which was brought from Newfoundland) and tiles. However, a terrible storm in 1575 closed the entrance to the estuary with vast sand dunes, so that ships could no longer enter. The town declined until 1808, when, after many years of construction work in which most of the stones from the old city walls were used, a canal, the Barra Nova, was cut through to drain the marshes, and an opening to the ocean was completed at Praia de Barra. This work was promoted by the most famous citizen of Aveiro, José Estevão Coelho de Magalhães, a great liberal and orator, who was also instrumental in bringing the railway to the town. In the years that followed Aveiro won back much of its prosperity. Later, though, it suffered new periods of recession, and many of its people emigrated to Brazil, Africa, North America and northern Europe.

Aveiro today

Today Aveiro has many new industries, but the traditional ones of fishing, salt-making, seaweed-gathering and tile-making still exist. The Vista Alegre porcelain factory, which is famous for its porcelain, is just to the south. Aveiro has also become an important centre for tourism: with its beautiful location, interesting buildings and good hotels and restaurants, it attracts many visitors.

What to see

Aveiro has so many Baroque buildings that it is often referred to as 'the Baroque city'. In Aveiro and all the other towns on the lagoon many of the houses are faced with tiles – an eminently practical covering in the very humid conditions. Some of the tiles are also very beautiful. The façades of many of the tiled houses are in *art nouveau* style.

The **Statue of José Estevão** in the centre of the town is the work of the sculptor Simões de Almeida. It was erected in 1892, paid for by public subscription among the people of Aveiro.

The eighteenth-century **Palace** has an elegant tower.

The **Misericórdia Church** was built in the early seventeenth century, but its main chapel is of a later date. It has an elegant façade and portal, and the interior is covered with glazed tiles.

The **Cathedral** has a Baroque portal. Inside there is a Renaissance bas-relief in wood depicting the Pentecost; a Renaissance panel depicting the Visitation; and a very early painted wooden triptych.

The **Carmelite Church** is Baroque. It has interesting seventeenth-century panels of figurative tiles.

The twin Churches of Santo António and São Francisco are interesting. The **Santo António Church** has a Baroque sacristy with gilt carvings and panels of figurative tiles. The **São Francisco Church** has frescoes on the ceiling.

The **Senhor das Barrocas Chapel** was built between 1707 and 1722, in an octagonal plan. The modern paintings inside were subscribed by devout local fishermen.

The **Aveiro Museum** is in the former Convent of Jesus, built in the fifteenth century but its style is mainly Baroque because of later remodelling. The museum contains the chapel and shrines of the convent, including the tomb of the saintly Princess Joana, daughter of King Afonso V and sister of King João II, who entered the convent as a nun after refusing marriage with various kings. She died in the convent in 1490. Princess Joana's tomb is Baroque, covered with polychrome marble and statues of angels, four of which serve as pedestals. The museum also has a number of seventeenth-century paintings of Princess Joana, as well as many other paintings, polychrome wooden statues, and other valuable objects.

Crafts

Ceramics, earthenware, tiles, fishing nets and painted fishing boats are made in Aveiro.

Festivals

The *Procissão dos Passos* takes place on the third Sunday of Lent. The *Feira de Marco* is held in March and April, and the *Festa da Ria* in the month of August.

Where to stay

Inexpensive

Hotel Imperial, Rua Dr Nascimento Leitão. Tel. (034) 22141. A three star hotel with 107 rooms with bath. It has a restaurant, three bars and money exchange.

Hotel Afonso V, Rua Dr Manuel das Neves 65. Tel. (034) 25191/2/

193

3. A three star hotel with eighty rooms with bath and TV, a pub, disco and one of the best restaurants in the city.

Hotel Arcada, Rua Viana do Castelo 4. Tel. (034) 23001/21885. A charming old hotel on the Central Canal with fifty-four rooms, forty-eight with bath, TV, bar and money exchange.

Pensão Residência Pomba Branca, Rua Luis Gomes de Carvalho 23. Tel. (034) 22529. A four star pension with nineteen rooms with bath and TV, a bar, money exchange and gardens.

Where to eat   **Cozinha do Rei**, in the Hotel Afonso V (see above). Tel. (034) 26802. The best in the town – beautifully decorated with fountains and green plants. Good fish and seafood.

Taverna Dom Carlos, Rua Dr Nascimento Leitão 46–48. Tel. (034) 22061. The decor is oak beams, wine bottles and wine bottling machinery. Good grilled meats and seafood. *Fado* music after 10.30 p.m. some nights.

Restaurante João Capela, Quinta do Picado. Tel. (034) 94450. Serves Portuguese specialities.

Cozinha Velha, Travessa da Rua Direita 7. Tel. (034) 20392. Laid out as a typical Portuguese kitchen with blue and white tiles and an open hearth, it serves regional dishes.

The Hotel Imperial (see page 193) also has a good restaurant.

What to eat   Try *mexilhões à moda de Aveiro* (mussels), *caldeirada de enguias* (eel stew), *bacalhau à zé do pipo* (a cod dish).

The Tourist Office is on the Praça da República. Tel. (034) 23680.

Ria de Aveiro   The Ria de Aveiro is a salt-water lagoon 45 km long, about 6,000 hectares in area, and roughly triangular in shape. The River Vouga empties into it. Except at the man-made opening at Praia de Barra, the lagoon is totally cut off from the Atlantic by wide sand dunes, which are criss-crossed by canals. Houses on the shores of the lagoon are faced with tiles. Many on the Costa Nova side of the Ria are painted in red and white, green and white, or blue and white stripes.

The whole region of the lagoon is covered with salt pans, crossed by bridges on stilts. In the late summer you can see thousands of pyramids of white salt standing everywhere. In the winter they are covered with straw for protection. At the south end of the dunes there is the São Jacinto Natural Reserve in the dunes and pine forest with elevated walks and observation towers for visitors to observe the birds and animals.

Boats   The *moliceiro* boats, used for dredging seaweed, are the most beautiful boats on the lagoon. They are Mesopotamian-style boats, 10 to 15 m long, with high, pointed prows that curl up out of the water. They are painted bright colours, and decorated with sea motifs, flowers and drawings of people. Each of the boats has a crew of two men, who sleep on board. They use long rakes to gather seaweed from the bottom of the lagoon. There are *moliceiro* races at Aveiro during the Festa da Ria in the last part of August or early September, and a *moliceiro* regatta in Torreira, a fishing village in the north.

The *mercantel* boats are used for transporting cargo, such as salt or fish. They are more conservatively painted and their prows are not so extravagantly curved.

The *bateiras*, which are fishing boats, have high prows and sterns and are 8 or 9 m long. They have sails, oars, and awnings for shelter. Near Vagueira, you can see the fishermen and their families launching these boats into the wild Atlantic waves to trawl fish, and pulling them back with the help of oxen.

The *caçadeiras*, also fishing boats, have flat prows, sails and oars.

The *erveiras* are only 5 m long and are painted black.

Water sports The lagoon is a good place for water sports of all kinds – surfing, fishing, water-skiing, boating. Unfortunately, however, around Aveiro the water can be polluted.

Tours A boat tour of the Ria leaves Aveiro daily at 10 a.m. from mid-June to mid-September. The tours include visits to the salt pans; to the port at Gafanha, where cod is dried; to the zone of the *moliceiro* boats, to see them gathering seaweed; and to the beaches on the lagoon at Torreira and Areinho. Lunch in the Pousada da Ria, and return at sunset.

There are also organized tours by road to the salt pans, the beaches, the Vista Alegre ceramic factory and museum, various little towns, grottoes and monuments in the region, the Buçaco mountains and palace, and the spas of Luso and Cúria.

For all these tours, inquire at the Tourist Office, Praça da República. Tel. (034) 23680.

Camp site **Parque de Campismo da Orbitur São Jacinto**, São Jacinto. Tel. (034) 48284.

Pousada **Pousada da Ria**, 3800 Aveiro. Tel. (034) 48332, telex 37061. A
Medium price pousada on a spit of land on the lagoon, 40 km north of Aveiro. It is a modern building with balconies over the lagoon where you can watch the colourful Ria boats go by and the birds circling over the water. There is a restaurant, and a swimming pool set in lawns.

Estalagem Riabela, Torreira. Tel. (034) 48137. A modern inn at the water's edge with thirty-five rooms with bath, a restaurant, bar, swimming pool and tennis courts.

Ílhavo Ílhavo is a small town to the south of Aveiro, on the way to Vista Alegre. It is said to have been founded by the Phoenicians. It has a museum showing regional costumes, Vista Alegre porcelain and objects related to the sea.

Where to stay **Albergaria Arimar**, Avenida Mário Sacramento. Tel. (034)
Inexpensive 25131. A four star inn with a good restaurant.
Vista
Alegre Vista Alegre is about 5 km south of Aveiro on a stretch of the lagoon. The famous Vista Alegre porcelain factory was founded in 1824 by José Ferreira Pinto Basto, and remains in the same family today. It produces lovely ornaments and table services which are sought after all over the world. It has a shop and museum with a collection containing almost all the patterns produced since the factory

began. Open afternoons except weekends and public holidays.

Vagos

Vagos is a small town south of Vista Alegre on the lagoon. There are many strange legends about its beginnings. It has a military fort nearly swallowed by the dunes, and traces of old shrines. The present shrine of Nossa Senhora de Vagos is in a pine wood where many pilgrims come on the feast of the Holy Spirit.

Mira

Mira is 16 km south of Vagos on the lagoon, on land claimed from the sea over the centuries. It may have been founded by the Romans. The houses in the town are of adobe, and some in the countryside nearby are made of sun-dried clay reinforced with straw. It got its name from the Moors, who called it *Emir*.

The Parish Church was built in 1690. It has carvings, glazed tiles and a painted ceiling.

Praia de Mira

Praia de Mira is on the lagoon west of Mira, near the sea. It still has some houses built on stilts in the water. The local people fish by taking nets far out from the shore and then pulling them in from the bank.

The highlands at the foot of the mountains that surround the lagoon have many rivers, lakes and thick forests, although the great pine forests that existed in the eighteenth century were destroyed during the French invasion in 1807. Many trees are planted to hold back the encroaching sand dunes. There are many old watermills. The people raise cattle and grow corn, potatoes, beans and grapevines.

As you go up into the mountains towards the spas of Cúria, Luso and Buçaco, you travel through a land of wine and water. Some of the best white wine in the country, Pocarica, is produced here, as well as the fine Bairrada reds. There are also champagne-type wines. The town of Mealhada is the centre of the sparkling white wine district.

Cúria

Cúria is a spa with all kinds of recreational facilities: tennis courts, swimming pools, a lake for boating, tea-houses, cinemas, beautiful parks and gardens. It is south of Aveiro between Lisbon and Oporto.

Where to stay, and eat Medium price

Palace Hotel, Cúria. Tel. (031) 52131. A three star hotel that was once the most elegant in the country. It has 122 rooms, 117 with bath. It has a bar, restaurant, nightclub, swimming pool and tennis courts.

Hotel das Termas, Parque da Cúria. Tel. (031) 52185/6/7, telex SOCURIA-CURIA. A three star hotel with thirty-five rooms with baths and twelve without. It has a swimming pool, a bar, and a good restaurant with a marvellous view.

Inexpensive

Pensão Imperial, Cúria. Tel. (031) 53235. A three star pension with twenty-five rooms, thirteen with bath, a bar and restaurant.

There are many other hotels, pensions and private rooms – the spa has accommodation for two thousand guests.

Luso

Luso is a spa on the side of a mountain, on the N234, 7 km off the N1 between Lisbon and Oporto. The mountain road is terribly crowded with lorries, so you will have to resign yourself to going very slowly.

Luso is a very old town, dating back to the twelfth century. The installation of the spa was begun in 1854.

The spa

The spa has thermal waters that gush from Saint John's Spring in the centre of the town. The water at spring source is at a temperature of 27°C/80°F, and is recommended for all sorts of diseases. A gym, therapy room, physiotherapists and doctors are available.

There are also various swimming pools and pleasant paths for walking or jogging, and you can row on the lake. In addition the town offers several cinemas and night clubs.

Where to stay Inexpensive

Grande Hotel das Termas do Luso, Rua dos Banhos, Luso, 3050 Mealhada. Tel. (031) 93450/1/2/3. A three star hotel with 157 rooms, all with bath. The hotel has a bar, a night club, a swimming pool, tennis courts, ping-pong and billiards.

Estalagem do Luso, Rua Dr Lúcio Pais Abranches, Luso, 3050 Mealhada. Tel. (031) 93114. A four star inn with seven rooms with bath. It has a bar and a children's playground.

Pensão Alegre, Rua Emídio Navarro, Luso, 3050 Mealhada. Tel. (031) 93251. A three star pension with twenty rooms, eleven of them with bath.

Pensão Restaurante Imperial, Rua Emídio Navarro, Luso, 3050 Mealhada. Tel. (031) 93171. A three star pension with eighteen rooms, thirteen of them with bath.

Manor house Inexpensive

Vila Duparchy, Estrada Nacional 234. Tel. (031) 93120. A large nineteenth-century house on a hill above the town, it has six double rooms with bath, three living rooms, a dining room, and pool.

Where to eat

Pensão Alegre and **Pensão Restaurante Imperial** have three star restaurants.

What to eat

Try roast suckling pig.

Buçaco

The beautiful town of Buçaco is in the forest preserve on the northwest slopes of the Buçaco mountains, in the wine region of Bairrada. It is on the N235, 45 km south-east of Aveiro and 100 km from Oporto. The roads are full of both bends and lorries, so be patient.

History

In the seventeenth century this place was almost inaccessible virgin forest. The Superior of the Order of the Barefoot Carmelites, who was looking for a place where his monks could pray and meditate far from the temptations of civilization, bought a piece of land here. And in 1629 six monks came and built a monastery, using the stones, cork and wood they found around them. The buildings were very simple, but the monks decorated the façades with designs in pebbles of different colours. They surrounded all of their land with a high wall, to which there was only one door, guarded by a monk. The wall had designs of skulls and bones, made of black and white stones.

The monks also planted more trees – native maple, laurel and oak, and, later, Mexican cypresses, some of which are still standing.

The monks built retreats for themselves, deep in the woods, where they often stayed alone for months on end. A chronicle of the Barefoot Carmelites tells of a hermit who taught a magpie to speak, but then decided that he had sinned by breaking the vow of silence. He sent the magpie away, and told him never to return. There are many magpies in the valley below, but it is said that none ever come up the mountain.

The monks also built fountains, crosses, and Stations of the Cross. Later, chapels were built at the Stations.

The friars were protected from the presence of women by a Papal Bull that threatened with excommunication any woman who entered there. In 1693, Catherine of Bragança, sister of the King of Portugal and widow of King Charles II of England, was given permission to visit the monastery, and the monks cut a new gate in the wall for her. As she was coming up the mountain, a terrible storm blew up and frightened her away. The monks walled up the gate, since then known as the Queen's Door. It was not until 1852 that a woman, Queen Maria II, finally entered the precincts of the monastery.

In 1810, after the third invasion of Portugal by Napoleon's troops under Masséna, Wellington and his 50,000 English and Portuguese troops stayed at the monastery. For a week Wellington slept by night in one of the cells, and by day, from under a tree on the mountain, he watched Masséna's troops as they came up the Mondego valley. The French were heavily defeated at the battle of Buçaco, losing 4,500 men. They did go on to capture Coimbra, but weakened and demoralized after Buçaco, it was the beginning of the end for them.

The English soldiers did not behave well during their stay: it is reported that they rioted, pillaged the monastery, and savagely attacked the prior.

In 1834 all religious orders in Portugal were suppressed, and their buildings and goods put up for sale. However, no one bought the Buçaco monastery, and twenty-four monks were allowed to return and live out their lives there.

At the end of the nineteenth century King Carlos commissioned Luigi Manini, an Italian scene-painter at the São Carlos Opera House in Lisbon, to design a summer palace to be built at Buçaco. Sadly, the refectory, the infirmary and the library of the monastery were all knocked down to make room for this building. Only the pebble-fronted church, some chapels in the woods, a small cloister and a few cells remain.

The monastery was replaced by a Manueline extravaganza of a palace, with turrets, towers, twelve-arched galleries, rotundas with pointed arches, an enormous marble stairway with glazed tiles depicting the battles with the French, public rooms the size of playing fields, and walls painted with landscapes.

In the end King Carlos never stayed in this palace. His son King Manuel stayed there in 1910 – it is said with his mistress – before going into exile in England. After that, the Palace became the Palace Hotel.

What to see   The wall around the 250 acres of forest now has nine gates – some for cars and some for pedestrians. The Queen's Door, which the monks opened in the wall to allow Queen Catherine to enter, is still there. The Victory Chapel, commemorating the victory over the French at the battle of Buçaco, is just outside it. Inside the wall you can see the Monastery Church, with its pebblework façade, and the cell in the monastery where Wellington slept before the battle. Look too at the Valley of the Ferns; the view from the Cruz Alta; the obelisk commemorating the battle; the Sula Windmill, where the English and Portuguese fought the French; the Military Museum, just outside the walls; the Fria Fountain; the São Silvestre Spring and waterfall; and the chapels in the woods.

Where to stay, and eat Expensive

The **Palace Hotel**, Buçaco, 3050 Mealhada. Tel. (031) 93101. A five star luxury hotel – one of the finest in Europe. As well as the suite that was occupied by King Manuel, it has eighty splendid rooms, some of them with adjoining terraces that overlook the woods. The hotel was totally refurbished in 1989. The service is superb.

The price for all this luxury is between 18,000 esc. and 22,500 esc. for a double room with breakfast. If you really want to splurge, for 62,000 esc. you can spend the night in the king's suite, with its large, ornate living room, dressing room, bedroom and bath.

The dining room of the Palace is beautifully furnished, with turn-of-the-century décor. The menu includes pheasant, lobster puffs, and all of the typical dishes of the region. The hotel also has a wine cellar with thousands of old wines. And again, the service is excellent.

Mealhada is a nearby town, with wine cellars and many hotels and restaurants.

Coimbra

Coimbra is a very old town on the River Mondego, just off the N1, halfway between Lisbon and Oporto. Unfortunately, the old town has been very largely spoilt by new buildings and factories which have been built without any thought for the ancient heritage of the town.

History

The city of Coimbra was the new town that grew out of the ancient Roman city of Conimbriga, after Conimbriga had moved nearer to the sea. Evidence of those times can be seen in the old Roman bridge over the Mondego, a Roman road, two towers and parts of a wall. The Romans called the town Aeminium. It was overrun by Germanic tribes and later by the Moors, and it became the most important centre of Mozarabic culture in Portugal. After the Christian reconquest in 1064, Coimbra grew into an important river port. The River Mondego has always been important in the lives of the people. It has been written about, sung about, and romanced about, but it has also brought floods and destruction.

After the University was founded in 1290 – at about the same time as Oxford and Cambridge – it became the heart and life of the city. It originated with the teaching by the monks in the Santa Cruz Monastery. It has produced many great men, including prime ministers, writers and judges.

The students of the University maintain many ancient traditions. Since the Middle Ages they have lived in *repúblicas* (republics) – a dozen students from the same region living in furnished lodgings and sharing expenses. Traditionally they wear long, black capes torn at the bottom: each tear is supposed to represent a conquest in love. Their faculty ribbons are pinned to their capes – blue for Arts, red for Law and yellow for Medicine – and at the end of each academic year they burn their ribbons in a ceremony called the *Queima das Fitas* (Burning the Ribbons). They also have a tradition of *fado* singing. The Coimbra *fado* is very different from the Lisbon *fado*, in feeling and in intellectual content. It is sung only by men and on special occasions such as the university graduation ceremonies when there is a *serenata* on the steps of the Old Cathedral.

Coimbra has played a large role in the history of Portugal. At one time it was capital of the country. Kings lived here, and Portugal's first two kings are buried here. The saintly Queen Isabel, wife of King Dinis, spent her last days here, in the Santa Clara Convent. King João I was crowned king here in 1385. Coimbra artists produced some of the country's finest Gothic and Renaissance work; and Camões, Portugal's greatest poet, lived here for a time.

What to see

Coimbra is divided into three districts: The *Alta* (Upper Town), the original site of the Iron Age *castro* where the university and many old palaces and churches are located; the *Baixa* (Lower Town), the maze of twisted streets and avenues near the river; and the Santa Clara, across the bridge on the west side of the river.

Alta

The **University** is on a hill high above the city. The old parts are very beautiful, but unfortunately some of the historic buildings were destroyed to make way for the new University City. You go into the courtyard around which the main buildings are grouped through the *Porta Férrea* (Iron Gate), where the ancient initiation ceremonies for new students take place. On one side of the square is an eighteenth-century clock tower and in the centre there is a statue of King João III, who donated his royal palace to the university in the sixteenth century. The main halls are up the exterior double staircase. The Sala dos Capelos, where degrees are traditionally awarded, is adorned with portraits of the Kings of Portugal and carpet tiles. It has a beautifully painted seventeenth-century ceiling. The Arms Room contains old arms and standards. From the open portico, there is a splendid view of the city.

The university's Baroque **Joanine Library** was built by King João V between 1717 and 1728. His coat of arms is over the grand entrance and his portrait at the back. The library has three rooms, all richly gilded and with trompe l'oeil ceilings. It is still used by the students.

The **University Chapel** is a mixture of Manueline and Baroque, with many panels of seventeenth-century glazed tiles, and a painted ceiling. The organ is Baroque. The **Museum of Sacred Art**, with gold and silver pieces, vestments, sculpture, paintings and furniture is in the annexe.

The **Machado de Castro Museum** is in the former sixteenth-century Bishop's Palace, near the University. It is one of the finest museums in the country and contains works from all periods between the twelfth and nineteenth centuries. There are many pieces by sculptor Jean de Rouen and his followers of the Coimbra school. Beneath the museum there is a cryptoportico – three levels of vaulted passageways built by the Romans as storerooms for their forum which once stood where the museum now stands. It houses a collection of Roman sculpture and other objects.

The first stone of the **Old Cathedral** was laid in 1162. The Gothic cloister was started in 1218. The Cathedral has been heavily restored, but on the left façade you can see the sixteenth-century door designed by Jean de Rouen. Inside you can see thirteenth- and fourteenth-century Gothic tombs, a large sixteenth-century Flemish retable, and retables of Saint Peter and the Sacrament in Coimbra Renaissance style. Saint Anthony of Padua was ordained priest here.

The **New Cathedral** was begun in the latter part of the sixteenth century. It belonged to the Jesuits until their Order was suppressed. It has many Baroque angels and carved gilt Baroque retables. The high altar is rich in gold, and the transept has silver shrines.

The **Aqueduct of São Sebastião**, near the university, was built in the sixteenth century, on the ruins of a Roman aqueduct.

The **Botanical Gardens**, by the Aqueduct, were laid out in terraces in the eighteenth century by Prime Minister the Marquês de Pombal. They are full of rare and exotic species of trees, flowers and shrubs from all over the world.

Church São João de Almedina beside the Machado de Castro Museum was founded in the twelfth century and used as a chapel for the Bishops. It was reconstructed in the seventeenth and eighteenth centuries.

The **Arco de Almedina**, the main pedestrian entrance to the upper part of the town, dates back to the ninth century, but was rebuilt in the fifteenth century. Above it is the **Torre de Relação**, which was the first Town Hall, and now houses the city's historical archives.

The ninth-century **Anto's Tower** is part of the defence walls of the old city and was home of the nineteenth-century poet Antonio Nobre. It now houses a craft centre.

The **Sup-Ripas Palace** was built in the sixteenth century with part of the old city walls incorporated in it. It has Manueline doors and windows and walls covered with bas-reliefs and busts by Jean de Rouen.

Baixa The **Monastery of the Holy Cross** belonged to the Augustinian Order. It was originally Romanesque, but the present façade is Manueline, with a Baroque porch. It has busts by Jean de Rouen and Nicholas Chaterene. Inside you will see the tombs of Portugal's first two kings, King Afonso Henriques and King Sancho I. The sixteenth-century Renaissance pulpit stands in the centre of the church. The Manueline choir loft has pink and gold choir stalls, and golden carvings showing the voyages of Vasco da Gama. The sacristy has several paintings, one of which is attributed to Grão Vasco.

The **Park of the Holy Cross** was once part of a monastery of the same name. It has monumental staircases, tile benches, an eighteenth-century waterfall and many statues.

The **Church of Saint James** is a Romanesque building dating from the late twelfth century.

The **Church of São Bartolomeu** dates back to the tenth century, and was originally Romanesque. Remodelling in 1756 gave it its present appearance.

Carmo Church and **Graça Church** were once church schools in the sixteenth century. They stand in Rua da Sofia, which means 'Street of Learning'.

Santa Clara

The **Old Convent of Santa Clara**, across the River Mondego from the city, is in ruins today, because of the flooding of the river. It was founded in the thirteenth century, and had as its patron the saintly Queen Isabel, the Aragonese wife of King Dinis. She spent the last years of her life in the convent, and was buried there. The Santa Clara nuns lived in this convent till 1677.

The **New Convent of Santa Clara** is up the hill from the Old Convent. Most of the relics of the church, and its decoration, are devoted to the saintly Queen Isabel. Her tomb was moved there. It has a carved polychrome figure of her in blue and pink, with her two dogs beside her. Around the bottom of the tomb there are small carved polychrome figures of Santa Clara nuns on one side and the Apostles on the other.

The **Quinta das Lágrimas** (House of Tears) is on Rua António Augusto Gonçalves, near the Old Convent of Santa Clara. Inês de Castro, beloved mistress of Pedro I, was murdered here by his enemies. Her body lay in the Old Convent before being transferred to Alcobaça. In the garden you will see a spring that is said to have gushed out of the ground after she was murdered. The water is her tears.

Portugal dos Pequenos (Portugal for Children), near the New Convent of Santa Clara, is a park containing models of all styles of Portuguese houses and all of its famous monuments, in a size to accommodate children. It is definitely worth a visit even if it is a long time since you were a child.

Environs

The **Celas Convent** was founded in 1215 by the daughter of King Sancho I. Each of the Gothic capitals in the cloister is different from all the rest.

The **Church of Santo António dos Olivais** is on the north-east side of the city. This church, rebuilt in the fifteenth century, is all that remains of a friary on this site. It has a profusion of Baroque gold woodwork, and blue and white tiles showing the life of Saint Anthony who taught here before going to Padua, Italy.

Crafts   It is worth looking out for pottery, shawls, high-heeled slippers, copies of fifteenth- to eighteenth-century Coimbra-style faience ceramics, hand embroidery, wrought-iron work, tin ware and basketry.

Festivals   The *Festa da Santa Clara* is celebrated in July, but the most important festivals in Coimbra are the *Festas da Rainha Santa Isabela*, the patron saint of the city, in June. In May the *Queima das Fitas*, when the students burn their college ribbons at the end of the academic year, is attended by thousands of townspeople and tourists.

Where   The following list gives just a small selection from the many hotels
to stay   and pensions in Coimbra.
Medium price   **Hotel Astoria**, Largo da Portagem. Tel. (039) 22055. Built in the 1920s in the shape of a triangle with cupolas, arches, pillars and wrought-iron balconies, this city landmark stands in the square by the old bridge where all the city streets converge. A three star hotel with sixty-four rooms with bath, bar, and restaurant.

Hotel Dom Luis, on the Lisbon highway 2 km from the city centre, Banhos Secos. Tel. (039) 841510 or 813196. A new, three star hotel with 105 rooms and suites, each with bath, telephone, TV, minibar. It has a panoramic bar and restaurant.

Inexpensive   **Hotel Bragança**, Largo das Ameias 10. Tel. (039) 22171/2/3, telex BRAGANZOTEL-COIMBRA. A three star hotel with eighty-three rooms with bath. It has a bar and restaurant.

Pensão Residência Almedina, Avenida Fernão de Magalhâes 203. Tel. (039) 29161/2. A three star pension with twenty-eight rooms with bath. It has a bar.

Pensão Avenida, Emidio Navarro 37. Tel. (039) 22155/6/7. A three star pension with twenty-five rooms, a bar and restaurant.

Manor house   **Casa dos Quintais**, Carvalhais de Cima-Assafarge, 3000
Inexpensive   Coimbra. Tel. (039) 28821. A manor house on a hill overlooking Coimbra. It has room for three couples.

Where to eat   There are also lots of restaurants in Coimbra. Again, the following list is only a small selection.

Alfredo, Avenida João das Regras. Tel. (039) 814669. A restaurant across the river that serves Portuguese cooking.

Piscinas, Piscinas Municipais, Calhabé. Tel. (039) 717013. An air-conditioned restaurant with a varied menu, and a marvellous view.

Trovador, Praça Sé Velha. Tel. (039) 25475. Located in the square by the Old Cathedral, this elegant restaurant serves excellent Portuguese and international dishes. It offers *fado* singing on weekends.

Espelho d'Agua, Parque Dr Manuel Braga. Tel. (039) 20634. A charming restaurant with a glassed-in terrace in the park by the river, it has good food and service. Dinner by candlelight in the evening.

What to eat   Specialities are *lampreia à moda de Coimbra* (lamprey), *perdiz fria* (cold partridge), *pudim de ovos* (a pudding made with eggs).

Tourist Office, Largo da Portagem. Tel. (039) 23886/33028.

Conimbriga

Conimbriga is the largest Roman archaeological site in Portugal. It is 17 km south-south-west of Coimbra on the N1, near the town of Condeixa. The site and museum are open every day except Mondays, Easter Sunday, Christmas Day and New Year's Day.

History

There was a settlement at Conimbriga long before the Roman occupation. A pre-Celtic tribe known as the Conii lived here until the Roman conquest in the second century BC. It was an attractive spot for a Roman settlement, because it was on the main Roman road between Lisbon and Braga. In the third century AD the inhabitants constructed a defensive wall, probably to protect themselves from the invading barbarians. All kinds of materials were incorporated in this wall, including stones with inscriptions, tombstones, and sculptures. But despite the wall, between 464 and 468 the town was captured and razed by the Swabians, and many of the inhabitants were taken as slaves. Conimbriga was later occupied by the Visigoths and became a centre of Christianity, but the Swabian attack caused the people to start moving to the more protected Aeminium (now Coimbra).

What to see

The most imposing buildings date from the end of the second century and the end of the fourth century. The defensive Roman wall 1,500 m long still exists. Outside the wall you can see a great part of the aqueduct, a building and the remains of three houses. Inside the wall, and close to it, you will see a large house with baths, water pipes, fountains, pools, columns, mosaic floors and vaulted passages.

The museum contains objects from the Roman and Visigothic periods. Those from the Iron Age are in the Ethnological Museum in Lisbon. There are funeral stones; altars; bronze figures; mosaics; tools; lamps; pottery; glass; personal jewellery and toilet articles; coins of bronze, silver and gold.

Maps and books about the site are available in the museum where there is also a good restaurant with a verandah overlooking the ruins.

Castles of the Mondego

The Castles of the Mondego were built as a line of defence for Coimbra. They were at the centre of constant battles between the Moors and the Christians. Among those still standing are Montemor, Santa Olaia and Soure.

Montemor-o-Velho

Montemor-o-Velho is on the River Mondego 21 km west of Coimbra on the N111. There has been a settlement on this site for at least 4,000 years. It was founded by the Lusitanians and later occupied by Romans and Moors. The Moors called it Munt Mahur. In the Middle Ages, it became Monte Mayor (Biggest Hill).

The castle

Its castle is one of the biggest and most beautiful in Portugal. An ancient legend says that there are two chests buried there – one containing gold, and the other calamitous plagues. No one has ever had the courage to look for them.

The castle also has a tragic story. Garcia, the adopted son of Abbot

João, Mayor of Montemor, jealous of the Abbot's nephew, Bermudo, went to Moorish Córdoba in Spain and got together an army of Moors to attack Montemor. After a long siege, the defenders cut the throats of their families and then set out to fight to the last man. The Moors were slaughtered by the Christians and, during the battle, the Abbot cut off Garcia's head. According to legend, the defenders of the castle and their families were miraculously restored to life, but for generations the people of Montemor carried a red mark round their throats.

After this, the castle was captured and recaptured many times by Moors and Christians. After the Mondego region was secured by King Fernando Magno of Castile, he gave Montemor to Count Sesnando. The castle was later rebuilt by Afonso of León and Castile.

In the thirteenth century King Afonso II quarrelled with his sisters, and they took refuge in Montemor Castle. Afonso laid siege to them there, but the Pope intervened to stop the dispute, and gave the castle to the Knights Templar. Later it passed back to the Crown, and the royal family continued to quarrel over it for generations. In 1808 it was sacked by the French.

Most of the present castle dates from the fourteenth century. The Chapel of São João, where Abbot João is believed to have said Mass, is in ruins. The Church of Santa Maria da Alcaçova, within the walls, dates originally from the eleventh century, but it has been reconstructed many times, and it is now mostly Manueline. The Santo António is outside the walls.

Soure

Soure is across the River Mondego, 17 km south of Montemor-o-Velho on the N342-1. It is on a fertile plain near the junction of the Arunca and Ancos rivers, which are tributaries of the Vouga. The town shows evidence of Lusitanian and Roman occupation. The castle, of which some walls and the watchtower remain on a hill, was attacked and damaged many times by the Moors. In 1211 it was given to the Santa Cruz of Coimbra Monastery.

What to see

The Parish Church, which dates from 1490, has a fine wooden barrel ceiling. The Chapel of São Mateus dates from the reign of King Afonso Henriques. The Misericórdia Church was built in the seventeenth century.

Figueira da Foz

Figueira da Foz is on the Atlantic, at the mouth of the River Mondego and 48 km west of Coimbra on the N111.

History

The site was inhabited in prehistoric times by the Lusitanians, then by the Romans, and then by the Moors. Throughout its history it has constantly been under attack from the sea. In 1602 it was sacked by English pirates. In 1807, during the Peninsular War, the fort at the entrance to the river was taken by the French. However, it was recaptured by the people of the town with the help of students from Coimbra University. In the following year 10,000 English soldiers under the Duke of Wellington disembarked at Figueira da Foz for a final push against the French.

There are a lot of new industries connected with fishing, salt, cement, glass and shipbuilding, but Figueira's prime claim to fame is as a watering place and tourist centre. It has a beach 500 m wide on the Atlantic (note, however, that the rollers there sometimes make it unsafe for swimming). It offers sailing, swimming pools, golf, tennis, bullfights and discos. There is a wide esplanade along the seafront with many modern hotels, restaurants, and a casino.

What to see
The **Casa do Paço**: a museum in this seventeenth-century mansion houses the largest collection of tiles in Portugal. The **Museu Municipal** contains archaeological artifacts, ceramics, paintings, sculpture, furniture and coins.

The **Santa Catarina Fort** was built in the eighteenth century. There is a sixteenth-century chapel within the fort.

*Where
to stay
Medium price*
Grande Hotel da Figueira, Avenida 25 de Abril. Tel. (033) 22146/7/8, telex GRANDEHOTEL-FIGUEIRA DA FOZ. A four star hotel with ninety-one rooms with bath. It has a restaurant, a bar, TV, and terraces facing the sea.

Inexpensive
Estalagem da Piscina, Rua de Santa Catarina 7. Tel. (033) 22420. A four star inn with twenty rooms with bath. It has a bar and a swimming pool.

Hotel Tamargueira, Marginal do Cabo Mondego. Tel. (033) 22514. A three star hotel on the coastal highway on the way to Cape Mondego. It has sixty-six rooms with bath and TV, a bar, and excellent restaurant.

Camp sites
Figueira da Foz Municipal Camping is well shaded, has electricity, hot showers, a restaurant, a grocer's shop, a swimming pool and facilities for water sports, such as canoeing. It is open all year round. Tel. (033) 23116.

Where to eat
Restaurante Tamargueira, Marginal do Cabo Mondego. Tel. (033) 22514. A restaurant with an esplanade and a marvellous view. It serves regional dishes and grilled food, and specializes in fresh shellfish.

O Pateo, Rua Dr Santos Rocha. Tel. (033) 26657. A regional restaurant with patio in the old part of town above the beach. Good food and *fado* music Saturday nights.

Restaurante Sagres, Avenida 25 de Abril. Tel. (033) 24354. A restaurant and snack bar that serves shellfish.

The Tourist Office is on the Avenida 25 de Abril. Tel. (033) 22610.

Buarcos
Buarcos is a fishing town on the Atlantic, just 3 km north of Figueira da Foz on N109–8. There are long sandy beaches and a camp site, and you can see the sardine fishing boats. A ruined castle stands on the beach.

In the seventeenth century Buarcos was a very rich town. It was, however, always subject to pirate attacks, especially by the English, Dutch and Algerians. The town would close its gates and keep watch all night against the pirates. But this did them little good in 1602, when English pirates invaded and sacked the town. They burned all the government buildings and historical records.

Where to stay
Medium price
Clube Vale do Leão, Vais, Serra da Boa Viagem. Tel. (033) 23001. A luxurious tourist complex on a hill above Buarcos. It has twenty-two apartments and villas furnished with antiques, a pool, piano bar, cinema, disco, health centre, boutique and hairdresser.

Where to eat
Teimoso, Marginal do Cabo Mondego. Tel. (033) 22785. A good seafood restaurant just outside Buarcos, specializing in *caldeirada* (fish stew).

Serra da Lousã
The Serra da Lousã, south-east of Coimbra, is a mountainous region covered with beautiful forests. There are many legends about this rather wild country.

Lousã
Lousã is in a deep valley on the River Arouce. The oldest paper mill in the country is located here – the great-grandfather of the paper factories that are polluting Portugal's rivers today. The town has a castle and a shrine set among dense vegetation. On Trevin Peak, at 1,204 m, you can see where snow and ice used to be taken out and sent to Lisbon for the royal court.

The castle
The castle is surrounded by legend. It is said that in 79 BC, when King Arunce, for whom the river is named, was the Roman King of Conimbriga, fleets of warriors arrived to steal his treasure. He escaped to the forests with his daughter Peralta, and built the castle on its present site. He buried his treasure there, put a magic spell on his daughter and household, and went off to Carthage, intending to get help to redeem Conimbriga. This was the last that was heard of him, but over the centuries treasure hunters have destroyed a great part of the castle in their vain search for his riches.

The castle still has structures dating from the eleventh century, and many more from the fourteenth. There is a massive, square watchtower. The entrance way has two semicircular towers, and there is a thick wall around the inside courtyard.

Where to stay
There are several pensions and restaurants in Lousã.

Penela
Penela is 27 km south of Coimbra on the N110. Its castle was important for centuries in the defence of Coimbra. It protected the Roman road that led from Conimbriga to Mérida in Spain. The Moors held Penela until Coimbra was liberated. The castle was repaired by King Sancho I and by King Dinis, and it was further enlarged in the fifteenth and sixteenth centuries. It was greatly damaged in the 1755 earthquake, and by people carrying away stone for other constructions, but it has been restored in this century. It has tall walls with turrets, square towers and a watchtower that totally dominate the town. The redoubt is set on a hill at the top of flights of narrow, steep steps. As usual, there is a legend about a beautiful Moorish girl who sits combing her hair by the fountain on Saint John's Eve.

Pombal
Pombal is 40 km south of Coimbra on the N1. The castle is said to have got its name from pigeons (*pombos*) that flew round its ramparts.

The castle gave its name to the town. And the famous eighteenth-century Prime Minister the Marquês de Pombal took his title from the town. His coat of arms is on the Casa do Celeiro, and his bones were kept in the Nossa Senhora do Cardal Church until 1856, when they were transferred to Lisbon.

What to see

The castle has high walls and a tall, square keep. It was built in 1160 by Gualdim Pais, Master of the Order of Knights Templar, on what must have been the site of a Romanized *castro* (see page 17). It suffered less than most Portuguese castles through the centuries, until the third invasion by Napoleon's forces in the Peninsular War, when the retreating French occupied and devastated Pombal.

The town is much spoiled by modern building, but you can see some fine old buildings in front of the Parish Church. They are, however, in bad disrepair.

Where to stay
Inexpensive

Pensão Cardal, Largo do Cardal. Tel. (036) 23006. A three star pension with twenty-seven rooms with bath and TV, a bar, hairdresser and shops.

Where to eat

Restaurante São Sebastião, Travassos. Tel. (036) 22745. A restaurant and snack bar that serves regional food.

Leiria

Leiria is 26 km south of Pombal on the N1. The road bypasses the town, but it is worth driving in and having a look. The town, which is at the confluence of the Rivers Lis and Lena, clusters round the sides of the hill where its castle stands, and is divided into the old town with its lovely monuments and the new town with its modern buildings and industries.

History

Leiria was probably a prehistoric hill-town. The Romans, who called the settlement Collippo, built the first castle here. Moors and Christians fought over it. King Afonso Henriques occupied it, and built a castle, in 1135, even before he became king.

There is a legend concerning the city's coat of arms, which is a castle between two pine trees on which two crows are sitting, with a star on top. It is said that King Afonso Henriques was waiting in Leiria to attack the Moors when he saw a crow sitting in a pine tree, flapping its wings madly. He took this as a good omen, and marched out and defeated the Moors. The star symbolizes this victory.

The Moors took Leiria for the last time in 1190. They were thrown out five years later, but the castle was badly damaged. It was rebuilt by King Sancho II and King Dinis. King Dinis lived in Leiria, and he planted the enormous pine woods to the west to provide wood for Portugal's fleet.

In 1254 King Afonso held a *Cortes* in Leiria, the first such assembly in Portugal to include representatives of the people.

What to see

The castle is situated on a nearly perpendicular rock. You can see the Moorish foundations on which it was built; the three-storey rectangular watchtower built by King Dinis; and the high, crenellated towers that flank the royal palace.

The palace has a beautiful atrium and a spacious fourteenth-century gallery with light arches. The loggia has eight arches set on columns. From the upper storeys of the palace there is a lovely view of the town and the countryside.

Other monuments in the town include the twelfth-century Romanesque church of **São Pedro**; the **Sé Cathedral**, a sixteenth-century building in pale stone; and the seventeenth-century **Santuario de Nossa Senhora da Encarnação** on a hill approached by 172 steps and filled with tiles.

Where to stay, and eat Medium price

Hotel Dom João III, Avenida Herois de Angola. Tel. (044) 33902. A modern, conveniently located hotel with sixty-four rooms with bath, a bar and restaurant.

Pensão São Francisco, Rua de São Francisco 29. Tel. (044) 25142. A three star pension with eighteen rooms with bath and TV, and a bar.

Inexpensive

Hotel Euro-Sol, Rua Dom José Alves Correia da Silva. Tel. (044) 24101/2/3, telex EUROSOL-LEIRIA. A three star hotel with fifty-four rooms with bath. It has a bar, a snack bar, a night club and a swimming pool.

Where to eat

Jardim, Jardim Luis de Camoes. Tel. (044) 32514. A modern restaurant in the central park with outdoor dining in the summer.

The Tourist Office is at Jardim Luis de Camoes. Tel. (044) 32748.

Pine forest

The pine forest west of Leiria towards the sea was planted by King Dinis six hundred years ago, to control shifting sand dunes and to provide timber for ships. It has been depleted by forest fires.

Marinha Grande

Marinha Grande, 12 km west of Leiria on the N242, is chiefly known as the site of the famous glass factories. The first factory was founded in 1748 by the Englishman John Beare. Later it was taken over by John and William Stephens. Some of the factories still produce glass by the old traditional methods, whereas others have switched to more modern methods. The Marinha Grande crystal is very beautiful. You can visit the Stephens factory, museum and showrooms.

Where to stay, and eat Inexpensive
São Pedro de Moel

Albergaria Nobre, Rua Alexandre Herculano 29. Tel. (044) 52226. A four star inn with twenty-two rooms with bath.

São Pedro de Moel is a charming beach resort, just 7 km from Marinha Grande off the N242-2. It has several hotels, pensions, restaurants and bars. There is an Orbitur camp site with cabins in the pine woods at the edge of the town. (Tel. [044] 59168.)

Batalha

Batalha (Battle) is just 11 km south of Leiria on the N1. It grew up around the Monastery of Santa Maria da Vitória, which was built to commemorate the Portuguese victory over the Spaniards in the battle of Aljubarrota, fought nearby in 1385. On the eve of the battle, King João I made a promise to the Virgin that he would build a monastery on the spot if he won the battle. He did, and work began on the monastery three years later, in 1388. The work went on through several of the succeeding reigns, and many architects contributed their talents. In fact the monastery was never completely finished.

What to see   It is a wonderful surprise to come down a hill from north or south and see in front of you on the flat plain below one of the most beautiful buildings in Europe. The **monastery** is constructed in the pale, golden stone of the region and is superb Gothic, with gables, flying buttresses, gargoyles and pinnacles all over the outside. The west side is richly decorated, with a sculptured portico above which there is a flamboyant Gothic window. The church is cruciform, with lancet windows. Inside it is very light, with tall, perpendicular columns. It is free of the clutter to be found in so many churches, so it is easy to appreciate its pure Gothic lines.

On the right side as you go into the church you will find the richly decorated **Founder's Chapel**, where lie the tombs of King João I and Philippa of Lancaster. Their statues carved in marble lie on the tombs hand in hand, under a beautifully embellished cupola. Their six sons, including Henry the Navigator, lie in niches along the walls.

The **Royal Cloisters** are, in style, a combination of Gothic and Manueline. The Gothic arcade openings are decorated with intricately carved marble columns sitting on slender columns carved with the shells, ropes and other sea motifs typical of Manueline.

The **Military Museum** is installed in a room near the fountain.

The **Chapter House** is off the Royal Cloisters. Each side measures nearly 23 m, with a vaulted roof without intermediate supports. It is said that the architect slept under the point of the roof to show sceptics that it would not fall down on him. The room houses the tomb of the unknown soldier.

The **Unfinished Chapels** must be entered from an outside door at the back. These seven chapels arranged around a central octagon were begun by one of the first architects, Master Huguet, but they were left unfinished, and never roofed. Nonetheless, with their soaring columns covered in every possible Manueline decoration, they are very beautiful.

In the small town next to the monastery you can still see some rather nice little eighteenth-century houses, although many of them were torn down to make way for the rather out-of-place equestrian statue of Nun' Alvares Pereira. There are also many hotels, restaurants, bars and souvenir shops.

Pousada   **Pousada do Mestre Afonso Domingues**, Largo Mestre Afonso
Medium price   Domingues. Tel. (044) 96260. A modern government inn with twenty rooms with bath, a bar, restaurant and an incomparable view of the monastery.

Fátima   Fátima is 20 km from Batalha on the N356. This is the place where, on 13 May 1917, three shepherd children from the village of Aljustrel said they had seen a vision of the Blessed Virgin. They said that the Virgin had told them to return to the same spot on the same day of each month for six months. They did this, and each time they, and many of the people who joined them, said they had seen the Virgin. The two younger children – a brother and sister named Francisco and Jacinta Marto – died young, but their cousin, Lucia dos Santos, is still alive. She is now a nun in the Carmelite convent in Coimbra.

In 1930 the Bishop of Leiria authorized pilgrimages to the site. People now come to the shrine from all over the world, especially on 13 May and 13 October, the first and last times the Virgin appeared.

Fátima is now absolutely full of hotels, pensions and restaurants, for the pilgrimage trade. However, many devout pilgrims camp out near the shrine.

Vila Nova de Ourém
History

Vila Nova de Ourém, 14 km east of Fátima on the N356–N113, has a story closely linked with the earlier history of Fátima.

Gonçales Hermigues, known as the 'Moor Eater', owned all of the land around here. He was a Knight Templar; and, as his name implies, a warlike person with a dislike of Moors. On an expedition to conquer the Moorish stronghold of Alcácer do Sal, south of Lisbon, he captured a Moorish girl named Fátima, daughter of the Mayor. They fell in love, she became a Christian and changed her name to Oureana, and they were married. They returned to his land and settled on his estate, which he named Fátima. Fátima/Oureana died young, and he went to Alcobaça and became a monk. Later, in the twelfth century, when King Afonso Henriques conquered the nearby town of Abdegas and gave it to his daughter Teresa, she named it Ourém, because she was fascinated by the love story of Oureana.

One of the later Counts of Ourém filled his castle there with Spanish noblemen, and became a favourite of the Dowager Queen Leonor. The Portuguese nobles feared and resented this, and one of them, the Master of Avis, who later becameKing João I, killed the Count. King João gave Ourém to his faithful follower Nun' Alvares Pereira, who passed it on to the Dukes of Bragança, later Kings of Portugal.

The castle is on the top of a high hill that must have been fortified before the beginnings of recorded history. It was probably taken and retaken many times by the Moors and Christians before it finally passed into Christian hands in the twelfth century.

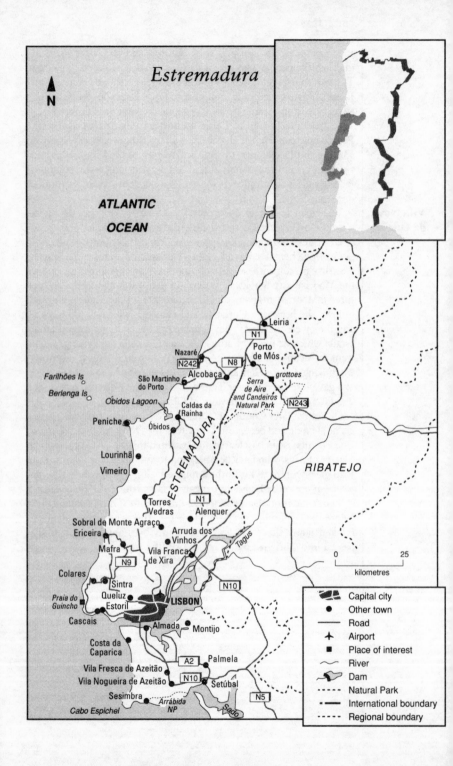

Estremadura

Introduction

If Portugal is a land of contrasts, the region of Estremadura seems to contain all those contrasts in microcosm. Within its boundaries that stretch from the Coastal Beira on the north to the Setúbal Peninsula below Lisbon on the south, and from the Atlantic Ocean on the west to the Ribatejo and Alentejo on the east, it has high mountains and lowlands claimed from the sea, backward villages and modern cities, subsistence farms and industrial centres.

Buildings Estremadura has some of Europe's most impressive buildings: the Mafra Monastery Palace, one of the biggest and most sumptuous in the world; the Alcobaça Abbey with its gigantic kitchens, cloisters and church and its tragic love story; and the Jerónimos Monastery in Lisbon, which is a perfect example of Manueline/Gothic architecture.

Fishermen The fishermen of Estremadura are like a people apart. Their life is difficult and dangerous, as they brave the strong Atlantic breakers in their open boats. The fishermen of Nazaré use open, flat-bottomed boats with high pointed prows on which they paint eyes to ward off evil spirits. The fishermen of Peniche have been fishing the waters off the coast since Peniche was an island, rather than the peninsula it is now. Cascais has turned from a little fishing village into an international tourist resort. But even now there is much excitement at the daily auction of the catch.

Piracy Estremadura has forts all along its coast which are monuments to the age of piracy, when Algerian, Dutch and English pirates raided the towns, stole cattle, burned forests, raided towns, and, in the case of the Algerians, carried the Portuguese off to the slave markets of North Africa or the Near East. The people locked up their towns at night, and kept watch.

Lisbon Lisbon, the capital of Portugal, is in Estremadura. Within a small radius it has an enormous amount to offer the visitor – a fascinating history, beautiful buildings and buildings of great historic interest, beaches, a variety of shops, good hotels, excellent restaurants.

Wines Estremadura has several demarcated areas within its boundaries. The wine of each area has its own distinct flavour and quality.

Bucelas wines are dry and white. Wines were being made around Bucelas in Roman times, but the Marquês de Pombal imported grape-

213

vines from the Rhine to improve their quality. Bucelas wines became known in England and France when the generals and soldiers confronting each other during the Peninsular War got a taste of them. The Duke of Wellington took Bucelas wine back to England with him, and it became fashionable to drink Bucelas at the court.

The region was demarcated in 1911. It is a small area 25 km north of Lisbon around Bucelas, near the River Tagus estuary. The vines are grown in limestone soil. The region has a microclimate with cold winters and mild summers. The wines are aged in wood, and are acid when young, so be sure to buy the older Bucelas.

King Afonso III brought vines from France in 1255 and had them planted near Colares. Many of the Colares grapevines are grown in an interesting way. They are planted in clay at the bottom of trenches some 3 m deep. The long vines are allowed to spread over the sand until the grapes appear, and then they are propped up. The climate is mild and humid, but the region is windy, so the vines are sheltered by bamboo fences.

The reds are ruby in colour when they are young, but turn brown with age. They are best if drunk when they are old. The whites are yellowish in colour, and they also age well.

Alcobaça is one of the most important wine-producing regions in the country. It also profited from the Peninsular War – as the French and English faced each other across the Lines of Torres Vedras, they learned to like these wines. The vines are grown on flat land around Alcobaça, Óbidos, Bombarral, Torres Vedras, Arruda and Alenquer. The region is cool, without extreme changes of temperature. The red wines are ruby and smooth. The whites are yellowish and fruity.

Western region and Leiria

Porto de Mós

Porto de Mós is a small medieval town approximately 20 km south of Leiria on the N1–N243. This region on the edge of the Serra de Aire and Candeiros Natural Park is one of high mountains, deep valleys, grottoes and underground rivers.

History

The site has been occupied since prehistoric times. Later Roman stonework with inscriptions has been found in the walls. It was fought over by Moors and Christians. After the reconquest in the twelfth century, its castle was restored and enlarged by King Sancho I and King Dinis. Later, it was given to Nun' Álvares Pereira and from him passed to the Dukes of Bragança. Duke Afonso of Bragança made improvements in the fifteenth century that reflect the influence of architecture he saw in Italy.

What to see

The castle has a charming airy look with its pointed green pinnacles on top of crenellated towers. It sits jauntily on a hill above the town. It has vaulted ceilings with interesting, carved keystones, a Renaissance patio and a cistern, and there is a restaurant.

The São Pedro church is in the Baroque style.

The Chapel of Santo António has seventeenth-century tiles.

The grottoes of Alvados, Mira de Aires and Santo António are all off the N243 about 14 km south of Porto de Mós.

The Santo António Grotto was discovered in 1955 by a child who crawled through a rock looking for a bird. The largest underground room has an area of 4,000 sq m with a height of 43 m. The caves are specially lit to give interesting effects to the stalactites and stalagmites. There is a restaurant/snack bar. The Mira de Aire Grotto is very deep, with a subterranean lake and underground river.

Alcobaça

Alcobaça, 20 km south of Batalha on the N8, is a bright, airy town. At one time, the sea used to come in almost to Alcobaça, but the area silted up over the years, and became fertile farming land. Fruit and some of the best wine in the country are produced there. It also has a large pottery industry. It is completely dominated by the great Cistercian Monastery of Santa Maria – the largest in the country.

History

Alcobaça began as an Arab castle; but the most significant moment in its history came in 1178, when King Afonso Henriques gave orders to build the monastery, to fulfil a promise he had made at the time of his conquest of Santarém from the Moors. He gave the monastery to the Cistercian Order, which had been invited to Portugal in 1138. The monks administered an enormous territory in which they were nearly as powerful as the monarchy. They brought in new methods of farming, and their expertise with grapevines probably accounts for the fact that Alcobaça wines are still among the best in Portugal. The monks remained until the suppression of the religious orders in the middle of the nineteenth century. The monastery was sold at auction in 1834.

Dona Inês de Castro

The monastery is most famous for the tragic love story with which it is connected. Prince Pedro, who later reigned as King Pedro I from 1357 to 1367, had as mistress a noble Galician lady, Inês de Castro, whom he loved very much. In 1336, his father King Afonso made him marry the Princess Constanza of Aragon, and banished Inês. After Constanza died giving birth to a son, Pedro called Inês back and installed her in a country house near Coimbra (now called Quinta das Lágrimas – House of Tears). They had several children, and Pedro refused to marry anyone else. But the King, concerned that Inês and her powerful brothers in Galicia would exert too much influence on the Portuguese throne, decided to have her killed.

On 7 January 1355, while Pedro was absent, the King and his henchmen went to the Quinta das Lágrimas and murdered her. Pedro revolted against the king and laid siege to Oporto, and Inês's brothers invaded Portugal. Peace was restored after a few months.

When King Afonso died in 1357 the murderers fled, but later King Pedro I got his hands on two of them and had them executed by drawing out their hearts. Declaring that he had been married to Inês, he set her decomposed body on a throne in the church of the monastery at Alcobaça, and forced every noble in the country to come and kiss her hand. He then gave her a sumptuous funeral. Inês became known as 'the queen who ruled after death'.

The story of Inês de Castro has been the subject of many books and plays. An episode in Camões' *Lusiadas* is dedicated to it.

The lovers Inês and Pedro are buried in the monastery, in tombs of carved limestone in flamboyant Gothic style. Their statues lie facing each other, so that the first thing they see on Judgement Day will be each other. Their story is recorded on their tombs: the lovers are depicted among the blessed on Judgement Day, while Inês's murderers, burn in hell.

What to see The Monastery of Santa Maria is a long, low two-storey Gothic building in white. The outside was altered in the seventeenth and eighteenth centuries. The refectory has a ceiling with superb ribbed vaulting. The kitchen, which is covered in pale glazed tiles, has ovens where you could roast six oxen at once. There is an underground stream – the Alcoa – where the monks fished for trout and eels and washed their dishes. The sacristy has a very ornate Manueline doorway decorated with entwined tree trunks and leaves carved in stone. The Hall of Tombs has lovely Gothic vaulting. The King's Hall, built in the eighteenth century, has statues of Portuguese kings carved by the monks in terracotta. There are glazed tile panels around the wall.

The Cloister of Silence, where the monks prayed and meditated, has ribbed vaulted ceilings, pillars and rose windows.

The Misericórdia Church in Rua do Castelo dates from the sixteenth century, and the Chapel of Nossa Senhora da Conceição is seventeenth century.

Festivals The *Festa da Nossa Senhora da Ascensão* takes place in May, the *Festa do Corpo de Deus* in June, the *Feira de São Bernardo* in August, and the *Feira de São Simão* in October.

Where to stay **Hotel Santa Maria**, Rua Dr Francisco Zagalo. Tel. (062) 43295.
Inexpensive A pleasant, two star hotel in the gardens in front of the monastery. It has thirty-one rooms with bath and TV, and a bar.

Where to eat **Restaurante Trindade**, Praça D. Afonso Henriques 22. Tel. (062) 42397. A restaurant and snack bar that serves regional food.

Restaurante Frei Bernardo, Rua Dom Pedro V 17–19. Tel. (062) 42227. It has an art-nouveau exterior and a huge dining room inside serving typical regional dishes. There is live Portuguese music and folk dancing.

Tourist Office, Praça 25 de Abril. Tel. (062) 42377.

Aljubarrota is 6 km north of Alcobaça on the N8. It was near here that on 14 August 1385 the famous battle of Aljubarrota was fought, and the Castilians were driven out of Portugal. Legend says a baker woman fought the Spaniards with a wooden bread shovel and killed them by pushing them into her oven. **Coz** is a small town just north-east of Alcobaça where there is another Cistercian monastery, founded in 1279 by Dom Fernando, Abbot of Alcobaça. When the sea used to reach here, it was on a lagoon.

Manor house
Inexpensive

Casa da Padeira (House of the Baker Woman), tel. (062) 48272, is a big inn with rooms at the entrance to the town. It has gardens, swimming pool, bar and billiard room.

Nazaré

Nazaré is 12 km west of Alcobaça on the coast. There are two Nazarés: the 'real Nazaré' with its fishermen often dressed in the traditional knee-length plaid trousers, bright shirts and stocking caps, who take their boats out into the dangerous waters to fish, or sit along the shore repairing their nets, helped by their wives in black shawls and full skirts with many petticoats; and the 'other Nazaré' of beach umbrellas, discos, seafront restaurants, hotels, tourists and noise.

History

Until three hundred years ago the site of what is now Nazaré was covered by the sea. When the sea receded in the seventeenth century the fishermen installed huts on the beach, but only in the second half of the last century did they begin to build a real town. Before that, the town was at Sítio on the high cliff you see to the north of Nazaré. You can reach it by funicular or by road. Sítio is a huge open square, like a veranda over the sea, bordered by a church, a chapel and houses, which sit far back as though cowering from the cliff's edge.

The people of Nazaré claim to be descendants of the Phoenicians. Their straight, thin noses and grey eyes are thought to be evidence of this, and so are their long, narrow boats with high pointed prows that have an eye painted on either side. Before a safe harbour was built for the boats, they had to be pulled back out of the strong currents to the shore by teams of oxen and later by tractors.

What to see

The São Miguel Arcanjo Fort is on the end of the promontory in Sítio, high above the ocean. Its walls follow the contour of the rocky cliff. It was built in the sixteenth century, to protect the coast from the English, French and Dutch pirates who preyed on it. In 1808, Napoleon's army attacked the fort and burnt the town and the boats.

The Church of Nossa Senhora de Nazaré is in the square in Sítio. It has glazed tiles with scenes from the Old Testament and a gilt carved main altar. The Memory Chapel is a tiny, white-painted chapel built into the side of the cliff by the square. If you look out from its window, you feel you are suspended over the ocean far below. The chapel was built on the spot where a miracle supposedly occurred. One Dom Fuas Roupinho was pursuing the devil disguised as a stag when it jumped over the cliff's edge and his horse followed. He and his horse were snatched back by the Virgin Mary – Our Lady of Nazaré – and saved. If you take a close look at the rocks on the edge of the precipice, you can detect what is said to be the mark in the rock left by his horse's hoof – but don't lean out too far.

Crafts

Long black fishermen's capes, Nazaré fishermen's caps, dolls with the typical costume of the Nazaré fisherwomen (including seven petti-coats), brightly coloured miniature boats.

Pilgrimage

The *Romaria da Nossa Senhora de Nazaré* takes place in September. There is a procession in which the image of Nossa Senhora de Nazaré is carried down to the sea.

Where to stay Inexpensive

Hotel da Nazaré, Largo Afonso Zúquete. Tel. (062) 51311. A three star hotel with fifty rooms with bath. It has a restaurant, bar and a night club.

Pensão Cubata, Avenida da República 6. Tel. (062) 51706. A three star pension with twenty-one rooms with bath.

Pensão Beira Mar, Rua dos Lavradores. Tel. (062) 51458/9. A two star pension with eighteen rooms with bath.

Where to eat

Restaurante Mar Bravo, Praça Sousa Oliveira. Tel. (062) 46180. A restaurant that serves both regional food and French cook-ing, and specializes in shellfish.

Restaurante Ribamar, Avenida da República. Tel. (062) 51158. A charming, glassed-in building with a lovely sea view. It specializes in seafood, fish and regional dishes.

The Tourist Office is at Rua Mouzinho de Albuquerque 23. Tel. (062) 46120.

São Martinho do Porto

São Martinho do Porto is a town on the beach with a quiet bay, 10 km south of Nazaré on the N242. It has some interesting nineteenth-century buildings and *art nouveau* houses, and several very good hotels, inns and pensions. There is a lovely view from Facho Hill.

Caldas da Rainha
Thermal waters

Caldas da Rainha is 25 km south of Alcobaça on the N8, just 10 km from the sea and 2 km from the Óbidos Lagoon.

For several centuries Caldas da Rainha (The Queen's Hot Springs) was best known for its curative mineral waters. In 1485 Queen Leonor – wife of King João II – discovered the healing powers of the water and had a hospital built there. In the centuries that followed many mon-archs frequented the spa to take the waters.

What to see

Our Lady of the People Parish Church is a fifteenth-century Manueline church built by Queen Leonor. It has a sixteenth-century octagonal baptismal font, a triumphal arch decorated by the six-teenth-century Lisbon school, eighteenth-century carved wooden altars and eighteenth-century silver. You can also see here some of Queen Leonor's clothes.

The São Sebastião Chapel was built during the sixteenth century and rebuilt later by King João V. The chapel walls are decorated with glazed tiles telling Saint Sebastian's life story.

There are many nineteenth-century houses with wrought iron balconies and glazed tile fronts.

The José Malhoa Museum has a collection of contemporary Portu-guese art and examples of Rafael Bordalo Pinheiro's pottery. The Stu-dio Museum of António Duarte exhibits contemporary sculptures. There is a bullfight museum in Rua Joaquim Alves.

Ceramics

Even before the fifteenth century, Caldas da Rainha was known for its ceramics. Clay from the nearby Oiteiros pits was being used as far back as Neolithic times. Some of the pottery is in a nice off-white or a bright green. The glazed green salad bowls shaped like huge cabbage leaves are especially attractive. However, many of the traditional pieces are incredibly gaudy and over-decorated, or simply representations of ugly creatures – including people.

The best known of the Caldas da Rainha potters was Rafael Bordalo Pinheiro, who as well as being a potter was a cartoonist and caricaturist. Some of his most famous figures include *Zé Povinho* (the typical fat peasant); *Ama das Caldas* (a Caldas da Rainha wetnurse); the *Sacristan*; the *Civil Guard*; and, oddly enough, *John Bull*. Perhaps you might find it amusing to have a gravy boat in the shape of John Bull lying on his back. Then again, you might not. The São Rafael Museum in Caldas da Rainha contains some of Rafael Bordalo Pinheiro's ceramic pieces.

Festivals

On Saturdays there is a big fair in the Praça da República. There are bullfights in the season and during the year other interesting festivals and fairs. The best known is the National Ceramics Fair in July.

Where to stay
Inexpensive

Hotel Malhoa, Rua António Sergio 31. Tel. (062) 35011. A three star hotel with 113 rooms with bath and TV, a bar, restaurant, money exchange and swimming pool.

Camp site

Parque Dona Leonor. Tel. (062) 32367.

Where to eat

Restaurante O Cortiço, Tornada. Tel. (062) 31328. A restaurant that specializes in cod dishes – and wild boar.

Restaurante Pátio da Rainha, Rua Camões 39. Tel. (062) 24672. A restaurant that serves regional dishes. It has live music.

The Tourist Office is in the Praça da República. Tel. (062) 34511.

Foz do Arelho is a resort just 8 km west of Caldas da Rainha on the N360. It has access both to the sea 2 km away and to the Óbidos Lagoon, and is good for swimming, sailing, rowing and fishing.

Where to stay
Inexpensive

Foz Palace Motel, Estrada Marginal, Foz do Arelho. Tel. (062) 97413/4. A three star motel with a restaurant, café, cocktail lounge, pub, swimming pool, tennis court, mini-golf and a children's playground.

Lagoa de Óbidos is the lagoon that remains from the time long ago when the sea reached almost as far as Alcobaça.

Óbidos

Óbidos is 5 km south of Caldas da Rainha on the N8. You can't miss seeing it on its high hill. It is a very beautiful little walled town. Its castle, cobbled streets, beautiful churches and whitewashed houses covered with flowers are like something out of a picture book.

You enter the town through a gateway in the wall which is really a shrine dedicated to Our Lady of Grace. There are also four doorways and one other gateway in the walls.

History

There is evidence that as far back as the fourth century BC there was a Celtic *castro* here, surrounded by water because the sea had not yet subsided. The Romans took it: for them it was a place of strategic importance. It was seized in 714 by the Moors, and taken from them in 1148 by King Afonso Henriques. He and subsequent kings, including King Dinis, improved and enlarged it. King Dinis gave Óbidos and the palace to his wife, the saintly Isabel. After it became the property of Leonor Teles, wife of King Fernando; Philippa of Lancaster, the English wife of King João I; Leonor of Portugal, wife of João II; and Catherine, wife of King João III, it became known as the Casa das Rainhas (House of the Queens).

In the seventeenth century Óbidos was the home of Josefa d'Ayala e Cabrera (Josefa de Óbidos), a famous primitive painter. She was the daughter of an Óbidos artist, Baltazar Gomes Figueira and a woman from Sevilla, and she lived in the Capeleira mansion near the town. She died in 1684, and is buried in the Church of São Pedro in Óbidos.

What to see
The **Castle** has crenellated battlements (Moorish) that run all round the town, and very tall square and cylindrical towers that reinforce the walls. The royal palace inside has been turned into a lovely pousada (see page 221).

The **Parish Church of Santa Maria**, in the centre of the town, was originally a seventh-century Visigoth temple. It is now an example of Renaissance architecture. Its walls are lined with blue and white tiles that extend to the ceiling, which is painted with designs representing Portugal's former African empire. There are eight paintings on wood by João da Costa dated 1616 on the high altar, and five paintings of Saint Catherine by Josefa de Óbidos in a side chapel.

There are several other churches of interest inside and outside the city walls, but they are often closed to the public; the **Misericórdia Church**, near the Church of Santa Maria, was built by Queen Leonor in 1498. Its Baroque porch was added in 1774. The **Chapel of São Martinho** dates from 1331. In front of it is the **Church of São Pedro**, which was originally Gothic but was reconstructed after the 1755 earthquake. The tomb of Josefa de Óbidos is in this church. The **Church of Nossa Senhora de Monserrate** is outside the town walls. It has a Baroque portal, and its façade is covered with sixteenth-century tiles. The **Church of Nossa Senhora de Carmo** is also outside the town walls. During the Roman occupation it was a temple to Jupiter; it became a Christian church under the Visigoths. The **Sanctuary of Our Lord of the Stone** sits alone in a field below the town. It was started between 1740 and 1744, but was never finished.

The sixteenth-century **Aqueduct** is 3 km long. It was built by Queen Catherine to bring water to the town fountains.

The **Santa Iria Chapel**, near the aqueduct, has a fifteenth-century carved stone statue of the saint. The **Cross of Memory** is a large stone cross erected outside the walls in memory of the place where King Afonso Henriques set up camp before attacking the Moors. You can still see the date of the taking of Óbidos, and the name Afonso. It was restored in the sixteenth century.

The **Pillory** inside town has the royal emblem of Queen Leonor, and is topped with an iron cross.

The **Museum**, in the sixteenth-century Town Hall, contains paintings, including a portrait by Josefa de Óbidos, sculpture, furniture and much carved gilt work.

Óbidos has become a cultural centre, and every two years sponsors an international arts exposition in the summer – BIO (International Bienal of Óbidos) with so many artists represented that often works of sculpture have to be exhibited in the streets.

Festivals

The *Romaria de Santo Antão* takes place in January, the *Procissão do Senhor dos Passos* at Easter, the *Romaria da Santa Cruz* in May, the *Feira da Santa Iria* in October.

Where
to stay
Inexpensive

Albergaria Residencial Josefa de Óbidos, Rua Dom João de Ornelas. Tel. (062) 959228. A four star inn at the town entrance. It has forty rooms, a restaurant and bar.

Estalagem do Convento, Rua Dr João de Ornelas. Tel. (062) 959217. Just outside the walls in a converted eighteenth-century nunnery, it has twenty-four lovely rooms with bath, an oak-beamed bar and restaurant and a garden for summer dining.

Medium price

Albergaria Rainha Santa Isabel, Rua Direita. Tel. (062) 959115. A charming four star inn in the centre of town with twenty rooms with bath, and a bar.

Manor house
Inexpensive

Casa do Poço, Travessa da Mouraria. Tel. (062) 959358. A house that dates back to the Moorish occupation of Óbidos. It still has Moorish doorways. There are four bedrooms, all with bath, and a bar.

Pousada
Medium price

Pousada do Castelo, Óbidos. Tel. (062) 959105/959146. A luxury pousada in the former royal palace. It has nine rooms, two tower suites, a bar and a nice restaurant with a beautiful view of the valley.

Where to eat

A Ilustre Casa de Ramiro, Rua Porta do Vale. Tel. (062) 959194. Just outside the walls, in an ancient house redesigned in Arabic style by Jose Fernando Teixeira, it has an open grill and good Óbidos wines.

Restaurante Alcaide, Rua Direita. Tel. (062) 959220. A restaurant with excellent views that specializes in Portuguese cooking.

Tourist Office, Solar da Praia da Santa Maria. Tel. (062) 95296.

Peniche

Peniche is on a peninsula which was once an island 23 km west of Óbidos by the N8–N114. In the sixteenth century a castle was built here as protection against attacks by pirates and slave traders.

Peniche today is a bustling fishing port. The peninsula has wide sandy beaches on one side and steep rocky cliffs on the other.

What to see

The **Castle** is a massive, sprawling structure covering 2 hectares. Used as a prison over the centuries, its dungeons have housed enemies of Marquês de Pombal, French soldiers defeated by Wellington, Absolutists and Liberals, German prisoners of war and dictator Salazar's political foes. After 1974 the castle was home to refugees from Portugal's former African territories. Its **Museum** contains archaeological artifacts, fishing and shipbuilding objects, and examples of *renda de bilros* (bobbin lace).

The sixteenth-century Church of São Pedro contains several large paintings. The Church of Nossa Senhora da Conceição was originally built in the sixteenth century, but it has been remodelled. It has interesting glazed tiles, gilt carved work, and some paintings attributed to the father of Josefa de Óbidos. The Misericórdia Church has seventeenth-century tiles and about a hundred paintings, five attributed to Josefa de Óbidos. The Church of Nossa Senhora dos Remédios is on the point of the cape. The Cape Carvoeiro Lighthouse was built in 1779. There is a restaurant there.

Crafts   Baskets, fishing nets and *renda de bilros* lace are made in Peniche.

Festivals   The *Festas da Nossa Senhora da Boa Viagem* take place at the beginning of August. During the *Romaria da Nossa Senhora dos Remédios*, in October and November, the people from all of the villages around carry the image of the Virgin from the Nossa Senhora dos Remédios Church down to the sea.

Where to stay, and eat Inexpensive   **Hotel da Praia Norte**, Estrada Nacional 114. Tel. (062) 71171/ 72085. A three star hotel with ninety-two rooms with bath, a bar, restaurant, pool, shops and disco.

Tourist Office, Rua Alexandre Herculano. Tel. (062) 72271.

Excursions   The **Berlengas** and the **Farilhões** are rocky islands off the coast that were once inhabited by monks expelled from the mainland by pirates. Today only a few fishermen and lighthouse keepers live on the Berlengas. The main island is covered by rare plants, and many migratory birds nest in the rocks. Boats run from Peniche to Berlenga every day from June through September. The trip takes about an hour. Tel. (062) 72153 or 72484.

The São João Batista Fort sits on an islet separate from the main island but connected to it by a dramatic winding stone bridge. It was once a monastery where monks prayed and helped sailors in distress, but the monks were so plagued by pirates that in 1665 it was decided to tear down the monastery and build a fort instead. It has seen struggles with pirates, Spaniards, absolutists, liberals, and assorted others.

The Jerónimos Convent is a small hermitage that was founded in 1513. It has been partially restored.

There are sea tunnels and grottoes that can be reached by boat.

Where to stay, and eat Inexpensive   **Casa Abrigo São João Baptista** in the seventeenth-century fort. Tel. (062) 72271. A hostel with twenty rooms open from June to mid-September run by the Friends of Peniche Association. Guests must bring their own bedding and food.

Pavilhão Mar e Sol, Berlenga Island. Tel. (062) 72031. A comfortable five-room pension run by the Peniche municipal authorities, it has a pleasant restaurant. Open from June through mid-September.

Lourinhã   Lourinhã, south of Peniche on the N114–N247, is on the coast. The countryside around is full of working windmills that have little

History | ceramic pots attached that sing in the wind as they spin around.

The town, called Laurinam by the Romans, was captured by the Moors, and held until 1160 when it was taken by King Afonso Henriques. Some say the ruined Moledo Palace was once a secret hideaway for Prince Pedro and his adored Dona Inês de Castro.

What to see | The Old Parish Church, which dates from the fourteenth century, stands on a high hill where the Moors had a castle. It has a lovely rose window, and pillars with exquisitely carved capitals. The engraved stone baptismal font is also worth seeing. The Misericórdia Church, built in 1626, has an interesting Manueline porch with a door carved in stone. It has a small art museum. The Santo António Church has seventeenth-century pictorial tiles. The Recoletos Franciscanos Convent has seventeenth-century tiles in the cloister, and several sixteenth-century paintings.

Beach | Areia Branca is a white sand beach 25 km long. It has some good hotels and restaurants, and a camp site.

Where to stay, and eat Inexpensive | **Estalagem Bela Vista**, Rua Dom Sancho I, Cascais de Santo Andre. Tel. (061) 42713. A four star inn with twenty-nine rooms with bath, a bar, restaurant and pool.

There are several good restaurants that specialize in shellfish.

Vimeiro is a spa south of Lourinhã. On 27 August 1808 the French under Junot were routed here by the Portuguese-English army under Wellington, during the Peninsular War.

Where to stay, and eat Medium price | **Hotel Golf Mar**, Porto Novo Beach. Tel. (061) 98157/8/9. A 257-room, three star hotel in a dramatic setting on cliffs above the beach. It has a restaurant and bar, two pools, shops, 9-hole golf course, horse riding and a disco.

Inexpensive | **Hotel das Termas**, Rua Joaquim Belchor – Maceira. Tel. (061) 98103. A well-known old hotel with eighty-eight rooms, forty-nine with bath, a 9-hole golf course, swimming pool and tennis.

Torres Vedras
History | Torres Vedras is 18 km south of Vimeiro on the N8-2. Prehistoric remains found nearby indicate that the site was inhabited at least 5,000 years ago. It was occupied by the Romans, and the Moors built fortifications here. In the twelfth century it was taken from the Moors by King Afonso Henriques. King Dinis enlarged the fortress and a century later King Fernando built the longer walls further down the hill. Many of the kings of Portugal lived in Torres Vedras. In 1414 King João I met with his court there to decide on the invasion of Ceuta in North Africa. But the town is most famous for the part it played in the defeat of Napoleon in the Peninsular War.

The Lines of Torres Vedras were a series of fortifications built at the beginning of the Peninsular War, under the direction of the Duke of Wellington, to impede the passage of the French. One line ran from the River Tagus at Alhandra through Torres Vedras and ended at the coast near Sesindro. A second line began in Póvoa da Santa Iria, went through Mafra and ended at the Atlantic. There was also a small defensive fortification at São Julião da Barra near Lisbon. By 1810, when the Portuguese and English troops under Wellington met the French, there were 108 forts on the lines, with 436 cannons. They effectively stopped the French army.

What to see

Very little remains of the fortifications disguised as windmills to fool the French, but on a hill at the entrance of town to the west, there is a carefully reconstructed fort that will give you an idea of how they were planned.

You will also see some traces of the defence works of the Lines of Torres Vedras inside the castle on the hill opposite, which was incorporated in the defence. Although the castle was badly damaged in the 1755 earthquake, you can also still see a Gothic entrance way, with a Manueline coat of arms and armillary spheres, the Santa Maria Church, the ruins of the castle residence, and a medieval cemetery.

Other things to see include: the **São Pedro Church**, with a Manueline portal, gilt work and Baroque tiles; the sixteenth-century **Graça Church**, with eighteenth-century tiles; and the **Museu Municipal**, with silver crowns, paintings, ceramics, coins and the archaeological artifacts dug up at the Castro do Zambujal site.

Marble

There are many marble quarries around Torres Vedras. Some of the companies will make tables, mantels for fireplaces, candlesticks, and other objects, to order, and will ship them.

Excursions

Castro do Zambujal, 3 km south of Torres Vedras, was a large fortified hill-town. Five thousand years ago there were copper mines here, and the first inhabitants of the site were undoubtedly people from the eastern Mediterranean who came to work the mines. Many findings from the site are in the Municipal Museum in Torres Vedras.

Castro do Povoadão was an Iron Age hill-top town on the Pena Hill near Torres Vedras. There are several early tombs here.

The **Varatojo Monastery** in the Varatojo Hills near Torres Vedras was built on the orders of King João, in thanksgiving for his success against the Moors in North Africa. It has a lovely two-storey cloister, a tiled patio and wall panels of eighteenth-century tiles. It is now occupied by Franciscans, who will allow you to visit.

Festivals

The Torres Vedras Carnival takes place in February. The *Feira de São Gonçalo* and the *Feira de São Pedro* are both in June, and the *Feira de Runa* is in September.

Beaches

There are several good beaches nearby. The Praia da Santa Cruz is on the Atlantic, 14 km west of Torres Vedras on the N247. It has a small airport.

Where to stay, and eat Inexpensive

Hotel Imperio, Praça 25 de Abril. Tel. (061) 25232. A light and airy two star hotel in Post-Modernist style in the centre of town. Twenty-six rooms with bath and TV, a bar and restaurant.

Restaurante Barrete Preto, Rua Paiva de Andrade. Tel. (061) 22150. Considered the most elegant in town and serving excellent regional food.

Sobral de Monte Agraço

The Tourist Office is in the Rua 9 de Abril. Tel. (061) 23094.

Sobral is 19 km south-east of Torres Vedras on the N248. On all of the hills there are old windmills, the most famous of which is the Moinho do Céu (Heaven's Windmill). This windmill bears the marks of Napoleon's troops. You can visit some of the working windmills.

Sobral played an important part during the French invasion. You can still see today some of the trenches and firing positions that were part of the Lines of Torres Vedras.

Arruda dos Vinhos

Arruda dos Vinhos is 8 km south-east of Sobral and 11 km west of Vila Franca de Xira on the N248. It is famous for its wine, which you can buy from the cooperative at the entrance to the town. In the middle of this century it was also famous for its *bruxa* (witch), who was widely consulted in matters of love, health and money. She handed out love potions, herbal remedies and cures for nearly everything.

The Lines of Torres Vedras also passed through Arruda. A large part of the French cavalry was billeted in the wine cellars here during the Peninsular War.

What to see

The sixteenth-century Parish Church has a beautiful Manueline portal. Its altars are richly carved gilt work, and it has lots of eighteenth-century tiles. The Misericórdia Church was built in 1574.

The Monastery of the Comendadeiras de Santiago is interesting, because this was the first community where the wives of the Knights of the military Order of Sant'Iago lived and carried out the duties of their husbands who were off fighting the Moors.

Where to eat

O Fuso, in the main street. Tel. (063) 95121. A popular, crowded regional restaurant with an enormous open fireplace where thick steaks, chicken and cod are grilled over a wood fire. They serve good Arruda wine – ask for the Reserve.

Alenquer

Alenquer, 16 km north of Arruda on the N115–4–N1 is a very old town which, because of its location near the River Tagus, was important from prehistoric times to the nineteenth century. During the time when the castle was still standing, several of the queens of Portugal made it their home. And many illustrious people were born in the town: Afonso de Albuquerque, who was Viceroy of India; and the poet Luis de Camões.

What to see

The castle was almost totally destroyed in the 1755 earthquake, but its unusual Couraca Tower and Door of Conception and a few fragments of wall remain.

The São Pedro Church was built in the twelfth century. It has sixteenth-century paintings, and the tomb of historian Damião de Góis. The Misericórdia Church has a marble altar and pulpit, a painted ceiling and a painting by Josefa de Óbidos. Its walls are covered in blue and white tiles. The Santa Catarina Chapel has two splendid seventeenth-century gilt carved altars.

The São Francisco Monastery was the first Franciscan monastery in Portugal. It has a Gothic portal, a lovely cloister and many paintings and pieces of sculpture.

Excursion

Meca, just north of Alenquer, has the eighteenth-century Santa Quitéria Church, one of the most beautiful churches in the region. It has two tall towers. The transept has gilded doors. In front of the church there is a raised dais where the priest stands to bless the cattle which are brought here decked out in flowers every May.

Mafra

Mafra is 33 km south of Torres Vedras on the N9–N116.

History

Mafra is one of the oldest towns in Portugal. The remains of *castros* in the area are evidence of prehistoric settlement. It was occupied by the Romans and later by the Moors. King Afonso Henriques took it from the Moors in the twelfth century, and King Sancho I granted it a charter in 1189 and gave the town to the Bishop of Silves. Over the centuries ownership of the town has been much contested among the crown, the Church and the nobility. It was a favourite residence of the nobility in the seventeenth, eighteenth and nineteenth centuries, and you can still see many of their fine old mansions.

Monastery Palace

Mafra Monastery Palace is an overwhelming building. Everything about it is enormous. It covers 40,000 sq. m, and has a façade 220 m long. It has 4,500 doors and windows. The marble statues tower over you like giants, and the towers and domes dwarf the whole town.

The monastery was commissioned by King João V in gratitude for the birth of a male heir. Thanks to the gold and other riches pouring in from Brazil, the King was fabulously rich, and he was ambitious to rival the splendours of Versailles. He brought in the architect Johann Friedrich Ludwig to plan the monastery; work on the building began in 1717, and it was completed in 1735.

The monastery is in the Baroque style and shows both German and Italian influences (Ludwig studied in Rome). The façade is cream-coloured, with a central pediment and two tall belfries. A huge coffered dome, beautifully painted, dominates the monastery.

The library is 65 m long, with a white plaster barrel ceiling, and is an outstandingly beautiful room. The royal apartments along the front and side of the monastery are lavishly painted and furnished.

The basilica is flanked by two imposing bell towers with 100 Flemish-made bells – the carillon of Mafra – considered among the finest in Europe. They are played on Sundays and religious holidays.

In the eighteenth century the monastery became famous as a school of sculpture under Alessandro Giusti, a well known Italian sculptor. The Mafra school of sculpture was responsible for much of the eighteenth-century sculpture seen today.

Crafts

Some of the prettiest pottery in the country is made near Mafra. It has discreet designs in pale blue on off-white.

Where to stay, and eat Inexpensive

Albergaria Castelão, Avenida 25 de Abril. Tel. (061) 52320. A modern four star inn with a glassed-in restaurant. It has twenty-seven rooms with bath.

Restaurante Frederico, Avenida 25 de Abril. Tel. (061) 52089. A pleasant, modest Portuguese restaurant.

Solar do Rei, Rua Detras dos Quintas 1, Tel. (061) 53149. A charming 'typical' bodega in a restored mansion, specializing in regional dishes. There is *fado* music the first Saturday night of the month.

Ericeira

Ericeira, on the coast 9 km west of Mafra on the N116, is a fishing town turned seaside resort.

It was from here that the royal family departed into exile after the republic was established in 1910. The Chapel of Santo António on the cliff has tiles portraying their departure.

A few kilometres north you will see remains of the eighteenth-century Santo Isidro Fort, built to protect the coast against pirates. It is now in ruins.

Ericeira has a sandy beach between cliffs. The water can be rough.

Where to stay, and eat
Medium price
Inexpensive

Hotel de Turismo da Ericeira, Rua Porto de Rezes. Tel. (061) 63545/6. A three star hotel with 154 rooms with bath. It has a bar, a night club, a swimming pool, tennis courts and shops.

Albergaria Casa Dom Fernando, Quinta da Calada. Tel. (061) 55204. A four star inn with rooms which have good views of the sea. It has a restaurant that serves homemade specialities. The restaurant is very popular – advance booking is essential.

O Barco, Rua Capitan João Lopes. Tel. (061) 62759. A well-known and popular restaurant by the harbour. It naturally specializes in seafood and fish.

Cesar, Estrada Nacional 247, 1 km north of town. Tel. (061) 62926. An enormous panoramic restaurant with a huge vivarium with all varieties of shellfish. It sits dramatically on the cliffs. There is a bar and music for dancing.

Tourist Office, Rua Eduardo Burnay 33-A. Tel. (061) 63122.

Sintra

Getting there

Sintra sits on a high peak, often shrouded in mist, 23 km south of Ericeira on the N247. It is visible from great distances – even from the top of Saint George's Castle in Lisbon. You can get there by car, bus or train. There is a train from the station in the Rossio in Lisbon.

Anything one could say about Sintra would be a cliché. It has been written about ecstatically by writers from the Muslims to Lord Byron to those of today. Their descriptions of the 'fairytale city' and the 'glorious Eden' only begin to describe this unbelievably lovely place. Its hillsides are covered in dense green forests, huge ferns and bright flowers, among which some of the most incredibly exotic and ornate palaces you have ever seen stand in gardens filled with statuary, gazebos, water fountains and exotic trees. It is a very romantic place, and when the frequent mists drift among the trees and hollows it becomes eerie and mysterious.

Perhaps that is why there are legends of fairies that dance in the moonlight and practise magic rites, of cults to the moon and the stars and of caves that reach to the very centre of the earth. (It was said that during the earthquake smoke and fire belched from these caves.)

History

The Romans called the place Promontorium Lunae (Lunar Promontory). Not much is known of their occupation of the mountain, or about any of the peoples that surely preceded them, but there is much evidence of the Moors who followed. The Moorish castle that stands out so starkly on the hillside is still very striking, even though it has been much restored and has fallen partially into ruin.

The Moorish King of Badajoz handed over the castle to Afonso VI of Leon in 1031, but it changed hands several times after that until King Afonso Henriques took it in 1147. The palace built on the foundations of another Moorish building in the centre of town became a favourite place for the Portuguese kings to pass the summer.

Sintra also became the favourite summer place for generations of English – writers, poets, dilettantes, nobles and members of the Factory House from Lisbon.

As all the world knows, Byron was in Sintra in 1809, when he was twenty-one and just out of university. He stayed nine days, pronounced Sintra a 'glorious Eden' and left to write about Sintra in glowing terms and to vilify the rest of the Portuguese nation.

Sintra today

Sintra today is a great tourist attraction for both Portuguese and foreigners, and it can be very crowded in summer.

You can hire a taxi to take you all round the town and up to the palaces: agree a price with the driver beforehand. Alternatively, during the summer you can rent a horse-drawn coach. The Tourist Office will furnish you with maps for walking tours in the hills.

What to see

The **Ramalhão Palace** is an imposing building at the entrance to the town before you cross under the old aqueduct when coming from Lisbon on the N249. It was built by King Dinis. William Beckford stayed here, and Queen Carlota-Joaquina, the Spanish mother of King Pedro IV and his brother Miguel, was kept under house arrest here while she plotted to help Miguel usurp the throne. The building is now an exclusive girls' school run by nuns.

The massive **Sintra National Palace** stands in the town square. Built on the ruins of a Moorish fortress, it was the favourite summer residence of the Portuguese royal family from the fifteenth century. It is a mixture of different styles of architecture. The Mermaids' Room has fifteenth-century raised black tiles. The Coat-of-Arms Room has a sixteenth-century ceiling painted with the arms of seventy-two noble Portuguese families, and some panels of tiles depicting hunting scenes. The Magpie Room has magpies all over it. The story goes that

King João I had the magpies painted after there was a lot of court gossip about the fact that the Queen had caught him kissing a lady in waiting – each magpie was said to represent a lady at court. The Swan Room has nineteenth-century diamond-shaped tiles in off-white and green, and life-size swans painted on the ceiling. The Chinese Room contains an ivory pagoda presented by the Chinese Emperor in 1806.

The Palace is closed on Wednesdays.

The **Seteais Palace** is on the very edge of the mountain, and has beautiful views. It was built at the end of the eighteenth century by Netherlands Consul Gildemaester, who later sold it to the fifth Marquês de Marialva.

Legend says the palace got its name from *sete* (seven) '*ais*' (an exclamation of surprise). The Portuguese nobleman Mendes de Paiva, so the story goes, fell in love with a Muslim princess who was escaping from the Moorish castle at Sintra when King Afonso Henriques captured it in 1147. It seems that a spell had been put upon the princess which would allow her to say '*ai*' only seven times before she died. She exclaimed '*ai*' when she first saw Mendes de Paiva. The two became lovers, but of course had to keep this secret. And in consequence of the precarious nature of their relationship the princess exclaimed '*ai*' four more times. When Mendes de Paiva heard of the spell, he left her, in order to protect her. However, his leaving caused her to exclaim once more. Her seventh '*ai*' was uttered when her Moorish former lover rushed in to kill her.

People with less romantic imagination suggest that the name comes from the 'seven sighs' breathed by the Portuguese because of their disappointment at the Treaty of Sintra, signed in the rooms of the Seteais Palace by the Duke of Wellington and the French after the first French invasion of the Peninsular War, when the French were allowed to carry off their booty.

The Seteais Palace is now a very elegant hotel (see page 230).

Music　　**The Sintra Music Festival** brings internationally famous musicians to perform in the palaces and castles of Sintra between 15 June and 15 July.

Ballet　　**Ballet in the Palace of Seteais** takes place during the first two weeks in August. Programmes available at the Sintra Tourist Office.

Monserrate, about 5 km beyond Seteais, is a strange three-domed Moorish palace that Francis Cook, who became the Viscount of Monserrate, built in 1864. There was originally a convent on the spot, but it was torn down by the Portuguese Viceroy of India, who built a palace there. In the eighteenth century this was bought by William Beckford, who made modifications and planted some of the gardens. The gardens have an extraordinary collection of rare plants and trees.

In the **Capuchos Convent**, often known as the Cork Convent, on the N375 west of the Pena Palace, you will find one of the most peculiar monasteries you can imagine. The cells are hollowed out of the rock, and lined with cork to keep out the damp. Much of the furniture is also cork. The monastery was founded by the Franciscans in 1560.

Cruz Alta is beyond the Capuchos Convent to the west. It is a peak 540 m high from which you can see as far as Lisbon, Cascais and Cape Espichel.

The **Moorish Castle**, which can be seen from the centre of the town, is half-way up the mountain on the way to the Pena Palace. It dates from the eighth or ninth century, but was greatly restored by King Sancho I and King Fernando I. There are five towers and a keep – not in a very good state – and long walls that climb up and down over the rocks and bridge chasms on the razor's edge of the mountain with precipices on either side. Inside the enclosure there are the remains of the little Romanesque São Pedro Church, which may originally have been a mosque. Nearby there is a vaulted cistern that carries water down to the National Palace in the town.

The **Pena Palace** is, as its name implies, on the mountain peak. It was built in the nineteenth century by Ferdinand Saxe-Coburg-Gotha, the consort of Maria II; the architect was Baron Eschwedge. The palace would have made Walt Disney very happy: there are turrets, domes, a drawbridge, tunnels, parapets, crenellated walls in every style imaginable, from mock-Arabic to Gothic to Victorian. It is quite fun, actually. The inside is royally furnished. The last kings of Portugal lived here before they were exiled. Open from 9 a.m. to 5 p.m. in summer and 6 p.m. in winter. Closed on Mondays.

The **Pena Palace Chapel** was part of the sixteenth-century monastery built by King Manuel I. It has a fine alabaster retable.

The **Pena Gardens** surround the palace. They were planted between 1846 and 1850 by King Fernando II. Trees and plants were brought from Portugal's territories all round the world. The Pena Gardens and the Monserrate Park have between them 3,000 different species of plants.

The **Church of Santa Maria** is a twelfth-century Gothic/Romanesque church under a hill in Santa Maria, a village that is actually part of Sintra. The **São Martinho Church** was built in the sixth century and restored in the eighteenth. It has painted wooden panels depicting the lives of Saints Anthony, Peter and Martin.

The **Museum Library** has a selection of prints and paintings of Sintra over the centuries.

Fair

The *Feira de Sintra*, takes place on the second and fourth Sunday of every month in São Pedro de Sintra. It is one of the most famous in the country. It sells everything from antiques (be careful) to pottery and vegetables. And you can eat grilled sardines or roast suckling pig and drink wine at the open-air stalls.

Where to stay
Expensive

Hotel Palácio dos Seteais, Rua do Bocage 8, Seteais, Sintra. Tel. (01) 9233200/9233250/9233225. A luxurious five star hotel built in the eighteenth-century Seteais Palace. It has eighteen rooms with beautiful furnishings, a restaurant, two swimming pools and tennis courts. There is a formal garden in front of the hotel.

Medium price **Hotel Tivoli-Sintra**, Praça da República. Tel. (01) 9233505/ 9233855. A modern hotel by the Nacional Palace, this four star hotel has seventy-five air-conditioned rooms with bath, a very good restaurant and a panoramic view.

Inexpensive **Pensão Sintra**, Travessa dos Avelares 12, São Pedro de Sintra. Tel. (01) 9230220. A three star pension with twenty rooms with bath.

Manor houses
Medium price **Quinta da Capela**, Estrada de Monserrate, 2710 Sintra. Tel. (01) 9230210. A beautiful old, noble house set in gardens with a swimming pool. It has a suite, four bedrooms with bath, and two apartments.

Inexpensive **Vila das Rosas**, Rua António Cunha 4. Tel. (01) 9234216. A large house on the northern outskirts of Sintra with four double rooms, a three-room suite, and a cottage, all with bath. Breakfast is served in the cool wine cellar in summer.

Where to eat The restaurant in the **Hotel Palácio dos Seteais** is wonderful. It is extremely elegant, has a marvellous view, and serves exquisite food.

Tulia, Rua Gil Vicente 4. Tel. (01) 9232378. A charming restaurant in what used to be three grain silos in an old house. Try the *bacalhau con natas* (codfish with whipped cream).

Cafe Paris, Praça da República 32. Tel. (01) 9232375. In the palace square, it has indoor and outdoor dining. Try the *arroz de Tamboril com gambas* (rice with fish and shrimp).

Adega do Saloio, Chão de Meninos. Tel. (01) 9231422. A rustic restaurant specializing in grills and shish kebabs.

The Tourist Office is in the Praça da República. Tel. (01) 923157.

Beaches **Colares**, 7 km west of Sintra on the N247, is famous for its wines. The beaches at nearby Praia das Maças and Azenhas do Mar have good seafood restaurants.

Praia do Guincho is a popular beach under the cliffs facing the Atlantic, 16 km south of Colares. The beach has a treacherous undertow, and the sea can be rough. In the winter the waves break violently on the rocks and can reach the tops of the cliffs. *Guincho* means 'a shriek' – which is an apt description of the wind. If you park your car on the cliff or in the pine woods, don't leave anything in it: if you do, the chances are it won't be there when you get back.

Where to stay, and eat Guincho has several good hotels and restaurants including **Hotel Guincho**, which is one of the nicest hotels in Portugal. With five stars and thirty-six rooms, it is a restored fortress, on a promontory looking out to sea. Tel. (01) 2850491.

Expensive

Medium price **Estalagem Muchaxo**, Praia do Guincho. Tel. (01) 2850221. A five star inn on the ocean with twenty-four rooms with bath, a bar, and swimming pool. It has one of the best seafood restaurants on the coast.

Cabo da Roca is a rocky headland standing 70 m above the Atlantic on the westernmost point of Europe. To get there, drive west along the coast road beyond Guincho, and turn left on to N247-4. There are several restaurants where you can get a certificate saying you have been to the westernmost point on the continent. There is a lighthouse on the point.

Cascais

Cascais is 13 km from Sintra by the N6-8-N9 and 32 km west of Lisbon on the coast road (called the Marginal). You can also reach it by local railway line from Lisbon. Once part of the defence for the port of Lisbon against pirates and other invaders, it is now a tourist resort and the home of a great many expatriate British businessmen and diplomats of many nations. The mansions of ex-kings and ex-dictators stand by the sea – some now occupied by rich Arabs.

There are vestiges of prehistoric occupation in the many grottoes and caves, and the area was also occupied by the Romans. Over the centuries it became a fishing village, from which brightly painted boats went out into the river and into the Atlantic to fish. You can still see the fishing boats pulled up on the beach in the little harbour, and there is still an auction of the day's catch every evening in the nearby market. Unfortunately, the little fishing village that was on the harbour was torn down to make way for a modern hotel.

What to see

On the west side of town towards Praia do Guincho there is a pine forest planted in the last century. This is the Marinha Grande, where many rich Portuguese and foreigners have houses. Within its area there are many sports facilities.

Along the coast road towards Guincho you will also come to the Boca do Inferno (Mouth of Hell). The name seems fairly accurate. It is a rocky promontory with underground caves into which the sea storms in great waves that hiss through the cavities and form whirlpools. There are stairways and viewing verandas in the rocks, but be careful: people have been swept away. There is a large roadside market selling all kinds of Portuguese crafts.

The Conde de Castro Guimarães Museum is in the mansion which belonged to the Castro Guimarães family, set in a large park on the way out of town on the beach road towards Guincho. It has an important collection of paintings, ceramics, sculpture, jewellery, old maps and furniture. The Nossa Senhora da Assunção Church has some paintings by Josefa de Óbidos. The São Jacinto Fort and the São Jorge Fort formed part of the defence works for Lisbon. The Citadel is a large military building dating from the seventeenth century.

Fairs

An auction of the day's catch of fish is held every weekday evening in the market. The Cascais market and fair is every Wednesday, in the centre of town.

Cascais Naval Club has a sailing school at weekends. There are yachts and motor boats for hire. You can also have lessons in water skiing and underwater fishing.

Entertainment

You will have no difficulty in finding a night life in Cascais. It is absolutely full of bars, discos and *fado* houses.

Where to stay

Hotel Albatross, Rua Frederico Arouca 100. Tel. (01) 282821. A

Expensive | luxury hotel on the water, originally a nineteenth-century villa for the royal family. Its modern addition has forty rooms with bath, a bar, swimming pool and an excellent panoramic restaurant.

Medium price | **Hotel Estoril Sol**, Parque Palmela. Tel. (01) 282831. A five star hotel on the beach with 310 rooms, several suites and every imaginable facility. It has its own 9-hole golf course.

Hotel Baia, Avenida Marginal. Tel. (01) 280055, telex BAIAOTEL-CASCAIS. A three star hotel with eighty rooms with bath. It has a terrace café-bar facing the fishermen's port.

Estalagem do Farol, Estrada da Boca do Inferno 7. Tel. (01) 280173/2864732. A four star inn with eighteen rooms with bath, a restaurant, bar, swimming pool and tennis courts.

Inexpensive | **Pensão Dom Carlos**, Rua Latina Coelho 8. Tel. (01) 2865154. A three star pension in a restored sixteenth-century mansion. It has eight rooms with bath, a bar and garden.

Manor house
Medium price | **Casa da Pérgola**, Avenida Valbom 13. Tel. (01) 2840040. A house in the centre of Cascais. It has a luxurious suite and five bedrooms with bath.

Casal de São Roque, Avenida Marginal. Tel. (01) 2680217. A charming, turn-of-the-century house not far from the beach with six rooms with bath.

Where to eat | There are many excellent seafood restaurants near the seafront and fish market: **João Padeiro**, Rua Visconde da Luz 12, tel. (01) 280232; **O Pescador**, Rua das Flores 10B, tel. (01) 282054; **Beira Mar**, Rua das Flores 6, tel. (01) 280152, and **O Pipas**, Rua das Flores 1B, tel. 286 4501. The English-style pubs **Duke of Wellington** and the **John Bull** also serve good English and other international fare.

What to eat | Fish, of course. Particularly grilled lobster, shrimps, *caldeirada* (a stew of assorted fish), *arroz de ameijoas* (rice with shellfish), grilled *robalo* (grey mullet), sole, cod.

Estoril | Estoril is next to Cascais on the coast road, 30 km from Lisbon and on the convenient local railway line that runs between Lisbon and Cascais. It has been a favourite resort for royalty and the rich since the last century. The turn of the century mansions and hotels with their large gardens are slowly being replaced by new hotels and modern houses, but the charm of the place has not been lost.

There are actually several Estorils bunched together, up on the hills above the coast road: São Pedro de Estoril, São João de Estoril and Monte Estoril. You should take a drive or a walk through them to see the old houses.

Casino | The world-famous Estoril Casino is in the lovely park in the centre of Estoril. It is a big, modern building that houses not only the casino but also a cinema, art gallery, restaurant and bars. The casino often sponsors events such as art exhibitions and craft fairs. The casino itself has the latest in slot machines with some of the biggest jackpots in Europe – more than 60 million escudos. It is open every day from 3 p.m. to 3 a.m. It offers baccarat, chemin de fer, vingt et un, bingo, roulette and slot machines.

Golf

The Estoril Golf Club, overlooking the sea, is open from 8.30 a.m. to sunset. Tel. (01) 2600176. The Hotel Estoril Sol Golf Club, 6 km north of Estoril on the Sintra road at Linho, is open from 9 a.m. to 7 p.m., except on Tuesdays. Tel. (01) 9232461.

Riding

There are several places where you can hire horses for riding, among them **Quinta da Marinha**, tel. (01) 289881, has a riding school and trails along the cliffs or in the pine woods west of Cascais.

Motor racing

Motor racing in the Estoril Autodrome attracts fans from all over the world, especially for the World Championship Formula 1. Ask at the Tourist Office for dates.

Art exhibitions

There are art exhibitions all the year round both at the casino and in the Estoril Tourist Office. There are also numerous art galleries.

Craft fair

A craft fair is organized every year by the Estoril Tourist Board. Exhibits come from every region of the country, and include tiles, wood carvings, embroideries, pottery, baskets, iron work, and so on. The fair is usually held in the casino. Inquire at the Tourist Office.

Music festival

The Estoril Music Festival offers concerts at reasonable prices in attractive settings. Inquire at the Tourist Office for dates.

Dog show

There is an international dog show in the park at Estoril every summer. It attracts hundreds of national and international dogs – and people. Inquire at the Tourist Office for dates.

Where to stay

Expensive

Hotel Palácio, Parque do Estoril. Tel. (01) 2680400. A luxurious five star hotel that has 200 rooms with bath and air conditioning. It has an excellent restaurant, a pleasant bar and a lovely open garden with a heated swimming pool.

Medium price

Hotel Atlântico, Estrada Marginal. Tel. (01) 2680270. A four star hotel with 183 rooms with bath. Some rooms have balconies and a wonderful view of the sea. There is a salt-water swimming pool with a terrace bar.

Estalagem Lennox Country Club, Rua Eng. Álvaro Pedro da Sousa 5. Tel. (01) 2680424. A four star inn with four suites, and thirty-two rooms with bath. It has a restaurant that serves buffet lunches and dinners. There is a heated swimming pool with a poolside bar, and there are also facilities for tennis, riding and golf.

Inexpensive

Pensão Pica-Pau, Rua Dom Afonso Henriques 48. Tel. (01) 2680803. A three star pension with forty-eight rooms with bath, a bar, restaurant and swimming pool.

Where to eat

Estoril Casino, Parque Estoril. Tel. (01) 2684521. An enormous, glittering restaurant/night club reminiscent of the Lido in Paris. The international show presents famous stars such as Julio Iglesias and Dionne Warwick. The food and service are impeccable. Surprisingly, for all this glamour, prices are reasonable – around 5,000 esc. for dinner and show, and only 3,000 just to see the show and have two drinks.

Four Seasons Grill, Parque Estoril. Tel. (01) 2680400. Changes its decor and menu each season. It is very elegant with excellent food.

Tamariz, Praia do Tamariz. Tel. (01) 2683512. A restaurant and snack bar next to the sea with a terrace garden.

English Bar, Estrada Marginal. Tel. (01) 2690413. A brown and white building overlooking the sea, decorated in the English manner, but serving Portuguese and international dishes.

Garrafão, Amoreira, on the outskirts of Estoril. Tel. (01) 2684195. An inexpensive seafood restaurant with its own vivarium.

The Tourist Office is in Arcadas do Parque. Tel. (01) 2680113/ 2687044/2681697.

Carcavelos

Carcavelos is between Estoril and Lisbon on the coast road. It has a wide beach that is good for surfing.

Fair

Every Thursday, in the main streets of Carcavelos, near the station, there is a big fair where you can buy anything you fancy, from whisky to carpets to clothes. Most of the sellers are gypsies. They set up their stalls early in the morning and pack up about 2 p.m. You can get some great bargains in clothes, especially T-shirts and pullovers, if you don't mind pushing. They sell lots of seconds of clothes destined for export to northern Europe, but look out for defects.

Oeiras

Oeiras is just along the coast road from Carcavelos, going towards Lisbon. There are several forts that formed part of the coastal defence of Lisbon. The Marquês de Pombal lived here when he was in power, and retired here after his fall, until he was banished to Pombal.

What to see

The Palace of the Marquês de Pombal is a pink eighteenth-century palace in the centre of the town. The São Julião Fort stands on the estuary facing south. It is an excellent example of a sixteenth-century Italian-style fortress. The work was under the direction of Miguel de Arruda, one of the architects of the Batalha Monastery. The Búgio Fort stands on a little islet in the middle of the estuary. It is a circular fort with a tall circular tower topped by a lighthouse. Work began on this fort in 1585, but it took many years to complete. Not even a lighthouse keeper lives here any more.

Where to eat

Saisa. Tel. (01) 2430634. A seafront restaurant on the coast road just before you get to Santa Amaro de Oeiras. It specializes in seafood, and produces one of the best paellas you will find anywhere.

Tourist Office, Largo Marquês de Pombal. Tel. (01) 2431500.

Queluz

Queluz is between Sintra and Lisbon on the N117. You can reach it by car or bus, or by train from Lisbon's Rossio station.

Queluz is best known for its pink Rococo palace that stands in a wide cobbled square. The palace was built between 1747 and 1752, on the orders of Prince Pedro, who was to become King Pedro III, consort of Queen Maria I. Poor, mad Queen Maria lived there.

The palace was planned by Mateus Vicente de Oliveira, a student of Ludwig, who built the Mafra Monastery. The Queluz Palace was considered to be a little Versailles, and although it is a little dishevelled now it is still very impressive. The main building has wings running off each side. There is a beautifully laid out garden with fountains, tiles and statuary. Inside, the walls are delicately painted and there are lovely tiles, period furniture, and paintings. During the month of August, each Friday, Saturday and Sunday night, there are presentations of eighteenth-century theatre, mime, music and ballet imitating those presented there in the court of the monarchs. The adjoining Cozinha Velha (see below) serves on those nights eighteenth-century dishes 'fit for a king'.

The palace is still used as a residence for visiting royalty and heads of state. Queen Elizabeth has stayed there. It is also used for state dinners, summer music concerts and special exhibitions.

Where to eat **Cozinha Velha**, Queluz. Tel. (01) 950232. A luxury restaurant in what was the old kitchen of the palace. The marble work table 5 m long, the copper utensils, the enormous spits and walk-in fireplace are all from the original palace kitchen. It has traditional cooking and special desserts. Closed on Wednesdays.

Lisbon

Lisbon, the capital city of Portugal, is on the estuary of the River Tagus. It sits on seven hills that have looked down on Phoenicians, Carthaginians, Romans and Moors, and on the ships of every seafaring nation in the world.

History
Prehistory There is evidence that there was a settlement here as early as the Mesolithic period: in the nineteenth century skeletons that can be dated to between 7700 and 7000 BC were discovered just north of Lisbon. By 3000 BC there was a densely populated settlement with houses, cattle and pottery. These early settlers were followed by Indo-Europeans – mostly Celts – with their Iron Age civilization. Then the Phoenicians and Carthaginians came, to trade in gold, tin and copper. It seems likely that the town's ancient name of Olisipo was of Phoenician origin (though indeed some say the town was founded by the Greek hero Ulysses during his ten-year odyssey following the Trojan war, and that it was called Olisipo after him).

Romans After the defeat of the Carthaginians in the Second Punic War (218-202 BC) the Iberian Peninsula fell under Roman domination. The Romans advanced to the Tagus, and in 137 BC Decimus Junius Brutus took Olisipo. From there he marched north, destroying Lusitanian strongholds, though for a long time he faced active and successful opposition from the Lusitanians under their leader Viriato (see page 171). Olisipo became the centre of Roman rule in the Peninsula, and it acquired the name of Felicitas Julia after Julius Caesar, who made the town a Roman municipality and granted the inhabitants Roman citizenship. Most of the Roman buildings, which included an amphitheatre dedicated to Nero, a necropolis, baths and temples, were destroyed by invaders or earthquakes, but some have been discovered under the city during excavations.

Germanic invasions Moors

After the Germanic invasions of AD 406 Lisbon was occupied by Swabians, and later by the Visigoths, who were Christians. In 714 the Moors drove out the Visigoths. The Moors stayed for four hundred years. Under their rule the town, which they called Aschbouna, flourished, becoming rich, and a centre of learning: many of the most illustrious of Moorish scientists, thinkers and writers came to Aschbouna. The Moors restored many Roman buildings, rebuilt the fortress, and turned the Visigoth cathedral into a mosque.

Crusaders

The town finally fell to the Christians, under King Afonso Henriques, in 1147, largely thanks to the help of English, Flemish and German Crusaders. These Crusaders were rough, tough men, some of them little better than pirates. King Afonso Henriques had promised that in return for their help they could have all the spoils of the city. After a siege of seventeen weeks the Moors in the city asked for a truce. An agreement was made that the Moors would be allowed to go in peace, if they would leave their goods behind. This agreement was not kept. As the Moors began to file out of the city, the Crusaders rushed in to rob, rape and slaughter. They even cut the throat of the Mozarabic Bishop of Lisbon. It took four days for the Moors to leave the city, and many of them were murdered before they could get out.

It is said that King Afonso Henriques gave the Crusaders land north of Lisbon (some Portuguese claim to be descended from these Crusaders). The King made an English priest, Gilbert of Hastings, the new Bishop of Lisbon. He also ordered the Church of Santa Maria dos Martires (Saint Mary of the Martyrs) to be built on the burial ground of the fallen Crusaders.

Building

King Afonso Henriques built a Romanesque cathedral where the Moorish mosque had been. The first Baixa (the town centre, where the shops and banks are today) was constructed, on canals crossed by bridges, as a branch of the Tagus still extended far inland at that time. His successor King Afonso III built the São Domingos Monastery in the Rossio. King Dinis of course supervised an extensive building programme. He built walls to protect Lisbon from pirates, and laid out two large squares where big fairs were held. At this time there was trade with Genoa, Flanders, Catalonia, England and Brittany.

Town life

By 1384 Lisbon had walls 6.5 km long, with seventy-seven towers and thirty-eight entrance ways. Its population was 60,000. It was not a healthy town. There was no sewage system – the people just threw out their refuse after dark. Town criers walked the streets warning against fire. Jews lived in their own separate quarter, as did Muslims, and they were required to wear identifying coloured badges.

João I and Philippa of Lancaster

Lisbon finally became the permanent capital of the country after King João I came to the throne, in 1385. During King João's reign Lisbon became a prosperous place. A glittering court surrounded him

237

and his English queen, Philippa, the eldest daughter of John of Gaunt, Duke of Lancaster. King João and Philippa of Lancaster had six children: Duarte, who studied law and philosophy, and succeeded to the throne; Pedro, a traveller and man of letters; Henry the Navigator, the instigator of the Portuguese Age of Discoveries; João, grand Master of the Order of Sant'Iago; Fernando, the Master of Avis, who died in Morocco; and Isabel, who married Philip the Good of Burgundy. The Queen also brought up the King's two illegitimate children, born before his marriage.

Queen Philippa, who was studious and very religious, had great influence on her husband and children. The King became quite pious, and apart from an occasional kiss for a lady in waiting (see page 228), it seems that after his marriage there were no royal escapades. Adultery became a crime at the court. Philippa was also much loved by the Portuguese people. She died of the plague in 1415, just as her husband and sons were setting off for Ceuta in North Africa on an expedition against the Moors. She and João are buried together at the Batalha Monastery (see page 210).

Age of Discoveries

By the fifteenth century Portugal had become a nation of traders. Ships were built beside the River Tagus and set off for faraway ports. Prince Henry set up an observatory and founded a school of navigation in the Algarve, and from there he sent out ships to explore the coast of Africa. He studied maps, navigational charts and nautical instruments. His explorers brought back from their voyages gold, ivory, spices, negro slaves – and information. In 1419 they discovered Madeira and in 1427 the Azores, both of which were subsequently colonized by Portugal. In 1434 Gil Eanes rounded Cape Bojador, and in 1436 Afonso Gonçalves reached the River of Gold.

Shortly afterwards Henry's men acquired a new and revolutionary kind of boat, the caravel. It was light, long and high, with lateen sails and a shallow keep that allowed it to go in close to shore. It was relatively very easy to manoeuvre, needed only a small crew, and could go very fast. The explorers set up *padroes* – stone pillars topped by crosses and the arms of Portugal – all down the coast of Africa. They reached Cape Verde and Guinea in 1448, and when Henry died in 1460 his explorers had reached Sierra Leone.

There was then a pause in the explorations, but they were resumed under João II, who came to the throne in 1481. In 1482 he sent out Diogo Cão, who reached the Congo and northern Angola, and brought back to Lisbon native chiefs, who became Christians.

In 1486 King João sent out two expeditions, one under Pero de Covilhã (see page 186), and one under Bartolomeu Dias. Bartolomeu Dias left Lisbon by sea in August 1487, heading for Walvis Bay in what is now Namibia. Heavy seas and contrary winds forced his caravels to turn out to the open sea to escape the mounting southerlies. He sailed for thirteen days south-south-west until the roaring forties forced him to turn east again and seek land. He did not find it where he calculated it should be. Finally he turned north to run before the wind. In early February, he sighted Africa to the west. He realized that he had rounded the southern tip of Africa – a discovery that opened the way to India and changed the history of the world. He re-entered Lisbon estuary in December 1488, having journeyed 16,000 miles and opened the Indian Ocean to the Portuguese.

To commemorate the 500th anniversary of the voyage of Bartolomeu Dias round the southern tip of Africa, a group of Portuguese emigrants to South Africa raised money and had a replica of Dias's caravel built in the Vila do Conde shipyards, using the same kind of wood and the same methods that were used for the first ship. The caravel, named the *Bartolomeu Dias*, sailed from Portugal in October 1987, skippered by Captain Emilio Carlos da Sousa and with a crew of sixteen, including doctors, architects, university students, naval officers, businessmen, yachtsmen and a Portuguese television team. It reached Mossel Bay, round the Cape of Good Hope, in February 1988 – just 500 years after Bartolomeu Dias.

The Portuguese will be commemorating the 500th anniversary of the discoveries up to the end of the twentieth century. There will be exhibitions in Lisbon, and other voyages to repeat those of antiquity.

After Bartolomeu Dias's momentous discovery, Portuguese navigators began to think about sailing to India west across the Atlantic, and calculated the distances; but a plague and other disasters intervened, and plans remained in abeyance. In 1481 Christopher Columbus went to King João II with the proposal that he should take an expedition across the Atlantic. The King rejected the idea, so Columbus took it to England, and to Spain. He sailed for Ferdinand and Isabella of Spain – and the rest is history. On his return voyage, he stopped at Lisbon. João II immediately prepared an expedition to go to America, but he was prevented by Spain, and by the Pope. In 1494, after much negotiation, the Treaty of Tordesillas was signed, designating the Spanish and the Portuguese spheres of discovery.

João II died in 1495, leaving no direct heir, and his cousin Manuel came to the throne. Manuel I introduced a constitution and an administrative system, and he continued the voyages of discovery. In 1497 he sent Vasco da Gama with three ships to sail round the tip of Africa to India. They battled their way through rough seas round the Cape and got beyond Mossel Bay on Christmas Day – so they called the place they landed Natal. They landed at Calcutta on 18 May 1498. The Portuguese Vasco da Gama had reached the India so many had sought in vain.

Lisbon in the sixteenth century

For a time after this discovery Lisbon was Empress of the World. Bankers and merchants from Germany, England, France, Flanders and Italy set up shop in Lisbon. You could buy anything: gold, precious stones, silk, ceramics, tea from China. . . . The city bloomed with great buildings in the Manueline style named for Manuel I – their Gothic structures adorned with motifs evoking the discoveries: ropes, seaweed, shells, almost anything that related to the sea. The Jerónimos Monastery and the Belém Tower, the churches of São Vicente and Madre de Deus, the great Misericórdia Hospital, seemingly endless palaces and monasteries were all built during this period. There were lavish parties, pompous religious processions and festivals.

The discoveries continued. Pedro Álvares Cabral, under the patronage of King Manuel, discovered Brazil and greatly extended the Portuguese empire in the Far East. For a time Manuel I was the richest ruler in Europe.

When Manuel died in 1521 he was succeeded by his son João III, who was nineteen years old. João spent great amounts of money colonizing Brazil. People were leaving their farms and moving into Lisbon, where life was easier. Many nobles were living at court. João got into debt.

Jews   Jews had lived in Portugal for centuries, under both Moors and Christians. They had become politically and economically powerful, as court doctors, artisans, astrologers – and bankers, financiers and money lenders. In 1492 the Jews were expelled from Spain, and some 60,000 of them took refuge in Portugal, many paying King João huge amounts of money for permission to settle.

In 1496, when Manuel I married the daughter of the Spanish monarchs, they required that he expel the Jews. He was reluctant to do this – he needed the Jews as advisers and bankers – so he thought of a very Portuguese solution: he would have the Jews baptized as 'New Christians'. When they would not agree to this, he had them dragged forcibly to the baptismal font. Still some committed suicide rather than submit, and some escaped to Morocco and Holland. He then decided that the Jews could have a 'technical conversion', after which no questions would be asked about their religious convictions for twenty years. On these terms, many stayed and lived as 'New Christians' – and 'Secret Jews'.

In 1506 a terrible incident occurred in Lisbon. During a religious ceremony in the Church of São Domingos, what was probably a play of light on a crucifix inspired some of the people attending to shout that a miracle had occurred. A 'New Christian' scoffed at the idea. He was killed by members of the congregation. Then two Dominican priests ran through the streets, inciting mobs to violence. During riots that lasted three days, several hundred Jews were slaughtered. Manuel had fifty of the culprits executed, closed the São Domingos Monastery, and extended the grace period for Jews by sixteen years.

But João III hated the Jews. In 1537 the Inquisition was established in Lisbon, in a palace in the Rossio. The 'New Christians' were pursued, tortured and burned to death. The *autos-da-fé* were days of great festivity in Lisbon, as the condemned filed into the Praça do Comércio in their *mamelucos* (hoods with their faces painted on them). Nobles – and many foreign dignitaries – enjoyed the spectacle from the balconies round the square. Before the Inquisition ended in the late eighteenth century, several thousand people had died.

Sebastião

João III was succeeded by his son Sebastião, born after his father's death and brought up by his grandmother, and Jesuit priests. A difficult, unruly boy, he became obsessed with the idea that he had been chosen by Christ to fight the infidels. He gathered together the nobles and 15,000 troops, and sailed off to Morocco in 500 ships. His army was overwhelmed at Alcácer-Quibir. Eight thousand were killed and almost all the rest were captured – less than a hundred got back to Tangier. For three weeks, no one knew where Sebastião was, and there was a widespread belief that he was still alive. Even after it was announced that his body had been buried under the house of the Governor of Alcácer, the legend grew up that he was alive and would return. This was the origin of what is referred to today as 'Sebastianismo' – the Portuguese longing for the return of a strong leader.

Spanish domination

Sebastião was succeeded by his elderly great-uncle, the Cardinal-King Henrique, who reigned for only two years. Then in 1580 the throne was claimed by Philip II of Spain, who became Philip I of Portugal. He was succeeded by Philip II (III of Spain) and Philip III (IV of Spain). Despite some popular unrest, the Spanish kings stayed in power until 1640, when the Spanish Governor of Lisbon was deposed in a coup led by a group of Portuguese noblemen. The Duke of Bragança, who was descended from the illegitimate son of João I, became King João IV.

João IV

Alliance with England

João IV inherited a country without an army or navy or border fortifications – without any horses to speak of, even. He entered a long period of strife with the Spaniards, French and Dutch. However, the old friendship with England was renewed, and it persisted through all the vicissitudes of the British régime. The Commonwealth Treaty of 1654 gave the English many rights in Portugal. The English in Lisbon were free to trade, they had their own judges, they were free to practise their own religion; and English warships were to be allowed into the Tagus. In 1662 the alliance was consolidated by the marriage of Charles II of England to João's daughter, Catherine of Bragança.

Afonso VI

But by that time João had been succeeded by his son, Afonso VI, who came to the throne in 1656. Unfortunately, Afonso was partially paralysed, and not quite right in the head. For much of his reign he was either kept in Brazil, or locked up in Sintra, while his brother Pedro ruled as regent. Pedro became king, as Pedro II, in 1683.

Gold rush

Pedro was fortunate in that during his reign gold was discovered in Brazil, in 1692 in the Mato Grosso. By 1705 there was an enormous gold rush that took 50,000 Portuguese to Brazil. The gold from Brazil produced another spate of lavish building and covered the churches in layers of gold leaf. In Lisbon the great aqueduct planned by architects

Gonçalo Vieira and Manuel da Maia was built to bring water from Queluz, and the ornate Necessidades Palace was built.

When Pedro II died in 1706 João V came to the throne, at the age of seventeen. He continued to spend Brazilian gold, and to try to imitate the splendours of the French court. He built the great Mafra Monastery. In 1750 he was succeeded by King José.

Earthquake All of the splendour ended suddenly one sunny morning. At nine a.m. on 1 November 1755 all of Lisbon began to shake and crumble, in one of the worst earthquakes ever known. Within five minutes Lisbon was demolished. The Senate House, the Palace of the Inquisition, the São Domingos Monastery, the Carmo Monastery, the Opera House, were all devastated. Because it was All Saints' Day, many of the people were in the churches, where there were lots of candles burning. These started a fire that spread over the entire city, consuming all that the earthquake had spared. All records were burned. A tidal wave carried much of the debris and many of the bodies out to sea. The Custom House and the Docks were washed away, along with the people who had taken refuge there.

The quakes continued for five days, with decreasing intensity. People slept in the fields, or took refuge on boats. The King and his family lived in tents in the gardens of the palace. Altogether about 20,000 buildings were reduced to rubble, and 40,000 people died, in the earthquake and in the epidemics and famine that followed. The King refused ever to live in a stone building again, so he had a wooden palace – *A Barraca* – built for himself and the court on a hill above where the Ayuda Palace now stands.

Only the Jerónimos Monastery, the Belém Tower and the aqueduct withstood the earthquake. The English traders of the British factory were virtually wiped out. Seventy-two English people, mostly merchants and members of their families, died in the earthquake. Their factories, homes and goods were destroyed. They never recovered.

Marquês de The Prime Minister at the time of the earthquake was the Marquês
Pombal de Pombal. He rebuilt central Lisbon as a planned city laid out in squares with straight parallel streets and underground sewers. The buildings (as you can see today in the Baixa) were almost uniformly five storeys tall, with rectangular windows. Their parts were prefabricated, and erected in series.

All this was laudably efficient. And in affairs of state too the Marquês instigated many reforms which made for greater efficiency. In particular, he worked hard to promote national industries. However, his methods were ruthlessly autocratic; and his régime was a reign of terror. Taking advantage of King José's predilection for pleasure rather than work, he took all power for himself, crushing anyone who stood in his way. He made his brother Inquisitor, and used the Inquisition for his own purposes. Determined to break the power of the Jesuits, he locked up 124 of them in the São Julião Fort, where some of them died, and he had one of their leaders, Father Malagrida, burned at the stake in a spectacular *auto-da-fé*. And in 1759 he dissolved the Society of Jesus in Portugal altogether, and expelled all Jesuits from Portugal, confiscating their possessions.

He also attacked the nobility. He accused the Duke of Aveiro, the Marquês de Távora, the Marquês de Gouveia, the Count of Atougis and their families of attempting to assassinate King José. They were arrested, tortured and finally executed in front of the Belém Tower. Some were beheaded; some were hanged; some were broken on the wheel and strangled. Then their bodies were burned, and the ashes scattered in the River Tagus.

It was typical of Pombal that he built the new university in Coimbra but shut down Évora University; and proscribed any book (including those of Voltaire and Rousseau) that might encourage independent thought.

As soon as King José died, in 1777, his successor, Queen Maria I, banished the Marquês to Pombal, in the Beira region. She released hundreds of political prisoners, and had many of his measures reversed. The people burned his effigy in the streets. He died in 1782, at the age of eighty.

Peninsular War

In the early years of the nineteenth century the Portuguese became involved in the Peninsular War between France and England, on the side of the English. The French invaded Portugal three times, but each time they were driven out by the combined forces of the English and the Portuguese under the Duke of Wellington.

At the beginning of the war João VI and his family and court had run away to Brazil, taking nearly all of Portugal's money with them. Even after the war was over, King João was reluctant to return, and he only went back in the end under the threat of a movement for popular suffrage and a constitution in Portugal. At a meeting in Lisbon in 1821 liberal representatives of the people drew up a constitution which included the institution of an elected parliament, and provisions to suppress feudalism and the Inquisition. When King João came back from Brazil he had to agree to this constitution.

Liberalism

War of Succession

João's death, in 1826, was followed by the civil War of Succession between his two sons, the liberal Pedro IV and his absolutist younger brother Miguel (see page 116). Miguel was finally defeated and went into exile, but Pedro lived for only a few months after his victory. He was succeeded by his daughter, Maria II.

Pedro had declared the extinction of all religious houses, and the sale of all their properties. There were at that time 402 monasteries and 175 convents in Portugal. But all the same, their sale could not discharge the terrible debts contracted during the civil war, and the royal jewels too had to be sold.

Political confusion

Political life in Portugal during the rest of the century was marked by repeated squabbles, and the rise and fall of governments. In some ways life did improve for the people. Attempts were made to set up a school system, roads and bridges were built, the death penalty, penal servitude and solitary life imprisonment were abolished. However, by the end of the nineteenth century the political system was in chaos, the state was virtually bankrupt, and the monarchy was deeply unpopular, and facing a great deal of republican opposition.

Assassination

In February 1908, King Carlos and his heir were assassinated in the Praça do Comércio. The younger son, Manuel, succeeded, and managed to hold out for two years during a deteriorating political situation. Then, convinced there was nothing more to be done, he departed with his family for exile in England.

The Republic

The Republican Party gained a huge majority in the elections for the assembly of 1911. They created a two-chamber parliament, abolished all titles of nobility, dissolved the Jesuits (again), and passed the Law of Separation between Church and State. They started free universities and supported unions and the right to strike. They also continued to squabble among themselves.

In 1916 Portugal entered the First World War on the side of the Allies. Throughout the war, and the years that followed, internal political agitation continued. Governments came and went, leaders were assassinated. The country was still heavily in debt.

Salazar

By 1926 the army had had enough. In a bloodless coup they deposed the government. Again, there were various rapid changes of leader over the next few years. But in 1928 Dr António de Oliveira Salazar, a professor of finance at the University of Coimbra, was invited to become Minister of Finance, and given absolute control over the finances of the state. Within an amazingly short time he had managed to balance the budget, reduce the national debt and the cost of living and generally put the economy in order. In 1932 he was made Prime Minister. From that time until 1968, when he was forced to retire because of ill health, Salazar, though constitutionally responsible to the president, held, and wielded, supreme power in Portugal.

Salazar supported Franco in the Spanish Civil War, and managed to keep Portugal neutral in the Second World War. During these years Portugal's neutrality made Lisbon into something like the setting for a comic opera drama, as spies of every country spied on one another. Allied and German planes were side by side on the airfield, and people of all nationalities and both sides mingled in the bar at the Hotel Tivoli. Lisbon became home for refugees from all over Europe. Thousands of Jews escaped to Lisbon, and from there were taken to other countries, especially the United States, in Portuguese ships or, later, clipper planes. Meanwhile many of the deposed crowned heads of Europe were also in Lisbon, sunning themselves on the beach at Estoril or gambling or dancing at the casino.

At the end of the war, Lisbon became the place of exchange for prisoners of war.

War for
independence

After the war, Portugal lost most of its Far Eastern territories. In 1962 war for independence started in all of its African territories: Angola, Mozambique, Guinea Bissau and São Tomé e Príncipe. The war lasted for twelve years, during which time Lisbon was the point of debarcation for the tens of thousands of Portuguese men going to fight in Africa. Lisbon also became increasingly the scene of pitched battles between the police and students protesting against the war. Several clandestine organizations put bombs in military installations and distributed anti-war propaganda.

Repression

The Salazar régime became more and more repressive. All newspapers were rigidly censored. Only one political party was permitted, and voting privileges were restricted. Anyone who tried to organize an opposition party would find himself pursued by the police. The Communist Party was banned, its members imprisoned. You could be sent to prison for trying to organize a union. The secret police were everywhere, the prisons were full of political prisoners, and many people were in exile abroad.

1974
Revolution

In 1968 Salazar was succeeded by university professor Marcelo Caetano. There was hope of a 'Portuguese spring', but this did not come about. Then, on 25 April 1974, a group of young military officers calling themselves the MFA (Movimento das Forças Armadas – Movement of the Armed Forces), staged a *coup d'état*. Called to arms by a song broadcast on the radio at 3 a.m., they converged on Lisbon and took it, with very few shots being fired. Marcelo Caetano was conducted to the airport and into exile in Brazil. The political prisoners were released. Workers were quickly organized into unions, and began to demonstrate in the streets of Lisbon. The radio broadcast revolutionary songs. Truckloads of red carnations were brought into Lisbon, and became the symbol of the Revolution.

A provisional government was set up, and elections were called. Soon, however, left-wing officers and political leaders began to take over. Under pressure, the new parliament wrote a Marxist constitution. Factories and lands were seized by the workers. Capitalists and professionals fled, and some were jailed without charges. There was a succession of takeovers by different groups of the radical left.

Finally, on 25 November 1975, moderate officers and political leaders, including the Socialists and Social Democrats, quelled a planned leftist putsch and in consequence were able to oust the radical left from power. A new constitution was promulgated in 1976. Parliament was to be elected by universal suffrage, in a system of proportional representation. The President was also to be elected by a popular vote. The Prime Minister and other ministers were to be responsible to the President and to Parliament. Independence was granted to Portugal's overseas territories: with the unforeseen result that about three-quarters of a million refugees fled to Lisbon. It is a tribute to the Portuguese character that these refugees have been absorbed into the population with very little friction – no mean feat, since they amount to an addition of almost 10 per cent to the population of Portugal.

After 1976 there was very little political stability, mostly because the large number of political parties made it almost impossible for any one party to have a majority in Parliament. There were sixteen different governments in the years between 1975 and 1987. In 1987 the right-of-centre Social Democrats finally won a majority. Economics professor Aníbal Cavaco Silva was named Prime Minister. In a separate election, former Socialist leader Dr Mário Soares, who had served three times as Prime Minister, was elected President.

You can still see political posters peeling from the walls, and slogans painted there, from all the elections and demonstrations that followed the Revolution; many are now plastered with posters of pop groups.

Ties with England
Crusaders

There were probably trade connections between Lisbon and England far before recorded time, but we know that contact became very close in the twelfth century, when English Crusaders helped the Portuguese kings to wrest Lisbon and other Portuguese towns from the Moors – and stayed to do a bit of raiding.

Philippa of Lancaster

Philippa of Lancaster, John of Gaunt's daughter, became the wife of King João I of Portugal, and had great influence on the Portuguese court in the late fourteenth and early fifteenth centuries. A pious and learned lady, she set a high tone for the court. She brought a great many of her English ladies with her, and many of them married Portuguese noblemen. Several Portuguese families trace their ancestry back to one or other of Queen Philippa's ladies. She passed on her love of learning to her sons, all of whom became outstanding men: the most renowned of them all being Henry the Navigator, who started Portuguese exploration and the Age of Discoveries.

Royalists v. Commonwealth

In the seventeenth century the kings of Portugal managed to maintain a friendship with England through all the vicissitudes of the Commonwealth and the Restoration. But King João IV was hard put to maintain impartiality when Prince Rupert, nephew of the executed Charles I, put into the Tagus with his ships, bent on pirating the ships of the English Commonwealth. The King wished to oblige his friend Prince Rupert, but did not wish to annoy the British merchants of the Factory, many of whom supported the Commonwealth. He ended by putting some of the Factory members in prison, much to their disgust.

British Factory

The Lisbon Factory was made up of rich merchants who had come from England and made their fortunes in trade. They have been described as a 'jolly bunch' who, along with the diplomats and assorted other English who came to Lisbon to winter or for their health, lived in a round of constant parties, balls and card-playing. Their heyday was in the sixteenth, seventeenth and early eighteenth centuries, until the 1755 Lisbon earthquake nearly wiped them out. They had their factories and warehouses on the river front, lived on the hills to the west, and spent their summers in Sintra. At times they had trouble with the Inquisition; at others with the Marquês de Pombal, who wanted to tax them and restrict their trade to encourage Portuguese manufacturing. After a great deal of struggle, they were allowed to have their own clergyman and cemetery.

Henry
Fielding

Lisbon was a favourite place for English poets and writers. The novelist Henry Fielding came in August 1754, hoping to improve his health. Sadly, he lived for only two months after his arrival, and he was buried in the little British cemetery in Estrela. Many have come to visit his grave, though for a long time it was left without a marker. Finally a large tombstone was placed there.

William
Beckford

Probably the Englishman who left the clearest picture of life in Lisbon was William Beckford, who wrote about it wittily and perceptively. When he first came to Lisbon in March 1787 he was a widower of twenty-six. Through his mother, who owned huge sugar plantations in Jamaica, he was one of the richest men in England, but he had been involved in a scandalous affair with a boy and had been boycotted by his family and society. In Lisbon, he expected to be received by the English consul, Mr Walpole, and presented to the court and English society. He was quite affronted to find himself snubbed, because his reputation had preceded him.

However, he was taken up by the Marquês de Marialva and his family. He loved the life they led, surrounded by costumed negroes, dwarfs, musicians, priests and assorted other characters, in their palaces in Lisbon and Sintra. They were the most powerful family in Lisbon; but, in spite of all their efforts, they could not get him presented to the Queen, Maria I. Finally, on a third visit in 1798, he was presented to the royal family in their palace in Queluz; but by that time the Queen had gone mad.

Beckford wrote of all his adventures in Lisbon and described in detail trips that he took to Batalha and Alcobaça. He bought the palace at Monserrate in Sintra, remodelled it and planted gardens. When he returned to England, he introduced a 'Marialva' life-style at his home at Fonthill.

Byron

Byron came in July 1809, on his way to Greece. He stayed long enough to visit Sintra, fall in love with it, take a swim in the Tagus and eat oranges. He took a dislike to the Portuguese, however.

The English
today

The English in Lisbon today do not have a fine Factory House, as those in Oporto do, but they have a hospital, a club, a theatre and a cemetery on a piece of crown land in the Estrela in Lisbon. There is a small Jewish cemetery in the grounds too, dating from the time when Jews could not be buried on Portuguese land.

River Tagus

The River Tagus begins high in the mountains of Spain, and flows down through Aranjuez and Toledo and across the plains into Portugal. Off and on for centuries there have been plans to make it navigable all the way from Lisbon to Toledo. It has always been an important river for trade, and its estuary has always been a busy place.

Large, flat boats called *fragatas* used to carry all of the goods in the river. Today most of them are rotting away. There are ferry boats that will take you across the river to Almada, where there are some good fish restaurants with views of Lisbon. You can also take tourist excursions up the river and down to the beaches at Cascais.

Lisbon today

Lisbon today is very different from the place it was even a few years ago. Streets in the centre have been closed to traffic, and little outdoor markets, restaurants and cafés have grown up. You will see painters drawing on the pavements, and musicians playing.

The influx of refugees from the former territories in Africa has meant that new bars and restaurants with African food and music have opened up. Emigrants returning from northern Europe have opened new boutiques, restaurants and bars. There are new fashion designers – for example, Ana Salazar – designing original and exciting clothes. There are many new art galleries showing the paintings of Portuguese contemporary artists. There are new shopping centres open day and night, where you can buy whatever you need.

Not all is good. Much of Lisbon is looking shabby. There are poor areas where old buildings are falling down. There are shanty towns all around. Ugly new buildings are replacing some historical ones.

Even so, Lisbon is still a beautiful little city, with its many parks, wide, tree-lined avenues and narrow, twisting streets, spacious squares, and the river. The best way to see it is on foot, but be sure to bring walking shoes, or gym shoes. The pavements with their decorated stones are pretty, but slippery and dangerous.

Transport

Buses

Buses are very convenient and cheap. But avoid travelling during rush hours! You can get blocks of tickets at a slight discount in kiosks belonging to the national bus company, Rodoviário Nacional. Tourists can get special passes at a big saving by presenting their passports at the ticket offices at the Praça dos Restauradores, the Rotunda, or the Santa Justa Elevator (see page 34).

Trams

Trams are old and rickety, but they take you slowly through the historic old parts of town, and some routes have spectacular views of the river. If you take the Graça tram from behind Praça da Figueira it will take you through the Baixa, up the hill past the Cathedral and all the way to Graça. It stops at the Santa Luzia Belvedere, where there is a lovely view of the Tagus and the Alfama, and it is only a short walk from there up to Saint George's Castle. A tram ride costs around 70 esc. You can use your tourist pass if you have one.

Metros

Metros are fast and cheap, and will take you to most places in the upper town. You can use a tourist pass.

Taxis

Taxis are cheap; however there are many complaints about taxi drivers overcharging. An average ride in town will cost you about 250 esc. The trip to the airport is approximately 500 esc. If you travel beyond the city limits, the driver will turn off the meter at the town boundary and compute the rest of the fare by kilometre.

What to see

Saint George's Castle and the Alfama

Most of the buildings that pre-dated the 1755 earthquake were destroyed. Only a few remain: they include the Jerónimos Monastery, the Belém Tower, and the aqueduct.

It is best to divide your visit according to districts: Saint George's Castle and the Alfama; the Ribeira; Belém; the Bairro Alto; the nineteenth-century Lisbon of Pombal; and the immediate outskirts.

Saint George's Castle is on a high hill above the city, surrounded by the ancient Alfama district. The castle is on a site that has been occupied since prehistoric times, and by Romans, Visigoths, Moors and Christians. The Moors made it a great centre of their civilization, gathering their most illustrious philosophers, theologians and scientists there. The present castle was built in the twelfth to fourteenth centuries – King Afonso Henriques may have built it to celebrate his victory over the Moors in 1147. The Alcaçova (palace) within the walls was built by King Dom Dinis and remained the home of the Portuguese monarchs until the late sixteenth century. The Castle has been greatly damaged over the centuries by sieges and earthquakes. You can stroll about its gardens where peacocks roam, or look at the spectacular views from the ramparts all around. You can easily reach the castle by tram or taxi, or you can park your car at the very top, in the grounds. It is also fun to walk up the steep stairs and passageways through the Alfama.

The **Cathedral** is just down the hill on the main street leading to the centre of town. The oldest church in the city, built in 1147 by King Afonso Henriques on the site of a destroyed Moorish mosque, it was badly damaged in the earthquake and repaired in this century. It has a massive, solid Romanesque façade with two side towers. Inside, the principal nave dates from the twelfth century, the chancel is Renaissance, and there is a lovely eighteenth-century organ. The Gothic chapels have interesting tombs. The cloister, which was constructed by King Dinis in the fourteenth century, was badly damaged, and is a museum of pieces collected during the restoration. Saint Anthony of Padua was baptized in the font in 1195. Beggars, lunatics and thieves on the steps of the Cathedral lend an authentic medieval touch.

Santo António da Sé church below the Cathedral was built in the early nineteenth century on the spot where Saint Anthony of Padua was born. It was paid for with alms collected by the children of Lisbon. It has a small museum dedicated to Saint Anthony.

The **Santa Luzia Belvedere**, just up the street, has a lovely view of the river and the Alfama, and a charming outdoor café.

The **Espírito Santo Museum-School of Decorative Arts**, in a seventeenth-century palace in the Largo das Portas do Sol beyond the belvedere to the north-east, has a collection of beautiful furniture, tapestries, European and Oriental china, silver, crystal, paintings and engravings. The adjoining school has about twenty-five workshops for

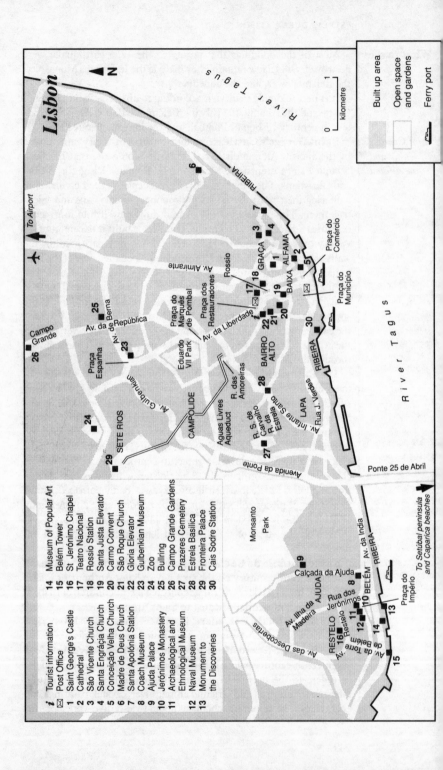

Lisbon

N ↑

To Airport ✈

River Tagus

i Tourist information
⊠ Post Office
1 Saint George's Castle
2 Cathedral
3 São Vicente Church
4 Santa Engrácia Church
5 Conceição Velha Church
6 Madre de Deus Church
7 Santa Apolónia Station
8 Coach Museum
9 Ajuda Palace
10 Jerónimos Monastery
11 Archaeological and
   Ethnological Museum
12 Naval Museum
13 Monument to
   the Discoveries
14 Museum of Popular Art
15 Belém Tower
16 St Jerónimo Chapel
17 Teatro Nacional
18 Rossio Station
19 Santa Justa Elevator
20 Carmo Convent
21 São Roque Church
22 Gloria Elevator
23 Gulbenkian Museum
24 Zoo
25 Bullring
26 Campo Grande Gardens
27 Prazeres Cemetery
28 Estrela Basilica
29 Fronteira Palace
30 Cais Sodre Station

Built up area
Open space
and gardens
Ferry port

0   1
kilometre

River Tagus

To Setúbal peninsula
and Caparica beaches

restoring antiques, making copies of eighteenth-century furniture, and teaching old methods of making gold leaf, wood carving, sculpture and other crafts. The Largo das Portas do Sol has outdoor restaurants and bars with splendid views. You can see part of the old Visigoth wall and, on top of the wall, the Santa Luzia church containing the tombs of Afonso III's family.

The **São Vicente Church**, across the valley from the Portas do Sol, was part of a monastery commissioned at the end of the sixteenth century by the Spanish King Felipe II, who had usurped the Portuguese throne, and designed by Filippo Terzi. Its severe majesty and grandiose size reflect the style favoured by the Spanish monarch in the Escorial he built outside Madrid. It was later reconstructed with a Mannerist façade. The church contains life-size wooden sculptures, and the cloisters are covered with eighteenth-century glazed tiles, representing fables by Fontaine. The pantheon of the Royal House of Bragança, whose kings ruled Portugal between 1656 and 1910, is located in the convent refectory.

The **Thieves Market**, held every Tuesday and Saturday in the Campo de Santa Clara behind the church, sells everything from antiques to hi-fis.

The **Church of Santa Engrácia** is a Baroque structure designed by João Antunes in the seventeeenth century, following an unusual centralized plan with undulating contours. It has a lovely domed roof and colourfully decorated marble floors. This is the third church on the site. It was ordered built in 1568 by Princess Maria in honour of the fourth-century Santa Engrácia, martyred in Spain; but desecrations, tempests, wars and the outlawing of the religious orders prevented its being finished until 1966, giving rise to the saying that anything that takes forever to do is *'uma obra de Santa Engrácia'*. It is now the National Pantheon, containing the cenotaphs of Portugal's most famous figures.

The **Conceição Velha Church** is down the hill from the castle in Rua da Alfândega, towards the Praça do Comércio. Built in the first part of the sixteenth century, the church was devastated in the earthquake, and only the south façade survives. It has a Manueline door showing Our Lady of Compassion sheltering Pope Leo X, King Manuel, Queen Leonor, bishops and others under her long mantle.

The **Manueline Gate** is near the Conceição Velha Church.

The **Casa dos Bicos** is nearby in the Rua dos Bacalhoeiros (Street of the Codfish Sellers). It was built by Afonso de Albuquerque, son of the Viceroy of India, around 1523. At this time, when Portugal's overseas trade was expanding so rapidly, most of the city's life centred on the port area. Even King Manuel I had built a palace near the waterfront. The Casa dos Bicos is also called the House of Diamonds, because of the diamond-shaped stones that stick out all over its façade. By the time of the 1755 earthquake it had become several shops. After the earthquake nothing was left of the Casa dos Bicos but its foundations and one layer of stones from the wall. It was totally reconstructed during the Year of Portuguese Discoveries and Renaissance Europe, sponsored by the Council of Europe in 1983.

You should take your time when walking through the Alfama, the old Moorish area of the city, where the Jews also lived. The streets are narrow, cobbled and perpendicular, with overhanging eaves, archways, stairs, courtyards and squares. It is a labyrinth rather like the souks of North Africa – perhaps not surprisingly, in view of its origins. You will see columns, lattice windows and tracery windows, and the remains of the old Moorish wall. Washing hangs from the balconies; street vendors push their carts along, and women collect water from the fountains. It is a very colourful place. There are many little bars and restaurants.

The **Church of Santo Estevão,** dating back to the thirteenth century and reconstructed in the sixteenth and seventeenth centuries, is in the Alfama, at the top of stairways leading from the Chancellor's Archway. It is built in marble, and follows an unusual octagonal plan. The high altar has a huge image of the crucifixion, flanked by two equally large angels. The **Church of São Miguel** is also very old, perhaps dating from the thirteenth century. It was totally reconstructed in the seventeenth century, but was knocked down in the earthquake. It was rebuilt and is rich in woodcarving and gilt work.

The sixteenth-century **Judiaria** (Jewish quarter) is off the Largo de São Rafael.

The **Casa do Menino Deus** and the **Casa da Rua dos Cegos** are two colourful Alfama houses that survived the earthquake. Both were built in the sixteenth century. The Casa da Rua dos Cegos is painted bright red and has a tiled roof and a green door. The Casa do Menino Deus, in the square of the same name, is pale yellow with green wrought iron balconies.

The **Madre de Deus Church** was ordered built in 1509 by Queen Leonor, related to the Emperor Maximilian of Germany, who sent her the many religious relics on display. The Holy Shroud of Jesus exhibited in the sacristy is one. Some Portuguese primitive paintings remain from that period, including parts of a panel illustrating the martyrdom of the Portuguese Saint, Auta, one of the 'Eleven Thousand Virgins' slaughtered by Huns as they were accompanying a Cornish princess on a pilgrimage to Rome in the fourth or fifth century. Maximilian returned the saint's body to Queen Leonor, who ordered a chapel built for it. Most of the building and cloisters, however, date from the seventeenth and eighteenth centuries, which accounts for the enormous amount of very ornate golden woodwork added when gold from Brazil was abundant. The portal is pure Manueline. The Nuns' Choir is enclosed in Baroque gilt woodwork.

The **National Tile Museum** occupies the large classic cloister and the Manueline cloister of the Madre de Deus Church and houses tiles from every period, from fifteenth-century Hispano/Arabic to modern tiles by Portuguese painters Paula Rego and Paulo Vieira. Many of the tiles depict animals, and there are some tiles in the famous *singerie* designs of monkeys dressed as people and carrying out human activities. But the most noteworthy exhibit is the priceless panel of blue and white tiles showing a panoramic view of pre-earthquake Libson, which runs the entire length of the upstairs gallery in the large cloister. Queen Leonor's tombstone stands in an angle near the door into the church. There is a nice bar/restaurant, displays illustrating tile making and videos flashing pictures of tiles from all over the country.

The **Military Museum** is in front of the Santa Apolónia railway station. It contains not only a fine display of cannons and other weapons, but also valuable coin collections, paintings, knights' armour, medallions and hundreds of curiosities – such as the waggon that transported the statue of King José I that stands in the Praça do Comércio.

Ribeira

The **Ribeira** is that part of Lisbon that stretches along the riverside from below the Madre de Deus Church and Convent, past the Santa Apolónia railway station and all the way west to the Jerónimos Monastery and Belém Tower.

The **Praça do Comércio** (also known as Black Horse Square and *Terreiro do Paço*) is on the river at the bottom of the streets that run up through the Baixa (Rua Augusta, Rua da Prata and Rua do Ouro). It is a beautiful rectangular square built after the earthquake, in the time of the Marquês de Pombal. In the middle of the square is an equestrian statue of King José I. The model for the horse was a Lusitanian horse from the royal stud in the Alentejo. On the north is the Arch of Rua Augusta constructed in the latter part of the nineteenth century in a style that contrasts with the Neoclassical whole. The arch of triumph has on its side columns statues of Nun' Álvares Pereira, Viriato, the Marquês de Pombal and Vasco da Gama. On top there are symbols of the River Tagus and the River Douro, crowned by symbols of Glory, Genius and Value. There are steps down to the river where boats used to dock. On the east side is the ferry point, where you can take boats to cross the river. The TransTejo excursion ferry will take you on a two hour trip to Motijo and Seixal, and on day trips down the river to Cascais. The square houses several ministries, and the post office. Unfortunately, it is also used as a car park!

Praça do Município is on the street that runs west behind the post office. The Town Hall, built in 1866 to 1875, is an excellent example of Neoclassical architecture. The pillory in the square is late eighteenth century.

The **Museum of Ancient Art** (Museu Nacional de Arte Antiga) is in Rua das Janelas Verdes. You can find it by walking west along the river through Largo dos Santos. Part of the museum is housed in the Janelas Verdes Palace, which has a Baroque façade. It was first the residence of the Counts of Alvor and later belonged to the family of the Marquês de Pombal.

The museum has very extensive collections of paintings, ceramics, and gold and silver. The collection of church plate includes an early-sixteenth-century monstrance made of the first gold to come from the Far East. And among the paintings is what is probably the most famous of all Portuguese paintings: the fifteenth-century polyptych of Saint Vincent by Nuno Gonçalves, which shows all the people of Lisbon surrounding the King and Queen. You can see Prince Henry the Navigator in a black hat, monks from the Cistercian Monastery at Alcobaça, various priests in the robes and hats of their orders, and an assorted group of other people. Two figures of Saint Vincent flank the King and Queen. The museum also has paintings by Grão Vasco and other Portuguese primitive painters. Works of other renowned European painters are represented by Albrecht Durer's 'Saint Jerome', Hieronymous Bosch's 'Temptation of Saint Anthony', Hans Holbein the Elder's 'Fountain of Life' and paintings by Piro della Francesca, Van der Wyden, Tintoretto, Memling and others. Many of the pieces reflect the 500-year relationship of Portugal with Africa and the Orient: the seventeenth- and eighteenth-century Oriental ceramics date from the time of the Companhia das Indias; the Japanese Namban screens, painted during the sixteenth and seventeenth centuries, showing scenes of Portuguese arriving in Japan, are among the finest in existence. In the summer you can have tea in the lovely garden.

Belém

The **National Palace at Belém** is the office of the President of Portugal, Mário Soares. It is the former royal palace, a lovely pink seventeenth-century building with formal gardens overlooking the street. There are black swans in the garden (President Soares complains that there is one cantankerous widowed swan who insists on attacking people – regardless of rank). You can watch the daily ceremony of the Changing of the Guard outside the palace, but the palace itself is not open to the public. The President holds private art exhibitions and music recitals in the garden.

You can visit the palace **Coach Museum**, housed in the former Royal Riding School. It has the finest coach collection in the world, with chaises, litters, calashes and berlins dating from the sixteenth to the nineteenth centuries, the golden Baroque coaches that brought the Portuguese ambassador from Rome in 1716 – and the pony carts used by the royal princesses for riding through the parks of the palace.

The **Chapel of Memory** is on Calçada da Ajuda, which goes up the hill beside the Belém Palace. It was erected by King José after he had escaped from an attempt on his life. The inside of the chapel is sumptuous, rich in sculptured marble, and there is a tableau depicting the attempted assassination.

The **Ajuda Palace**, in Largo da Ajuda up the hill above the Belém Palace, was built between 1796 and 1826 on the site of the wooden palace *A Barraca* (Royal Hut) built by King José after the great earthquake, and occupied by the royal family when they returned from exile in Brazil. It was enlarged for the marriage of King Luís to Maria Pia of Savoy, but the work was never completed. King Luís lived there, and his widow – the grandmother of the last King of Portugal – continued to live there until the proclamation of the Republic in 1911. It has been restored and is used for state occasions, such as the visit of the Prince and Princess of Wales. It has jewels, beautiful carpets and many treasures in porcelain, crystal and bronze which are on display to the public. There is an attractive Oriental Room and an impressive set of silver for the State Dining Room.

In the streets west of Belém towards the Jerónimos Monastery there are old houses that date from the time when the river came in almost as far as the Jerónimos. Many of them have been turned into little restaurants, some with terraces.

Beco da Chão Salgado (Alley of Salted Earth) is a small cul-de-sac between the restaurants with a pillar commemorating the execution by Prime Minister Marquês de Pombal of the nobles and their families who supposedly tried to assassinate King José in 1759. Their palaces were razed to the ground and salt spread there.

The **Praça do Império** in front of the Jerónimos Monastery has an illuminated fountain in the midst of formal gardens in which the flowers are planted to represent the coats of arms of all the regions of Portugal – they used to include also the countries of the Portuguese empire.

The **Jerónimos Monastery** is the finest example of Manueline architecture in Portugal. Sited near the spot from which Vasco da Gama and his fleet set sail on their momentous journey to India, it was built as a monument to Portugal's great discoverers, and was paid for with profits from the spice trade. Building probably started about 1502, and the first master of the works was Diogo Boitac, who worked on it till 1517, when João de Castilho took over. He was followed by the great Renaissance architect Diogo de Torralva. Many of the sculptures are by French Renaissance sculptor Nicolas Chanterene. Work on the building was completed by classicist architect de Rouen. The monastery is of white marble, and it is covered with Manueline decorations based on motifs taken from the sea and the discoveries. The original monastery was the section to the east. There are later Renaissance and Neoclassical additions, and the long galleries on the west are neo-Manueline, dating from the nineteenth century. The Royal Pantheon contains the tombs of King Manuel and other monarchs.

The church contains the tombs of several monarchs of Portugal, and those of Vasco da Gama and the poet Camões (but Camões's tomb is empty, because he died in penury elsewhere).

The **Archaeological and Ethnological Museum** (Museu Nacional de Arqueologia e Etnologia), in an annexe to the monastery, has a collection of prehistoric artifacts from all over Portugal.

The **Naval Museum** (Museu da Marinha) is in another annexe. It has models of Portuguese ships, including royal galleons, fishing boats, and the caravels used in the Age of Discoveries. There is also a lovely white, gold and pale green royal barge in which Queen Elizabeth and the Duke of Edinburgh were rowed ashore from the royal yacht during their visit in 1957.

The **Planetarium**, built by the Gulbenkian Foundation, is next to the Naval Museum. There is a list of times of showings posted outside.

The **Monument to the Discoveries** is near the river, facing the Jerónimos. It was built in 1960 to commemorate the 500th anniversary of the death of Prince Henry the Navigator. It is in the shape of the prow of a caravel, surrounded by people involved in the discoveries, being led by Henry the Navigator. Nearby there is a pleasant park and museum.

The **Museum of Popular Art** (Museu de Arte Popular) has crafts from all over Portugal, arranged according to regions. You can see here Portuguese embroideries, ceramics, lace, jewellery, rugs, wrought iron work, and much else.

The **Belém Tower** (Torre de Belem) is further west along the river in a large park on the water's edge. It was built to house cannon to defend the Tagus, and especially the Jerónimos, against corsairs and pirates, but it is also a work of art. It was constructed between 1515 and 1520, under the supervision of the architect Francisco de Arruda. At that time the water of the River Tagus reached almost to the Jerónimos Monastery, and the tower was built on rocks out in the river. The square tower is richly decorated with statues, pillars, stone tracery, Moorish balconies and Manueline sea motifs and armillary spheres. It was used many times in the past as a prison for political prisoners. It now contains a permanent exhibition of fifteenth- and sixteenth-century arms, armour and navigational instruments.

The **St Jerónimo Chapel** is on top of a hill in Restelo, near the Belém Tower, between Avenida das Descobertas and Avenida Ilha da Madeira. Go up from the tower on Avenida da Torre de Belém, or from the Jerónimos on Rua dos Jerónimos. Built in 1514, it is a sober little chapel in white marble with tiny pointed towers and a cross on top. It was here that the Portuguese explorers came to pray before leaving on their voyages.

Baixa

The Baixa is the lower part of central Lisbon laid out on a grid system and rebuilt by the Marquês de Pombal after the 1755 earthquake. Its buildings date from the seventeenth and early eighteenth centuries. The entire Baixa was once an arm of the River Tagus.

The **Rossio** square in the Baixa was the centre of Lisbon by the mid-thirteenth century. It had a main fair and market place and many palaces. Later, it housed the dreaded Palace of the Inquisition. The square and its buildings were totally destroyed in the 1755 earthquake, but lovely eighteenth-century houses were built around it in the time of the Marquês de Pombal. The restored **Teatro Nacional Dona Maria II** stands on the north side. There is a lovely fountain with cavorting nymphs and by it some colourful flower stalls, and some popular outdoor cafés, including the famous Pastelaria Suiça.

Praça da Figueira is the large square east of Rossio. The equestrian statue is of King João I, who defeated the Spaniards at the famous battle of Aljubarrota, defeated the Moors at Ceuta in North Africa, married Phillipa of Lancaster and was father of Prince Henry the Navigator.

The **Rossio Train Station** is a Manueline revivalist building from the Romantic period. Trains depart for Sintra, Queluz and Óbidos.

Between the Rossio and Praça do Comércio three streets run down to the river: Rua do Ouro (Street of Gold), that was the street of the goldsmiths; Rua da Prata (Street of Silver), where the silversmiths worked; and Rua Augusta. They are now the banking and commercial centre of Lisbon.

The **Chiado** is the area up the hill to the west of the Rossio, along the streets of the Rua do Carmo and Rua Garrett, where there are many smart shops. Chiado is best known for its coffee houses – like the Brazileira – which have been the haunt of generations of famous artists and writers. A statue of Fernando Pessoa, the greatest Portuguese poet of his time, sits at a table on the terrace of the Brazileira, his favourite café. Many historic buildings in Chiado were razed by a disastrous fire in 1988. It is being rebuilt according to a plan executed by architect Siza Vieira.

The **São Carlos Opera House** in nearby Largo do Directorio is an eighteenth-century copy of the San Carlos in Naples.

The **Museum of Contemporary Art** (Museu de Arte Contemporaneo) in Rua Serpa Pinto contains a large collection of paintings and sculpture of the nineteenth and early twentieth centuries.

The iron **Santa Justa Elevator** takes you from Rua do Ouro in the Baixa to the ruins of the Carmo Convent. You have a lovely view of Lisbon and there is a restaurant on top. The lift is often attributed to Eiffel, but it was actually built in 1898 by the Cardoso Dargent company to a plan by R. Mesnier.

The **Carmo Convent** was built in the fourteenth century and destroyed by the earthquake and fire in 1755. Its ruins stand above the town, floodlit at night, like a monument to Portugal's age of glory. Inside it has a museum of inscribed stones dating all the way back to prehistoric times. Concerts and other events are often held in the ruins. Inquire at the Tourist Office for details.

The sixteenth-century **São Roque Church** is in Largo Trindade Coelho near Praça da Misericórdia. Its **Chapel of São João Batista** was commissioned in Rome by King João V and sent to Lisbon by sea. It is made of marble, alabaster, lapis lazuli and other semi-precious stones in soft colours – the most expensive structure of its kind ever built. The Cornish Sir Francis Tregian is buried there, with an inscription telling of his imprisonment under Queen Elizabeth I. He lived in Portugal for twenty years, and was considered a saint.

The **Treasury Museum**, attached to the church, contains the treasure from the Chapel of St John the Baptist. There are two candlesticks weighing 400 kilos each, altar pieces in gold and silk, vestments the Pope wore when blessing the chapel in Rome, and many other valuable objects.

Praça dos Restauradores, north of the Rossio, has an obelisk commemorating the Restoration of 1640, when the Spaniards were driven out and a Portuguese king was restored to the throne. The main Tourist Office is on the west side and the main post office is on the east.

The **Parque Mayer** is just off Avenida da Liberdade north of Praça dos Restauradores. It is a crumbling old theatre district where musical reviews are still staged. There are many little restaurants.

The **Gloria Elevator** takes you up a nearly perpendicular street from Praça dos Restauradores to the **Bairro Alto**, an old district on the hill opposite Saint George's Castle and the Alfama. It is an area of narrow streets and old houses where you will find dozens of little restaurants, *fado* houses, pubs and taverns. Recently it has become the centre of Lisbon by night. The Solar do Vinho de Porto, where you can sample dozens of kinds of port wine, is at the top of the Gloria Elevator.

The Botanical Gardens are in Rua Escola Politécnica, near Avenida da Liberdade. There are lots of rare trees and plants, many from Africa and Brazil.

Praça do Marquês de Pombal, also known as the Rotunda, is north of Praça dos Restauradores at the top of Avenida da Liberdade. There is a marble equestrian statue of the Marquês de Pombal in the square.

The **Eduardo VII Park** is a large green park north of Praça do Marquês de Pombal. One of the sights of Lisbon is the **Estufa Fria** (cold greenhouse) in the park. It is a latticed plant house set in a hollow below the Ritz Hotel. The atmosphere is lush and tropical, and plants grow in profusion among rocks and streams. It also has a large auditorium where Lisbon's symphony orchestra and other musical groups hold concerts. Inquire at the Tourist Office for details.

The Gulbenkian Museum and Foundation is in Avenida de Berna, at the edge of Praça Espanha. Tel. (01) 734309. This foundation was started by the Armenian oil millionaire Calouste Sarkis Gulbenkian, who spent the last years of his life in Lisbon, after escaping from Paris during the Second World War, and left his fortune and his marvellous art collection to Portugal. The foundation building has two concert halls, a library, two galleries for temporary art exhibitions, lecture halls and the museum. The Gulbenkian also has what is at the moment one of the best contemporary ballet companies in Europe, and it sponsors a symphony orchestra.

The **Gulbenkian Museum** contains the founder's collection of paintings, sculpture, furniture, tapestries and ceramics, ranging from early Egyptian to *art nouveau*. Many of the paintings were bought from the Leningrad Hermitage Museum in the 1920s, when the Soviet Union needed cash. Some of the most noteworthy are: the Egyptian collection; Islamic ceramics and carpets; a roomful of Lalique jewellery, and paintings from the French Impressionists and Barbazon Schools.

The **Modern Art Centre** is in the gardens at the back of the Gulbenkian Foundation. It has a fine collection of nineteenth- and twentieth-century Portuguese paintings on the ground floor. Upstairs there is a long gallery of foreign paintings and engravings. The Centre sells some good reproductions and has a nice cafeteria that looks out on to the gardens. It also presents theatre and dance productions by visiting groups.

The **Zoo** is in a lovely garden with pools, lakes and trees at the north of town in Sete Rios, not far from the Praça Espanha. The polar bears don't seem to be too happy with Portugal's climate, but the tropical birds look fine. There are some American buffaloes, donated to the zoo by the American School in Lisbon. The giraffes are friendly. There is an elephant that will ring a bell if you give him money.

The **Bullring** is at the other end of Avenida de Berna, in the Avenida da República. It looks like a rather strange version of a mosque, with minarets all around its red stone walls. Bullfights are held there regularly in the season. It has a tauromaquia museum.

The **Municipal Library** is in the Palácio Galveiras in Campo Pequeno near the bullring.

The **City Museum** (Museo da Cidade) is in the eighteenth-century Palace of Mitra, in Campo Grande, near the viaduct at the end of Avenida da República. It has paintings, engravings, maps, projections and many other objects that illustrate the history of the city of Lisbon.

The **Rafael Bordalo Pinheiro Museum** is in Campo Grande. Tel. (01) 7590816. It contains sketches by the nineteenth-century cartoonist and caricaturist Rafael Bordalo Pinheiro.

The **Campo Grande Gardens** in Campo Grande have outdoor cafés and boats.

The **Costume Museum** (Museu do Trajo) is at Largo São João Batista 5, Parque do Monteiro-Mor, Lumiar. Tel. (01) 7590318. You can see here regional costumes from all over Portugal, as well as collections of foreign clothes, including many Oriental costumes. There are Coptic fabrics dating back to the fourth century. And the collection of eighteenth-century costumes is particularly extensive and impressive. There is a lovely restaurant and tea-room in an old mansion in the grounds.

Open 10 a.m. to 1 p.m. and 2.30 p.m. to 5 p.m. Closed Mondays and public holidays.

The **National Theatre Museum** (Museu Nacional do Teatro) is at Estrada do Lumiar 10, Monteiro-Mor Park, Lumiar. Tel. (01) 7582547. This museum has collections of theatrical costumes, scenery, drawings, programmes, cartoons, posters, photographs, books and everything else you can think of related to the theatre.

The **Aguas Livres Aqueduct** in Campolide can be seen from the bridge on the road leading out of Lisbon towards Cascais. This aqueduct was constructed by order of King João V and designed by Manuel da Maia and Custódio José Vieira in the first half of the eighteenth century. The aqueduct stretches 28 km from Canecas to the Casa do Agua near Amoreiras. It contains 109 arches in solid stonework that tower 65 metres above the Alcantara Valley. It is open to the public now on weekends after being closed for 137 years after a madman named 'Pancada' (the Clubber) had the unfortunate habit of bludgeoning people and tossing them into the abyss.

The **Prazeres Cemetery** (Pleasure Cemetery) at the end of Rua Saraiva de Carvalho, covers 110,000 sq. metres with seventy-three streets lined with tombs in every style imaginable: Romanesque, Manueline, Gothic and Baroque, covered with a plethora of statues, columns and opulent decorations. The empty tombs are inhabited by families of cats.

The **Estrela Basilica**, in the Estrela Gardens, is an imposing eighteenth-century Neoclassical church. Lisbon's last great church – built by Queen Maria I to give thanks for the birth of her son José. The sumptuous interior is decorated in pink, grey and ochre marble. Queen Maria's tomb is on the right side of the transept.

The English Cemetery, the British Hospital and the British Club and Theatre are near the Estrela Gardens.

The **Fronteira Palace**, São Domingos de Benfica, was built in the second half of the seventeenth century. It has formal gardens, and some of the most beautiful glazed tiles in Portugal. The tiles, dating from the seventeenth to the nineteenth centuries, cover the interior and outsides of the galleries and terraces, and depict historical events.

Open on Mondays and Wednesdays, from 10 a.m. to 12 noon, and on Saturdays from 3 p.m. to 6.30 p.m.

The **Bridge** over the River Tagus was built in the 1960s by an American company. It is one of the longest single-span suspension bridges in the world – longer than the Golden Gate in San Francisco. It leads from Lisbon to the Setúbal peninsula and the beaches of Caparica. It is also the way to the Alentejo, the Algarve, and Spain. The present toll for an average car is 80 esc. You pay on the way out of

Lisbon, but not on the way back in. If you possibly can, avoid crossing on Sundays or holidays, or on sunny days in summer when everybody is heading for the beach. Particularly coming back in the evening, you can be stuck in traffic jams for hours.

Odivelas, at the end of Calçada de Carriche, is a dormitory town that has grown up around a Cistercian monastery. If you can find it through the urban sprawl, you should pay a visit to the tomb of King Dinis, who built so many castles and monasteries and did so much for agriculture in the early years of the Portuguese nation. His stone tomb is surrounded by carved figures showing a man fighting a bear, which refer to an incident in the King's life when he killed a bear single-handed. King Dinis deserves a more worthy resting place.

The **Statue of Christ** is a tall stone statue of Christ standing on the hill opposite Lisbon where it can be seen from nearly every vantage point. There is a lift up to it. From the top you have a marvellous view of Lisbon and the beaches.

Art exhibitions

Art exhibitions are held at the following centres.

Gulbenkian Museum, Avenida de Berna 45. Tel. (01) 762146.

Palácio Foz, Praça dos Restauradores. Tel. (01) 362531.

The **Almada Negreiros**, Avenida da República 16. Tel. (01) 579037.

Fado

Lisbon *fado* is more sober than Coimbra *fado* (see page 53), in content and tune. Most of the *fado* houses are in the old districts of Lisbon: Alfama, Bairro Alto, Madragôa and Alcântara. Go late at night: the music continues till about 3 a.m. The *fado* house below is *the* place to go for pure *fado*.

Senhor do Vinho, Rua do Meio à Lapa 18 (Lapa). Tel. (01) 672681. Don't talk during the singing as you will be hushed by the other customers who take their *fado* very seriously.

Adega Machado, Rua do Norte 91. Tel. (01) 3460095. More fun because it offers folk dancing in addition to *fado* and the customers can talk, sing and take part in the dancing.

Festivals

The June *Festas dos Santos Populares* are in origin a celebration of the ancient summer solstice, but have been turned by the Catholic Church into a celebration of the feast of Saint John the Baptist. In Lisbon the celebrations begin on 13 and 14 June, the Feast of Saint Anthony, who was born in the Alfama. The entire Alfama is decorated, and all night long the people sing, dance, drink wine and eat grilled sardines. Pots of sweet basil are sold. On 23 and 24 June, the Feast of Saint John, the people make bonfires sprinkled with scented herbs and thistles and jump over them. There are marches through Lisbon in costume, with each district singing its own song. The last night of the celebration is the Feast of Saint Peter, on 29 June.

The *Festas de São Pedro*, held on 28 and 29 June in Montijo near Lisbon are festivals in honour of Saint Peter that have been celebrated since the Middle Ages. On 29 June there is a procession and a blessing of the boats. Everyone eats sardines. The bull farms bring their bulls into town and release them, and the young men race them through the streets – sometimes with disastrous results. There are also bullfights. On the last night there is an old pagan rite: a skiff is burned and offered to the River Tagus as a sacrifice.

Shopping

There are many good buys to be had in Lisbon. It is worth seeking out ceramics, especially glazed tiles (see page 53). Some of the shops will pack and ship. Sant'Anna shop at Rua Alecrim 95 has lovely decorative tiles and other ceramics. You can get the famous Vista Alegre porcelain in Largo do Chiado 18, Rua Ivens 52/54, Edifício Castilho and Avenida Igreja 4F; and the Loucas de Sacavém shop in Avenida da Liberdade has lovely hand-painted china.

Paintings by contemporary Portuguese artists are a good financial, as well as artistic, investment (see pages 22–4).

Tapestries in traditional patterns or in modern designs by leading artists are sold in the shop in the Rua da Academia das Ciências 2.

If weight is no problem it is also well worth taking home a rug or a carpet. Jewellery is also an excellent buy, and there are many reputable jewellers in the Baixa.

Shoes and other leather goods, ready-made clothes and hand-embroidered linen are moderately priced and of good quality. You can get Madeira lace and embroideries and Minho coarse linen embroideries in several shops. Fishermen's sweaters in thick wool are also a bargain.

Shopping centres

The **Amoreiras Shopping Centre** is so big and flashy you can't miss it. On Rua das Amoreiras and Avenida Duarte Pacheco between Praça do Marquês de Pombal and the bridge on the N7 to Cascais, it is a Post-Modernist building in pink and green and glass designed by architect Tomás Taveira. It stays open from early in the morning to midnight, and it is a city in itself, with banks, estate agents, smart boutiques, shoe shops, wine shops, restaurants of every possible variety, a supermarket, bars, health clubs, cinemas, jewellers, gift shops, stationers, chemists and so on. It has two floors of parking facilities under the building. This is the New Lisbon. Don't miss it.

In the centre of town is the **Centro Comercial Imaviz**, Avenida Fontes Pereira de Melo 35, Edifício Aviz. This shopping centre is next to the Sheraton Hotel.

Post offices

The two main post offices are in Praça dos Restauradores and Praça do Comércio. The one in Restauradores is open from 8 a.m. to midnight. There is a 24-hour post office at the airport.

Hairdressers

Isabel Queiroz do Vale, Avenida Fontes Pereira de Melo 35. Tel. (01) 548238. Also at Centro Comercial Imaviz. Tel. (01) 549142.

Bruna, Largo São Carlos 8. Tel. (01) 363821.

Churches

Corpo Santo Church (Irish Dominican), Largo do Corpo Santo, has Mass at 7 a.m., 8 a.m. and 9 a.m. during the week. On Sundays there is an additional Mass at 11 a.m.

Saint George's Church (Church of England), Rua da Estrela 4, holds services at 8.30 a.m. and 11 a.m. on Sundays.

Baptist Evangelical Church, Rua Filipe Folque 36-B, holds services at 10 a.m. and 9.30 p.m. on Sundays and 9.30 p.m. on Wednesdays.

Shaare Tikva Synagogue, Rua Alexandre Herculano 59, holds services at 8.30 a.m. and 7.30 p.m. every day except Saturday, when there is a service at 9 a.m.

Hospitals

São José Hospital, Rua José A. Serrano. Tel. (01) 871684/775171. A state hospital. It accepts emergencies.

Santa Maria Hospital, Avenida Professor Egas Moniz. Tel. (01) 775171. A state hospital.

British Hospital, Rua Saraiva de Carvalho 49. Tel. (01) 602020/603785. A private hospital with English-speaking doctors and nurses. It will accept emergencies.

Street car trips

Special **scenic street cars** with plush-covered seats and panelled interiors depart from the Praça do Comércio daily at 10.30 a.m., 2.30 p.m. and 4.30 p.m. for rides by most of the historic monuments with various stops. Tickets are sold on board.

Boat trips

TransTejo, Estação Fluvial do Terreiro do Paço. Tel. (01) 875058/369201. Offers two-hour scenic trips on the River Tagus during which you get a lovely view from the water of all Lisbon's famous monuments, the bridge over the Tagus and the statue of Christ. The boat is specially fitted out for tourists. Between April and October departs daily at 3 p.m. from the marina near Praça do Comércio, and returns at 5 p.m. Tickets are a bit pricey.

Where to stay
Luxury

Ritz Inter-Continental, Rua Rodrigo da Fonseca 88-A. Tel. (01) 692020. Lisbon's top luxury hotel, overlooking the Eduardo VII Park in the city centre. It has 260 rooms and 40 suites with air conditioning, mini-bars and satellite TV. The Ritz also has a famed Grill restaurant, a piano bar, a coffee shop, a tea room, and its own boutiques and art gallery.

Hotel Lisbon Sheraton, Rua Latino Coelho 2. Tel. (01) 575757. A five star hotel in the centre of Lisbon. It has 400 rooms with air conditioning, TV and a view of Lisbon. It has two restaurants, bars, a health club, swimming pool, shops and an art gallery.

Expensive

Hotel Tivoli, Avenida da Liberdade 185. Tel. (01) 530181. A five star hotel conveniently located close to the centre of town on Lisbon's main avenue. It has 350 rooms and 15 suites. Of its two restaurants, the roof top grill is a favourite Lisbon dining spot. Its spacious lobby and bar are popular meeting places. It has a heated swimming pool and a tennis court.

Medium price

Hotel Penta, Avenida dos Combatentes. Tel. (01) 7265050. A modern, four star hotel away from the city centre near the Gulbenkian Museum. It has 588 rooms with bath, TV and balcony, a disco, restaurants, bars, shops and swimming pool.

Inexpensive

Hotel da Torre, Rua dos Jerónimos 8. Tel. (01) 630161/637332/636262. A three star hotel with fifty-two rooms. It is near the Jerónimos Monastery in Belém, and has a good restaurant.

Senhora do Monte, Calçada do Monte 39. Tel. (01) 862846. A four star inn up in the old Graça district with a view of St George's Castle. It has twenty-seven rooms with bath, and a bar with terrace.

Residência York House (+ annexe), Rua das Janelas Verdes 32-1. Tel. (01) 662435. A four star inn near the river in a house that once belonged to Portuguese writer Eça de Queiros. It has fifty-eight rooms, a nice interior patio, bar and restaurant.

Pensão Residência Capital, Avenida Elias Garcia, 87-2. Tel. (01) 767330. A three star pension with twenty-two rooms. It has a bar, but you will need to find your own restaurant.

Manor house
Inexpensive

Quinta Nova da Conceição, Rua dos Soeiros 5, São Domingos de Benfica. Tel. (01) 780091. A rare example of late eighteenth-century houses that were country homes of Lisbon nobility. Set in gardens, it offers two rooms.

Where to eat
Alfama

Faz Figura, Rua do Paraiso 15-B. Tel. (01) 868981. Overlooks the River Tagus with a veranda for dining and watching the ships go by. Its wood panelling and leather chairs give it the flavour of an exclusive club. A long and varied menu. Closed Sundays.

Michel, Largo Santo Cruz do Castelo 5. Tel. (01) 867763. A restaurant located in Saint George's Castle. It specializes in French cuisine. It is advisable to book. Not open on Sundays.

Casa do Leão, Castelo de São Jorge. Tel. (01) 875962. Also located in Saint George's Castle. A first class restaurant that serves regional cooking. It is essential to book in advance.

Belém

The streets near Belém have many little restaurants.

Varandazul, Restelo Stadium, Avenida Restelo. Tel. (01) 612006. A lovely restaurant with a view of the River Tagus. It serves fresh fish, and Portuguese specialities.

Caseiro, Rua de Belem 5. Tel. (01) 3638803. An attractive restaurant, near the Jeronimos Monastery, specializing in Portuguese cooking and seafood. Closed Mondays.

Pastelaria de Belém, Rua de Belém. A century-old café. Does not serve meals but is famous for its little hot custard tarts.

Baixa

Aviz, Rua Serpa Pinto 12-B, 1. Tel. (01) 328391. An elegant restaurant with an attractive bar, impeccable service and excellent international cuisine. It was founded by the chef from the old Aviz hotel, where oil millionaire Calouste Gulbenkian spent the last years of his life. Not open for Saturday lunch or on Sundays.

Tagide, 18 Largo da Biblioteca Publica. Tel. (01) 3460570. Its marble staircase leads up to the dining room, completely surrounded by picture windows with views of St George's Castle and the river. The food and service are impeccable.

Bairro Alto

Pap d'Açorda, Rua da Atalaia 57. Tel. (01) 364811. A restaurant that serves Portuguese specialities – such as *açorda* (a sort of kedgeree). Not open for Saturday lunch or on Sundays.

Bota Alta, Travessa da Queimada. Tel. (01) 327959. A noisy, typical bistro with good Portuguese food. Closed Sundays.

Lapa **Sua Excelência**, Rua do Conde 40/42. Tel. (01) 603614. A small restaurant which serves very good specialities ranging from Mozambique prawns to hazelnut ice cream with hot chocolate. Not open on Wednesdays, for Saturday lunch or during September.

Principe Real/ **Varina da Madragoa**, Rua das Madres 36. Tel. (01) 665533. An
São Bento old tavern, near Parliament, converted to a tiled restaurant.

Conventual, Praça das Flores 45. Tel. (01) 609196. A restaurant that specializes in old convent and monastery cooking that goes back to the seventeenth century. It is decorated with objects from churches. Closed Saturday lunch and Sundays.

Rato **Casa da Comida**, Travessa das Amoreiras 1. Tel. (01) 685376. One of the best restaurants in Lisbon. It is set around a lovely interior garden and serves beautifully decorated and tasty dishes. Closed Saturday lunch and Sundays.

Entre **Feira Popular**, Entre Campos. An amusement park with restau-
Campos rants that serve Portuguese food and wine from different regions of the country. Most of them specialize in charcoal-grilled sardines. The park is open from April to November after 6 p.m.

What to eat You can get the specialities of all the different Portuguese regions in Lisbon. Fish is particularly delicious - try *ameijoas na cataplana* (shellfish steamed in a covered copper pan), *sardinhas assadas* (grilled sardines) *ameijoas à bulhão pato* (shellfish with garlic and coriander), *bacalhau à çomes de sá* (cod with potatoes, eggs, olives and olive oil), *lulas recheadas* (stuffed squid), *espadarte fumado* (smoked swordfish). Of meat dishes, *cozido á Portuguesa* (stew with boiled vegetables, sausages and different types of meat) and *coelho à caçadora* (rabbit stew with tomato sauce) are good. And for dessert: *bolo de chocolate e amêndoa* (almond cake covered in cream and chocolate), *tarte de laranja* (orange tart), *pudim molotofe* (whipped egg whites with caramel on top), and the famous *pastéis de Belém* custard tarts.

Discos **Banana Power**, Rua de Cascais 51/53. Tel. (01) 631815. One of the 'in' places to go. It also has a bar and restaurant.

Alcantara Mar, Rua da Cozinha Economica 11, is in the dock area in a converted factory. It holds 2,000 people and has lots of loud music. Very popular. Closed Mondays and Tuesdays.

Whispers, Avenida Fontes P. de Melo. Tel. (01) 575489.

Bairro Alto, Travessa dos Inglesinhos 50, in the Bairro Alto. Tel. (01) 322717. A huge, converted sawmill, imaginatively decorated to tell Lisbon's history. The entertainment is also imaginative.

Night club **A Caravela**, a night club with floor show in the Ritz Inter-Continental.

Bars **Pavilhão Chinés**, Rua Dom Pedro V 89. Tel. (01) 324729. Near the antique shops in the Bairro Alto, it is decorated in antiques and Chinese objects, and has a lovely mahogany bar.

Praça das Flores, Praça das Flores 30A. Tel. (01) 604789. A simply decorated pub with a pleasant atmosphere. It has all kinds of live music, ranging from Brazilian to Portuguese to American.

Botequim, 79 Largo da Graça. Tel. (01) 871523. A small piano bar which is a favourite late-night haunt for Lisbon's intellectuals. It is owned by Natália Correia, a well known poet and member of parliament.

Travel agencies

Several travel agencies offer tours of Lisbon, the Estoril Casino, bullfights, night clubs, palaces and other cities. Some are: **Mundial Turismo**, Avenida António Augusto de Aguiar 90-A. Tel. (01) 563521/2. **Cityrama**, Avenida Praia da Vitoria 12B. Tel. (01) 575564. **RN Tours**, Avenida Fontes Pereira de Melo 33. Tel. (01) 560016.

The main Tourist Office is in the Palácio Foz, Praça dos Restauradores. Tel. (01) 3463624/3466307/3469113.

Warnings

Like other capitals, Lisbon has a drug problem, and it is quite common to be approached by pushers. There are also a great many pickpockets and purse-snatchers, especially in the metro. Sometimes they will kindly abandon the papers they may find in your purse or wallet – and then again, they may not. If you are robbed, go to the police immediately. Do not leave anything at all in your car if you park it in the street or in a car park. It might not be there when you come back, and you might also have a smashed window. Don't buy 'cheap' gold watches or carved ivory from people in the streets. The watches aren't gold, and the ivory is likely to be plastic.

Costa da Caparica

The Costa da Caparica is the bit of the Atlantic coast south of Lisbon across the River Tagus bridge. There are long stretches of sandy beaches backed by dunes and yellow cliffs, and the water is unpolluted. A little narrow-gauge railway line with an umbrella-covered coach runs from the town to the end of the beaches – you can get off whenever you see a spot that appeals to you.

In the past these beaches were the haunt of Moorish pirates. Caparica got its name from the belief that these pirates buried their treasures in the sands there – *capa-rica* means 'a cover for riches'.

The town of Caparica is not very nice. It is full of beach shacks and ugly modern buildings. (Though it does have some good fish restaurants on the seafront.) But if you drive along a bit or take the little shuttle train south along the beach, you will find lots of nice beaches with names like Praia do Rei (King's Beach), Praia da Sereia (Mermaid Beach) or Praia do Infante (Prince's Beach).

The Costa da Caparica can be very windy. It is a matter of luck. It is better to take day trips to the beach from Lisbon rather than plan to stay there during the summer because rooms are scarce and camping space minimal. Avoid weekends as traffic jams are horrendous.

Where to stay
Inexpensive

Caparica Oceano, Rua Mestre Manuel 26. Tel. (01) 2904253. Has 124 apartments, bar and swimming pool.

Hotel Praia do Sol, Rua dos Pescadores 12, Caparica. Tel. (01) 2900012. A two star hotel with fifty-four rooms, all with bath. It has a bar.

Camp sites

Parque de Campismo da Orbitur, Estrada da Trafaria, Monte de Caparica. Open all year. Tel. (01) 2900661.

There are many other camp sites, but they are extremely crowded in the summer.

Where to eat

Restaurante Centyonze, N111, Caparica. Tel. (01) 2903968. A nice restaurant with a bar and a fireplace. It serves its own specialities, as well as Portuguese dishes.

Varanda do Oceano, Avenida Gen. Humberto Delgado, Caparica. Tel. (01) 2903092. A restaurant with a view of the sea. It serves fish, shellfish and other Portuguese dishes.

Tourist Office, Praça da Liberdade, Caparica. Tel. (01) 2400071.

Arrábida Peninsula

The Arrábida Peninsula stretches all the way from Setúbal to Cabo Espichel. Three of its towns – Setúbal, Palmela and Sesimbra – have fine old castles that were built to protect the peninsula from marauding pirates. There are many good sandy beaches in the coves at the foot of the mountains.

What to see

Turnatur, sponsored by the Costa Azul Tourist Office, offers walking tours, bicycling tours and photographic safaris of the region. Contact Tourist Office in Setúbal or Turnatur, tel. (01) 2073748.

Wine

The peninsula is also famous for its wine. Seventy per cent of the region is covered in vines. These strong, sweet wines, made from muscatel and other white grapes, are pale to burnt amber in colour, and have a very high alcohol content (18° to 20°) and an unmistakable taste. The Moscatel de Setúbal is world famous.

The red table wines produced in the area are some of the best in the country. Periquita is a very popular red table wine and Bacalhôa – named after a famous palace – is one of the best.

Palmela
History

Palmela is on the A2 between Lisbon and Setúbal. It is believed that Palmela was first inhabited at the end of the Neolithic period. The town was later occupied by the Moors, and was finally taken from them by King Afonso Henriques in 1166.

What to see

Palmela Castle is at a strategic point overlooking the Tagus and Sado estuaries, a spot chosen by the Roman governor Aulio Cornelio Palma. In 1148 King Afonso Henriques captured the castle from the Moors, in a surprise attack. The Moors got it back in 1165, but the following year King Afonso recaptured it. From 1288 it was the headquarters of the Portuguese Order of Sant'Iago. It was badly damaged in an attack by Almansor, and was reconstructed in the fifteenth century. In the 1755 earthquake it again suffered considerable damage, and after that it was abandoned. It has now been restored, and accommodates a pousada.

The fifteenth-century Santiago Church contains the tomb of Dom Jorge de Lencastre, the last Grand Master of the Order of Sant'Iago, who died in 1551. It has sixteenth-century decoration and seventeenth- and eighteenth-century tiles. The Misericórdia Church is decorated with beautiful seventeenth-century tiles.

There is a seventeenth-century pillory.

The Town Hall dates back to the seventeenth century. The salon is decorated with portraits of the Portuguese kings up to Manuel I.

There are also the remains of the Church of Santa Maria do Castelo, which was destroyed during the 1755 earthquake.

Pousada
Medium price

Pousada do Castelo de Palmela, 2950 Palmela. Tel. (01) 2351226/2351395. A luxury pousada in Palmela Castle. It has twenty-seven rooms, an excellent bar and regional restaurant.

Palmela Tourist Office is in Largo do Chafariz. Tel. (01) 2350089.

Setúbal

Setúbal is on the Sado River Estuary at the southern end of the A2 from Lisbon.

History

Archaeological finds dating back to the Neolithic period indicate that there was a prehistoric settlement here. During the Roman occupation, Setúbal became an important centre of the salt trade and of the fish-salting industry. Factories were located along the River Sado and the Tróia Peninsula. In the time of the Moors the factories were abandoned and soon covered by the sand of the river.

Setúbal was resettled after the Christians took the region from the Moors, and the Order of Sant'Iago was established here. In 1458 King Afonso V sailed from Setúbal to conquer Alcacer Ceguer in Morocco.

As a consequence of economic and social development in the nineteenth century, Setúbal again became a significant commercial and industrial centre with an important fishing fleet. However, during recent years it declined because most of its industries became obsolete. It is now enjoying a revival.

What to see

The **Church of Jesus** belonged to the Monastery of Jesus, which was built in the fifteenth century. It is a very early example of Manueline architecture.

Setúbal Museum is in what used to be the Monastery of Jesus. It has collections of paintings, jewellery, items of architectural interest, archaeological finds from the Setúbal area, documents dating back to the fourteenth century and books in editions dating back to the sixteenth century. The ethnographic section of the **Archaeological and Ethnographic Museum** has an interesting exhibition of the fishing and agricultural traditions of the region.

The **Santa Maria da Graça Church** was built during the thirteenth century and then rebuilt in a classical style during the sixteenth century. It has sixteenth- and seventeenth-century paintings and wooden sculptures with gold leaf, and eighteenth-century tiles.

Casa do Bocage, the house where the Portuguese poet Bocage was born in 1765, is now the Municipal Gallery of Visual Arts.

The **Fortress of São Filipe** was built in the late sixteenth century, on the orders of King Philip II. The chapel is covered in glazed tiles by

Policarpo de Oliveira Bernardes. There is now a pousada in part of the fortress.

The **Fishing and Oceanographic Museum** contains collections of marine species.

The **Church of São Julião** was reconstructed after the 1755 earthquake, but there are still two doorways remaining from the original Manueline church. It contains thirteenth-century statues and jewellery, a sixteenth-century box and panel, and eighteenth-century wood carvings and tiles.

Where
to stay
Inexpensive
Hotel Esperança, Avenida Luisa Todi 220. Tel. (065) 25151/2/3. A three star hotel with seventy-six rooms, all with bath. It has a bar, a night club and a billiard room.

Albergaria Laitau, Avenida General Daniel de Sousa 86. Tel. (065) 37031. A four star inn with forty-one rooms with bath, a bar and TV.

Pensão Bocage (+ annexe), Rua de São Cristovão 14. Tel. (065) 21598. Have thirty-four rooms with bath, and a bar.

Manor house
Inexpensive
Quinta do Patrício, Encosta de São Filipe. Tel. (065) 522088. An eighteenth-century, pink farmhouse on a slope overlooking the sea and the River Sado. There are three rooms with bath, sitting room and dining room.

Pousada
Medium price
Pousada de São Filipe, 2900 Setúbal. Tel. (065) 23844/24981. A luxury pousada with fifteen rooms with bath, a restaurant, a bar and a terrace.

Camp site
Parque de Campismo Municipal, Toca do Pai Lopes, Setúbal. Tel. (065) 22475.

Where to eat
The restaurant in the **Pousada de São Filipe** is very good. Regional specialities are served.

Beco, Rua Misericórdia 24. Tel. (065) 24617. A typical Portuguese restaurant with a bar.

The Tourist Office for the town is in Praça do Bocage. Tel. (065) 24204. The Regional Tourist Office is in Largo do Corpo Santo. Tel. (065) 24284/29507.

Arrábida Natural Park
The Arrábida Natural Park covers 10,800 hectares of the Arrábida Peninsula, from Setúbal to Sesimbra. It is a mountain range which is covered with rare Mediterranean vegetation. There are many paths for walking, and there are beautiful views of the sea.

Vila Fresca de Azeitão
Vila Fresca de Azeitão is to the west of Setúbal on the N10. It has the Quinta da Bacalhôa palace, which was originally a hunting lodge belonging to King João I. In 1528 it was bought by the illegitimate son of the famous Portuguese Viceroy of India Afonso de Albuquerque. He added many features that turned it into what looks like a Portuguese fort in India. The wonderful Bacalhôa wine comes from this estate.

Manor house
Inexpensive
Quinta do César, Vila Fresca de Azeitão. Tel. (01) 2080387. A house that was originally built by the Prime Minister of King Carlos.

It has been reconstructed since, and it offers one suite, two bedrooms with baths and a big living room with a fireplace. Outside the house has a courtyard with a beautiful garden and a swimming pool.

Vila Nogueira de Azeitão

Vila Nogueira de Azeitão is a lovely little town just south of Vila Fresca. It originally belonged to the wife of King Pedro. Later, it passed into the possession of the Order of Sant'Iago, and it belonged to them till 1759. It has many beautiful sixteenth-, seventeenth- and eighteenth-century mansions, including the palace of the Dukes of Aveiro, built in 1520. Near the palace you will find the Nossa Senhora da Piedade Convent. The original building, dating from 1435, was destroyed in the 1755 earthquake, but you can still see tiles and other remains, which were integrated into the reconstructed convent. The São Lourenço Church has an altar with tiles attributed to António Bernardes. The town has several restaurants, antique shops, an enormous open market on Sundays, and famous wineries.

Wineries

The José Maria da Fonseca company in Vila Nogueira de Azeitão have an old palace with lovely gardens where you can go and taste their wines. The famous Lancers Rosé wines are also made in Vila Nogueira de Azeitão.

Where to stay
Inexpensive

Quinta das Torres, Vila Nogueira de Azeitão. Tel. (01) 2080001. A beautiful eighteenth-century, ivy-covered four star inn in lovely grounds. It has eleven rooms with bath, and a restaurant.

Cabo Espichel

What to see

Cabo Espichel is on a promontory high over the Atlantic on the very end of the peninsula. To get there, you drive down the N379 over a high, barren cliff top where the trees are bent and gnarled by the wind. It was called the Cabo da Santa Esperança (Cape of Saint Hope) because sailors returning from their voyages sighted it and knew they were almost home to Lisbon. A small white chapel, called the Chapel of Memory, was built there in the fifteenth century. When you stand inside and look out, you feel almost engulfed by the Atlantic.

The Nossa Senhora do Cabo Sanctuary was a pilgrims' inn in the Middle Ages. It has two long arcaded buildings that face a wide courtyard at the end of which is a church dedicated to Our Lady of the Cape. The sanctuary was self-contained, with kitchen, ovens, cisterns, shops, and even a small eighteenth-century aqueduct. The pilgrims who came here were first farmers from the region, then the court from Lisbon, and finally fishermen. It is now abandoned.

Fossilized dinosaurs' footprints and tail-marks have been found on the cape at the north and south ends of Lagosteiros beach, below the cliffs, an area which was originally a lagoon. The marks indicate that the dinosaurs were about 15 m long. Before it was confirmed that the footprints had been made by dinosaurs, a legend had grown up around them – the legend of the Pedra da Mula (the Mule's Rock). It was believed that the Virgin came up out of the sea riding a mule, and rode on up the cliff. The mule's hoofs left the marks.

Sesimbra

Sesimbra is 34 km west of Setúbal on the N241. There was a pre-

History | historic settlement here, and the site was later occupied by the Romans. In the twelfth and thirteenth centuries it changed hands several times between the Moors and the Christians, until it was finally captured by King Sancho I. In 1236 King Sancho gave it to the Knights of Sant'Iago, and in order to populate the area convicts were brought in and fishermen who lived here were granted special privileges. The town was granted a charter in 1323, by King Dinis. By the fifteenth and sixteenth centuries Sesimbra had become an important trade and fishing centre, and it played a great part in the Age of Discoveries. Later, Dom Henrique and Dom João, the commanders of Sant'Iago and Aveiro, built two forts in order to defend the port.

Sesimbra today | Sesimbra remains quite an important fishing centre, but today it is mainly a tourist resort.

What to see | The castle was built during the twelfth and thirteenth centuries. Inside the Santa Maria do Castelo Church there are ruins that date from the second half of the twelfth century. The church was reconstructed in the eighteenth century. The Parish Church, which dates from the sixteenth century, is a perfect example of the transition between the Manueline and the Renaissance styles. It has seventeenth-century carvings. The Misericórdia Church was built in the sixteenth century, but there are later modifications. Among the paintings in the annexe is the *Nossa Senhora da Misericórdia* by Gregório Lopes. The Espírito Santo dos Mareantes Chapel was built as an annexe to a fifteenth-century hospital. It was rebuilt in the seventeenth century, but there are still traces of the original building.

The Santiago Fort was constructed by King João IV during the seventeenth century. It served as a fort and a prison.

The Porto de Abrigo is a busy sheltered harbour with many colourful fishing boats.

The Municipal Museum contains a good archaeological collection. It also has collections of coins and of sacred art.

Where to stay
Medium price | **Hotel do Mar**, Rua General Humberto Delgado 10. Tel. (01) 2233326/2233422. A four star hotel with 120 rooms. It has a bar, restaurant, swimming pool, tennis, and a night club.

Inexpensive | **Pensão Espardarte**, Avenida 25 de Abril 10–11. Tel. (01) 2233189. A three star pension with eighty rooms with bath, a bar and restaurant.

Camp sites | **Atlantico Camping Club**, Praia das Bicas – Altarim. Tel. (01) 678971. A luxury camp site with many amenities and trees.

Forte do Cavalo, Sesimbra. Tel. (01) 2233694. Overlooks the fort and sea.

Where to eat | **Chez Nous**, Largo do Município 11/3. Tel. (01) 2230141. A nice restaurant with an open kitchen. It serves French food.

Angelus, Santana. Tel. (01) 2231340. A restaurant that serves typical Portuguese food and its own specialities.

The Tourist Office is in Avenida dos Náufragos. Tel. (01) 2233304.

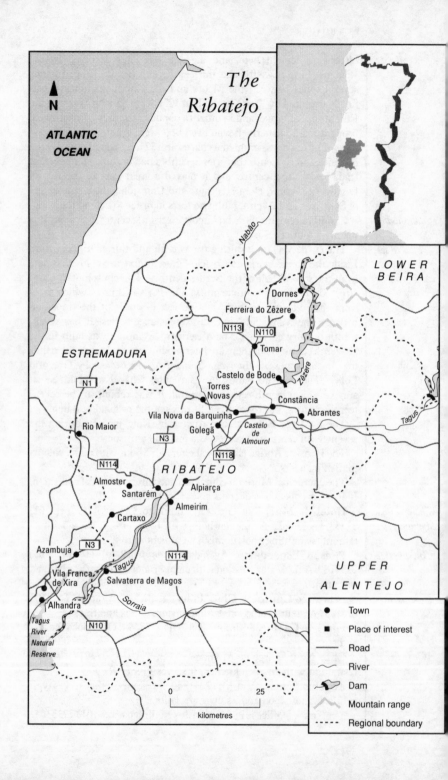

The Ribatejo

Introduction

'Ribatejo' means, literally, 'Tagus river bank'. The Ribatejo occupies both banks of the river from the north-western border of the Alentejo to the eastern edge of Estremadura, and from Tomar in the north to Vila Franca de Xira in the south, in a roughly triangular shape. A great part of the land is flat, and there are many heaths and barren, sandy wastes. The region is susceptible to severe flooding, and there have been some catastrophic floods.

River Tagus

The Tagus has always been an important highway for transportation. Towns like Abrantes and Constância were important river ports in early times: you can still see the quays that were built in the Middle Ages. In those days the river was navigable from Lisbon to the Spanish border. When the Spanish kings Philip I and Philip II governed the entire Iberian Peninsula, there were attempts to make the river navigable from Lisbon to the city of Toledo, near Madrid, but in the end nothing came of these efforts.

Horses and bulls

The Ribatejo is horse and bull country. There are thousands of hectares given over to the raising of horses, bulls and cattle. In the Ribatejo you can still ride to hounds, attend bullfights, and watch *campinos* (cowboys) herd bulls.

Campinos

The *campino* is a common sight on the Ribatejo plains as he rides along on his horse with his herds of bulls, punching them with his long wooden pole to keep them in line. His costume is colourful – a white shirt, red cummerbund, black breeches, scarlet waistcoat, green stocking cap with a red tassel, and a black coat flung over his shoulder. The *campino* herds the bulls, brands them, chooses those to go into the ring and those to be used for beef or breeding, and organizes private bullfights to judge the animals with the best 'caste'.

Horses

In the fourteenth century King Fernando promulgated the first laws governing the breeding and raising of Portuguese horses. Kings of subsequent dynasties continued to be very involved in the important work of breeding horses, which were so necessary to the army. In 1746 King João V established an official stud farm at Portel in the Alentejo; this was later transferred to Alter do Chão, also in the Alentejo. He appointed the famous horseman the Marquês de Marialva to be in charge, and the Marquês raised Lusitanian horses of international fame. But during the Napoleonic invasions of the nineteenth century most of the horses were lost – except for one small group that happened to be on an estate in Azambuja in the Ribatejo.

There is great new interest in horse-breeding today, and Lusitanian horses are being sold all over the world. The Estação Zootécnica Nacional (National Stud Farm), whose brand is CN (Coudelaria Nacional) is at Quinta da Fonte Boa in Vale de Santarém in the Ribatejo.

There are many private stud farms in the Ribatejo around Santarém, Cartaxo, Azambuja, Alpiarça, Golegã (where the famous horse fair is held), and in the Alentejo around Elvas, Monsaraz, Évora and Ourique.

Haute École   The Portuguese School of Equestrian Art, with horsemen dressed in traditional eighteenth-century costumes, have recently put their horses through the exacting and spectacular *Haute École* paces for both Queen Elizabeth and President Reagan.

Wines   You see vineyards everywhere. The Ribatejo was producing wine even before Portugal became a nation. However, in the eighteenth century the Marquês de Pombal prohibited the growing of vines, to encourage the cultivation of wheat. Vines were recently reintroduced, and the Ribatejo now produces some good regional wines, both red and white, such as Cartaxo and Almeirim.

Tomar

Tomar is in the centre of Portugal, on the River Nabão, 135 km north of Lisbon. The countryside around consists of rolling plains with many trees and farms, surrounded by high hills where neat little towns overlook the rivers. As you come down the hill on the road from Lisbon, you see at the highest point of the town the immense and beautiful castle and the Monastery of Christ.

History   Inscription, monuments and other remains show that the site was occupied in prehistoric times and then by Romans, Visigoths and Moors before, in 1157, it was given to the Order of the Knights Templar, who made it a stronghold of Christianity.

The Templars carefully chose the site to defend the road from Santarém and prevent the Moors from attacking Lisbon. Using to a large extent stone from the old Roman town of Selium nearby, they built what was essentially a military fortress like the ones they had built all across Europe to Jerusalem. The old town is laid out in the form of a cross.

In 1190 the castle was besieged by the Emir of Morocco. The Moors broke down the gate of the outer walls and rushed the inner courtyard, but they were beaten off by the Christian soldiers, with the help of the townspeople, who had taken refuge in the castle. The Moors abandoned their attack on the castle, but destroyed the town.

Early in the fourteenth century the Order of the Templars was suppressed by papal decree, but in Portugal King Dinis founded, as a replacement, the Order of Christ, which inherited the Templars' property. In 1356 Tomar became the headquarters of the Order. The Order of Christ was very important during the Age of Discoveries, when Prince Henry the Navigator was Grand Master, and used part of the Order's income to send his ships on their voyages of discovery around Africa and to India.

Later kings – Portuguese and Spanish – enlarged Tomar's castle and built additions. But during the nineteenth-century French invasions Tomar was sacked and pillaged, and all of the contents of the castle disappeared. Then in 1834, when all the religious orders were suppressed in Portugal, the castle was abandoned. It deteriorated and became a home for squatters. However, it has now been rescued and has become one of Portugal's national monuments.

Tomar today

Tomar is a beautiful town, with the River Nabão running through its centre. It has a lovely park, many buildings of historical interest, pleasant hotels and lots of outdoor restaurants and cafés.

What to see

The **Castle** and the **Monastery of Christ** form a complex at the top of the hill above the town. You come in from the east through the impressive Porta do Sol. The buildings, with their arches and towers, sprawl through the gardens. Of the original twelfth-century castle there still remain the walls that encircled the citadel, the Tower of Homage, a circular temple, the Charola, seven cloisters, and the Templars' Church.

The **Charola** is an octagonal temple built in the twelfth century in the style of Byzantine mosques the Templars had seen in the east. It is said that the Templars used to attend Mass on horseback, each sitting on his horse under one of the sixteen arches. After it was struck by lightning, King Manuel I had it restored in the Manueline style. A nave occupied by the choir was added, along with turrets and steeples. The outside of the choir has the famous Chapter Window, which is the most extravagant example of Manueline art in Portugal. It has every sea motif you can possibly imagine. There is also the Order of the Garter, conveyed on Prince Henry the Navigator.

Four of the seven **Cloisters** are open to the public. The main cloister, built in the reign of King João II, is in the style of the Italian Renaissance. The cloister built in the reigns of the Spanish kings Philip I (crowned king of Portugal here) and Philip II is the largest, an intricately carved two-storey structure. Under the buildings were rooms used by the Inquisition. The tomb of Balthazar de Faria, who introduced the Inquisition into Portugal, is on the upstairs terrace.

The twelfth-century **Templars' Church** has a splendidly carved main doorway. The whole of the wall behind the high altar is painted with frescoes.

The **Church of Nossa Senhora da Conceição**, on the side of the hill below the monastery, is a small, bare church built in the sixteenth century in the Renaissance style.

The sixteenth-century **São Gregório Chapel** is a polygonal structure surrounded by a porch supported by columns.

The Church of **São João Baptista** is in the Praça da República, the main square of the old town. It has three naves separated by arches resting on Manueline columns. There are several interesting primitive paintings, and some sixteenth-century painted panels attributed to Gregório Lopes.

The **Synagogue**, in the nearby Rua Dr Joaquim Jacinto, is the only really well preserved ancient synagogue in Portugal. It was bought in 1929 by Samuel Swartz, who had a particular interest in the history of the Jews in Portugal. He donated it to the State in 1939. The building is rectangular and with its high thin columns and vaulted roof it rather resembles a mosque. It was probably built sometime in the fifteenth century, and used only briefly as a synagogue. It seems later to have been a Christian church and then, in the sixteenth century, a prison. It now houses the Abrahão Zacuto Museum, containing tombstones and inscriptions in Hebrew collected from all over Portugal.

The **Church of Santa Maria dos Olivais** is just outside Tomar, alone in a field. Twenty-two Grand Masters of the Templars and of the Order of Christ are buried here. At its zenith, this church was the Mother Church for all of Portugal's churches in Africa, Asia and America – but this is hard to believe when you see it today.

The **Chapel of Santa Iria** is on the River Nabão, on the site where, according to legend, Santa Iria was martyred in the seventh century.

The waterwheel on the River Nabão in the central park is often called the Moorish Wheel. There are many such wheels on the river, though most of them are no longer in use, having being replaced by modern machinery. They usually measure from 7 to 19 m in diameter, and have twenty-eight to fifty spokes and about fifty ceramic buckets. They make a pretty, rhythmic sound as they turn in the water.

You can also see many watermills all along the river.

Festivals

The *Festas dos Tabuleiros* takes place every four years, in the first half of July. It seems likely that it was originally connected with a bread cult that can be traced back to the worship of the Mother Goddess in ancient times. In the fourteenth century the nature of the festival changed, under the influence of the saintly Queen Isabel, wife of King Dinis, and it became a festival in honour of the Holy Spirit.

The procession, which is very beautiful, is now a famous tourist attraction. Young girls dressed in white walk through the streets of the town, each carrying on her head a *tabuleiro* or platter piled with thirty loaves of bread fixed on rods, interspersed with flowers and topped with a crown. The bread is later distributed among the poor.

The other two, smaller festivals of Tomar take place every year, the *Festa do Círio da Santa da Piedade* at the beginning of September, the *Feira da Santa Iria* in October.

Excursion

A short drive north-west along the N113 will take you to a signposted track leading to a lovely valley spanned by some of the 180 arches of the graceful Pegões Aqueduct. The nineteenth-century Nossa Senhora da Piedade church, with its stairway of 365 steps, is nearby.

Where to stay
Medium price

Hotel dos Templários, Largo Cândido dos Reis 1. Tel. (049) 31321, telex HOTEMPLARIOS-TOMAR. A four star hotel with eighty-four air-conditioned rooms. It has a restaurant, a bar, a disco, shops, a swimming pool, tennis courts and billiard room.

Estalagem Santa Iria, in the park by the river, is an elegant four star inn with twenty-one rooms with bath, a bar and restaurant. Somerset Maugham stayed here.

Ilha do Lombo, Serra de Tomar, 16 km east of Tomar. Tel. (049) 371128. A four star inn on a beautiful island in the middle of the River Zêzere, reachable by boat. It has fifteen rooms with bath, swimming pool, bar, TV, restaurant and boating.

Inexpensive

Pensão União, Rua Serpa Pinto 94, 1° and 2°. Tel. (049) 322831. A three star pension with twenty-nine rooms with bath, a bar and restaurant.

Residencial Trovador, Rua Dr Joaquim Ribeiro, Lote 1. Tel. (049) 311582. A four star inn with thirty rooms with bath, a bar and TV.

Camp site

Tomar Municipal Camping, on the River Nabão in the Municipal Park at Tomar. Tel. (049) 313950.

Where to eat

Marisqueira de Tomar, Avenida Norton de Matos 9. Tel. (049) 313903. A large, air-conditioned bar-restaurant, specializing in seafood and *arroz de lampreia* – River Nabão lamprey, done in a black earthenware pot with rice, wine and garlic. Closed Mondays.

Chez Nous, Rua Dr Joaquim Jacinto 31. Tel. (049) 312294. Small and prettily decorated, in the old quarter of town. Serves French and Portuguese fare. Closed Saturdays.

Bela Vista, Fonte do Choupo 4. Tel. (049) 312870. An old restaurant, a landmark, by the river. Serves good Portuguese food. Closed Tuesdays.

What to eat

Try *lampreia com arroz* (lamprey with rice), *achegã*, *cabrito assado* (roast kid), *queijo de Tomar* (a small white cheese), and, for dessert, *fatias de Tomar*.

Bar

Quinta Bar, Quinta do Falcão. Tel. (049) 381767. Just out of town, has live music.

The Tourist Office is on the Avenida Dr Cândido Madureira. Tel. (049) 313095.

Ferreira do Zêzere

Ferreira do Zêzere is 20 km north of Tomar by the N110–N238–N348. It is a peaceful little town, a good place to fish, or to relax.

Where to stay, and eat Inexpensive

Estalagem Lago Azul, Estrada Nacional 348. Tel. (049) 361441/ 5/6. A four star inn on the banks of the River Zêzere. It has twenty double bedrooms with air conditioning and bath, a restaurant, a bar, a terrace, a swimming pool and tennis courts.

Estalagem Lago Azul has an excellent restaurant that serves Portuguese specialities. Ferreira do Zêzere also has several other good restaurants that serve Portuguese and regional food.

What to eat

Try *cabrito com grelos* (kid with green vegetables), *leitão com batatas* (suckling pig with potatoes).

Dornes

Dornes is 27 km north of Tomar by the N110–N238, beside the River Zêzere. The road curves up through hills, pine and eucalyptus woods and past many pretty old houses. When you get to Dornes you will find a quaint, unspoiled little town.

History

Dornes now sits on a little peninsula in the lake formed on the Zêzere by the Castelo de Bode dam. It grew up around the church which Queen Saint Isabel, wife of King Dinis, had built there (she built churches as he built castles). Near the church is a pentagonal tower which was probably built by the Templars.

Name

Dornes got its name from the image of *Nossa Senhora dos Dores* (Our Lady of Pain). This statue of the Virgin Mary with the dead Jesus in her arms was found on the river bank. The image was said to give forth loud lamentations. *Dores* became Dornes.

Where to stay, and eat Inexpensive

Estalagem Vale da Ursa, Cernache do Bomjardim, Sertá. Tel. (074) 67511. A four star inn overlooking the lake just 3 km from Dornes across the bridge. It is surrounded by pine woods and has spectacular views of the lake. Each room has a bath, terrace, telephone, radio and TV. There is a large terraced swimming pool and a restaurant with excellent regional cooking. The kid and the river fish are especially good. On Saturdays you can get a dish of sheep's belly stuffed with mint and other herbs, and sausages.

Vila Nova da Barquinha

Vila Nova da Barquinha is a small town on the banks of the River Tagus 20 km south of Tomar, off the N110 on the N3 towards Constância. Its life has always depended on the river, and at one time it was an important river port. There are several little restaurants on the river that serve river fish.

Castelo de Almourol

Castelo de Almourol is on an island in the River Tagus between Vila Nova da Barquinha and Constância. The best way to reach it from Tomar is to take the N110 for 8 km south and then turn off on the N358-1 towards Constância until you come to the river. Turn right and you will see the castle. You can also reach Castelo de Almourol from Vila Nova da Barquinha. But whatever you do, don't leave this area without visiting it. There is usually a man on the river bank who will row you across.

History

Castelo de Almourol probably began as a Lusitanian fortified town and was then captured by the Romans. The little island was mentioned in the writings of Strabo two thousand years ago. Part of the lower walls are of Roman construction, and Roman coins have been found on the island. It was later occupied by Visigoths and Moors, until it was taken by the Christians under King Afonso Henriques, who gave it to the Order of Knights Templar. They rebuilt the fortifications in 1171, when Gualdim Pais was Master of the Order. You can see his name and the date of the building over a door in the castle. After the Order of the Templars was suppressed, the castle belonged to their successors, the Order of Christ.

What to see
The walls follow the contours of the rocky island. Near an inner gate you can see the remains of a tunnel that local people believe once connected the castle with the shore. The outer wall has ten towers, and there are battlements, turrets, arrow slits, ramparts, terraces. There are marvellous views from the ramparts.

Legends
The island has a fascinating collection of stories of giants, knights fighting for damsels, and ghosts of Moorish boys. Legend says that it was occupied at one time by a giant named Almourol, who guarded two young princesses in the castle – Miraguarda and Polinarda. An English crusader named Palmeirim who stopped in Oporto on his way to Constantinople heard of the giant Almourol and his charges and decided to go and win one of the princesses for himself. In one version he fights the giant and takes away Polinarda. In another he fights but fails to capture a princess. Anyway, Almourol was eventually defeated by another giant, Dramusiando.

Another story explains why the castle is haunted by a Christian girl and her Moorish lover. The Christian Mayor of Almourol Castle murdered the mother and sister of a young Moorish boy, and forced the boy to act as a page in his castle. But he and the Mayor's daughter, Beatriz, fell in love and ran away, and the father died of a broken heart. The lovers appear on the keep tower on Saint John's Eve.

Constância
Constância, 11 km from Vila Nova da Barquinha on the N3, is a pretty little town that climbs the slopes of the hill where the Tagus and Zêzere rivers meet. It is a white town, with many flowers. It is believed that the poet Camões lived in a house on the river front between 1547 and 1550. During the Peninsular War Wellington assembled the British troops here for his march into Spain to fight the French. The view is somewhat marred by a polluting paper mill.

Manor houses
Inexpensive
Casa do Paláçio, 2250 Constancia. Tel. (049) 93371/93224. A stately, nineteenth-century mansion on the banks of the River Tagus. It has four bedrooms with bath, spacious living rooms, bar and boating. Queen Maria II stayed here.

Casa de Santa Bárbara, Quinta de Santa Bárbara. Tel. (049) 93214. An historic house, with an old Jesuit chapel, on a big farm. It offers six bedrooms with bath, large living rooms, garden, swimming pool and riding ring.

Castelo de Bode
Castelo de Bode is 10 km from Constância on the N358-2 and 13 km from Tomar on the N110-N358-2, on the reservoir of the River

Zêzere, good for fishing and all kinds of water sports, while the crest of the dam gives a good view of the Zêzere valley.

Boat trips

A boat trip up the river is a pleasant way to spend the day. The São Cristovão river boat, which runs a regular service from Castelo de Bode, is a modern, two-storey boat with a restaurant.Tickets can be obtained at hotels.

Pousada
Medium price

Pousada de São Pedro, Castelo de Bode. Tel. (049) 94244. Has fifteen rooms with bath, a restaurant, a bar and a terrace. The restaurant specializes in regional cooking, and has a lovely view of the lake.

Abrantes

Abrantes is on the north bank of the River Tagus, 15 km east of Constância on the N3. It centres around its castle, which sits high above the river where you have a view with a radius of 80 km. It was an important river port in the days when the Tagus was navigable from its mouth to the Spanish border. Abrantes got its name from the gold that was found in the sands of the river banks – *aurantes* means golden.

History

It was inhabited in pre-Roman times, and was taken in 130 BC by the Romans under Decimus Junius Brutus. The Romans fortified the town. Later it was occupied by the Moors until it was taken from them in 1148 by King Afonso Henriques. King Afonso III enlarged the castle, and his son King Dinis gave it to his wife, Queen Isabel. Many kings stayed in the castle, and many princes were born there.

The French captured Abrantes during the Peninsular War (Napoleon went so far as to create Junot Duc d'Abrantes), but they were driven out by the Portuguese and the English under Wellington.

What to see

The castle has two lines of walls with lovely gardens in between. Inside it has vaulted corridors and great vaulted chambers. The main entrance is on the north-east. The Santa Maria Church in the castle is now a museum. It has collections of Roman statuary, sixteenth- and seventeenth-century tomb sculptures, and Mozarabic tiles.

The Monastery of São Domingos has a Renaissance cloister and a vestibule with glazed tiles.

The Misericórdia Church has a Renaissance portal and sixteenth-century paintings attributed to Gregório Lopes.

Festivals

The *Feira de São Matias* takes place in February, the *Feira Mourisca* in March, the *Feira do Artesanato* in May and June, the *Festas de São Pedro* in June and July, and the *Festas de Verão* in July. The *Festa de São Lourenço* and the *Festa da Arrifana* are in August, and the *Festas da Nossa Senhora do Rosário* in September.

Where to stay
Inexpensive

Hotel de Turismo de Abrantes, Parque de Santo António. Tel. (041) 21261. A three star hotel with twenty-four rooms with bath, a bar, and a good restaurant that serves Portuguese and regional specialities.

Manor house
Inexpensive

Quinta dos Vales, Tramagal, Tramagal, 10km from Abrantes. Tel. (041) 97363. A lovely, white country house offering six rooms with bath, common lounge and dining room, riding ring and stables for wonderful rides along the banks of the Tagus.

Where to eat

Casa do Pastor, 12 km from Abrantes on N244–3 and N358 toward Mouriscas. Tel. (041) 95255. A rustic lodge serving excellent regional dishes.

Torres Novas

Torres Novas is 18 km south of Tomar, on the N3 to Lisbon. It is a pleasant town on the River Almonda.

History

Legend says that some of Ulysses' men came up the Tagus and built the fort that is now Torres Novas. It is rather more likely that the first fort was the Roman Nova Augusta. The Visigoths came, then the Moors, and then the Christians. The conflicts between the Moors and the Christians inflicted great damage on the town. Later, more damage was caused by the Spaniards, the French, and the 1755 earthquake. After the War of Succession, in which Torres Novas supported Dom Miguel, the town was virtually abandoned, and its walls and towers were pulled down. It is now being restored.

What to see

The São Salvador Church and the Santiago Church both date from the thirteenth century, and the São Pedro Church from the fourteenth century. The Misericórdia Church has a lovely ceiling painted in 1678.

Festival

The Blessing of the Cattle takes place early in May.

Golegã

Golegã, just 7 km south of Torres Novas on the N365, is a town of low white houses on a wide plain where cattle graze.

What to see

The Misericórdia Church has seventeenth-century tiles.

The Quinta da Cardiga, which belonged to the Order of Christ, is one of the finest palaces in Portugal, with interior patios, towers with cupolas, a private chapel with a sixteenth-century door, and a great farm around it with buildings for making cheese, wine, and so on.

Horse fair

Anyone who likes horses should really try to see the Golegã Horse Fair, held for eight days in November every year. It has become a real event – the finest horses in the Ribatejo are paraded and there are festivities of all kinds.

Where to stay, and eat

Café-Restaurant Central has rooms and a restaurant. Tel. (041) 72187. Portuguese cooking and regional specialities.

Santarém

History

Santarém is 37 km south of Golegã by the N365–N3 and 79 km north of Lisbon by the E1 or the N3. It is on the River Tagus.

Santarém has been occupied since the Neolithic period. It was conquered by the Romans and later by the Moors. King Afonso Henriques took it from the Moors in 1147. In 1325 King Dinis died here.

Santa Iria

The Romans called the town Scallabis. It derives its present name from its patron saint, Santa Iria, a nun who was martyred in Tomar in the seventh century. It is said that her body was flung into the Nabão and after floating down the Tagus was washed ashore at Santarém. In a shrine high off the ground on the river bank there is a statue which was found in floodwater, and which the people of Santarém call Santa Iria. They believe that if the river water ever reaches the feet of the statue it will be the Deluge, and even Lisbon will be swept into the sea.

Santarém today

Today Santarém is a bustling agricultural town with modern shops and busy, crowded streets. It has, however, kept its character, and it is a pretty town. The hillsides that stretch down to the river have many fine old buildings and houses with lovely views of the river and plains.

What to see

There is not much left of the castle or the royal palace, but Santarém is full of churches. The town divides into five sections.

The **Alcáçova** or royal residence was on a hill above the plain. The castle and palace were completely walled for defence. Today only the tower, the castle walls and two Gothic doors remain.

The area known as **Marvila** is reached by a long, tree-lined avenue at the end of which are the Portas do Sol (Gates of the Sun). There is a formal garden from which there is a fantastic view. This was the original walled town, but most of the walls were pulled down in this century and the last. The Marvila Church was built in the sixteenth century. It is a tall, austere building with three aisles entirely covered with diamond-patterned tiles that get progressively bigger as they climb to the ceiling.

Fora da Vila is a section outside the old walls where Franciscan and Dominican priests and nuns lived. There are several Gothic churches, including the thirteenth-century São Francisco Church, and the fourteenth-century Graça Church and Santa Clara Church. The Graça Church has the tomb of Pedro Álvares de Cabral, the discoverer of Brazil, and the finest rose-window in Portugal. The thirteenth-century São João de Alporão Church is now the Archaeological Museum, containing the tomb of the Count of Viana. The tomb has only his tooth inside, because that was all that was left of him after he was hacked to death by Moors. The Donas Convent also dates from the thirteenth century.

The riverside is divided into two parts: the Ribeira on the north and the Alfange on the south.

In the days when the River Tagus was navigable from Lisbon the **Ribeira** was the old river port. It is now a poverty-stricken area where life centres around fishing and the making of small boats. You can see Santa Iria here on her pedestal watching over the river.

The **Alfange** is a very old area. The ruins of the pre-Roman São João Evangelista Church are here.

Agricultural fair

At the end of May or beginning of June every year, Santarém holds the greatest agricultural fair in Portugal. It is known variously as the *Feira Nacional da Agricultura* and the *Feira do Ribatejo*. Cattle and horses from all over the country are displayed here. There are bullfights, horse shows, and pavilions with foods of different regions.

Excursions

Vale de Lobos in Azoia de Baixo, 3 km from Santarém on the N3, is a 40-hectare estate where the writer Alexandre Herculano invented all kinds of new methods to improve agriculture.

The **Estação Zootécnica Nacional** (National Stud Farm) is at Quinta da Fonte Boa in Vale de Santarém, 7 km south of Santarém on the N3. The farm has Lusitanian and Arab horses.

The town of **Almoster**, 10 km west of Santarém on N365–N114–2, grew up around Almoster Monastery, which was founded in 1289. The monastery is now in a very dilapidated state.

Where to stay
Inexpensive

Hotel Abidis, Rua Guilherme de Azevedo 4. Tel. (043) 22017/8. A two star hotel with twenty-seven rooms, only six with bath. It has a restaurant and a bar.

Pensão Jardim, Rua Florbela Espanca. A three star pension with twenty rooms with bath, a bar and restaurant.

Manor houses
Inexpensive

Casa dos Cedros, Azoia de Cima. Tel. (01) 800986. A white manor house with wrought-iron balconies in Aldeia, near Santarém. It has four bedrooms that share two bathrooms.

Quinta da Sobreira, Vale de Figueira. Tel. (043) 42444/42221. A nineteenth-century country house that offers three rooms with bath, and a living room. There is a swimming pool, and horse riding.

Casal da Torre, Rua Nova da Torre 29, Vale de Santarém. Tel. (043) 75227. A small manor house in the town of Vale de Santarém. It has three bedrooms, several living rooms, a kitchen and a garden.

Where to eat

Mal Cozinhado, Campo da Feira. Tel. (043) 23584. A restaurant that serves regional dishes.

Restaurante Portas do Sol, Jardim das Portas do Sol. Tel. (043) 23141. A restaurant that offers Portuguese as well as regional dishes. There is a lovely view.

Castiço, Campo da Feira. Tel. (043) 23891. A rustic restaurant in the fair grounds that serves good regional food. Closed Sundays.

What to eat

Try *sopa da pedra* (stone soup), roast cod, and, for a sweet, *celestes de Santa Clara* (almonds, sugar and eggs).

There are Tourist Offices at Rua Capelo Ivens 63, tel. (043) 23140 and Portas do Sol, tel. (043) 23141.

Almeirim

Almeirim is 4 km from Santarém on the N114. The road goes through lines of trees and past many beautiful old country houses. This was a favourite place of residence for the kings of the Avis dynasty – largely because of the abundance of game.

Almeirim is known for its wine, but above all for its *sopa da pedra* – a soup of meats, beans and vegetables, the base of which is a stone. Local legend says the soup originated with a beggar-priest who tricked local housewives into giving him the ingredients by pretending to boil a stone.

Where to eat

Touçinho, Rua Macau. Tel. (043) 52237. A big, authentic Ribatejo restaurant with an open country kitchen and a brick bread oven. The *sopa da pedra* and grills are the specialities. Closed Wednesdays and all of August.

Alpiarça | Alpiarça is 7 km north of Almeirim on the N118. Alpiarça was inhabited in Neolithic times, and important archaeological finds have been made at the castle, and in several necropolises in the neighbourhood. There are also the remains of a Roman road.

The Casa dos Patudos is a museum in the house which José Relvas left to the town. The collection contains paintings from the sixteenth to the nineteenth centuries, glazed tiles, furniture, ceramics – including rare Chinese porcelain made especially for the European market – tapestries, and Arraiolos carpets. Open Saturdays and Sundays and Thursday afternoons.

Salvaterra de Magos | Salvaterra de Magos is 34 km south of Santarém on the N114–N118, on the east side of the River Tagus. The road is flat, lined with vineyards and pine trees.

The town was a favourite place for the kings of the Bragança dynasty. It was originally built by Prince Luis, brother of King João III. It had a magnificent palace, opera house and bullring, built for royal entertainment. But all of this, except the royal chapel, was destroyed by a fire that started under mysterious circumstances.

The royal falconry is fascinating. There are 310 cages for falcons – all now empty.

Rio Maior | Rio Maior is 33 km west of Santarém on the N114. Most of its old buildings have been pulled down to make room for new ones. The town prides itself on being a centre of political conservatism and for stopping the advance of communists marching north during the 1974 Revolution. You can get a brass-studded wooden club for bashing heads, as a souvenir of that time. The town has a famous onion fair in summer.

What to see | The castle, which is in ruins, was originally an Iron Age *castro*.

The Misericórdia Church has a three-tiered wooden ceiling, a Baroque gilt carved altar and seventeenth-century tiles.

Where to stay
Inexpensive | **Pensão Rio Maior**, Rua Dr Francisco Barbosa. Tel. (043) 92087/8. A four star pension in the centre of Rio Maior, with rooms with bath, telephone, and bar.

Where to eat | There are several restaurants on the roads that lead into town, and others in the town itself.

The specialities of Rio Maior are *frango Rio Maior* (chicken with walnuts) and the famous Rio Maior *pão de ló* (sponge cake).

Cartaxo | Cartaxo is 14 km south of Santarém on the N3. It is a very old town that got its first charter from King Dinis in 1313. Junot stationed his troops here during the Peninsular War, and Wellington had his troops here between 1810 and 1811. Cartaxo's wine is famous.

What to see | The Parish Church was built in the sixteenth century, but has been much restored. There is a Manueline cross by the Parish Church.

The Senhor dos Passos Chapel dates from the sixteenth century.

Azambuja | Azambuja is 13 km south of Cartaxo on the N3. In the year 1200 it was given to Flemish Crusaders, who had helped in routing the

Moors. In the eighteenth century the pine woods nearby became notoriously infested with bands of robbers. Today the town has been much modernized, but its centre is still interesting.

Vila Franca de Xira

Vila Franca de Xira is 32 km north of Lisbon on the E1, by a bridge over the River Tagus. It is also on the main railway line. It is a busy agricultural centre, and a dormitory town for Lisbon.

History

The town was founded in the twelfth century, as part of the domain of the Templars. It was here that, in 1823, a *coup d'état* put an end to the short-lived 1820 constitution.

Festival

It has one of the best bullrings in the country. On the first or second Sunday in July there is a festival called *Colete Encarnado*, which involves bull-running in the streets and big bullfights in the ring. The festival is also animated with fandango dancing, and with riding and bull-herding competitions among the Ribatejo *campinos*.

You should not leave the Ribatejo without visiting a bull and horse farm to see the *campinos* herding the bulls. You can see a show of bull-running in the Centro Equestre da Lezíria Grande, Estrada Nacional 1, Povos Vila Franca de Xira. Tel. (063) 22781.

Where to stay

Estalagem da Lezíria, Rua Alves Redol 56. Tel. (063) 22129. A four star inn with a restaurant.

Inexpensive

Pensão Restaurante Flora, Rua Noël Perdigão 12. Tel. (063) 23127. A three star pension with twenty-one rooms, fourteen with bath, a bar, TV and restaurant.

Where to eat

The **Estalagem da Lezíria** has a good restaurant that serves local dishes.

Comboio, Rua Serpa Pinto 126. Tel. (063) 23080. A restaurant with good Portuguese cooking. Closed on Wednesdays.

Redondel, Praça Touros (Bullring). Tel. (063) 22973. A restaurant with regional cooking, a bar, air conditioning and parking. Closed on Mondays.

Alhandra

Alhandra is near Vila Franca de Xira on the N10, on the west side of the River Tagus. It has been marred by the polluting effects of a cement factory, but you can still see nineteenth-century houses faced with tiles, and the colourful little fishing boats on the river.

The castle and the Parish Church were built in 1558.

There is a statue of Hercules standing on a pedestal on a high hill up the river. This statue marks the end of the Torres Vedras Lines, the fortifications erected by the Duke of Wellington against the French in the Peninsular War. A plaque honours the Portuguese engineer, Neves da Costa, who planned them, and the English officer, J. Fletcher, who built them.

Tagus River Natural Reserve

The Tagus River Natural Reserve includes all of the estuary between Vila Franca de Xira and Sacavém. It is part of a rather belated attempt to save the fish and wildlife of this very polluted river. The dolphins, the oysters and many of the species of fish that used to be here have disappeared.

The Alentejo

Introduction

The Alentejo is a vast, rolling upland that stretches from the Spanish border to the Atlantic Ocean, and from the mountains that separate it from the Algarve on the south to the River Tagus 150 km north of Lisbon. It makes up one third of the total area of Portugal, but has only 12 per cent of the population; and almost all of the people are in agriculture. It has contrasts of temperature – very hot summers and cold winters.

The Alentejo is one of the most beautiful regions in the country. Its bright white towns with houses trimmed in blue or yellow – a tradition inherited from the Moors, who believed these colours deterred evil spirits – are in sharp contrast to the grey, granite villages of the north. The people are very friendly and hospitable. In spring, the entire countryside is covered with red, yellow and purple wild flowers and poppies.

History   For centuries the Alentejo was a battleground, invaded by Romans, Visigoths, Moors, Spaniards and French by turns. The legacy from that time can be seen in the magnificent old walled towns and castles that guard every hilltop. The presence in the Alentejo of the Romans

Moors   and Moors – especially the Moors – over a period of some 1,100 years

Land   set the pattern for the land distribution and way of life which persists
distribution   today. They divided the land into enormous estates, called 'Montes', on which the local people were forced to work. After the Moors were finally expelled by the Portuguese Christian kings, the system merely changed hands. The vast tracts of land were handed out to the military and to religious orders, who fortified them and continued as before, with the people working for them. When the religious orders were suppressed in the seventeenth century, their land and property was sold off intact to rich men, who also continued the system and finally became absentee landlords of huge estates that produced fortunes in cork for them, or were used as private hunting reserves for them and their friends. There were no small landowners, as there always were in the north of the country, in the Minho, Trás-os-Montes and other regions. The labourers worked the land for the landowners – a few living on the estates, but most of them part-time itinerant workers. This situation continued until the 1974 Revolution.

Agrarian reform   After the 1974 Revolution, the new Parliament passed the Agrarian

287

Reform Law, calling for the expropriation of any estate over 500 hectares in size if it were pasture land and 50 hectares if it were irrigated land. In October 1975 the Communists led the farmworkers in taking over the land. There were clashes with the National Republican Guard, but they succeeded in setting up Cooperative Production Units – known as UCPs. A total of 1.2 million hectares of land was confiscated. The UCPs numbered more than nine hundred. Housing was provided for workers and those living in villages were transported to and fro by truck. (You can see truckloads of women in the Alentejo hats and costumes being driven back from the fields every evening.) However, the system had really not changed that much: the vast estates now belonged to one political party rather than one landowner, but the conditions of the people did improve greatly.

The Communist party has regularly received between 50 and 60 per cent of the vote in the elections since 1974, so most local government is run by Communists. However, the Social Democrats and right-wing parties who came to power after 1975 tried to relieve the Communists of their fiefdom and give the land back to absentee landlords. They cut off credit and did not provide needed technicians. In 1989, they did away with the Agrarian Reform altogether. The landowners are back on their bull farms and hunting preserves. Only those UCPs able to buy or lease land have survived. Many workers have been forced to emigrate or go as seasonal workers to France or other countries.

Cork and marble

Portugal is the largest exporter of cork in the world, and 90 per cent of Portugal's cork trees are in the Alentejo. As early as 1310 King Dinis, the farmer king and builder of castles, recognized the value of the cork industry and established laws for taking care of the trees. Later, in the nineteenth century, the British played a big role in the cork industry, just as they had in Oporto with the port wine industry. Today, however, most of the industry is Portuguese-owned.

The Alentejo has some of the largest deposits of marble in the world. The Romans began the excavations. Today 90 per cent of the marble quarried is exported – mostly to Spain and Italy, where it is worked and re-exported. But still even the most humble homes in the Alentejo have marble sinks, tables, tanks, and so forth.

Songs and singers

The *Cantares Alentejanos* (Alentejo songs) are very important to the people of the Alentejo region, especially the Lower Alentejo. These songs are of very remote origin, and are passed down from generation to generation. The themes cover everything from the most simple act of everyday life to life itself, and death. A village will have its own singers – a large group of men who sing together without accompaniment in tunes of two parts, sometimes with a third added (see page 322).

Hunting

The owners of more than eighty-five Alentejo estates, covering many thousands of hectares of hunting preserves, are participating in a programme sponsored by the Ministry of Tourism to offer shooting and hunting holidays which will include full board, horses and other equipment. Among those taking part are the famous bullfighters João Moura and Paulo Caetano, whose bull and horse farms are show places in the Alentejo, and one of Portugal's most famous hunters in Africa, when Portugal had vast territories there. Inquire at the Tourist Office for a complete list of the tours.

Wines

The wines of the Alentejo tend to be heavy, and high in alcohol content, the reds sweet, full-bodied and robust, the whites pale yellow. Most of the vineyards are around Portalegre, Évora and Beja. The areas are just about to be demarcated.

The Upper Alentejo

Castelo de Vide

The famous spa of Castelo de Vide is a good starting-off point for an exploration of the Upper Alentejo. Castelo de Vide is on the N246, 170 km from Vila Franca de Xira. With its many parks and trees, it is one of the prettiest towns in the Alentejo.

History

Castelo de Vide was a border defence post for centuries, as you can see by its old walled town and ruined castle. The story of its founding is the familiar one of the beautiful girl who is carried away by the man she loves against the will of her wicked father. Guiomar, daughter of Rui Nunes of Asturias in Spain, wanted to marry Martim Gil, a young Portuguese, but her father was adamant against it. So Martim put her on his horse and galloped away with her to the top of a faraway hill where Portuguese King Afonso II had given him land to colonize. Because there was a grapevine growing there, they called it Terra de Vide (Land of the Vine). After they built the castle, they changed the name to Castelo de Vide.

Actually, the site was first fortified by the Romans because of its excellent position for defence and because of its location on the Roman road leading to Mérida in Spain.

By 1232 it was Portuguese. Later, it came into the possession of King Dinis's brother, Prince Afonso. The brothers were at odds for years over strategically positioned Castelo de Vide, and Prince Afonso built walls around the town in defiance of the king. Finally, however, he agreed to exchange Castelo de Vide, along with other fortified border towns (such as Marvão and Portalegre) which also belonged to him, for Sintra and other towns away from the border.

King Dinis, acting true to form, built stronger walls and made major repairs to the castle. The town was involved in and suffered from all of the wars of subsequent centuries. It was occupied at various times by both French and Spanish armies, who damaged many of its fortifications.

What to see | The castle, which stands at the top of the town, still has within its walls the old town with its ancient military quarters and old houses. It was rebuilt in 1327 and has five towers, but the keep built by King Dinis was damaged by an explosion at the beginning of the eighteenth century. The São Roque Fort is a bastioned structure with thick walls built in the eighteenth century.

Castelo de Vide has several interesting old churches. The São Salvador do Mundo Church dates from the twelfth and thirteenth centuries; the Misericórdia Church from the fifteenth; the Sant'Iago Maior Church from the fifteenth and seventeenth; the São João Baptista Church from the fifteenth and eighteenth.

In one of the narrow, cobbled streets of the old Jewish quarter you can see the door of the ancient synagogue.

Crafts | Wickerwork, wrought iron objects, embroideries, and wood and cork objects are made in the town.

Festivals | The *Feira de Santo Amaro* is held in the middle of January, and the *Festas de São Pedro e São João* is at the end of June.

Excursion | It is worth going to see the Senhora da Penha Chapel on the mountain peak opposite the town.

Where to stay
Medium price | **Hotel Sol e Serra**, Estrada de São Vicente. Tel. (045) 91337. A three star hotel, near the park, with fifty-one rooms with bath and balconies, a bar, restaurant and swimming pool. The hotel has its own game preserve across the Spanish border where guests can hunt partridge, deer, pheasants and wild boar during the season.

Inexpensive | **Albergaria Jardim**, Rua Sequeira Gameiro 6. Tel. (045) 91217. A four star inn with twenty rooms with bath, a bar and restaurant.

Pensão Casa do Parque, Avenida de Aramanhã. Tel. (045) 91250. A three star pension with twenty-four rooms, a bar and restaurant.

Manor house
Inexpensive | **Casal dos Lilases**, 7320 Castelo de Vide. Tel. (045) 91250. A manor on a farm, with a beautiful view of the town. Offers three bedrooms, one bathroom, kitchen and living room.

Where to eat | **Dom Pedro V**, Praça Dom Pedro V. Tel. (045) 91236. A three star restaurant, bar and disco. The restaurant serves Portuguese and regional dishes. Not open on Mondays.

What to eat | Specialities are *sarapatel* and *cachola* soups, and *cachafrito de cabrito* and *ratata de cabrito* (two kid dishes). As a sweet, *toucinho do céu* or *fatias douradas* (fried bread with sugar, cinnamon and orange sauce).

The Tourist Office is on Rua Bartolomeu Álvares da Santa. Tel. (045) 91361.

Marvão | Marvão is 12 km south-east of Castelo de Vide, on a road, off N246-1, that curves up to the summit of a mountain. The town sits 1,000 m above the plain, on an escarpment with a sheer precipice all round. It is totally walled, and its thirteenth-century castle is at the tip of the pinnacle. If you look over the battlements you can see for many kilometres in every direction – and realize why this tiny fortress on its nearly impregnable rock was so important over the centuries.

History   Marvão must have been fortified in very ancient times, but there is no documentation concerning the Romans, or the Swabians and Visigoths who followed them. It is said that the town got its name from Marvan, the Moorish ruler of Coimbra, who slaughtered all of the Visigoth Christians in the valley in 715, repaired the fortifications in Marvão and had it settled. It was taken by King Afonso Henriques in the twelfth century, and it received an official charter in 1214.

It was constantly in the centre of wars, and all of the male population were required to render military service at all times. After it was extensively damaged by Castilian attacks, King Dinis, the perpetual builder of castles, transformed it into an impressive fortress guarding the northern border of the Alentejo.

From 1640 on, Marvão took part in the wars to drive out the Spaniards and restore a Portuguese king. In 1641, it withstood a heavy attack by the Spaniards. The attacks continued on and off for twenty years. During the War of the Spanish Succession, Spanish and French forces occupied Marvão until they were driven out by Count São João. The Spanish and French tried again in the Seven Years War, but were repelled. In 1808 Napoleon's forces were expelled.

In the 1960s, emigration emptied the town of most of its inhabitants and left its old houses empty. An international tourist resort company wanted to buy the town outright and turn it into a mecca for coach tours. To prevent this desecration, Portuguese artists and writers started to move to buy up the old houses themselves and restore them. Many of the old houses have been carefully restored and Marvão remains as it has been for centuries.

What to see   The castle sits on the rocky pinnacle surrounded by buttressed walls and towers. You enter by a wide gate into the courtyard, where there is an enormous, vaulted cistern. There are square towers and a bastion standing out over the precipice. The high tower of the keep, thought to be the work of King Dinis, dominates the entire countryside.

The Nossa Senhora da Estrela Monastery (Our Lady of the Star Monastery) was founded in 1445. It is built on a rocky terrace outside the walls, near the spot where a shepherd – guided by a shooting star – discovered an image of Our Lady of the Star. It is thought that this statue was probably buried by Christian Visigoths when they fled from Marvão to the mountains of Asturias to escape the invading Moors. It is now kept in the monastery, and the people of Marvão believe that it has on several occasions protected them from invaders.

Crafts   Wrought iron work, wicker baskets and chairs, and chairs made of chestnut are produced in Marvão.

Excursion   At São Salvador de Aramenha, in the valley near Marvão, there are the remains of a large Roman city, Medóbriga. Most of the artifacts found here are in the Ethnological Museum in Lisbon.

Where to stay
Inexpensive
Pousada
Medium price

Pensão Dom Dinis, Rua Dr Matos Magalhães. Tel. (045) 93236. A small pension with a restaurant.

Pousada de Santa Maria, Marvão. Tel. (045) 93201/2. A pousada near the castle. It has nine rooms, seven of them with bath, a bar, and a restaurant with a spectacular view of the valley.

There are also rooms to rent in the town. For further information, telephone (045) 21815.

Where to eat

The restaurant in the **Pousada de Santa Maria** has regional food, and a marvellous view.

Varanda do Alentejo, Largo do Pelourinho. Tel. (045) 93272. Has a restaurant upstairs over its snack bar and outdoor dining.

Travessa da Praça, Caso do Povo. Tel. (045) 93160. A rustic restaurant.

Restaurante Marcelino, Rua da Cima. Tel. (045) 93138. A homey restaurant where the town postman is the cook and waiter. Good Portuguese dishes.

What to eat

Specialities are *sopa de miúdos* (giblet soup), *açorda à Alentejana* (a sort of kedgeree), *cachafrito* (fried rabbit or lamb), sheep's milk cheese, olives, cured sausages, black pudding, almond sweets.

The Tourist Office for Marvão is in Rua Dr Matos Magalhães. Tel. (045) 93226. Another is open at the Frontier post during July, August and September.

Portalegre

Portalegre is 14 km south of Marvão on the N359, on a plateau in the São Mamede mountains. It is a bustling town with many shops and industries: it is one of the largest manufacturers of tapestries in Europe, and is also famous for its textiles.

History

Legend says it was founded 2,000 years before Christ, by Lysias, son of Bacchus, on the site of what is now the São Cristovão Hermitage. The remains of Lysias are said to be in a wooden coffin covered in Greek writing that was discovered in the eighteenth century during the remodelling of the Hermitage.

Lysias named the town Amaya, which it remained in Roman times. Those times are wrapped in mystery. In the thirteenth century King Dinis acquired the town from his brother Prince Afonso (see page 289), and, naturally, built a castle. In 1704, Portalegre became involved in the War of Spanish Succession and was occupied by Spanish and French forces. At the beginning of the nineteenth century, when the Alentejo was invaded by the armies of Napoleon, Portalegre

What to see

and other towns revolted and drove them out.

The **Castle** and its walls have to a great extent been destroyed to make way for the modern town. You can find parts of them used to form archways over streets or walls of houses. The keep, with its Gothic windows, vaults and doors, is at the top of the town. Parts of the ramparts remain, and so do two towers.

The **Cathedral** was founded in 1556, and dedicated to Nossa Senhora da Assunção. It is an enormous church with three naves and lateral altars in classical style. It has a beautiful groined and painted ceiling, and the sacristy is lined with blue and white glazed tiles depicting the Flight from Egypt. There is an interesting collection of pre-Reformation English embroidered vestments.

The **São Bernardo Monastery**, now a military barracks, has an impressive Baroque portico. Inside there is a marble fountain with sixteen spouts and the imposing, sumptuous tomb, 12 m long and 6 m high, of the founder of the Monastery, Jorge de Melo.

The **Church of the Monastery of São Francisco** was built in 1275. It has a chapel with a marble tomb of its founder, Gaspar Fragoso. It is now a cultural centre.

The **Bom Fim Chapel** on the outskirts of town was built in 1720. It has tiled panels, gilded altars and Rococo paintings with scenes from the Passion.

The José Régio Museum is in the house that belonged to the poet José Régio. It has objects that he collected in his lifetime.

In Avenida da Liberdade there is a plane tree 23 m tall.

Manueline windows can be seen on the lovely old houses in many of the streets inside the walls.

Tapestries Portalegre's tapestry industry was founded in 1947, and since then the town has become one of the most important centres of tapestry manufacture in Europe. Many of the tapestries are really beautiful, with marvellous designs – nearly all of Portugal's greatest artists have contributed designs. You can buy the tapestries in Portalegre, or in Lisbon at Galeria Tapeçarias de Portalegre, Rua da Academia das Ciências 2-J, H and I, 1200 Lisbon. Tel. (01) 321481/368202.

Festivals The *Feira de Portalegre* is held on the last Wednesday of January, on 5 to 7 June and on 13 to 15 September. The *Romarias a Senhora da Penha* takes place in early May, the *Festas dos Aventais* during the first weekend in August, the *Romaria ao Senhor do Bom Fim* at the end of September. There is a market every Wednesday and Saturday.

Excursion The small walled town of **Alegrete** is 10 km south-east of Portalegre on a little road that winds through vineyards and olive groves. In origin it was probably a fortified hill town of the Iron Age, and the many Roman remains found there indicate lengthy Roman occupation. The castle (built by King Dinis) is in ruins, but you can still see the medieval battlements, ramparts and tower, and Gothic doorways.

Where to stay
Inexpensive **Hotel Dom João III**, Avenida da Liberdade. Tel. (045) 21192. A three star hotel with fifty-six rooms with bath. The hotel has a restaurant, bar, swimming pool and gift shops.

Pensão Restaurante Quinta da Saúde, Quinta da Saúde. Tel. (045) 22324. A three star pension with a restaurant. It has nineteen rooms, fifteen of them with bath.

Camp site   **Quinta da Saúde**. Tel. (045) 22848. An Orbitur camp site with bungalows, electricity, gas, hot showers, first aid, post office and grocery. It is open from 16 January to 15 November.

Where to eat   The restaurant in the **Quinta da Saúde** pension serves good regional food, and has a marvellous view. Or you might like to try one of the following.

O Tarro, Avenida das Forças Armadas. Tel. (045) 22901. A restaurant, bar and café.

Alpendre, Rua 31 de Janeiro 21. Tel. (045) 21611. A restaurant that serves Portuguese and regional dishes. It has air conditioning for the summer and a fireplace for the winter.

What to eat   Specialities are *gata* and *cachola* soups, *alhada de cacão* (dogfish cooked with garlic), meat pasties, *miolada* (brains) and sweets such as *doces de ovos, tocinho do céu, fatias douradas* and *boleimas*.

The Tourist Office is at Rua 19 de Junho 40–42. Tel. (045) 21815.

Alter do Chão
History   Alter do Chão, 33 km south-west of Portalegre on the N119–N245, was an important town at the time of the Romans, who called it Elteri. It was on the old Roman road that linked Lisbon with Mérida in Spain. But the Emperor Hadrian ordered the destruction of Elteri for its part in a revolt against him.

In the thirteenth century the Bishop of Idanha granted a franchise to Alter do Chão. King Dinis granted it important privileges, and in 1349 King Pedro I gave orders for a castle to be built there. King João I gave Alter do Chão to his comrade-in-arms Constable Nun' Álvares Pereira. When the Constable's daughter inherited it, the town became part of the domain of the House of Bragança, later to be the Kings of Portugal.

The town was made the royal stud farm in 1748, by King João V, who imported Andalucian horses. The rare Lusitanian breed that resulted became world-famous. When other breeds were introduced the stud farm lost its prestige. However, it is now being restructured successfully.

What to see   The castle, in the centre of the town, is an irregular pentagon with three rectangular towers and two cylindrical ones. A marble plaque states that it was built in 1359. The Palace of the Counts of Alter, and the marble fountain, dated 1556, are also interesting to see.

Crafts   Lace, ropes, and cork and wood objects are made in Alter do Chão.
Festivals   The *Festa da Senhora da Alegria* takes place in September, the *Feira de São Marcos* in April, the *Feira de São Domingos* in August.

Where to   **Pensão Ferreira**, Avenida Dr João Pestana. Tel. (045) 62254. A
stay, and eat   one star pension with fifteen rooms.
Inexpensive   **Pensão Restaurante Avenida**, Avenida Dr João Pestana 35. Tel. (045) 62259.

What to eat	Try *sarapatel* soup, *pezinhos de porco de coentrada* (pig's trotters with coriander), *ensopada de borrego* (mutton), *cabeça de xara* (pig's head). The Tourist Office is at the Largo do Pelourinho. Tel. (045) 62179. Open in July, August and September.
Fronteira	Fronteira is 17 km south of Alter do Chão on the N245. Not much is known of its past, but some believe it was founded by King Dinis, while others say that it was founded by Fernão Rodrigues Monteiro, a Master of the Order of Avis. The famous battle of Atoleiros was fought near Fronteira, in 1384. The young nobleman Nun' Álvares Pereira led a band of farmers in routing a Castilian army of invaders. He became the hero of the Alentejo, and led a widespread farmers' revolt. The Parish Church was built in 1577, by King Sebastião, and the Nossa Senhora Vila Velha Church was built in 1604. You can also see the pillory, the ruins of the thirteenth-century walls, and the clock tower, built in 1613.
Crafts	Tapestries, wooden dolls, cork objects and objects made of horn are all produced in the town.
Festivals	The *Festa da Santa Cruz* is celebrated at the beginning of May, the *Feiras de São Pedro* on 29 and 30 June and the *Festa da Nossa Senhora da Vila Velha* at the end of August and beginning of September.
Where to stay *Inexpensive*	**Pensão Central**, Rua Miguel Bombarda 11. Tel. (045) 65212.
What to eat	Specialities are cured sausages, *sarrabulho* (stew with pig's blood), *ensopado de borrego* (mutton stew). For sweet, try flaky pastries, biscuits or honey cakes.
Monforte	Monforte is 20 km east of Fronteira on the N243 and 29 km south of Portalegre on the N18, on a high hill near the River Avis. Monforte was a Neolithic hill-town that was taken over by the Romans, and both Neolithic and Roman remains abound in the area. Later, the Moors occupied the town till they were expelled in 1139 by King Afonso Henriques. You can see nearby the ruins of a Roman town and of a fourth-century Roman/Christian basilica. The Madalena Church, built in the fifteenth century, is painted in white on the outside and covered in tiles inside. The Nossa Senhora da Conceição Church has seventeenth-century tiles. The Parish Church was reconstructed in the eighteenth century. There is a Tourist Office in the Praça da República. Tel. (045) 53115.
Campo Maior	Campo Maior is 34 km east of Monforte on the N243, a short distance from the Spanish border. It is an agricultural centre and has one of the biggest coffee-producing factories in Portugal.
History	According to legend, Campo Maior got its name when three men were looking for a place to build a town. One of them found a big, open space and called out, 'Aqui é o campo maior!' ('Here is the best tract of land!'). You can see carvings of the heads of the three men on what was supposedly the first house built in the village. More likely, Campo Maior was a Roman settlement, then Visigoth,

Moorish and, after the reconquest, Christian. King Dinis granted it a charter, rebuilt the castle on a larger scale and walled it in. He also built the Parish Church of Santa Clara. King João II built the giant three-storey keep of the castle.

During the War of Restoration against Castile, Campo Maior took the side of Castile and remained loyal to the Kings of Castile even after Portugal had won its independence. In 1388 the Portuguese King João I laid siege and finally took it. In 1580, when the Spaniards invaded, Campo Maior stayed loyal to Portugal. More walls and bastions were added for defence. During the War of Spanish Succession, it was besieged by the Spaniards under the Marquis of Bay in 1712 with 25,000 men. The fortress held out for thirty-six days, until Bay retreated, leaving behind artillery and 5,000 dead.

In 1732 the keep tower, full of ammunition, was struck by lightning and exploded. Thirteen hundred people were killed or wounded, and the castle and town were reduced to rubble. King João V had it rebuilt.

During the invasion of the Spaniards under Godoy, the garrison held out under siege for eighteen days. During the Peninsular War it was forced to surrender to the French after a heroic resistance, but four days later it was liberated by a Portuguese/English force under Lord Beresford, who was made Marquis of Campo Maior.

What to see The walls, bastions and the damaged keep of the castle are still standing. The Parish Church is white, trimmed in yellow, with two bell towers. Its Capela dos Ossos (Bones Chapel) is completely decorated with human bones fashioned into designs (there is a similar one in Évora). The Church of the Misericórdia dates from 1592 to 1726. The Church of São João Baptista and the Church and Cloister of the Santo António Monastery are also worth seeing.

Crafts Look out for embroidery, pottery, artificial flowers, wooden objects, wrought iron.

Festivals The *Festa da Senhora da Enxara* takes place at the beginning of April, the *Festa de São João* on 24 June.

Excursion The Castro de Segóvia, 5 km south of Campo Maior, is one of the most important Iron Age hill-top towns in southern Portugal. Walls of stones without mortar stretch over a great distance. Excavations have uncovered three different periods of habitation, and pottery, jewellery and coins have been unearthed.

Where to stay, and eat **Albergaria Progresso**, Avenida Combatentes da Grande Guerra. Tel. (045) 68657/8/9. A four star inn. It has a bar and a restaurant that serves Portuguese food.

Inexpensive

What to eat Try *ensopado de borrego* (mutton stew) and, for sweet, *tortilhas de amêndoa* (almond tarts) and *nogado* (nougat).

Ougela Ougela is 8 km north of Campo Maior 4 km from the Spanish border, on the N373, which ends in the town. To get there you drive through high, open country with fields of lavender and scrub. Ougela is separated from Spain by the pretty valley of the River Xevora – you can see the Spanish town of Albuquerque on the other side. On the Portuguese side there are remains of an old Templars' monastery.

The town was originally a Romanized settlement called Budua. Later it was occupied by the Visigoths and the Moors. It was finally taken by the Christian Portuguese. The castle at Ougela was one of the many restored by King Dinis. It was subject to siege in the centuries that followed.

An old chronicle relates how one dispute between the Castilian Spaniards and Portuguese for possession of the town in 1475 was settled by hand-to-hand combat between the two commanders of the opposing armies. João da Silva Portuguez, Governor of Ougela, and Juan Fernandes Galindo, Governor of Albuquerque, fought a joust on the field beneath the walls of Ougela Castle. Juan Galindo was killed on the field, and João da Silva Portuguez died twenty-eight days later.

There are thick walls around the entire medieval town. Within the wall is an enormous open area surrounded by houses – all the life of the town takes place here. The castle keep stands on top of the redoubt, beside the Nossa Senhora da Graça Church built in the wall facing outward.

Elvas

Elvas, about 15 km south of Campo Maior by the N371, is on the N4, the main road between Lisbon and Madrid, just 10 km from the Spanish border near Badajoz. It has been called the Queen of the Frontier.

Elvas has a split personality. On one side of the road sits the uninteresting modern town with hotels and restaurants, where cars dash through day and night. On the other side of the road is the beautiful, ancient walled town with its exciting history. So, on your way to or from Lisbon or Madrid, don't fail to stop a while and have a look.

History

Some Portuguese historians say that Celts and Goths arrived in Tavira in the Algarve and came up the River Guadiana to the site where Elvas now stands and built a hill fort. The Carthaginian General Maharbal supposedly found them there later. There are many dolmens and other prehistoric remains around to reinforce a belief that something along these lines happened. The Moors took the town in 714, built a castle and walls, and stayed for five hundred years, leaving behind them wells for water (the Alcala well was used for several hundred years after they were expelled), customs, and street names like Almovar, Alcáçova, Alcamim, Alcaiza. In 1166 it was taken from them by Geraldo Sem-Pavor of Évora fame (Gerald the Fearless), but it was not permanently under Christian control until 1229, when King Sancho II claimed it.

In 1580 Elvas was treacherously sold to Philip II of Spain and was only won back in 1644, during the War of Restoration with Spain. During that war Elvas was made headquarters for the Alentejo military government under General Matias de Albuquerque, who strengthened the fortifications. The total population of the town and countryside pitched in to fight the Spaniards, who attacked with 15,000 men. After ten days of siege, they were forced to retreat to Badajoz. Elvas was further fortified with bastions, curtain walls, arsenal, barracks and a cistern with a capacity of 2,300 cu. m – enough to last the town for four months. It became the strongest fortress in the country, almost impregnable. Other forts were built around it, including the impressive Graça Fort on an adjoining hill. But by January 1659 Elvas was under siege and an epidemic had reduced its defenders to 1,000 men. On 14 January of that year General Albuquerque took his men out under cover of a thick fog to join forces from Estremoz who had come to the aid of Elvas. When the fog dispersed, the Spaniards saw that they were surrounded. They were decimated. It was a brilliant victory for the Portuguese, and Elvas and Portugal were free of the Spaniards for the time being. Unfortunately, General Albuquerque died in the battle.

In 1663 Elvas again resisted attack by Spanish forces, led by John of Austria, and in 1808 Napoleon's army under Godoy was beaten off. Wellington used Elvas as his general headquarters during the Peninsular War, after the Treaty of Sintra was signed.

Emblem The emblem of the city, showing a warrior on horseback carrying a standard, is the subject of much dispute. Legend says that the figure is one João Paes Gago, who, in 1438, on Corpus Christi Day, ran into the adjoining Spanish town of Badajoz, grabbed the Castilian standard from the Spaniards' religious procession and ran back to the walls of Elvas. As he was pursued by hordes of irate Spaniards, the people of Elvas were afraid to open the gates to let him in, but he ran around the walls and hung the Spanish emblem against them. He was caught and killed by the Spaniards, who then fried him in a cauldron of boiling oil. As he died, he cried, 'The man dies, but his fame lives on' – as, indeed, it has – but was it worth being fried in oil? The legend is interesting, but historic documents show that the emblem was registered in the national archives as early as 1258. And a rather more likely explanation is that it is a representation of King Sancho II, who took Elvas from the Moors.

Elvas today You enter the town over a drawbridge that spans a dry moat. It has two wide avenues and squares, but most of the streets are narrow and twisting, with names from Moorish and medieval times. The streets are full of pots of all kinds of flowers.

What to see The **Aqueduct**, which brings water from Amoreira, 7.5 km away, is a national monument. And it is not, repeat not, Roman. The people of Elvas get very cross when they hear someone say it is. It was built between 1529 and 1622, paid for by a royal tax on the people of Elvas. It is 7.5 km long, and it has 1,367 m of underground galleries, 4.5 km of galleries at ground level, and 1,238 m in overhead arches – some as high as 30 m. There are 371 main arches and 462 supplementary ones.

The Moorish **Castle and Walls** were remodelled after the Christian reconquest. Three lines of walls were built on Moorish foundations. The first line had three gates, two of which still exist: the Porta da Alcáçova and the Porta do Miradeiro. The remains of the second wall show it had four gates. The third wall had twenty-two towers, eleven gates and a watchtower. The tower was built at the orders of King Dinis. King João II went on with the work and built the keep, which has a beautiful vaulted room. Between the gate and the balcony you can see a plaque with the arms and pelican of King João.

The **Graça Fort** stands on a hill opposite Elvas, at a distance of 1 km from the town. It is dug deep into the rock of the hilltop, and has four bastions, extensive walls, a wide fosse and a deep cistern, with enough water to keep a garrison for several months. Its main entrance is the highly decorated Door of the Dragon. The main building contains the governor's house, a chapel and a great hall with a veranda from which there is a fantastic view. When Napoleon's army invaded, they bombarded the fort but inflicted only slight damage.

The **Santa Luzia Fort** was built during the War of Restoration between 1641 and 1648.

The **Nossa Senhora da Consolação Church** was built in 1543 on the foundations of an old Templar church. It has marvellous tiles from the seventeenth century, and a wrought iron pulpit.

The **Nossa Senhora da Assunção Church**, built in the sixteenth century, was the Cathedral between 1570 and 1882. The church, designed by architect Francisco de Arruda, is essentially Manueline. It has a sumptuous interior with three naves. There are paintings of the Assumption of the Virgin by Lorenzo Grameira and of Saint Anthony by Bento Coelho da Silveira.

The **Santo Domingos Church**, which dates from the thirteenth century, is the largest church in Elvas. It has a marvellous Gothic high altar.

The **Ordem Terceira de São Francisco** has a sumptuous high altar with gilt carvings. Its ceilings are 7 m high, with six figures that spout water representing the River Guadiana and lesser rivers.

The **São Pedro Church** has its original Romanesque/Gothic portal from the thirteenth century.

The **Salvador Church** was an old Jesuit monastery. It has frescoes by Luis de Morales.

The **English Cemetery** is next to the hermitage of São João de Corujeira.

In the eighteenth century, seven chapels representing the seven Stations of the Cross in carved white marble were built around the

Crafts town – two form part of the Cathedral and the Salvador Church.

Fur coats, carpets and objects in copper and tin are made in Elvas.

Festivals The *Romaria ao Senhor Jesus da Boa Fé* takes place at the beginning of September, and the *Feira de São Mateus* is at the end of September.

Where to **Hotel Dom Luis**, Avenida de Badajoz. Tel. (068) 22756/7/8. A
stay three star hotel with sixty-one rooms with bath and TV, a bar and res-
Medium price taurant.

Albergaria Eixadai-Parque, Varches, on the highway from Lis-bon 3 km out of town. Tel. (068) 63036. A four star inn in a lovely con-verted mansion in wide grounds with fifteen rooms with bath and TV, a swimming pool, tennis, bar and restaurant.

Inexpensive **Estalagem Dom Sancho II**, Praça da República 20. Tel. (068) 62684. A four star pension in the centre of town, with twenty-four rooms with bath, a bar and restaurant.

Pousada **Pousada da Santa Luzia**, Avenida de Badajoz. Tel. (068) 22194.
Medium price A pousada on the highway with eleven rooms, nine of them with bath. It has a restaurant and a bar.

Where The restaurant in the **Pousada da Santa Luzia** has a very high
to eat reputation, and attracts many Spanish customers from over the bor-der. There are also several other restaurants in Elvas.

O Cristo, Parque da Piedade. Tel. (068) 623512. Big and popular, has good fish and seafood.

Chimarão, Vila Justo, off the road from Lisbon. Tel. (068) 629956. Brand new, built like a castle in the woods. Serves Brazilian food.

Flor do Jardim, Jardim Municipal. Tel. (068) 623174. Has an esplanade in the town garden.

The Tourist Office is in the Praça da República. Tel. (068) 62236.

Vila Viçosa Vila Viçosa is 32 km south-west of Elvas on the N4–N255.

History Vila Viçosa may have been a Roman settlement originally – a Roman road passed nearby, and there are many Roman inscriptions. It was occupied by the Moors till the Christian reconquest in 1226. It was granted a charter in 1270; and later King Dinis built a powerful castle and strong walls, which still stand.

Vila Viçosa became a royal city after the Dukes of Bragança, who became kings of Portugal, settled there. The fourth duke, Dom Jaime, went to live in the castle after his father had been executed for con-spiring against the king. He didn't like the old castle, so built a country house which became the nucleus of the present great palace. Duke Jaime, motivated by unfounded jealousy, murdered his Spanish wife Leonor in the palace.

The town today is very lovely, with its historic buildings and its streets lined with orange trees. It is certainly worth a visit.

What to see The **Ducal Palace**, built in 1501 by Duke Jaime, has three floors. The very long façade is entirely covered in cream-coloured Montes Claros marble, and each floor has twenty-three windows stretching in a line across the front. It stands in an enormous square and has at its side a chase surrounded by 18 km of walls which was the private hunting ground of the kings. It is now a game reserve. Inside the palace you will find a museum, a library and a collection of coaches and carriages. The last King of Portugal left all of his possessions to his country when he died in exile in England in 1932.

The **Castle** stands in ruins at the other side of the square. It has an archaeological museum.

The **Agostinhos Church** was built in the twelfth century and restored in the sixteenth. It contains the Pantheon of the Dukes of Bragança with their tombs resting on the backs of black lions.

The **Chagas Convent** is Renaissance in style. The nave is panelled in tiles. It contains the Pantheon of the Duchesses of Bragança. The **São Bartolomeu Church** was built in 1636. The **Esperança Church** has sixteenth-century frescoes.

Crafts Clay pottery and marble sculptures are produced in Vila Viçosa.

Fairs The *Feira de Maio* is held towards the end of May. The Horse Fair, held in the Campo da Restauração in August, is the largest animal fair in the Alentejo.

Where to stay **Casa dos Arcos**, Praça Martim Afonso de Sousa 16, Vila Viçosa.
Inexpensive Tel. (068) 98518 or (01) 664488. An enormous Alentejano manor house with antique furnishings. It has four suites, each with two beds and kitchen, two rooms each with two beds, two double bedrooms and one single bedroom. All the rooms have central heating and bath.

Where to eat **Restaurante Ouro Branco**, Campo da Restauração 43. Tel. (068) 42556. A restaurant that specializes in shellfish and Portuguese cooking. Not open on Mondays.

What to eat Try *empadas de galinha* (chicken pasties), goat's milk cheese, and, as a sweet, *tibornas de ovos do Convento da Esperança* (eggs, sugar and almonds).

The Tourist Office is in the Praça da República. Tel. (068) 98584/ 98305.

Estremoz

Estremoz is 54 km west of Elvas on the N4. It is a totally walled city with white buildings surrounding its impressive castle and towers on a very high hill.

History Estremoz was a fortified Roman city on the road between Olisipo (Lisbon) and Emerita (Mérida in Spain). The Romans exploited the marble quarries there. The invaders who followed added to the fortifications. When it was finally retaken from the Moors in the thirteenth century, King Afonso III began to rebuild the castle. The untiring, ubiquitous King Dinis completed the great tower of the keep. He also built a royal palace, while he was negotiating for the hand of the Princess Isabel of Aragon. He and Queen Isabel lived in it during much of his reign, and she died there in 1336.

In 1384, when King Juan of Castile invaded Portugal to claim the throne in the name of his wife Beatriz, Estremoz remained loyal to the Portuguese contender for the throne, the Master of the Avis Order, who was to become King João I. Nun' Álvares Pereira, Commander of the Alentejo, set up his headquarters there and led his army to Atoleiros, where he defeated the Castilians.

In 1580, when the Duke of Alba invaded the Alentejo to assure the Portuguese throne for Philip II of Spain, the Mayor of Estremoz surrendered the town to prevent loss of life.

During the War of Restoration, Estremoz sent out an army of 10,000 men to aid Elvas, which was besieged by Spaniards. The Elvas commander, General Albuquerque, slipped out under cover of fog and joined the Estremoz army. Together they defeated the Spaniards at Elvas Lines in 1665. Estremoz came once again to the aid of a besieged Elvas during the War of the Spanish Succession, when they forced Spanish troops under the Marquis de Bay to withdraw.

In 1698 an explosion totally destroyed the castle, along with several nearby houses. King João V had the castle reconstructed. He also restored the garrison and turned it into a military museum. All were sacked by the French in 1808.

Many of the kings of Portugal lived in Estremoz. And Vasco da Gama was living there when King Manuel I gave him command of the fleet which first sailed to India.

Estremoz today

Estremoz today is actually two towns: the bustling agricultural centre with modern buildings and houses, and the old town around the castle with its narrow streets, where houses with lovely carved doors lean against one another. The large town squares are full of gardens and fountains.

What to see

The **Castle** and **Royal Palace** are definitely worth seeing. Their walls, the tall keep tower and smaller cylindrical towers are still standing. The great tower of the **Keep**, built of white marble and 27 m high, is known as the Tower of the Three Crowns, because it was built by three kings: King Sancho II, King Afonso III, and King Dinis.

The **Raínha Santa Isabel Chapel** is inside the castle. In 1659 the Queen Regent, Dona Luisa de Gusmão, had the room where Queen Isabel died turned into a chapel, in thanks for the Portuguese victory over the Castilians at the battle of Elvas. The chapel was badly damaged in the explosion of 1698, but King João V repaired it, and had it decorated with tiles depicting scenes from the life of Queen Isabel – including the famous Miracle of the Roses. According to this legend, the queen disobeyed her husband, King Dinis, and took food to the poor. He saw her and demanded to see what she was carrying in her shawl. When she opened it she found that by a miracle the alms had been turned into roses.

The **Archaeological and Ethnological Museum** contains many artifacts of historical interest, and a large collection of the polychrome clay figures that are typical of the art of Estremoz. These figures are true peasant art, representing religious themes, people working, animals and the seasons. I particularly like the figure of *Spring* – a young girl in bright dress, around whom flowers are whirling in a ring.

The **Parish Church** is dedicated to Santa Maria. It has two sixteenth-century painted panels depicting *The Adoration of the Kings* and *The Beheading of Saint John the Baptist*.

The **São Francisco Monastery**, which is now a cavalry barracks, is basically Gothic. Its Gothic church has extensive gilt work from the seventeenth and eighteenth centuries. The Gothic tomb of Vasco Esteves Gatus has a carved figure of him with his head on pillows and his feet on two dogs.

The **Tocha Palace** in the Largo Dom José was built in the seventeenth century. It has glazed tile panels depicting Portugal's war of independence against Spain.

The **Gadanha Artificial Lake** is now completely dry. Its statue of Saturn stands high and dry in the middle.

The **Rossio** is a very large square surrounded by seventeenth-century ramparts, in the lower part of town. Every Saturday it has a weekly fair.

Crafts

Look for glazed pottery dolls, limestone sculptures, earthenware, woodwork, horn, straw and bamboo articles, leatherwork.

Festivals

The *Feira de Agricultura* takes place in May, the *Feira de Artesenato de Santiago* in July, the *Festas da Cidade de Estremoz* at the beginning of September, the *Festas de Santo André* in November.

Where to stay
Inexpensive

Hotel Alentejano, Rossio do Marquês de Pombal 50. Tel. (068) 22717. An old, turn-of-the-century, one star hotel with twenty-one rooms. Only two of the rooms have bath.

Residencial Mateus, Rua Dr Gomes Resende 26. Tel. (068) 22226. A two star pension with ten rooms with bath.

Pensão Restaurante Estremoz, Rossio Marquês de Pombal 15. Tel. (068) 22834. A two star pension and restaurant. It has nine rooms, without bath.

Manor house
Inexpensive

Quinta do Monte dos Pensamentos, Estrada da Estação do Ameixial, 2 km from town. Tel. (068) 22375. A magnificent nineteenth-century country house with a red tile roof and turrets. It has four rooms with bath, breakfast and a help-yourself bar.

Pousada
Medium price

Pousada da Raínha Santa Isabel, Largo Dom Dinis. Tel. (068) 22618. This luxurious pousada is in the old royal palace. It has twenty-three rooms with beautiful furnishings, a restaurant and a bar.

Where to eat

The elegant restaurant at the **Pousada da Raínha Santa Isabel** serves regional dishes, and has a magnificent view.

Águias d'Ouro, Rossio Marquês de Pombal 27. Tel. (068) 22196.

What to eat

An air-conditioned restaurant known for its roast lamb.

Specialities are *cozido à Alentejana* (boiled meat, vegetables and sausages), roast or fried mutton, stuffed tongue, a stew of white beans with pig's head (or ear), *sarrabulho* (a stew of meat and sausages with pig's blood), *entrecosta assado* (roast spare ribs), *migalha com carne de porco* (bread with pork), *sopa de hortelã* (mint soup), tomato soup with eggs, asparagus soup, wild boar and rabbit in season.

Évora

Évora is 46 km south of Estremoz on the N18, and 110 km from the Spanish border near Elvas, on the N18.

In 1986 UNESCO declared Évora a World Patrimony, because of its many beautiful and valuable monuments. The town has been artistically, culturally and politically important since the country's history began. Over the centuries it has been a centre for great painters, sculptors, architects, writers and other talented people.

History

By the time the Romans came Évora was the capital of the Celtic kingdom. The town was captured in the second century BC by Decimus Junius Brutus, who pacified the territory between the Tagus and Guadiana rivers. In 59 BC Julius Caesar named Évora Liberalitas Julia and made it a Roman city; he also sent a group of Romans to live in the town as citizens. Some historians believe that Évora was the headquarters of the legendary Roman Quintus Sertorius, the one-time Roman official in charge of Hispania, who, around 80 BC, revolted against the Roman emperors and attempted to set up territories independent of them.

In the fifth century Évora came under the dominion of the Visigoth Ataulfo. The Arabs took the city after the battle of Guadalete in 711, and remained there until 1165, when they were driven out by Geraldo Sem-Pavor (Gerald the Fearless). He then handed Évora over to the Christian King Afonso Henriques.

Throughout the Middle Ages Évora was an important centre of learning and government. The University was founded in 1557 by Archbishop Henrique (later to be Cardinal-King Henrique). During the first and second dynasties the court of the kings of Portugal was at Évora. The town was also the original headquarters of the religious and military Order of Avis. And during the regency of Queen Leonor Teles the people of Évora burned down the royal palace and declared the head of the Avis Order King João of Portugal. A long struggle for power followed. Later, the kings of the Avis dynasty often lived in Évora, and the *Cortes* met there.

In the seventeenth century, during the Spanish occupation, Évora suffered badly. It suffered also under the autocratic Prime Minister the Marquês de Pombal, who in 1759 shut down the University. And in 1808, during the Peninsular War, Évora was invaded by French troops under Loison. During the rest of the nineteenth century and the first half of the twentieth century Évora diminished in importance. Then after the 1974 Revolution it became a centre for agrarian reform. It was also discovered by tourists from every country, who come in great numbers every summer to see its ancient monuments. The present local government of Évora is making a great effort to preserve its buildings and at the same time make it possible for people to continue to live in the old houses, to maintain the life of the city.

The University of Évora reopened in 1975.

Exploring Évora

Basically, the streets of Évora lead out and downwards from the Marquês de Marialvas Square, but it is very easy to get lost. I suggest that you get a good map in English from the Tourist Office.

What to see

There are three sets of **Walls**. The Old Walls, which belong to the Roman, Visigothic and Moorish period, and date from as far back as the first century BC, had a perimeter of 1,080 m. Many lengths of Roman walls, with gates and towers, are still standing. The New Walls, which were built in the time of Afonso IV, Pedro I and Fernando, were almost 4,000 m long and had forty towers, ten entrance ways, fosses and a watchtower. Many stones from the Old Walls were used. Much of the New Walls remain, as do sixteen towers and six entrance ways. The most impressive is the Porta de Alconchel. The third set of walls was built in the period of King João IV and King Afonso VI.

The **Old Castle** was built on the flat land protected by the walls. It was vast and strong, containing the royal palace and the headquarters of the Order of Calatrava – later Avis. It was partially destroyed when the townspeople revolted and burned it, before declaring the head of the Avis Order King of Portugal. Two towers of the São Miguel Palace remain, as do the towers of the Cadaval Palace and the Salvador and São Paulo Convents.

The **Ancient University** at the end of the Old Castle was built in Baroque style in the mid-sixteenth century, by Archbishop Henrique. It has marble cloisters and some interesting tiles from the sixteenth, seventeenth and eighteenth centuries.

The **New Castle** was designed by the architect Diogo de Arruda, by order of King Manuel, in the sixteenth century. It is in Manueline style and somewhat resembles an Italian Renaissance fortress. It has a large courtyard and thick towers. Bastions were added during the War of Restoration in the seventeenth century. It was made a cavalry barracks in the eighteenth century. In 1808 it was occupied by the French army under Junot.

The **Roman Temple**, in the Marquês de Marialva Square, probably dates from the third century AD. It is often called the 'Temple of Diana', but according to historian Túlio Espanca it was not given that name until the seventeenth century, when the Jesuit priest who wrote *Évora Ilustrada* referred to it as such. The temple is rectangular, made of granite and marble, with Corinthian columns. It appears to have been partially destroyed at the end of the fourth century or the beginning of the fifth, during persecutions of paganism. Later it was partially walled up with brick and used as a storehouse – which probably saved it from further destruction. It was restored in the late nineteenth century.

The **Cathedral**, a grandiose Romanesque/Gothic structure with three naves, was built in 1186. Its façade is flanked by two unequal towers, and it has strange conical structures built over the dome. The bell tower dates from the thirteenth century, the organ and the richly carved choir stalls from 1562. The **Museum of Sacred Art** contains many valuable pieces, including a large amount of silver and a thirteenth-century carved ivory image of the Virgin and Child.

The **Regional Museum** near the Cathedral has many archaeological pieces, and primitive paintings by Frei Carlos, a priest of Flemish origin who was painting in Évora in the sixteenth century. There are also Flemish paintings of the Bruges school.

The **Praça do Giraldo** at the end of the Rua Cinco de Outubro has many charming arcades with shops, a sixteenth-century fountain and the **São Antão Church**, built in 1557. This church has lovely Baroque altars and polychrome marble statues.

The **Houses of the Inquisition** (the Inquisition was very powerful in Évora) are off the square containing the Cathedral.

The **Espírito Santo Church** was begun in 1566, and is a fine example of Jesuit architecture. It was one of a complex of buildings that made up the old University, and since the University was shut down it has been used as various other things.

The **São Francisco Church**, in the Praça 1° de Maio on Rua da República, was built between 1460 and 1510. It has the form of a simple Latin cross, but it shows strong Moorish influence in its arches and windows. The interior is in dark stone ribbed in white.

The **Bone Chapel** forms part of the São Francisco Church. This macabre place is decorated in complicated designs constructed entirely of human bones, and over the main door there is a Latin inscription which translates as 'We bones that are here wait for yours'.

The **Cadaval Palace** and the **Church of São João Evangelista** are near the Roman Temple. They form an interesting group of Gothic buildings from the era of King Manuel. The church has eighteenth-century tiles and picturesque cloisters.

The **Portas de Moura Square** has fifteenth-century arcades and a Renaissance fountain – the Fonte da Bola – built in 1556.

The **Misericórdia Church** in the Rua da Misericórdia has Baroque bas-relief work and polychrome tiles dating from the eighteenth century. Its high altar is elaborate gilt work.

The **Graça Church** was built around 1537. The architects Miguel de Arruda, Diogo de Torralva and Manuel Pires worked on its construction. What has fascinated everyone since the church was built are the four huge figures on top of pillars, below burning globes. Legend says they represent the first four supplicants burned in *auto-da-fé* (quite common in Évora during the Inquisition). The church is partially in ruins.

The **Porta Nova Aqueduct** was built in 1531 by Francisco de Arruda, on the orders of King João III. You can still see its galleries and old arches running along through the walls in the old town.

The **Lóios Convent and Church** is in the Marquês de Marialvas Square. In the fifteenth century, Dom Rodrigo de Melo, an adviser to King Afonso V and governor of Tangiers, asked the king and the Bishop of Évora if he could found a monastery on his family's lands near the old palace, so that he could be buried there later. He was given permission and the first stone was laid in 1485. The church was called São João Evangelista and belonged to the Order of the Lóios. The founder died before it was finished in 1491. He was buried in the church and so were a long line of his descendants. His burial chapel is a good example of Manueline style.

The monastery – now a pousada – has a porch with Neoclassical columns. The two-storey cloister has the ground floor in Gothic Manueline and the upper floor in Renaissance style.

The **Nossa Senhora das Mercês Church** is now the Museum of Decorative Religious Art. The church was opened in 1698, but it was totally transformed in the eighteenth century. It is in Baroque style with an opulent front and extravagant altars. The transept is richly adorned with gilt Rococo work with flowers. The church also has glazed tiles in the sacristy and the presbytery. In the museum, you will find carved Baroque gold furniture, sculpture, rich tapestries and Baroque and Rococo jewellery.

The **Church and Convent of Santa Clara** were founded in 1452. Like the rest of the numerous nunneries in Évora, the convent was a refuge for many women of distinguished family. The façade of the church is sixteenth-century Baroque. It has a Baroque gilt retable from the seventeenth century.

The **Calvário Convent** was founded in 1570 by the Infanta Dona Maria. The noble Isabel Sousa Coutinho lived cloistered here for many years, because she refused to marry the man the Marquês de Pombal had chosen for her. She later married the man she loved, from the family of the Dukes of Palmela. The convent suffered in the War of Restoration in 1663. The church has a number of interesting paintings, from the seventeenth century.

The **São Braz Hermitage** is located outside the city walls. It was built in 1490 on the spot where there had been a shelter for people suffering from the plague. It is a square building with cylindrical outside buttresses with conical spires. Granite gargoyles of zoomorphic creatures protect the whole building.

Nossa Senhora do Espinheiro is a fortified monastery 5 km north-west of Évora. It was here that the sixteenth-century mystic painter Frei Carlos lived and worked. The monastery is said to be built on the spot where a miracle happened: in the fifteenth century, so the story goes, a shepherd boy saw a tree that burned without being consumed, and nearby a splendid image of the Virgin. He built a little chapel there, and with the proceeds from devotive offerings built the monastery, which he gave to the Jerónimos monks. Actually the monastery was founded, in the fifteenth century, on the spot where there had been a Moorish mosque. It was greatly modified in the eighteenth and early nineteenth centuries, and it has an enormous nave covered with ornate plasterwork from 1801.

The **Judiaria** (Jewish quarters), west of Giraldo Square, still have a medieval look, with narrow streets and old houses. The **Bairro da Mouraria** (Moorish quarter) is north of the old wall.

The **Porta de Alconchel** is a square tower that is the main gateway to the city. It existed in 1402. At one time it was used as a prison.

The **São Bento de Castris Convent**, 3 km outside Évora, is the oldest convent in the south of Portugal. It grew out of a modest chapel where Bishop Soeiro saw a mysterious phosphorescent light on the night of 21 March 1169 – the feast of São Bento. Later a rich widow obtained permission to build a hermitage to which she and her daughters and sister could retire from the world. Permission was given, and in 1274 the hermitage became a convent. The church was consecrated in 1384. The convent was closed in 1890, and it is now a home for the rehabilitation of invalids. It has styles for all periods. There are fine eighteenth-century Rococo tiles, a carved gilt altar and a Gothic cloister.

There are many other churches and old buildings in Évora that are not listed here, which you may enjoy discovering.

Crafts

It is worth looking out for ceramics and basketwork, hand-painted furniture, decorated cork objects.

Handicrafts Museum, Praça 1° de Maio 7, in an imposing eighteenth-century building, exhibits and sells regional crafts. **João Cutileiro's studio**, Estrada de Viana do Alentejo 13. Tel. (066) 23972. The workshop of Portugal's internationally known sculptor; can be visited in the mornings. Works can be bought or commissioned.

Festivals

The *Festa da Senhora das Candeias* is held on 2 February, the *Feira do Gado* on the Friday before Palm Sunday, the *Feira de São João* at the end of June, the *Feira Nova* in October.

Where to stay
Inexpensive

Estalagem Monte das Flores, N308. Tel. (066) 25018. A five star inn on a farm 4 km from Évora. It has seventeen rooms with bath, a pool, tennis courts, horse riding and a regional restaurant.

Residencial Riviera, Rua 5 de Outubro. Tel. (066) 23304/25111. A four star modern inn in the centre of the town. It has twenty-two rooms, all with TV and radio.

Hotel Planície, Rua Miguel Bombarda 40. Tel. (066) 24026/7/8. A three star hotel with thirty-three rooms with bath and TV. It has a bar and a good restaurant.

Hotel Santa Clara, Travessa da Milheira 19. Tel. (066) 24141. A two star hotel with twenty-two rooms, restaurant and bar.

Vitoria, Rua Diana de Lis. Tel. (066) 27174. A comfortable, modern inn with forty-eight rooms with bath, TV and air-conditioning, and a bar.

Diana, Rua Diogo Cão 2. Tel. (066) 22008. A three star pension with fifteen rooms, in the centre of town, with a bar and restaurant.

Manor houses
Inexpensive

Casa do Conde da Serra, Rua do Conde da Serra da Tourega 1. Tel. (066) 31257. A historic fifteenth-century house situated in one of the towers of the town gate, Portas de Moura, with four rooms with bath, living rooms and terrace.

Casa de São Tiago, Largo Alexandre Herculano 2. Tel. (066) 22686. A historic aristocratic house that dates back to the time of King Manuel in the sixteenth century; it has three rooms with bath, and a bar.

Quinta da Nora, Estradas dos Canaviais. Tel. (066) 29810. A rustic house on a farm 4 km from Évora with five rooms with bath, and a swimming pool.

Pousada
Medium price

Pousada de Lóios, Largo Conde de Vila Flor, 7000 Évora. Tel. (066) 24051. A pousada in what used to be the Lóios Convent (see page 307). It has thirty-two beautifully decorated rooms with bath, a lovely Moorish-style restaurant round the cloisters, and a comfortable bar with a large fireplace.

Where to eat

Restaurante Cervejaria Fialho, Travessa das Mascarenhas 14. Tel. (066) 23079. An award-winning restaurant and beerhouse, famous for its regional dishes and marvellous *petiscos* (appetizers).

Restaurante O Guião, Rua da República 81. Tel. (066) 23071. A restaurant that serves typical regional food.

Cozinha de Santo Humberto, Rua da Moeda 39. Tel. (066) 24251. A restaurant famous for game in season (Saint Humberto is patron saint of hunters). Out of season, try the *porco a alentejano*.

What to eat

Typical dishes are *açorda* (kedgeree), broth with croûtons, *sarapatéis de bacalhau*, stews, lamb, *queijadas* (Portuguese cheesecakes).

The Tourist Office, the Comissão Municipal de Turismo de Évora, is at Praça do Giraldo 73. Tel. (066) 22671. There is also the Posto de Turismo da CMT, at Avenida São Sebastião. Tel. (066) 31296.

Around Évora

The roads from Évora to outlying towns and places of historical interest lead out from the town like spokes from the hub of a wheel.

Valverde

Valverde is on the N380 near Évora. The Bom Jesus Monastery here was founded in the sixteenth century by Cardinal Henrique. The large white building with its red tiled roofs and Renaissance arches is now part of the University of Évora.

Alcáçovas

Alcáçovas is a little town 26 km south-west of Évora at the crossroads of the N2 and N257. They make *chocalhos* – cowbells – here. The cowbells are now used mostly for decorative purposes, but they are still made in the traditional way. They are made in different sizes, out of tin, bronze and copper. Designs are hammered on, the bells are shaped, and then they are covered in clay and fired. The clay is then hammered off. There is a small museum of cowbells.

The **Nossa Senhora de Aires Sanctuary** stands out in an open space off the N384 near Viana do Alentejo, 30 km south of Évora. It is an imposing white and yellow building with two towers and a cupola built in 1743. Pilgrims come here to ask for miracles, and the whole of the inside of the sanctuary is lined with votive offerings.

Monsaraz

Monsaraz is a small, totally walled town on the N319, 7 km off the N256 between Évora and Moura. It is near the River Guadiana and the Spanish border. From a distance the town is very beautiful, with its whitewashed houses and church spires standing within the walls. When you go into it, you feel you have stepped back into the Middle Ages. The town has a bullring and bullfights are still held there.

It seems likely that the town was originally a prehistoric *castro*, and later a settlement occupied in turn by Romans, Visigoths and Moors. After the Christian reconquest it was handed over to the Templars, and later to the Order of Christ.

The castle dates from the fourteenth century, from the time of King Dinis. Most of the walls with their square towers are still standing. The pentagonal keep has two floors with ogival vaulting.

Where to stay
Inexpensive

Estalagem de Monsaraz, Largo de São Bartolomeu. Tel. (066) 55112. A four star inn with seven rooms, all with bath, a bar and restaurant.

Manor house
Inexpensive

Casa Dom Nuno, Rua do Castelo 6. Tel. (066) 55146. An ancient house built on several levels within the old walls. Beautifully restored with eight rooms with bath for guests.

Reguengos de Monsaraz

Reguengos de Monsaraz was founded by people from the old town of Monsaraz. It is 35 km south-east of Évora on the N256, and 15 km west of the old town of Monsaraz. It is famous for its wine, and its pottery.

Festivals

Reguengos is a town of many festivals, pilgrimages and fairs. The *Feiras da Freguesia de Reguengos de Monsaraz* takes place in January, May and August; the *Feira de São Marcos do Campo* in late April; the *Romaria de Santo Isidro* at the end of May; the *Festejos de Santo António* in June; the *Feira da Santa Maria da Lagoa* and the *Festa de Nosso Senhor Jesus dos Passos* in September.

Manor house
Inexpensive

Casa das Palmeiras, Praça de Santo António. Tel. (066) 52362. A house built at the beginning of this century. Eight double bedrooms, several living rooms and a garden are available.

The Tourist Office is at Praça Dom Nuno Álvares Pereira 5. Tel. (066) 55136.

Mourão

Mourão is close to the River Guadiana, 20 km south-east of Reguengos de Monsaraz on the N256, and just 7 km from a frontier post on the Spanish border. The original town of Mourão was on a site now known as Vila Velha. Some ruins remain from that time – notably the castle, with its three high towers. The people probably moved away from Vila Velha because it was too near the river to be healthy.

Azaruja

Azaruja is 17 km north of Évora on the N18. You can see there the prehistoric São Matias dolmen and the São Bento Parish Church.

Évoramonte

History

Évoramonte is 10 km north of Azaruja on the N18. The fortress castle – which has recently been restored – looks down from a high hill. Excavations have shown that the hill has been occupied since the Paleolithic period. Many graves, carvings, and bone and stone tools have been discovered. These early settlers were followed by Romans, Visigoths and Moors. In 1160 King Afonso Henriques and Geraldo Sem-Pavor freed Évoramonte from the Moors. King Afonso III started to build fortifications, and King Dinis enlarged the castle and threw up a strong set of walls in the form of a triangle round the hilltop. The castle and walls collapsed in a 1531 earthquake, but were quickly built up again, and round towers were added to give them strength.

During the fourteenth-century wars with Castile, the King of Portugal asked King Richard II of England for help. He sent troops who, according to Portuguese historians, behaved as badly in the Alentejo as their Castilian enemies. This was one reason why Count Fernandes Andeiro of Évoramonte made a separate peace with the Castilians – a decision that later cost him his head, when the national-ist Master of Avis became King of Portugal and the Castilians were expelled. The king gave Évoramonte to his comrade-in-arms Nun' Álvares, and it later passed into the domains of the Dukes of Bragança. The fourth Duke, who, out of unfounded jealousy, murdered his Spanish wife in Vila Viçosa, afterwards locked himself up in Évoramonte in remorse, to do penance. He later returned to Vila Viçosa, but he always had a soft spot for Évoramonte. When it was flattened in the earthquake of 1531 he had it rebuilt finer than ever. Later, Évoramonte was involved in all of the turmoil of the wars with the Spaniards and the French. And the treaty that ended the War of Succession between the two brothers Pedro IV and Miguel was signed by the walls of the castle at Évoramonte in 1834.

Manor house
Inexpensive

Monte da Fazenda, Évoramonte. Tel. (068) 95172. A white, Alentejo house on a farm with olive and cork trees. It offers two rooms with bath, a bar, riding, hunting and shooting.

Arraiolos

Arraiolos, 22 km north of Évora on the N370, is famous for its rugs. The making of rugs probably originated with the Moors, who were in Arraiolos for eight hundred years. The stitch used is what is known as the 'Greek stitch' or 'Slavic stitch': it is a cross stitch used to make geometric designs or designs with flowers or animals. Originally natural dyes were used for the wool, and the designs were passed down from mother to daughter. Now there are two factories, which between them employ a hundred women on the factory floor and many more in their homes. It takes eight hours to stitch one square metre of a rug.

Montemor-o-Novo

Montemor-o-Novo is 30 km north-west of Évora by the N114, and is on the main N4 between Lisbon and Madrid. It is an agricultural town which sits astride the road, and at first sight it seems to be not much more than a bus stop. But if you go into the old part of town you will find a castle and some fine old buildings.

History

The town was originally a Roman military fortress. It was taken by the Moors, who held it for seven hundred years until it was captured by King Afonso Henriques. The Caliph of Morocco recaptured Montemor and destroyed it, but King Sancho finally drove the Moors out for good, and rebuilt the town. King Dinis built walls and added to the castle.

King João I planned the invasion of Ceuta in the castle at Montemor-o-Novo. And Vasco da Gama came here to see the King in preparation for his voyage to India.

The most famous man of Montemor, though, was São João de Deus (Saint John of God), who built a hospital and devoted his life to taking care of the poor and insane.

What to see

The São João Parish Church has the baptismal font that was used for the saint's baptism in 1495. The Chapel of Santo André dates from the fourteenth century. The Castle rebuilt by King Sancho.

Festivals

The *Feira de Maio* takes place at the beginning of September and the *Festa da Senhora da Conceição* early in December.

Where to stay, and eat Inexpensive

Pensão Monte Alentejano, Avenida Gago Coutinho 8. Tel. (066) 82141. A three star pension with nine rooms with bath, and a restaurant.

Restaurante Sampaio, Avenida Gago Coutinho 12. Tel. (066) 82237. A restaurant that serves Portuguese and regional food. Not open on Tuesdays and Monday nights.

The Lower Alentejo

Tróia Peninsula

The Tróia Peninsula lies between the Atlantic Ocean and the River Sado. You can reach it from Setúbal by ferry boat across the Sado Estuary (you can put your car on the ferry, and the boat trip takes only twenty minutes); or take the N253 from Alcácer do Sal, or the N261–N253 from cities to the south.

The peninsula, which is 20 km long, is a strange, rather eerie place, with the rotting hulls of huge old river boats on the river, and wide, deserted sand dunes that slope down to the sea. There is water everywhere in flat lagoons and bays. There are little fishing villages on the shore, and in the pine woods little lost towns were time has stood still. And it has been said that there are more poltergeists on the Tróia than anywhere else in Portugal.

Well, that was the way the peninsula was for centuries, until about fifteen years ago when a large tourist development got a toehold on the tip of land just across from Setúbal. Actually the development is quite nice and quite discreet, occupying only a small portion of the peninsula, and has not changed Tróia's character very much.

Tróia was inhabited in Paleolithic times. The Romans built a big town here, but it was abandoned after their empire fell. The ruins of this city, which was called Cetobriga, are being excavated.

Cetobriga
Cetobriga was built in the first century BC, and it was probably inhabited till the sixth century AD. It occupied an area 1 km long beside the River Sado, and was one of the most important fish-processing towns in southern Europe. You can see the fishing and fish-processing equipment that has been uncovered, as well as a boat dock, baths, a gymnasium, a chapel with wall paintings, many houses, a crematorium, and several necropolises with tombs.

The **Torralta Tourist Development** is on the tip of the peninsula just across from Setúbal. It has nearly everything you could want on a holiday: hotels, apartments, restaurants, cafés, long sandy beaches, several swimming pools, water sports, tennis courts, horse-riding, an excellent 18-hole golf course, a cinema, boutiques. At the same time it is just a few minutes away from the calm, beautiful Sado Estuary Natural Reserve, with birds, animals, tiny villages, and the Roman ruins at Cetobriga.

Film festival
There is an international film festival in Tróia every June.

Where
to stay
All of the hotels and restaurants are on the beach.

Medium price
Aparthotel Magnoliamar, Tróia, 2900 Setúbal. Tel. (065) 44151/4, telex 18138 TROIAM P. A four star hotel with 129 spacious modern apartments. Each apartment has bath, small kitchen, balcony, air conditioning, telephone and radio. Most have spectacular views of the sea and the Arrábida mountains.

Aparthotel Tróia, Tróia, 2900 Setúbal. Tel. (065) 44221/4, telex 18138 TROIAM P. A three star complex of 429 apartments. Each apartment has bath, fully equipped kitchen, balcony, telephone and heating.

Where to eat
Troiamar. A restaurant with excellent food and service.

Bico das Lulas. A restaurant that serves regional dishes.

Sado Estuary Natural Reserve
The Sado Estuary Natural Reserve covers 23,000 hectares, and includes part of the River Sado, some of the Tróia Peninsula, and lots of mudflats and marshes. There are many dolphins, otters, foxes, civet cats and other mammals, and nearly a hundred different species of birds, including storks, water hens, eagles, herons, ducks, and migratory birds of all kinds.

There have been men in this area for 5,000 years: Neolithic towns dating from 3500 BC to 2800 BC have been discovered. The people lived by fishing and by gathering crustaceans and molluscs, and large dumps (*concheiros*) of shells have also been found.

This is a region to discover. Bring your binoculars. It is easily accessible by car or boat from Setúbal, or from the Tróia tourist complex.

What to see

The **tidal watermill** at Mouriscas near Setúbal uses the force of the tides to move its machinery. **Pinheiro**, on the eastern side of the Sado opposite Cavalo Island, is a pine wood with groups of white houses trimmed with yellow, and a rather strange collection of huts made of reed and thatch, and used for storing farm products. **Cavalo Island** is a breeding ground for many species of birds. The **Bem Pais Lagoon** near Pinheiro is a good place for walking and birdwatching. **Roman kilns** near Pinheiro were used for making amphoras.

Carrasqueira is a town on the west side of the River Sado at the south end of the peninsula. The people divide their time between farmwork and fishing. Its fishing port looks almost like a prehistoric lake settlement, with walkways and houses built on stilts over the lakes. Many of the houses are made of wood and cane.

Comporta, at the southern end of the peninsula, is also beside a series of lakes and lagoons. Rice is grown here.

The **salt flats** at the end of the Mitrena Peninsula on the Setúbal side of the river extend all the way up the river to Alcácer do Sal, 40 km away. They are worked from June to September.

Alcácer do Sal

Alcácer do Sal, 52 km south-east of Setúbal on the N10–N5 and 43 km south-east of Tróia on the N253–1–N253, is a pretty white town that climbs the sides of a hill beneath its impressive castle fortress.

History

The site has been occupied for more than 5,000 years. In the Iron Age it was called Eviom, and traded with cities in the Mediterranean. It became an important Roman municipality, with the name of Salatia Urles Imperatoria, coining its own money. The Romans collected and traded salt and dried fish.

After the town was conquered by the Visigoths it became an important centre of Christianity. The Moors conquered it in 715, named it Al-Qsen, and made it one of the strongest fortifications on the Iberian Peninsula. In 1217 it was retaken by the Christians, with the help of English and Flemish crusaders, who were allies of the Portuguese kings.

Alcácer today

Today Alcácer do Sal still produces salt, along with rice, wheat, cork, tomatoes, cattle and lumber.

What to see

The old part of the town remains much as it has been since ancient times.

The **Castle** was built in the twelfth century, on the foundations of an earlier Moorish castle. King Dinis made later additions to it. The **Santa Maria Church** in the castle dates from the thirteenth century, but was modified in the sixteenth. The **Aracelli Convent**, also within the castle walls, is sixteenth century.

The **Santiago Church** is a medieval church that was rebuilt by King João V. It has interesting wall tiles and gilded wooden carvings.

The **Santo António Convent** was built in the sixteenth century.

The **Sanctuary of the Martyrs** is a medieval building with chapels from the thirteenth, fourteenth and fifteenth centuries.

The **Municipal Museum** is in the Espírito Santo Church, which was built in the fifteenth century. It contains many archaeological finds from the region.

The **Fountain** has panels of sixteenth-century glazed tiles depicting the origins of the town.

The houses in Rua de Marquês de Pombal, better known as Rua Direita, are worth seeing.

Crafts Look out for decorative cork, wooden benches and chairs, leather articles and wicker baskets.

Fairs The *Feira do Torrão* takes place at the beginning of August, the *Feira de Alcácer do Sal* in early October.

Where to stay **Estalagem Herdade da Barrosinha**, Estrada Nacional 5. Tel.
Inexpensive (065) 62363. A four star inn with eleven rooms, ten with bath.
Pousada **Pousada do Vale de Gaio**, Torrão, 27 km from Alcácer on N5.
Inexpensive Tel. (065) 66100. A pousada with a splendid view and a lovely restaurant. There is good hunting nearby, and it also offers fishing and various water sports on the Vale de Gaio dam.

Where to eat The restaurant in the **Pousada do Vale de Gaio** is excellent. It serves regional dishes.

Avenida dos Aviadores is a wide street along the riverside which has many restaurants and cafés. Most of them have good regional food.

What to eat Try *açorda à Alentejana* (kedgeree), *chispe no forno* (roast pig's trotters), *migas de bacalhau* (a cod dish), and, for dessert, pine nut cakes and sweets with an egg base.

Grândola Grândola is 22 km south of Alcácer do Sal on the N120. Its greatest claim to fame comes from the 1974 Revolution. The folk song *Grândola, Vila Morena*, written by Portugal's great modern folk singer and composer José Afonso, about a peasant uprising in Grândola, became the call to arms and the theme of the Revolution.

There are several pensions and restaurants in Grândola.

Santiago do Cacém Santiago do Cacém is 25 km south of Grândola on the N120. The town occupies the slope of the hill on which its imposing castle sits.

History Santiago's beginnings date back to prehistory. It was first fortified about 500 BC, by the Celts, on the site now known as Miróbriga. Around 300 to 200 BC it established relations with towns on the south of the Iberian Peninsula.

The Romans took Miróbriga and developed it into an agricultural, cattle-breeding and horse-training centre. Miróbriga was also well known for its medicinal waters.

After it was invaded by the Visigoths in the third century the town lost much of its importance. At some time it was moved to its present site, nearer the coast. Many of the stones from the old Miróbriga were used to build the new town. The Moors built a castle on the hill.

In 1158 King Afonso Henriques seized the town from the Moors, and gave it to the Order of Sant'Iago. Five years later the Moors under Caliph Yakub recaptured it. They held it till 1217, when the Christians finally liberated it. From then on it was called Santiago do Cacém. It seems probable that the name 'Santiago' came from the order of Sant'Iago, but no one seems to know where 'Cacém' came from, though there are various rather improbable stories.

Between 1315 and 1336 the castle belonged to the Byzantine Princess Dona Vetácia, a maid of honour and friend of Queen Isabel, the saintly wife of King Dinis. It was then returned to the Order of Sant'Iago. In 1594 King Philip II gave it to the Dukes of Aveiro. In 1759, possession passed to the crown.

Santiago today Santiago is now a delightful town of hilly streets with fine old houses and many flowers.

What to see The **Castle** is rectangular, with walls that form a perimeter more than 600 m long. Some traces of the old Moorish walls remain. The remaining tops of the old support towers of the barbican make perfect verandas for viewing the countryside. Since the nineteenth century there has been a cemetery in what was the courtyard.

The **Parish Church** is an old Romanesque/Gothic church built into the castle walls in the fourteenth century, by the Order of Sant'Iago. It was damaged in the 1755 earthquake, and later restored. There is an interesting sculpture of Saint James fighting the Moors. The church also has a fourteenth-century silver cruciform *relicário* (a casket for keeping relics), containing a relic of the Holy Cross. The fraternity of the Holy Cross was founded in 1765 to venerate it. The casket used to be taken out in processions to petition for rain.

The **Municipal Museum** is in the old prison. It has an interesting collection of archaeological finds from the Bronze Age and the time of the Roman occupation (especially objects from the site at Miróbriga), a realistically reconstructed prison cell and an Alentejo kitchen, complete to the last pot and pan.

There is a working windmill on the hill opposite the town.

Crafts Wooden chairs, wicker chairs, cork objects and tapestries are all produced in Santiago.

Fair The *Feira do Monte* is held in early September.

Where to stay **Albergaria Dom Nuno**, Avenida Dom Alvares Pereira 88 to 92.
Inexpensive Tel. (069) 23325. A four star inn with seventy-five rooms with bath, and a bar.

Pousada **Pousada de São Tiago**, Estrada Nacional, 7540 Santiago do
Medium price Cacém. Tel. (069) 22459. A pousada with seven rooms with bath. It has a very pleasant atmosphere and from its terrace there is a wonderful view of the castle and the Roman ruins at Miróbriga.

Where to eat | The **Pousada de São Tiago** has an excellent restaurant, with good home cooking and regional dishes.

Martins, Largo de Santo André. Tel. (069) 76113. A popular restaurant that serves seafood.

What to eat | Specialities are *caldeirada* (fish stew), *ensopado de enguias* (eel stew), *açorda à Alentejana* (kedgeree), goat's milk cheese, pine nut cakes.

Miróbriga | Miróbriga was the original site of the Celtic prehistoric town that grew into Santiago do Cacém. It is only 3 km from the present Santiago. The site has been excavated, beginning in 1808.

History | Miróbriga probably originated as a Celtic *castro* in the Iron Age, around the fourth century BC. Quantities of pottery from this period have been found. It is evident from the coins and other imported objects unearthed that by the second and first centuries BC the people were trading with towns in the south of Spain. The site was occupied by the Romans, who, in the first century AD, made it a city. There are stones with inscriptions from that period. There are also the remains of temples to Venus and Aesculapius, with inscriptions, and of several houses, with traces of frescoes. And there are well-constructed Roman baths, including cold, tepid and hot baths and a sauna. All of the baths are covered with grey marble. You can still see the stone pipes and water tanks that make up the heating system. Miróbriga also had a Roman circus or hippodrome that could seat 25,000 people to see the horse races that were staged there. Unfortunately, it is in a bad state of disrepair. Many of the finds from Miróbriga are in the museum in Santiago do Cacém.

Sines
History | Sines is on the coast, just 17 km south-west of Santiago do Cacém. Sines has been a fishing and trading port since very early times, and it had early trading links with Mediterranean towns. It was occupied by the Romans, and later by the Moors. In 1217 it was taken from the Moors by the Knights of the Order of Sant'Iago. In the fifteenth century Vasco da Gama, the discoverer of India, was born in Sines. In the nineteenth century, after his defeat in the War of Succession, Dom Miguel embarked from Sines into exile.

Sines today | The town has been somewhat marred by the building of a large oil refinery and deep-water ports for tankers. The old part of the town, though, is much as it was.

Castle | The Castle of Sines may have been built during the reign of King Fernando, for protection against pirates. It is possible that Vasco da Gama was born in the Castle, as his father was mayor of the town.

Fairs | The *Feira de Sines* is held in the middle of August and at the end of October. There is a market fair on the fourth Monday of each month.

Where to stay
Inexpensive | **Residencial Malhada**, Rua Deputado António Santos Silva 1. Tel. (069) 634065. A four star inn.

Residencial Búzio, Avenida 25 de Abril 14. Tel. (069) 632114. A three star inn with thirty-nine rooms with bath, a bar and restaurant.

Camp site

The **Parque de Campismo** is open all the year round. Tel. (069) 634011.

Where to eat

The restaurant of **Residencial Búzio** specializes in fish and shellfish.

Varanda do Oceano, Rua Rampa 1. Tel. (069) 632303. Also specializes in fish.

The Sines Tourist Office is at Largo Municipal 44. Tel. (069) 632952.

There are several beaches and interesting little towns on the coast south of Sines.

São Torpes is a beach next to Sines. It has an interesting legend. It is said that in ancient times a boat came to shore at the mouth of the river with the body of São Torpes (Nero's chief steward), a rooster and a dog on board. The chapel that was erected on the spot was said to be the first Christian church in Portugal.

The fishermen in São Torpes used to use one-man paddle boats made of reeds – which seems to indicate ties with the eastern Mediterranean going back several thousand years.

Porto Covo

Porto Covo is a small fishing village between Sines and Vila Nova de Milfontes. It is a beautiful little town, with low-built, snow-white houses trimmed in blue or red. It has a beach on an inlet protected by high cliffs and other beaches of soft sand broken by giant rocks.

Porto Covo was often attacked by Algerian and Moroccan pirates. King Pedro II had two forts built to protect the town: one, the Fort of Ilha de Dentro, on the shore of the mainland, and the other on the island of Pessegueiro, a few hundred metres offshore.

The **Fort of Ilha de Dentro** still has its walls and some of its other structures intact. There are lovely views of Pessegueiro Island from its wide terraces.

The **Fort of Pessegueiro** was never repaired after the 1755 earthquake, and it is totally in ruins. However, it is very interesting to visit, if you can get a fisherman to take you over, or join an excursion from Sines. It was probably built on the remains of an older fort, perhaps destroyed by pirates. There are also the remains of a Roman harbour and a sixteenth-century chapel on the island.

There is a story that in 1660 pirates killed a hermit on the island, and threw his image of the Virgin into a fire. The people of Porto Covo found the image intact, which they considered a miracle, and they took it with them to the mainland, where they built a chapel called the Capela da Nossa Senhora da Queimada (Our Lady of the Burning), to which pilgrimages were made.

Vila Nova de Milfontes

Vila Nova de Milfontes is at the mouth of the River Mira, 41 km south of Sines on the N120-1–N330. It is a lovely little town with good beaches – now very crowded in the summer.

Castle

The castle was built on the ruins of an old Moorish fort, to protect the town from pirates. Arab pirates, based in Algiers, would swoop

318

down on Vila Nova de Milfontes at intervals, sacking and burning it, and carrying away the people to be sold in the slave markets, or ransomed. The castle was given to the Order of Sant'Iago. King João made the town a sanctuary for fugitives from justice, if they would commit themselves to defending the place against pirates.

The castle has now been turned into a hotel.

Where to stay Medium price

Castle Hotel, Vila Nova de Milfontes. Tel. (083) 96108. A lovely hotel with twelve rooms with bath. All of the furniture is antique, and quite beautiful. In the high season it is necessary to book quite far ahead.

Moinho da Asneira, 7645 Vila Nova de Milfontes. Tel. (083) 96182. A tourist complex near an eighteenth-century watermill, a short distance from town. It has rooms, suites, fully equipped houses to rent, swimming pool, fishing and water sports.

Inexpensive

Residencial Mil Reis, Largo Marechal Carnona. Tel. (083) 96223. A three star inn with rooms with bath.

The Tourist Office is at Avenida General Humberto Delgado. Tel. (069) 634011.

Manor house Inexpensive

Quinta do Moinho de Vento. Tel. (083) 96383. A modern, white Alentejo house 800 metres from the beach with pool and tennis courts. Three rooms and two apartments with bath.

Camp site

Parque de Campismo de Milfontes. Tel. (083) 96104.

The **Barragem de Santa Clara** is an extensive dam and reservoir on the River Mira, about 30 km south-east of Odemira on N123–N266–N393. There are water sports on the lake.

Pousada Inexpensive

Pousada de Santa Clara, Santa Clara-a-Velha. Tel. (083) 52250. A pousada with six rooms, a restaurant and bar – and a wonderful view over the lake.

Aljustrel

Aljustrel is in the centre of the Alentejo, 58 km north-east of Odemira on the N263. It is a very ancient mining town. Objects found in the old pyrite mines, and an extensive necropolis nearby, indicate that the Romans worked the mines intensively. A set of bronze tablets on which the Roman laws governing the working of the Aljustrel mines are inscribed, and the rights and duties of each person are set out, is in the Archaeological and Ethnological Museum in Lisbon. Most of the other objects from Roman times found in the mines are in Aljustrel's own Mine Museum, which is well worth a visit.

What to see

The castle is in ruins, but it has a lovely view.

The Nossa Senhora do Castelo Hermitage, at the top of a long, steep staircase, belonged to the Order of Sant'Iago, and played an important part in the struggles between the Moors and the Christians.

The Parish Church has two large panels of glazed tiles on its façade.

Ferreira do Alentejo

Ferreira do Alentejo is a crossroads for anyone travelling from Lisbon to the Algarve, or between the south of Spain and the coast. It is 25 km north of Aljustrel on the N2, and 24 km north-west of Beja on the N121. There are many vestiges of Roman occupation. After the

Christians recaptured the Alentejo from the Moors, Ferreira do Alentejo was given to the order of Sant'Iago.

The **Santa Maria Madalena Hermitage (Calvário)** is an extraordinary chapel, totally round and painted white, with stones sticking out all over it in an irregular pattern. There is a small tower with a cross perched on top. Inside there are images of Saint John and Mary Magdalen.

The **Parish Church** is very beautiful. It has an image of Santa Margarida, the city's patron saint, which is said to have been taken along on Vasco da Gama's voyage of discovery to India. Santa Margarida was the daughter of a Moorish king. She became a convert to Christianity, and was baptized in the River Jordan. When her father found out he had her killed, but the Virgin healed her wounds by washing them in the River Jordan. Whereupon her father was so impressed that he became a Christian himself.

The **Misericórdia Church** has an interesting Manueline door from an older church that was demolished.

Festivals

The *Feira de Ferreira do Alentejo* takes place in September, and the *Festa da Nossa Senhora da Conceição* early in December. The Ferreira do Alentejo market is held twice a month.

Where to stay, and eat Inexpensive

Pensão Santo António, Avenida Gago Coutinho e Sacadura Cabral. Tel. (084) 72320. A three star pension with fourteen rooms with bath.

Pensão Restaurante das Picanheiras, N121. Tel. (084) 72381. A three star pension with thirty-nine rooms with bath, and a regional restaurant.

Alvito

Alvito, 28 km north of Ferreira do Alentejo by the N2–N257, is a beautiful little town, with whitewashed houses from the sixteenth and seventeenth centuries. The site was occupied by Romans and Moors, who left behind many archaeological remains. Alvito received its town charter in 1249, and it was the seat of the first barony in Portugal.

Castle

The castle, which dominates the town, was built in 1482 by the first Baron of Alvito. He had been the first man in Portugal to receive the title of Baron, and now became the first private individual permitted to own a castle. Over the centuries, many kings and queens were guests in the castle; King Manuel was born and died here. But by the nineteenth century it had fallen into disrepair. It has recently been restored.

The castle is a square structure, half-fortress and half-mansion, with circular towers and a square keep. Around the top there is a parapet with battlements. It has big, beautiful arched Manueline windows, a great hall, many rooms and a large courtyard.

Church

The yellow, sixteenth-century Parish Church has a large interior with three naves held up by decorated pillars. It has many decorative tiles, and an ornate gilt altar from the seventeenth century.

Moura

Moura, 52 km south-east of Alvito on the N258, is a very old town. It was an Iron Age hill-top *castro* which was then occupied by the Romans, who made it into an important town, Nova Civitas Arrucitana. Some of the Roman fortifications can still be seen in the Velha do Carmo and Câmara Towers. It has a spa.

History and legend

There are still many remains of the Moorish occupation, which lasted four hundred years. The Arab name for the town was Al-Manijah. According to legend, it got its present name for a Moorish girl who inadvertently helped the Christians to retake it in 1166. Salukia, the daughter of the Moorish governor of the region, was betrothed to Brafama, the Moorish mayor of the nearby town of Aroche. On the day planned for the wedding the bridegroom and his party were on their way to the ceremony when they were attacked and killed by a band of Christians. The Christians then disguised themselves in the dead men's clothes and went on to Al-Manijah. When Salukia saw them coming, thinking it was her bridegroom and his party, she had the drawbridge lowered and the gates opened to them. The Christians rushed in and massacred the Moorish defenders. In grief and remorse, Salukia threw herself from the tower. The town became known as Moura (Moorish Girl), and the spot 5 km away where the bridegroom was killed is still known as Brafama de Aroche.

History says that Moura was taken from the Moors by Geraldo Sem-Pavor (Gerald the Fearless) in 1165. He is said to have used the same method as he used to take Évora, making a ladder of lances to scale the walls at night. It changed hands between Christians and Moors many times after that, and in later centuries it was also taken several times by the Spaniards.

What to see

Over the centuries much of the castle has been destroyed, but the keep, nine rather battered towers, parts of the wall and watchtower, the Arab gates, and the Gothic tower and arch are still standing. The keep has a large chamber with medieval vaulting.

The *Mouraria* (Moorish quarter) still remains, with its narrow, cobblestone streets, low houses and picturesque chimneys.

Noudar Castle is east of Moura on the very border with Spain, near Barrancos. You can see the ruins of the castle constructed in 1346 by King Dinis: it is reputedly haunted by a tragic Moorish girl, who turns into a snake if you see her.

Festivals

O Corso de Carnaval and the *Feira Anual de Moura* take place in September.

Where to stay
Inexpensive

Hotel de Moura, Praça Gago Coutinho 1. Tel. (066) 22494. A lovely old hotel, once an eighteenth-century convent, with marble staircases, wrought-iron balconies and beautiful tiles. It offers thirty-seven rooms with bath and TV, a bar and restaurant.

The Tourist Office is in the Praça Sacadura Cabral. Tel. (066) 22589.

Serpa

Serpa is south of Moura on the N255, in the midst of fertile fields, lakes and rivers.

History

The site was occupied in prehistoric times. Under the Romans it became an important fortification, with the name of Cidade das Rosas. The Moors, who called the town Sherberina, stayed for four hundred years, and were difficult to dislodge – they did not leave for good until 1232, when King Sancho drove them out. King Dinis built the castle and the strong fortifications you can see today. In the centuries that followed, the castle withstood most attacks, but was badly damaged when the Spanish Duke of Ossuna blew it up in 1707. You can still see giant pieces of the wall collapsed on each other.

Serpa today

The town today is a busy agricultural centre with wide squares and many fine old houses. It is famous for its round, creamy *Queijo de Serpa*

Cheese

(Serpa Cheese), made of sheep's milk. This cheese is much sought after, as it is made only in small quantities. You can buy it between April and June at Senhor Abraços, Rua dos Barrigos', or Senhor Bul, Rua da Nossa Senhora.

Alentejo singers

Serpa is also famous for its Alentejo singers. These groups of men, dressed in sheepskin trousers and sheepskin vests, with colourful blankets and bags over their shoulders, sing old songs handed down from the Middle Ages and before. You can often hear them in the countryside or in the cafés.

What to see

The walls and towers of King Dinis's castle are still standing. In a room to the left of the entrance as you come into the courtyard you will find bigger-than-life-size iron figures of Jesus Christ and the Twelve Apostles, seated round an enormously long table partaking of the Last Supper. They are disconcertingly real-looking.

The Porta de Moura and the Porta de Beja are enormous entrance ways flanked by tall, circular towers. They are all that remain of the five built by King Dinis. You enter the town through the imposing Porta de Moura.

The aqueduct that soars above the walls is thin and graceful.

There are several interesting churches: the Parish Church is Gothic; the Church of Santa Maria dates from the fourteenth century; the Salvador Church from the sixteenth century; the Nossa Senhora da Saúde Church has a seventeenth-century carved gilt altar; and the Misericórdia Church has eighteenth-century tiles. The São Francisco Monastery was built in the sixteenth century, the São Paulo Church and Monastery in the seventeenth century.

The Palace of the Marqueses of Ficalho, built in the seventeenth century, is furnished in that period. There are many other interesting houses in Rua dos Farizes and Rua das Amendoeiras.

The fourteenth-century Nossa Senhora de Guadalupe Hermitage is 1 km out of town. Every Easter Sunday there is a festival and pilgrimage there.

Festivals

The *Festas do Concelho* are at Easter, the *Feira de Serpa* in late

August, the *Feira da Aldeia Nova* and the *Feira de Pias* in early September.

Pousada de São Gens, Alto de São Gens. Tel. (084) 90327. Has eighteen rooms, twelve with bath, a bar and regional restaurant.

Casa de São Bras, 4 km along the road to Pulo do Lobo. Tel. (084) 90272. An enormous nineteenth-century house surrounded by gardens and orchards. It offers six rooms with bath, a bar, swimming pool, tennis and riding. English run.

The Tourist Office, Largo Dom Jorge de Melo 2. Tel. (084) 90335.

Beja

Beja, the leading town of the Lower Alentejo, is 27 km west of Serpa on the N260. It is in the heart of the wheat-producing area, on top of a high hill surrounded by vast plains dotted with cork and olive trees.

History

Beja was an important town several hundred years before the birth of Christ. The Romans named it Pax Julia because it was here that the peace treaty with the Lusitanians that ended the indigenous opposition to Roman occupation was signed. It was the capital of one of the three Roman provinces in Lusitania.

The city remained important during the time of the Visigoths, who made it their capital and episcopal see. When it was conquered by the Moors in 713 it became a centre of Muslim learning: many of their most illustrious men gathered in Beja – poets, philosophers, theologians and historians.

Beja was disputed back and forth for hundreds of years between the Moors and the Christians, so that several times it was virtually destroyed and had to be rebuilt. Finally, in 1254, the Christians gained permanent possession of it. Naturally, King Dinis reconstructed it, and he had the castle built in 1303. His coat of arms and the date are on one of the towers.

Beja suffered damage in all the wars that followed with the Spanish and the French, and the civil wars. The town supported the Portuguese Master of Avis in his struggle for the crown against the Spanish queen, and later led the revolt against the forced rule of Philip II of Spain. During the Peninsular War Junot's French troops were garrisoned in Beja. On 24 June 1808 a revolt against them broke out. Junot began reprisals, and 1,200 people of Beja were killed fighting in the streets, almost totally unarmed, against the French.

After the War of Succession between the liberal supporters of King Pedro and the supporters of his absolutist brother Miguel, the liberals murdered many priests and other clerics. From that time the Alentejo has been noticeably anti-clerical. The priests have none of the hold on the people that they have in the north of the country.

Beja and the rest of the Alentejo was a stronghold for the opponents of the Salazar dictatorship, which lasted for forty-two years, from 1932 to 1974. The army several times tried to foster an uprising in Beja.

Portuguese letters

Three hundred years ago there lived in the Conceição Convent in Beja a nun, Mariana Alcoforado, who is thought to have written the famous *Letters from a Portuguese Nun*, to a French officer who had been her lover. These letters were published in French in 1669, and in an English version nine years later.

The *Letters from a Portuguese Nun* are said to have inspired Elizabeth Barrett Browning's *Sonnets from the Portuguese*. And in this century they inspired three remarkable Portuguese women, the poet Maria Teresa Horta, the novelist Maria Isabel Barreno and the social writer Maria Fátima Velho da Costa, to write *The New Portuguese Letters*, to draw attention to the appalling plight of women under the antiquated laws of the Salazar dictatorship, and also to defy the strict censorship laws. They went on trial but were absolved after the 1974 Revolution.

Beja today

Beja today is a prosperous agricultural centre. The town has been modernized, with new roads, housing developments, sports pavilions and restaurants, but now some effort is being made to preserve its historic buildings. Unfortunately, many of the fortifications and the old town gates were torn down in 1850.

What to see

The Conceição convent was founded in 1467, and was once among the richest in Portugal. It now contains the Queen Leonor Museum. This museum has a very fine collection of Visigoth remains and Roman coins and mosaics, and also collections of paintings, religious vestments, church plate, and a fine Ming bowl from 1541.

All that is left of King Dinis's castle is the keep, with its impressive double battlements. Originally it had forty towers.

There are some interesting churches: the Visigoth Santo Amaro Church, the oldest in Beja; the Santa Maria Church and the São Luis chapel, which are both Gothic; the Misericórdia Church.

Crafts

Look for copper work, wooden forks and spoons, rope rugs, miniature clay statues.

Fairs

The *Feiras de Beja* take place in May and August.

Excursion

The Roman ruins of Pisões are 10 km from Beja, near the village of Penedo Gordo. The site was occupied from the first to the fourth century AD. Since 1967, when excavation began, a large house, some small houses, baths (perfect arched structures), storehouses, stables, and many other contructions have been unearthed. There are lovely polychrome mosaics with geometric designs and figures of birds and animals. The name of the owner of one house is on a stone dedicated to a goddess.

Where to stay

Pensão Cristina, Rua de Mértola 71. Tel. (084) 23035/6. A four star pension with thirty-one rooms with bath, a bar and TV.

Inexpensive

Pensão Residência Coelho, Praça da República 15. Tel. (084)

24032. A three star pension with twenty-six rooms with bath.

Pensão Tomás, Rua Alexandre Herculano 7. Tel. (084) 24613. A two star pension with nine rooms with bath, and a regional restaurant.

Where to eat **Aficcionado**, Rua Açoutados 38. Tel. (084) 23964. A restaurant with a varied menu.

Restaurante Luis da Rocha, Rua Capitão João Francisco de Sousa 63. Tel. (084) 23267. A restaurant that serves regional dishes.

The Tourist Office is at Rua Capitão João Francisco de Sousa 25. Tel. (084) 23693.

Mértola Mértola is 50 km south of Beja on the N122, and only 16 km from the Spanish border. Although it is only 72 km north of Vila Real de Santo António on the Algarve, it is definitely off the beaten tourist track. As you come down from the adjoining mountain and cross the bridge, you see the whole town with its white houses climbing up the hill dominated by its ancient castle.

History The Phoenicians, Carthaginians, Romans and Arabs all came to Mértola, because its position on the navigable Guadiana made it a convenient trading post for the Mediterranean. The Romans called the town Mirtilis: it was on the important Roman road that connected Beja with Seville, and Roman coins were minted there. You can still see the Roman quay on the river, and many other remains. The Romans were followed by the Swabians and the Visigoths. Then the Moors conquered the town, and called it Mirtolah. They tore down most of the old buildings and built their own. The town was taken from them in 1238 by King Sancho II, who handed it over to the Order of Sant'Iago. The town walls were built by King Dinis.

What to see The Parish Church, painted a brilliant white and with twelve conical towers, is a fascinating example of the influence of Arab architecture. It was an old Moorish *mesquita*, probably from the eleventh century, that was reconstructed in the thirteenth century by the Christians. It has Moorish columns and a *mihrab* – a prayer niche that indicates the direction of Mecca.

The castle has Moorish walls and much Roman stonework. In the vaulted keep, which was built in 1292, there is an impressive collection of Roman, Visigoth, Moorish and Christian carved stone pieces. There is a cistern, which can be visited, in the middle of the castle courtyard.

A workshop for making hand-carded, hand-loomed blankets has been set up down the steps from the town square. You can see women carding, looming and weaving these beautiful blankets from the wool of the region's sheep. You can also buy the blankets there.

Manor house *Inexpensive* **Casa das Janelas Verdes**, Rua Dr Manuel Francisco Gomes 40. Tel. (086) 62145. A rustic house in the old, historic part of town, with three rooms and three bathrooms.

Where to eat **Alengarve**, Rua Dr Afonso Costa. A restaurant that serves good, simple food. Tel. (086) 62210.

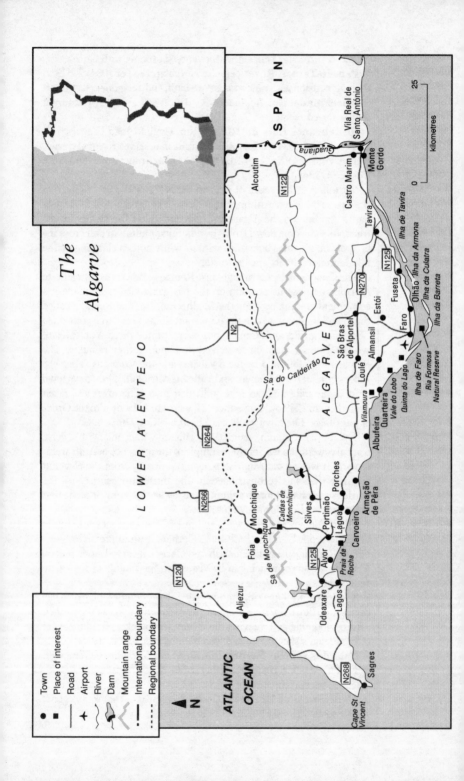

The Algarve

Legend
- ● Town
- ■ Place of interest
- Road
- ✈ Airport
- River
- Dam
- Mountain range
- International boundary
- Regional boundary

N (north arrow)

ATLANTIC OCEAN

LOWER ALENTEJO

SPAIN

ALGARVE

Cape St Vincent
Sagres
N268
Aljezur
N120
Odeaxaxe
Lagos
Praia da Rocha
Alvor
N125
Portimão
Lagoa
Carvoeiro
Porches
Armação de Pêra
Silves
Caldas de Monchique
Monchique
Foia
Sa de Monchique
N266
N264
Sa do Caldeirão
N2
Albufeira
Vilamoura
Quarteira
Vale do Lobo
Quinta do Lago
Ilha do Lago
Ria Formosa Natural Reserve
Ilha de Faro
Loulé
Almansil
São Bras de Alportel
Estói
Faro
Olhão
Fuseta
Ilha da Armona
Ilha da Culatra
Ilha da Barreta
N270
N125
Tavira
Ilha de Tavira
Alcoutim
N122
Castro Marim
Guadiana
Monte Gordo
Vila Real de Santo António

0   25
kilometres

The Algarve

Introduction

The Algarve is the tourist mecca of Portugal. Many tourists fly direct to Faro, spend their days on the beaches and their evenings in the restaurants and night clubs, and fly out with a sun tan. But there is much more to the Algarve than sun and fun. There are fishing villages that saw the comings and goings of Phoenicians and Carthaginians. There are Roman ruins with the remains of streets and palaces, a reminder that Rome once considered this region a very important part of its empire. There are vivid traces of the hundreds of years of Moorish occupation, in the remnants of castles and forts and in the dark features of the people. The place names, dialogue and character of the place are Moorish. There are some very fine old churches with glazed tiles and gold work from the period that followed the Christian reconquest. And, importantly, in the extreme west you can see the places where Prince Henry the Navigator, son of King João I and his English Queen Philippa, had his famous school for navigators, and from which he sent out Portuguese explorers down the coast of Africa on their voyages to discover an all-water route to India.

The region was occupied by fishermen for at least 4,000 years. Phoenicians, Carthaginians, Greeks and Romans came to trade. The Carthaginians had settlements from which they exchanged goods and recruited the local Lusitanians as warriors to fight with them against Rome. After Carthage fell, they left and were replaced by the Romans; they were displaced by the Visigoths, who were later driven out by the Moors who invaded between 711 and 713 and were not ousted until 1250. The Algarve gets its name from the Moorish word *el gharb*, meaning the farthest west of the Moorish kingdom. The towns – especially Silves – were centres of culture under the Moors.

Finally in the thirteenth century, the Portuguese kings, with the help of English and German Crusaders drove out the Moors. In the fifteenth and sixteenth centuries, Prince Henry the Navigator made the Algarve – especially Loulé and Sagres – his headquarters. It was the starting point for invasions of North Africa to attack the Moors.

The Algarve suffered raids by pirates and the English during the Spanish occupation that left many of its cities in ruins. Earthquakes and tidal waves completed the destruction. Most of what you see in the Algarve was built after the eighteenth century.

The Algarve faces south on the Atlantic Ocean, cut off from the

Alentejo region by the Monchique and Caldeirão Mountains. It stretches 150 km from the Spanish border on the east to Cape São Vicente on the west.

Climate The land is cooled by the Atlantic in summer and warmed by the air from Africa in winter, so its climate is generally enjoyable the year round. It has an average of 3,000 hours of sunshine a year. Its sea water is often warmer in the autumn than in the summer, although unexpectedly cooler than the Mediterranean.

Sports The year-round good climate makes the Algarve the sports mecca of Portugal. Many of the region's most attractive tourist developments are built around golf courses. There is an abundance of tennis courts, and stables that rent out horses. The underwater caves and rock formations are a scuba diver's paradise. There is both shore- and deep-sea fishing, and all the ports have boats to rent.

Buildings The typical buildings of the Algarve – the whitewashed houses with their interior patios and painted doors, and white churches with round domes and blue decorations – show a strong Moorish influence. During the 1980s there was a spate of uncontrolled construction which resulted in the hodgepodge of buildings seen in some towns today. The situation has improved: a ban on building during the tourist season, new and wider roads and more high quality structures.

The land The Algarve has three different types of terrain. Just a few kilometres north of the coast you will come to the mountains, where there is a great abundance of water providing spas, forests and gardens. The land to the west of Faro has sandstone cliffs that back beautiful, wide, sandy beaches. The sea coast, especially between Albufeira and Lagos, is full of grottoes and strange rock formations that you can visit by boat. Westward the beaches become more deserted until you come to the region of Cabo de São Vicente where the beaches and the sea are wild, but beautiful. East of Faro the land is flatter and the sand beaches even wider, all the way to the Spanish border.

Life Like the terrain, life in the Algarve exists on several different levels. There is the old Algarve of the villagers, the farmers and the fishermen, who live the way they have for 4,000 years. There is the rather shoddy new Algarve thrown up in the 1980s where hamburger huts, pubs, discos and fish and chip shops abound. And then there is the make-believe world of the posh tourist developments populated mostly by foreigners, where smart white villas with swimming pools, tennis courts and golf courses are set among green manicured lawns.

Special features In spring (early February), the entire region becomes a white sea of almond blossoms. The almonds become the main ingredient of the sweets for which the Algarve is famous. Every town has a pre-Lenten carnival; during May and June there is an International Music Festival, and a beer festival in June introduces you to the excellent Portuguese beer. In August you can buy sackfuls of shellfish at the Shellfish Festival, and September sees the colourful national Folklore Festival.

What to drink The hot, dry climate of the Algarve is ideal for growing vines.

Wines

Wines have been produced in the Algarve for centuries. The Moors were exporting them in the eighth century. In the eighteenth century, when the Douro vines were affected by phylloxera, the Algarve sold its wine to the Douro to substitute for the Douro wine in making port.

The majority of the wines produced in the Algarve are red. The Algarve also produces two kinds of muscatel (dry and sweet).

Aperitifs and liqueurs

Cruz de Portugal is a sweet wine made from a mixture of black and white grapes. Licoroso de Tavira is a sweet, dark wine with a high alcohol content. Medronho is a strong liqueur made from red, fuzzy berries that grow in the Monchique mountains. Amêndoa Amarga is a liqueur of bitter almonds, best drunk very cold.

You can visit the wine bodegas. Ask at the local Tourist Office.

Faro

Faro is 52 km from the Spanish border and just 7 km from the international airport. It divides the western half of the Algarve from the eastern half and is just 40 minutes from Lisbon by plane.

History

The Romans called it Ossonoba and made it an important administrative centre. The Visigoths made it the centre of a cult of the Virgin. The town was known as Santa Maria, and an image of the Virgin was kept in the city walls. Legend says that the Moors threw the image into the sea, and the Virgin in consequence took away all the fish and did not put them back until the image was restored.

The Christians took Faro from the Moors in 1249. In 1596 Faro was sacked by English soldiers under the Earl of Essex. The Earl carried off the library of the Bishop of Faro, and presented it to Sir Thomas Bodley for the library he had recently founded in Oxford. A fire set by the troops reduced Faro to ashes. It later regained its importance until it was all but razed to the ground by the 1755 earthquake, but once again it was restored. In 1808 it was occupied by Napoleon's forces under Juno until the townspeople revolted and drove them out. It has been the capital of the Algarve since 1756.

Faro today

Today Faro is a modern city with luxury hotels and restaurants and a sophisticated night life. Many of the streets near the port have been closed off to traffic and cobblestoned, and are lined with charming sidewalk cafés and shops. But much of the charm of the old city remains in the narrow streets with their houses fronted with wrought-iron balconies, and some late eighteenth-century palaces. Especially interesting is the district around the Church of São Pedro.

What to see

The **Cidade Velha** (old city) is by the port near the Jardim Manuel Bivar garden. You enter through the **Arco da Vila**, a huge arch that was once the door to a palace built by the Bishop of Faro. The inside is an Arab portico.

The **Cathedral** and the **Bishop's Palace** stand inside the old city in a lovely spacious square. The Cathedral was built in 1251, probably on the site of a Moorish mosque. Originally in Romanesque/Gothic style, it was rebuilt after the earthquake with little attention to harmony of styles – a mixture of Gothic, Renaissance and Baroque. The Bishop's Palace also has eighteenth-century polychrome tiles.

The sixteenth-century **Convent of Nossa Senhora da Assunção**, behind the Cathedral, houses the **Prince Henry Archaeological and Lapidary Museum** with its collection of Roman and pre-Roman remains, paintings, tiles and militaria.

The statue in the square is of **King Afonso III**, who led the Christian forces who drove the Moors out of Faro in 1249.

The sixteenth-century **Church of São Francisco**, east of the old city, has a plain exterior, but the interior walls are completely covered in Baroque gold work. The **Church of São Pedro**, in the Rua do Santo António, is also originally from the sixteenth century, but it has been largely rebuilt. It has fine Baroque gold work and a Rococo chapel with glazed tiles. A statue of Saint Anne is attributed to Machado de Castro. The **Church of Santo António do Alto** was built on the site of an old watch tower and Gothic chapel. Its chapel houses the **Saint Anthony Museum**. The church tower provides a fine view. The **Carmo Church** is an important Baroque church on the north side of town and has a statue of Our Lady of Carmel by Machado de Castro. For lovers of the macabre, there is the gruesome **Chapel of Bones**, decorated with bones from the cemetery.

The **Ramalho Ortigão Maritime Museum** is in the Harbourmaster's Building on the port. The **Regional Ethnographic Museum** in the District Assembly Building has reconstructions of typical Algarve houses, models of dress and all types of handicrafts.

Excursions

The **Ilha de Faro** is a long spit of land with the sea on one side and the river on the other. It has a fine beach, water sports, restaurants, bars, changing rooms, and a camp site. The adjacent **Ilha da Barreta** with sand beaches can also be reached by boat.

The **Ria Formosa Natural Reserve** is 50 km long and 6 km wide, and includes all the wetlands between Anção and Cacela Velha. It is a favourite stop-over point for migratory birds. You can hire a boat for an excursion among inlets and islands.

Estói is a charming little town just 11 km north of Faro on N2–N2–6. It has a beautiful palace and gardens just behind the church in the centre of town. The palace is a magnificent eighteenth-century building that originally belonged to the Carvalhal family. Upon the death of the last woman heir, the palace was sold and the proceeds divided among the poor. It is now part of the Algarve patrimony.

The **Ruinas de Milreu** (the remains of a Roman villa) are just down the road west from the Estói Palace. Several imperial busts were found at the site. They are now in the museums in Faro and Lagos.

Follow the yellow signs from the church square in Estói to the **Monte do Casal**, a charming country inn with an excellent restaurant. Tel. (089) 91503. Closed Mondays. Nearby in Santa Bárbara de Nexe, **La Réserve** has excellent French and other international cuisines. Tel. (089) 90234. Closed Tuesdays.

Boats

The **Lusitania Car Ferry** leaves Faro for Tangier three times per week. Reservations can be made in Faro travel agencies or in Lisbon in Rua Dom Luis 1–5C/D. Tel. (089) 674111/2/3/4.

The three-masted schooner '**Odemirense**' sails daily from the dock behind the Faro old city wall and goes through the Ria Formosa Wildlife Sanctuary islands and out to sea.

Tour agencies

Agencia Abreu, Avenida da República 124. Tel. (089) 25035/6. **Miltours**, Rua Verissimo de Almeida 14. Tel. (089) 802030.

Crafts

Look for plant pots, earthenware, tin oil lamps and pitchers. It is possible to visit the potteries. Inquire at the Tourist Office.

Where to stay
Medium price

Estalagem Aeromar, Praia de Faro. Tel. (089) 817542. A four star inn with eighteen rooms, bar, restaurant, boat rental and shops.

Hotel Eva, Avenida da República. Tel. (089) 803354. A four star hotel overlooking the port, with 138 rooms and 12 suites, all with bath and air conditioning. The hotel has all amenities.

Inexpensive

Hotel Faro, Rua Dom Francisco Gomes. Tel. (089) 803276. A three star hotel in the centre of town, it has forty-four rooms and eight suites, all with bath, a bar, restaurant, games and TV rooms.

Casa de Lumena, Praça Alexandre Herculano 27. Tel. (089) 801990. A historic family mansion which has been converted into a three star inn with eleven rooms with bath, a restaurant and bar.

Pensão Condado, Rua Conçalo Barreto. Tel. (089) 22081. A three star pension, it has seventeen rooms with bath, a bar and TV.

Camp site
Where to eat

Parque de Campismo, Praia de Faro. Tel. (089) 817876.

Cidade Velha, Rua Domingos Guieriro, Largo da Sé. Tel. (089) 27145. An intimate, elegant restaurant with excellent international cuisine. Closed Sundays. **O Gargalo**, Largo Pe da Cruz 30. Tel. (089) 27305. A typical Algarve restaurant specializing in codfish *Se do pipo* and the famous *cataplana*. **A Gruta**, Estrada Nacional 125. Tel. (089) 26245. On the road out of the city, this is a typical Algarve restaurant. It offers *fado* music after dinner from 11 p.m. to 3 a.m. **Lady Susan**, Rua 1° Dezembro 28. Tel. (089) 28857. Specializes in fish and fresh meat dishes. Closed Sundays.

What to eat

Grilled sardines with local bread and a tomato salad are the most common fare, but perhaps even more popular is the *cataplana* (cockles or other shellfish steamed in a covered pan with various additions) and sweets made from figs or almonds.

Entertain-ment

There are many 'in' bars and discos at the back of Faro near the Hotel Faro. Some are very chic. Some have live music. Try the **Joia** or the **Ubis**, or the discotheque **Sheherazade** in the Hotel Eva. Tourist Office, Rua da Misericórdia 8–12. Tel. (089) 25404/24067.

São Bras de Alportel

Some 18 km north of Faro on N2, this town was founded by the Moors in the mountains surrounded by almond, cork and carob trees. Its white houses have terraced roofs for drying fruit. Try the almond cakes and local brandy. There are archaeological sites nearby.

Where to stay **Pousada São Bras**. Tel. (089) 842305. A relatively modern, state-run inn on the mountain above the town, it has twenty-three rooms with bath, a swimming pool and spectacular views.

West of Faro

Loulé

Loulé is 17 km north-west of Faro on the N125–N125–4. The 1755 earthquake knocked down the castle and most of the houses. However, the castle has now been restored, and you can still see the streets of the old town with their whitewashed houses.

What to see

The castle is in the centre of the town. Its walls surround the Tourist Office and the Museum.

Churches

The thirteenth-century Parish Church has lovely glazed tiles, carved gilt work and a Manueline arch. The Misericórdia Church has an interesting Manueline portal. The sixteenth-century Nossa Senhora da Piedade Church contains the image of the patron saint of Loulé. The market was built at the beginning of this century.

Festival

The Carnival in February is a celebration of the almond blossoms.

Fairs

At the National Handicraft Fair in August, you can buy hand-made products from every region of Portugal at low prices.

Travel agent

Turalgarve Travel Agency, Praça da República 96. Tel. (089) 62143/4. Offers jeep safaris.

Where to stay
Inexpensive

Pensão Dom Payo, Rua Projectada a Antero de Quental. Tel. (089) 64422. A three star pension with twenty-six rooms with bath.

Where to eat

O Avenida, Avenida Jose da Costa Mealha 13. Tel. (089) 62106. Offers Portuguese and international food and live entertainment. Closed Sundays.

What to eat

Grilled fish, lamb stew (*Ensopado de Borrego*) and almond cakes.

The Tourist Office is inside the old castle. Tel. (089) 63900.

Almansil

Almansil is on the N125, 13 km west of Faro. The town is uninteresting except for its ochre pottery painted in blues and reds.

What to see

The **São Lourenço Church** is 3 km east of town. This tiny Baroque church is one of the finest in Portugal. Its walls and vaulted ceiling are covered with blue and white glazed tiles dating from 1730, the work of the famous artist Policarpo de Oliveira Bernardes. They depict the life and martyrdom of Saint Laurence. The church withstood the 1755 earthquake, and local people consider that a miracle.

A visit to the **Centro Cultural São Lourenço** is a must. Located in restored buildings beside the church, it exhibits works by famous and unknown Portuguese and international artists. There are also Portuguese antiques and old wines. Tel. (089) 395475.

Where to stay
Luxury

Quinta do Lago, near Almansil and 24 km from Faro Airport, is one of the most elegant tourist estates in the Algarve. Accommodation rental can be for the season or for just a day or two. It is possible to book in the UK.: Clube da Quinta Reservations, Leisure Estates

International, P.O. Box 2, Great Glen, Leicestershire LE8 0QZ. Tel. 053 759 3400.

Expensive **Four Seasons Country Club**, Quinta do Lago. Tel. (089) 396150/72. Has villas, apartments, and a golf course.

Where to eat **Shepherd's** is next to the Quinta do Lago Country Club. Tel. (089) 934541. It is run by Richard Shepherd, who started the renowned Langan's Brasserie in London with Michael Caine. **Cheers**, Fonte Coberta, between Almansil and Vale do Lobo. Tel. (089) 935547. A typical Algarve restaurant with Portuguese and international food. Also has live music and *fado*. **The T-Club**, Almansil, in the luxurious Buganvilla Plaza shopping centre at the entrance to the Quinta do Lago. Tel. (089) 936755. The newest and most spectacular culinary spot in the Algarve with international and traditional food.

Entertainment **Trigometria**, Buganvilla Plaza, Quinta do Lago, is a popular night club/disco in the shopping centre.

Riding **Pine Trees Riding Centre**, Quinta do Lago. Tel. (089) 394369.

Where to stay **Vale do Lobo**, 1,000 villas and apartments, just 20 minutes from
Expensive Faro Airport near Almansil, claims to be 'Europe's finest luxury resort'. It literally has every facility under the sun. The price of a studio apartment or a one bedroom apartment is approximately the same as that for a five star hotel.

What to do There is a 27-hole golf course, the Roger Taylor Tennis Centre and the Clube Barrington Health and Fitness Centre.

Where to eat **Clube de Golf**, tel. (089) 394444, ext. 5406. A restaurant with a terrace by the golf course, serving Portuguese and international food.

Mr Freddie's, Escanxinas, on the Vale do Lobo road. Tel. (089) 95302. A good restaurant-pub.

Entertainment **Smokey Joe's** is a classy night club on the square.

There is a regular bus service to the outside world. For bookings Vale do Lobo, Reception (089) 8994444.

Quarteira Quarteira is on the beach 6 km off the N125 on the N396. It was once a fishing village, but has now been turned into a tourist dormitory. The narrow beach gets packed. However, should you need to stay there, there is plenty of accommodation from which to choose.

Where to eat **Restaurante Bar Gida**, Semino. Tel. (089) 315164. Specializes in fish, meat, fondue and *cataplana*. Folklore and *fado* once a week.

Restaurante Zé do Norte, Estrada Nacional 125 – Quatro Estradas. Tel. (089) 97321. Features a genuine regional kitchen.

Vilamoura Vilamoura is an enormous tourist complex west of Almansil. The first tourists there were the Romans, and they left traces of their presence at the Cerro da Vila archaeological site.

Sports There are three golf courses and a golf club. Most of the tourist villages and hotels have tennis. The Centro Desportivo Squash has several squash courts. The Clube de Tiro, just outside the main entrance, is one of the largest gun clubs in Europe with facilities for hiring guns. The Riding School near the highway is excellent, with horses for hire and lessons. There are all types of water-based sports.

Sailing

The yacht marina has hotels, restaurants and 1,000 berths for yachts. To join a boat tour or rent a yacht, call the **Vilamoura Marina**, tel. (089) 314867, or the **Algarve Marina Travel Agency** in the Marina Shopping Centre, tel. (089) 312772.

Where to stay
Medium price

Hotel Dom Pedro Marina. Tel. (089) 313222. A four star hotel with 154 rooms with satellite TV, minibar and air-conditioning, and suites with private jacuzzi. It has a pool, bar and restaurant.

Inexpensive

Estalagem da Cegonha, Poco do Boliqueime. Tel. (089) 66271. A four star inn with ten rooms with bath, a bar, restaurant and riding.

Bookings of apartments and houses can be made through the Services for Owners, tel. (089) 313278, or directly at the developments.

Where to eat

There are more than twenty restaurants in Vilamoura. Two good ones are: **A Margarida**, overlooking the marina. Tel. (089) 312168. **O Vapor**, Parque Mourabel. Tel. (089) 35646.

What to eat
Entertainment

Cataplana, caldeirada de peixe (fish stew), *bife de atun* (tuna steaks).

The **Vilamoura Casino**, tel. (089) 312999. Open daily from 7 p.m. to 3 a.m. Also has a restaurant and nightclub with international show.

The **Discoteca Zebra**, in the Aldeia do Mar. **Skipper's Club** is a discotheque in the Marina shopping centre. All the tourist villages, hotels and the Marina shopping centre have attractive bars.

Praia da Falesia
Where to stay
Medium price

This town has pine woods that slope down to the sea, where there is a beautiful wide beach backed by sandstone cliffs. The beach has a large tourist development with villas, restaurants, all amenities, and the four star **Alfa-Mar Hotel**, tel. (089) 50351.

You can reach undeveloped beaches by taking the little roads that lead off the coast road to the sea.

Albufeira

Albufeira is on the coast on the N395 off the N125 west of Faro. One of the most popular of the resort towns of the Algarve, what was once a little fishing village with narrow, steep streets and white houses has grown into a city with modern hotels spread out across the hills above the sea. A few of its Moorish characteristics remain, and you will still see the colourful fishing boats and the fishermen mending their nets.

History

Albufeira was occupied in turn by the Romans, the Visigoths and the Moors. The Moors gave it the name of Al-Buhera, meaning 'castle of the sea'. During the Moorish occupation it flourished through trade with North Africa, but its prosperity declined after it was taken by the Portuguese King Afonso III, in the thirteenth century.

The town had a famous priest, Vicente de Santo António, who was a missionary among the Japanese. You can see a statue of him in the upper part of the town.

What to see

Albufeira's castle, which protected it against foreign pirates, was reduced to ruins by the 1755 earthquake and burned in the nineteenth-century War of Succession. There are now only a few remains.

The Parish Church, which was reconstructed after the 1755 earthquake, still has vestiges of Manueline style and valuable statuary.

Beaches

Albufeira has marvellous beaches, some among giant rocky outcroppings. There are splendid grottoes that you can visit by boat, and excursions to Malpique and Lajem do Cónego in the mountains above.

A favourite place to be is the town square with its outdoor restaurants, fountains and shops. A tunnel leads down to an esplanade around the beach with more terraced restaurants under the cliffs.

Where to stay
Medium price

Hotel Carlton, tel. (089) 858261. A new four star hotel in Moorish style in the hills above the town near the beach, with 310 rooms with TV and air conditioning, and all amenities.

Hotel Sol e Mar, Rua José Bernardino de Sousa. Tel. (089) 52121. A three star hotel with seventy-four rooms with bath, two pools, air-conditioning, bars and restaurant.

Inexpensive

Estalagem do Cerro, Cerra da Piedade. Tel. (089) 52191/2. A four star inn with eighty-three rooms with bath, a swimming pool, health club, bar and restaurant.

Pensão Polana, Rua Candido dos Reis 32. Tel. (089) 55859. A two star pension in the centre of town with thirty-one rooms with bath, a breakfast room and bar.

Camp site

Parque de Campismo de Albufeira, Estrada Nacional 125. Tel. (089) 53851. Luxury camp site, five minutes from the beach.

Where to eat

A Ruína, Cais Herculano. Tel. (089) 52094. By Fishermen's Beach, it serves seafood. **Palaçete**, Rua Almeida Garrett, Areias de São João. Tel. (089) 52114. Specializes in typical Algarve food. **Jardím d'Allah**, located opposite the Sol e Mar Hotel in the ancient Moorish quarter. Tel. (089) 52190. Decorated in Arab style, but the food is regional Portuguese – and very good. **Michael's**, at Montechoro Park. Tel. (089) 55997. Presents an international show.

What to eat

You can get excellent shellfish and fish, served in the typical *cataplana* (copper steamer). Grills are also a good choice.

Entertainment

Harry's Bar, Largo Eng. Duarte Pacheco 37–38, in the main square. A very smart, popular bar. **Cave do Vinho do Porto**, Rua da Liberdade 23, is really a cave, lined with bottles of all kinds of port wine for tasting by the glass or buying by the bottle. **Boîte-Restaurant Kiss**, Areias de São João. Tel. (089) 53116. The oldest and most famous of Algarve's discos. **Crazy Bull e Magix**, in Black Bull tourist complex by the bullring in Areias de São João. Tel. (089) 54671. One of the biggest discos in Portugal with constant music.

Bullfights

There are **bullfights** in the Albufeira Bullring every Saturday during the season. Book at the bullring, Tourist Office, hotels, camp sites.

Folk dancing

There are exhibitions of folk dancing and singing in the town square. Tourist Office, Rua 5 de Outubro. Tel. (089) 52144.

Armação de Pêra

Armação de Pêra, a few kilometres west of Albufeira, is a resort full of high-rise hotels and apartments, but it has one of the finest beaches in the Algarve. A wide esplanade runs along the clifftop with staircases leading down to the beach where there are many restaurants. At the eastern end, you will find the fishermen's beach and at the western end, is a tiny Romanesque chapel perched high on a cliff top. It is Nossa Senhora da Rocha (Our Lady of the Rocks), who is said to have

What to see

saved a fisherman from the rocks by miracle. Further west still, near **Furnas**, are famous grottoes that can be visited by fishing boat from Fishermen's Beach.

Fishing   **Cruzeiros Sul e Mar**, Rua Dr Martinho Simões 26. Tel. (082) 312729. Offers fishing and pleasure cruises.

Where to stay   **Hotel Garbe**, Avenida Marginal. Tel. (082) 312194. On the cliffs,
Medium price   it has ninety rooms and eleven suites and all amenities.
Inexpensive   **Albergaria Cimar**, Rua das Redes 10. Tel. (082) 312171. A four star inn with nineteen rooms with bath, and a bar.

Pensão Hani, Rua Rainha Santa 4. Tel. (082) 312230. A three star pension with twenty-six rooms with bath, and a bar.

Rural tourism   **Casa Bela Moura**, tel. (082) 313422. A charming inn with two Algarve, Moorish-style houses, with fourteen rooms with bath, a swimming pool and bar.

Where to eat   **Restaurante Lino**, Edificio Vista Mar, Avenida Infante Dom Henrique. Tel. (082) 313099. Specializes in seafood. **O Gatsby**, Rua Dr Manuel Arriaga 109. Tel. (082) 313535. A very popular restaurant.

Two other good restaurants are: **Restaurante Bar a Grelha**, Rua do Alentejo 4. Tel. (082) 312245; and **Restaurante Pontal**, Rua General Humberto Delgado 5. Tel. (082) 312379.

Entertainment   **Charlie Chaplin's**, Rua Dr Jose António dos Santos. A bar with pool, music and dancing.

Sports   **The Big One**, Estrada Nacional 125, Alcantarilha. Tel. (082) 312827. Is the biggest aquatic park on the Algarve.

Camp site   **Parque de Campismo de Armação de Pera**, tel. (082) 312260. Tourist Office, Avenida Marginal. Tel. (082) 312145.

Porches   Porches, on the N125 on the way to Lagoa, has steep, tortuous streets, believed to be of Roman origin. It was wrested from the Moors by King Afonso III. It is an important pottery-making centre.

What to see   The **Parish Church** has the chancel of the original sixteenth-century church, rebuilt in the last century.

Handicrafts   The Olaria Pequena Pottery factory and showroom are on N125 at the turn-off for Porches. Tel. (082) 53213. Open Monday to Friday.

Wine tasting   Try the wines of Porches at the Oleiros wine tasting adega.
Where to eat   **O Leão**, in a seventeenth-century farmhouse in the town centre. Tel. (082) 52384. Serves excellent food in a charming atmosphere.

Lagoa   Lagoa, famous for its wines, is presumed once to have been on the banks of a lagoon. It is 5 km west of Porches on a hilltop amongst vineyards. Entrance to the town is through a gate in the bell tower.

What to see   The **Parish Church** has a nineteenth-century Baroque façade. Its polychrome statue of Our Lady of Light is attributed to the eighteenth-century sculptor Machado de Castro. **Church of the Misericórdia** has lovely carved gilt work from the eighteenth century. **Tower-belvedere** was part of the convent of São José. It has been restored completely, but you can still see the window with the turntable which was used for receiving abandoned babies.

Wine tasting   The **Co-operative Wine Cellar** should be visited to try the Lagoa wines, known for high alcohol content and velvety flavour.

Motel Parque, Estrada Nacional 125 (Sitio do Carmo). Tel. (082) 52265. A three star motel with forty-two rooms and two suites with bath, a swimming pool, children's park, restaurant and bar.

Restaurante Escondidinho, Rua Comendador Teófilo Trinidade 12. Tel. (082) 52497. Near the church, serves typical Portuguese food, and will prepare Arab food on request.

Carvoeiro

Carvoeiro is a beach resort 5 km south of Lagoa. It is a beautiful little town, a blend of fishing village and tourist centre, that sits in a cove surrounded by cliffs.

There are many secluded beaches in the area, some of which you can reach only by sea – you can hire boats. The coast here is full of strange rock formations, grottoes, caves and isolated inlets. At **Algar Seco**, 1 km east of Carvoeiro, there are especially spectacular rock formations. The beach at **Vale de Centianes** near Algar Seco is set among rocks and cliffs with conditions for surfing. The quaint village of **Benagil** has a small beach and boats for hire.

Hotel Dom Sancho, in the square by the beach. Tel. (082) 57301. A four star hotel with forty-seven rooms with bath, a swimming pool, bar and restaurant.

Togi Apartments, next to the Togi restaurant in town. Tel. (082) 57517. Offers five two-room and four fully furnished apartments.

Novo Patio, on the square. Tel. (082) 57367. Specializes in fish and seafood at lunchtime and French dishes in the evening. **Restaurante Togi**, a tropical-style restaurant in lush gardens above Algar Seco. Tel. (082) 58216. Serves both French and Portuguese food.

The Tourist Office is right on the square. Tel. (082) 57728.

Silves

Silves, 8 km north of Lagoa, makes an impressive picture as you come down into its river valley and see the red stone battlements and castle on a hill opposite against a backdrop of mountains.

It was founded by Phoenician traders who came up the River Arade. In the time of the Moors it became the most important city in the Algarve, and one of the most important in Portugal. But divisions among the Moors weakened it, and so the Christians were able to attack it. King Sancho I, with the help of English and German Crusaders, laid siege to Silves in 1189. Silves fell, and the Crusaders were so cruel during the sacking of the town that the Portuguese army finally had to drive them back to their ships by force.

In 1191 the Caliph of Morocco retook Silves and held it until 1231 when it was finally won for the Christians by Paio Peres Correia. There followed a series of calamities. The River Arade silted up, then repeated earthquakes between the fourteenth and the eighteenth centuries finally left only five houses standing.

The **Castle**. You can still see traces on the north side of what was the castle of the last Moorish ruler. The Cistern of the Moorish Girl, an impressive, vaulted structure with square pillars supporting the arches, had the capacity to supply the castle for a whole year. The Cistern of the Dog, which is 70 m deep, was originally a copper mine worked by the Romans. There are underground storerooms and a crematorium.

The **Cathedral** was built on the site of the mosque. It is a Gothic building that survived the 1755 earthquake. It contains fifteenth-century tombs. **Church of Nossa Senhora dos Martires** was a twelfth-century Romanesque church. Later additions are Manueline. It contains the tombs of the Portuguese and Crusaders who died in the conquest of the city against the Moors. **Cruz de Portugal** (Cross of Portugal) is an intricately carved stone lacework cross from the sixteenth century. It stands at the edge of the town under a stone canopy on the road to Messines. **Medieval Bridge** on the site of a Roman one, was built in the thirteenth century.

Where to stay
Inexpensive

There are a few simple, but clean, pensions: **Residencial Castelo**, Rua 1° de Maio. Tel (082) 43316; **Residencial Central**, Rua Policarpo Dias 18. Tel (082) 42747; **Residencial Sousa**, Rua Samora Barros, 17–1°. Tel. (082) 42502.

Where to eat

Casa Velha, Rua de Abril 11–13. Tel. (082) 443417. In the lovely arcades by the castle gate, it serves typical Algarve food.

Café Ingles, inside the castle walls with tables under the trees, is famous for its cakes and bread baked in an outdoor oven.

Entertainment

Centro Hípico de Silves, Rua Comendador Vilarinho 37. Tel. (082) 43754. The Silves riding school offers rides on horseback.

Tourist Office, Rua 25 de Abril. Tel. (082) 42255.

Portimão
History

Portimão, 8 km west of Lagoa on the N125, probably originated as a prehistoric settlement and was later occupied in turn by Phoenicians, Carthaginians, Romans and Moors. The Christians captured Portimão in the thirteenth century. In the centuries that followed it suffered attacks from the Spanish, the English, and the Dutch.

Portimão
today

Today Portimão is a bustling seaport surrounded by ever-mushrooming tourist complexes, hotels and apartment buildings. Traffic is a problem, especially in the summer. However, the river port area and the gardens and promenades near the river with their outdoor cafés and markets retain some original characteristics.

What to see

The fortified **Castle** in Ferragudo across the river is a ruined monument to the days when Portimão had to defend itself against invaders. The **Parish Church**, constructed in the fourteenth century, was rebuilt after the 1755 earthquake, but traces of the original church remain. It has seventeenth- and eighteenth-century tiles.

At the Fishing Port, dozens of boats unload their catches.

Where to stay
Medium price

Hotel Globo, Rua 5 de Outubro 26. Tel. (082) 22151. A three star hotel in the centre of town. It has sixty-eight rooms with bath, beach facilities, bars and a good restaurant.

Inexpensive

Pensão Denis, Rua da Guarda. Tel. (082) 24273. A three star inn with lovely guest rooms.

Pensão Pimenta, Rua Dr Ernesto Cabrita 7. Tel. (082) 23203. A three star pension with thirty rooms and five suites, all with bath, and a bar.

Camp site | **Parque de Campismo de Ferragudo**. Tel. (082) 24321.

Where to eat | To get a taste of the real Portimão, try charcoal-grilled sardines with a salad and home-made bread in one of the taverns by the bridge. For more conventional dining try one of the following:

A Lanterna, near the bridge on the Ferragudo side. Tel. (082) 23948. A reasonably priced Portuguese restaurant specializing in fish. Closed Sundays.

A Casa de Jantar, Rua de Santa Isabel 14–18. Tel. (082) 22072. An excellent new restaurant decorated in nineteenth-century style.

The Old Tavern, Rua Judice Fialho 43. Tel. (082) 23325. A bar-restaurant with Moorish decor. Seafood and international cuisine.

What to eat | Try the *cataplana*; grilled sardines; almond sweets.

Entertainment | **Melody Inn**, Rua Judice Fialho. Tel. (082) 27299. Has piano music. **Boîte Chaminé**, Largo Rainha Dona Leonor 12, across the river in Ferragudo. Tel. (082) 21179. Music and dancing.

Water sports | **Slide and Splash**, on Estrada Nacional 125, Vale de Deus, between Carvoeiro and Portimão. Tel. (082) 53411. A big aquatic park with all facilities.

Boats and fishing | Portimão's river port is lined with boats that will take you out sightseeing or deep sea-fishing. **Cepemar**, Centro de Pesca Desportiva no Mar, Praça da República 24-A. Tel. (082) 25866. Operate two big-game fishing boats. **Actividades Maritimo Turistico**, Rua Santa Isabel 35. Tel. (082) 415136. Offer fishing or cruises.

Travel agencies | **Star Travel Service**, Rua Judice Biker 26-A. Tel. (082) 25031; **Agencia Abreu**, Rua Infante Dom Henrique 83. Tel. (082) 35182. **Viagens Rawes**, Rua da Hortina 34, Centro Comércial Tropical. Tel. (082) 23092.

Tourist Office, Largo 1° de Dezembro. Tel. (082) 23695.

Praia da Rocha | Two km from Portimão, this is the Algarve's most famous beach. It is wide and sandy with giant outcroppings of yellow and red sandstone rocks that form caverns and grottoes. Above the beach on the cliffs there are some fine old turn-of-the-century houses.

What to see | **Fortress of Santa Catarina de Ribamar** was built in the sixteenth century to defend Portimão. It has a small chapel with a Gothic doorway, spectacular views and an open-air café.

Where to stay
Medium price | **Hotel Jupiter**, Avenida Tomás Cabreira. Tel. (082) 22041. A four star hotel near the beach with 180 rooms with bath and balcony, and all amenities.

Inexpensive | **Hotel da Rocha**, Avenida Tomás Cabreira. Tel. (082) 24081. A three star hotel with 158 rooms with bath, a bar and restaurant.

Hotel Alcalá, Avenida Tomás Cabreira. Tel. (082) 24062. A two star hotel with twenty-two rooms with bath, a bar and restaurant.

Albergaria 3 Castelos, Avenida Marginal. Tel. (082) 24087. A four star inn with ten rooms with bath, a bar and restaurant.

Where to eat | **Restaurante A Balança**, Avenida Tomás Cabreira, Edificio Vista Mar. Tel. (082) 26514. Has a terrace overlooking the sea and serves regional and international dishes, especially *cataplana*.

Tropical Beach, Areal. Tel. (082) 26738. Has beautiful views and serves excellent fish stews and kebabs.

Entertainment The **Hotel Algarve**, Avenida Tomás Cabreira. Tel. (082) 24001. Has a night club with picture windows showing the sea through the fantastic rock formations. Floor show three times a week. Closed Mondays. **Night Star Club**, in the Hotel Jupiter. Tel. (082) 22041. One of the Algarve's classiest discos.

Just 3 km from Portimão, **Praia do Vau** is a development with bright, luxurious apartments, swimming pools, and water sports.

Alvor Alvor, just 4 km from Portimão, is another well known resort.

History Alvor is believed to have been founded by the Carthaginian General Hannibal in 436 BC and later became an Arab stronghold. In the fifteenth century King João II died there.

What to see The **Parish Church** is notable for a portal that shows Moorish influence in the lacy fretwork, the round arch and doorway, and the use of floral motifs. Later Manueline architecture was incorporated.

Where to stay **Hotel Dom João II**, Praia de Alvor. Tel. (082) 459135. A four star *Medium price* hotel on the beach with 202 rooms and 18 suites, each air-conditioned with balcony, and all amenities.

Inexpensive **Aparthotel Alvor**, Praia de Alvor. Tel. (082) 459211. A tourist complex with apartments and villas by the beach.

Pensão O Pinheiro, Quatro Estradas, Alvor. Tel. (082) 459881. A three star pension with twenty rooms with bath, a bar and restaurant.

Where to eat **Restaurante Taberna Velha**, Rua Pedro Alvares Cabral 34-A. Tel. (082) 459713. **Restaurante Amsterdam**, Rua Dr Afonso Costal 3. Tel. (082) 459445.

Entertainment The **Alvor Casino**, Alvor. Tel. (082) 23141.
Where to stay The **Penina Golf Hotel**, on the N125 towards Lagos. Tel. (082)
Expensive 22501. A fine hotel with three golf courses, plus tennis courts, swimming pool, dining rooms, and dancing. Its 200 rooms and 14 suites with bath are air-conditioned and most have balconies.

Caldas de Monchique Some 24 km north of Portimão, the road winds up through forests with many springs and brooks to Caldas de Monchique, a spa used originally by the Romans and surrounded by woods. Plants growing there have been used for centuries for medicinal purposes. The spa itself is rather shabby and not very exciting, but all around there are fountains, paths and look-out points. If you feel like a walk, you can climb up to the ruins of Our Lady of Desterro, which was built by the Franciscans. The spa has craft shops, restaurants, inns and a wine-tasting (not water-tasting as one would expect) bar.

Where to stay **Albergaria do Lageado**, tel. (082) 92616. A four star inn with
Inexpensive twenty-one rooms with bath, a swimming pool, restaurant and bar.
Crafts Wooden and wickerwork articles, woollen rugs and sweaters are made in the hills.

Monchique The town of Monchique itself is not very attractive either, except for its setting in the mountains. For centuries it dedicated itself to making wooden barrels and casks, and rough woollen cloth.

What to see

The Parish Church is sixteenth-century Manueline with polychrome decorative tiles. The woodwork statue of Our Lady of the Immaculate Conception is attributed to Machado de Castro.

Where to stay,
and eat
Inexpensive

Albergaria Bica-Boa, on the Lisbon road N266. Tel. (082) 92271. A four star inn, it has an oak-beamed dining room with terrace, and a wine cellar. Its four rooms have bath, heating and telephone.

Manor house
Inexpensive

Casa da Paz, Acor-Alferce, 8550 Monchique. Tel. (082) 92576 or (01) 537035. Hidden in the Serra de Monchique valley, this manor house is run as a health resort. It offers an apartment for two people.

Most of the other inns and restaurants are on the road to Foia, which, at 920 metres, is the highest point in the Algarve and is 8 km almost straight up from Monchique. From Monchique they are:

Teresinha, tel. (082) 92392. A restaurant in a rough, stone building with a great view of the valley, that serves regional dishes.

Inexpensive

Estalagem Abrigo da Montanha, Corte Pereiro. Tel. (082) 92131. A four-star inn in the woods with six rooms with bath, a bar and restaurant. **Estalagem Mons Cicus**, Estrada da Foia. Tel. (082) 92650. A three star inn with two pools, tennis courts, restaurant, bars, and sauna. It has eight rooms with bath. A real bargain.

Paraíso da Montanha, 3 km from Monchique. Tel. (082) 92150. A very large, popular restaurant.

Jardim das Oliveiras (Garden of the Olive Trees), 500m off the Foia road to the right, is definitely a place to be 'discovered'. Tel. (082) 92874. A farm house converted into a restaurant, it has an outdoor grill, walk-in bread oven, and a beer garden. Closed Tuesdays.

Foia
Medium price

Estalagem da Montanha is a new inn on top of the mountain at Foia, where there is also a look-out point and a very big shop selling honeys, liqueurs and crafts of the region.

Inexpensive

Pensão Restaurante O Planalto, Foia. Tel. (082) 92158. A two star pension with a restaurant in the little town.

What to eat

Traditional recipes are used to cook rabbit, pheasant, hare and pork. The area is also famous for smoked ham, honey, and Medronho brandy made from strawberry-tree wine.

Lagos
History

Lagos is on the coast, 17 km west of Portimão on the N125.

Lagos was probably founded about 2000 BC. It was a flourishing town in the time of the Romans, who called it Lacobriga. It was taken by the Visigoths, and later by the Moors. The Portuguese kings finally got possession of Lagos from the Moors in the middle of the thirteenth century. King Dinis reconstructed the fortress.

It was from Lagos that Portugal's great armada set off to conquer Ceuta. And it was at Lagos that Prince Henry the Navigator built his caravels to send off on voyages of discovery. He also installed his personal court and men of commerce in what is now the Governor's Palace. In 1578 King Sebastião set off from here with his army of 15,000 men to conquer the Moors. Mass was said on the beach at Meia Praia, before they embarked for Morocco on 500 ships in the bay (see page 241). The objects used in the Mass are in the Lagos Museum.

Sir Francis Drake tried to take Lagos in 1587, during England's war with Spain, but he was driven off. The 1755 earthquake razed Lagos.

Lagos today

Today Lagos is a flourishing resort but it has maintained much of its historical character. The forts still guarding the bay, the sixteenth-century walls and the huge bronze statue of Prince Henry are constant reminders of its role in the Age of Discoveries. Many of its old streets have been turned into pedestrian malls, but its old houses with wrought-iron balconies, covered with flowers, and its wide, palm-lined boulevards around the bay are still beautiful.

What to see

The **Forte da Porta da Bandeira** is a fort with a drawbridge that was built as a defence against pirates.

The **Church of São Sebastião**, on which construction began in the fifteenth century, contains a cruficix brought back from the battle of Alcácer-Quibir and a statue of Our Lady of Glory taken from a wrecked eighteenth-century ship. The **Santa Maria Church**, a sixteenth-century church restored in the nineteenth, has a famous statue of São Gonçalo, the patron saint of Lagos, who is venerated by local fishermen because, it is said, he multiplies the shoals of tuna.

The **Church of Santo António** in Rua Henrique Correia da Silva is a national monument. It has magnificent gilded, carved woodwork and eighteenth-century decorative tiles. The **Municipal Museum** has many archaeological finds, religious art, paintings and the town charter dated 1504. The **Slave Market**, under a series of arcades in Rua da Senhora da Graça by the Praça da República, was, according to tradition, the first place African slaves were sold in Portugal.

The **Statue of King Sebastião**, in the Praça de Gil Eanes, executed by contemporary sculptor João Cutilerio, depicts the king as very young, very wistful and very lost – which he was.

Handicrafts

You can get beautifully made copper utensils here and articles made of palm leaves.

Beaches

The nearby sandy beaches of São Roque and Meia Praia have all kinds of facilities for water sports and fishing. There is an 18-hole golf course at Palamares. The Praia da Dona Ana is off the promontory south of Lagos, partly hidden by cliffs. You reach it by steps carved in the side of the cliff. Praia do Camilo and Porta de Mós are within walking distance; Porta de Mós has a large camp site.

Excursion

Ponte de Piedade is a high promontory 2 km south of Lagos. You can take a boat trip from Piedade or from Dona Ana beach to see the strange rock formations and tunnels in the sea.

Sports and fishing

Inquire at the Tourist Office, or the Water-Sports Centre, tel. (082) 768967.

Skytours

Algarve Airsport Centre, in the Municipal Aerodrome of Lagos, tel. (082) 62906, offers flightseeing tours and paragliding.

Bullfights

The Lagos Bullring presents bullfights every Saturday during the season. Tickets for sale at the bullring or at hotels.

Tours

Miltours, Praia da Rocha. Tel. (082) 82798.

Falcon shows

Casa dos Falcões, Rua Dr José Formosinho, on the road to

Pinhão Beach. Exhibitions of falcons, eagles and vultures in flight.

Where to stay
Medium price

Hotel de Lagos, Rua Nova da Aldeia. Tel. (082) 62011. A four star hotel with 287 rooms with bath, a restaurant, bars, disco, swimming pools, tennis and water sports.

Inexpensive

Hotel da Meia Praia, Meia Praia. Tel. (082) 62001. A modern three star hotel 2 km from Lagos, only 100 metres from the beach. It has sixty-five rooms with bath, and all facilities.

Hotel Riomar, Rua Candido dos Reis 33. Tel. (082) 63091. A three star hotel in town with forty rooms with bath and bar.

Pensão Lagosmar, Rua Dr Faria e Sousa 13. Tel. (082) 63523. A three star pension with twenty-one rooms with bath, bar and TV.

Manor houses
Medium price

Casa do Pinhão, Praia do Pinhão, on the road to Sagres. Tel. (082) 62371. On cliffs overlooking the beach, it has three rooms with bath, a lounge, dining room and terrace.

Inexpensive

Quinta da Alfarrobeira, on the road to Palamares, Odeaxare. Tel. (089) 68424. A big, traditional Algarve house on a farm next to the Palamares Golf Club. It offers two rooms with bath.

Camp sites

Parque de Campismo de Lagos, Estrada de Porto de Mos on N125. Tel. (082) 60031. **Parque de Campismo de Valverde**, Praia da Luz. Tel. (082) 69211.

Where to eat

The streets of Rua 25 de Abril and Rua Marquês de Pombal near the Tourist Office in the historic part of town have been closed to traffic and are lined with restaurants, many of them with open-air dining.

Alpendre, Rua António Barbosa Viana. Tel. (082) 63705. One of the oldest restaurants in Lagos, also has a bar. **O Galeão**, Rua Laranjeira. Tel. (082) 63909. Serves international and regional dishes.

What to eat
Bars and boîtes

Fish and shellfish, and sweets made of almonds and eggs.

Lançarote Clube, Rua Lançarote de Freitas 26. Tel. (082) 60890. A combination of bar–restaurant–disco, with entertainment for all ages. **Shaker Bar**, Avenida 25 de Abril 68. Tel. (082) 63316. **Boîte Satelite**, Rossio da Trinidade. Tel. (082) 63711.

Tourist Office, Largo Marquês de Pombal. Tel. (082) 63031.

Praia da Luz

Praia da Luz, 2 km from Lagos, is a British enclave with tourist developments and sports clubs.

Where to stay
Medium price

Beach Villas of Cambridge, Luz. Tel. (082) 69401. Converted fishermen's cottages and villas with private swimming pools.

Inexpensive

Apartamentos Turisticos Luz Beach, Avenida dos Pescadores. Tel. (082) 69642. Offers twenty-one fully furnished apartments.

Where to eat

O Jardim at the Luz Bay Club. Tel. (082) 69555. Open to all, it is set in sub-tropical gardens. Charcoal grills a speciality.

Darcy's International Restaurant, Rua da Praia 14. Tel. (082) 69140. One of the Algarve's best restaurants.

Sports

Luz Bay Sea Sports Club, Avenida dos Pescadores 4. Tel. (082) 69538. A diving and water sports centre.

Sagres

Sagres, 26 km west of Lagos on the N125–N268, is on top of high cliffs. It is very windy and almost without vegetation. There are caverns in the cliffs and the noisy sea shoots up through dark tunnels.

History

Prince Henry the Navigator was given, by his brother the King, a large grant of land around Sagres. He set up an observatory and a school of navigation and brought in men of skill and learning from all over the world. He mortgaged all of his personal possessions, pledged the money of the Order of Christ, of which he was Grand Master, and raised huge loans to finance the enormous programme of exploration that began the Age of Discoveries. From Sagres he watched his caravels sail off down the coast of Africa.

After Prince Henry's death, in 1460, the town declined. Then in 1587 it was attacked, pillaged and burnt by Sir Francis Drake. The archives and library of Prince Henry were destroyed. What was restored was wrecked during the 1755 earthquake and tidal wave.

What to see

Sagres Fort. In 1793 Queen Maria I gave orders for the fort to be rebuilt, but it was never finished. During the past twenty years, however, much of it has been restored. You can see the famous *rosa do ventos* (wind compass) made up of lines of stones set in thirty-two directions of the compass. **Prince Henry's house** and the **Graça chapel**, with a fifteenth-century image of St Catherine, can also be seen. From the Aspa tower you get a panoramic view of the open sea. Incredibly, fishermen sit on narrow ledges around the walls and line-fish into the water hundreds of feet below.

Where to stay
Medium price

Pousada do Infante, tel. (082) 64222/3. A luxury inn standing on the cliffs with balconies all around. It has fifteen rooms, a swimming pool, restaurant and bar. The decor evokes the Age of Discoveries.

Hotel Apartamentos Navigator, Sitio da Baleeira. Tel. (082) 64354. Has fifty-five fully furnished apartments, and all amenities.

Inexpensive

Hotel da Baleeira, Praia da Baleeira. Tel. (082) 64212. A three star hotel in a cove, with 122 rooms with bath, a bar, restaurant, disco, tennis court and swimming pool.

Where to eat

A Tasca, Praia da Baleeira. Tel. (082) 64177. A typical fisherman's restaurant with a fantastic view overlooking the bay.

What to eat

Fresh seafood, especially lobsters.

The Tourist Office is in the Fort.

Fort Beliche

On the road to São Vicente, this fort once guarded the coast. It is now an annexe to the Pousada do Infante (see above), and has four rooms with bath, a bar and restaurant, and in its garden there is an old chapel with a gilt polychrome altarpiece. The restaurant is open all year, but the hotel closes between 15 October and 15 February.

Cabo de São Vicente

Cabo de São Vicente (Cape Saint Vincent) is the most westerly point of the Algarve. It is a lonely promontory standing on sheer cliffs that are cut by the sea into frightening, unreal shapes. For centuries, sailors have called it *O Fim do Mundo* (World's End).

Legends

It is a place of legend. It is said that the gods often came here to sleep when they left Mount Olympus at night, that the hero Hercules was buried here, and that the body of Saint Vincent was washed ashore here and guarded by ravens. A chapel, called the Temple of the Ravens, was built on the spot where Saint Vincent's body rested.

344

What to see

The fortress is on the point, built into the cliffs. There is a new lighthouse which throws beams 80 km out to sea.

Aljezur

Aljezur, 42 km north of Sagres on N268, originally settled by the Moors in the tenth century, was conquered in 1246 by the Christian Kings. Situated in a valley by a little river, history passed it by for centuries. The road from Sagres to Aljezur follows the coast. The mountains are terraced for farming and there are thousands of goats everywhere. Strange trees and shrubs dot the hillsides.

Aljezur itself is a white town spread around the sides of the hills with its ruined castle on top. It has old copper mines.

What to see

The **Castle**, on the site of what was a prehistoric *castro*, was originally built by the Moors, restored by King Dinis and later destroyed by the 1755 earthquake. There are spectacular views from the castle but the road up to it is better for mountain goats than for cars.

Where to stay, and eat Inexpensive

Hotel Vale da Telha, Vale da Telha. Tel. (082) 72180. A two star hotel with twenty-six rooms with bath, and a bar, and a rustic restaurant with good Portuguese cooking.

East of Faro

Olhão

Olhão is 8 km east of Faro on the N125. It is an important fishing centre, and has a good fish market. Arab influence is apparent in its cube-shaped houses with inside staircases and roof-top terraces.

In the nineteenth century a group of fishermen went from Olhão in a little boat called the *Bom Sucesso* all the way across the Atlantic to Rio de Janeiro to tell the exiled King João VI that the armies of Napoleon had been driven from Portugal.

What to see

The **Parish Church** is a Baroque structure built in the seventeenth century with contributions from the fishermen. Inside is the Capela dos Aflitos (Chapel of the Sufferers), where wives of fishermen go to pray during storms. The Church of Nossa Senhora da Soledade, also built by the fishermen, has a cupola like a mosque.

The **Bairro da Barreta** has whitewashed houses along very narrow streets. The **Rua do Comércial** has tile-covered buildings with wrought iron balconies.

Notice the **Water Dogs** in Olhão and in the nearby fishing villages. Strong dogs with long, curly hair, they have been of valuable assistance to Algarve fishermen for centuries – reputedly diving down into the water to depths of over 4 m to guide the nets or to save fishermen from drowning. They always formed part of the crew of caravels.

Where to stay Inexpensive Where to eat

Hotel Ria Sol, Rua General Humberto Delgado 37. Tel. (081) 72167. A two star hotel with fifty-two rooms with bath, a bar and TV.

Restaurante Kinkas, an excellent, unpretentious restaurant in front of the fish market on the waterfront. It specializes in fish.

Excursions

From Olhão, you can take a boat to the islands of Culatra, Armona, Hangares, Fuseta and Farol, at the entrance to Faro.

Fuseta is a typical old fishing village with boats drawn up along the riverside. Boats go over to the island of Armona all summer. There are excellent conditions for windsurfing on the Fuseta lagoon.

Quinta Palmeiras Garden Centre on N125 between Olhão and Tavira. Tel. (081) 96189. Has thousands of trees and plants.

Tavira

Tavira, 20 km east of Olhão on the N125, is one of the prettiest towns in the Algarve. The River Gilão runs through the town and is crossed by a Roman bridge. All around are vineyards.

History

It may have been founded by the Greeks about 400 BC and later occupied by the Romans. It became an important Moorish centre until it was taken in 1242 by the Christian Kings. King João II lived in Tavira in the fifteenth century, during which time it was a very important port. Catastrophes like the plague in 1645, the earthquake of 1755 and the silting up of the river caused its decline.

What to see

The **Castle**, reached by stone staircases from various points in town, has lovely gardens enclosed by the old walls, and good views.

Tavira has twenty-seven churches, many closed and it is difficult to track down the keys, but it is worth trying to see some of them.

The **Church of São Francisco** has an interesting cupola, and an image of Nossa Senhora da Conceição that the men of Tavira took with them when they went to fight the Moors in North Africa. **Santa Maria do Castelo**, by the castle, is actually built on a mosque. It was here that the sons of King João I were knighted after their victorious return from the battle against the Moors in Ceuta. The **Misericórdia Church** is one of the finest examples of the Renaissance style in the Algarve. It has fourteen magnificent panels of glazed tiles. The **Carmo Church** has a beautiful eighteenth-century polychrome altar. The **Ondas Church** (Church of the Waves) has a seventeenth-century painted wooden ceiling.

The **Roman bridge**, reconstructed in the seventeenth century and again in 1990 after it was seriously damaged in a winter storm, was part of the Roman via from Faro to Mertola. The **Market** is a turn-of-the-century building, with lots of decorative ironwork, in the park by the river. It sells fish, fruit, vegetables and Algarve handicrafts.

Excursions

Ilha de Tavira is an island 2 km from town. Boats leave from the pier every 30 minutes in the summer for the 5 minute trip.

Miltours, tel. (089) 802040, offer various tours in the area.

Where to stay
Expensive

Aldeamento Turistico Quinta das Oliveiras, Estrada Nacional 125, Quinta das Oliveiras. A beautiful development with sixty-one apartments with every luxury.

Inexpensive

Eurotel Tavira, Quinta das Oliveiras. Tel. (081) 22041. A three star hotel with eighty rooms with bath and balconies.

Apartamentos Turisticos Nora Velha, Sitio da Nora Velha. Tel. (081) 23131. Has ninety-six fully furnished apartments, and all amenities.

Pensão Princesa do Gilão, Borda D'Aqua de Aguiar. Tel. (081) 23171. A two star pension with eighteen rooms with bath.

Manor house
Medium price

Quinta do Caracol, São Pedro. Tel. (081) 22475. A seventeenth-century farmhouse, set in lawns, with seven apartments in an annexe to the main house. It has a bar, swimming pool and tennis court.

Camp site

Ilha de Tavira, Ilha de Tavira. Tel. (081) 23505.

Where to eat

There are many little seafood restaurants on the esplanade near the market by the river in Rua Jose Pires Padinha, such as the **Imperial**, tel. (081) 22306, and the **Europa**, tel. (081) 881745.

Crafts

Look out for delicate cast iron work and regional embroidery.
Tourist Office, arcade of Praça da República. Tel. (081) 22511.

Beaches

Cabanas is a typical fishing village with many small restaurants specializing in shellfish caught locally. It is 1 km off N125 on the way to Vila Real de Santo António. **Caçela** is the next beach just 1 km off the road. **Manta Rota**, the next beach, is enormously wide and rather savage. It has a four star hotel and several little beach restaurants.

Monte Gordo

Monte Gordo is 18 km east of Tavira on the N125. It has one of the most beautiful beaches in the Algarve. This new, attractive town has a wide esplanade lined with hotels, shops and restaurants.

Where to stay
Medium price
Inexpensive

Hotel dos Navegadores, Rua Gonçalo Velho. Tel. (081) 42490. A three star hotel with 356 rooms with bath, a restaurant, bar, and pool.

Pensão Paiva, Rua 11. Tel. (081) 44187. A three star pension with twenty-five rooms with bath.

Albergaria Monte Gordo, Avenida Infante Dom Henrique. Tel. (081) 42570. An American-run four star inn with twenty-five rooms with bath, a bar, and an excellent restaurant with sea views.

Camp site
Where to eat

Parque de Campismo de Monte Gordo, tel. (081) 44188.

Copacabana, on the main beach avenue. Tel. (081) 42464. Run by the Hotel Navegadores, it specializes in grills.

Restaurante Bar Mota, Praia de Monte Gordo. Tel. (081) 42650. A restaurant on the beach serving regional and international cuisine.

Entertainment

The Casino is on the beach, and has a restaurant and floor show. Tel. (081) 42224. **Al Tech**, Residencial Catavento. Tel. (081) 42003. A large, loud and flashy disco. **Giovani Club**, Avenida Infante Dom Henrique 3–64. Tel. (081) 44767. Music and dancing.
Tourist Office, Avenida Marginal. Tel. (081) 44495.

Vila Real de Santo António
History

Vila Real de Santo António is 23 km from Tavira on the N125, and on the River Guadiana, the frontier with Spain. There is also a good, wide highway that goes near the beach through the pine woods.

Originally there was a Roman town on the site. It later became an important centre for fishing and preserving sardines and tuna. The town was completely engulfed by the sea at the end of the sixteenth century. In 1774, after the sea had receded, King José ordered his Prime Minister, the Marquês de Pombal, to build another town. He built it in the same style as he had rebuilt the Baixa section of Lisbon after the 1755 earthquake. He then ordered the people from the old towns around to move to the new town or have their houses burned – not surprisingly, many chose to emigrate to Spain. The town remained empty until this century.

Excursion   You can get a ferry boat to take you and your car across the river to Spain. It is fun and cheap, so do make the trip. Seville and Cadiz are quite near. An international bridge will open in 1991.

Where to stay
Inexpensive   **Hotel Apolo**, Avenida dos Bombeiros, near the fire station. Tel. (081) 44448. A two star hotel with forty-two rooms with bath and balcony, a bar and restaurant.

Camp site   **Praia Verde**, Praia Verde. Tel. (081) 42382.

Where to eat   **Caves do Guadiana**, Avenida da República 89. Tel. (081) 44498. On the main street near the ferry boats, it serves seafood and Portuguese dishes. **Dom Jotta**, Ponta da Areia. Tel. (081) 43151. On the point by the river with a splendid view, it specializes in *cataplana*, fish and meat on the spit, and grilled shrimps.

Excursion   **Tranguadiana**, Rua Almirante Candido Reis 96. Tel. (081) 42752. Runs excursions up the River Guadiana.

The Tourist Office is by the port. Tel. (081) 43272.

**Castro
Marim**   Castro Marim is 4 km north of Vila Real de Santo António on the N122, by the Guadiana River Nature Reserve, where you can see rare migratory birds.

History   Casto Marim was an important sea and river port even before the Phoenicians came. Later, the Romans and the Moors fortified it. In 1238 it was taken by the Christian King Sancho II. Because it was so far away from other Christian towns it was constantly under attack by the Moors. In order to attract inhabitants, it was made a sanctuary for fugitives. Later it became the headquarters of the Order of Christ and during the Inquisition was a place of exile for those sentenced by that dreaded court.

What to see   King João IV built the castle of São Sebastião in the seventeenth century. It was destroyed by the 1755 earthquake, but you can see many of the old walls and towers. The present castle was built by King Afonso III and houses the Church of Sant'Iago and a small museum. The buildings are fine examples of Algarve architecture.

Where to eat   **Restaurante Manel D'Agua**, Estrada Mouro Vaz 4. Tel. (081) 43880. A typical Portuguese restaurant with good food.

Alcoutim   Alcoutim is 40 km north of Castro Marim on the banks of the River Guadiana across from the Spanish town San Lucar.

History   It was a river fort during the time of the Phoenicians, Greeks and Carthaginians. The Romans and the Moors occupied it for its strategic position. After the Christian reconquest in 1240 its walls and castle were fortified. In 1371 King Fernando I of Portugal and King Henrique II of Castile met in the middle of the river there and signed a peace treaty between their two countries. As trade moved down to the mouth of the Guadiana, Alcoutim declined, but today it is awakening.

What to see   The **Castle** is in ruins, but its walls provide beautiful views of the river. The **Parish Church** has a Renaissance-style portal, sixteenth-century coloured bas-relief and an eighteenth-century monstrance.

What to eat   The river produces delicious lamprey, eels, grey and other types of mullet that are served in little restaurants by the water.

Index

Abrantes 273, 280–1
Afife 83–4
Afonso Henriques, King of
    Portugal
  in the Alentejo 291, 295, 311
  in the Beiras 176, 189, 208
  in Estremadura 215, 220, 222,
    223, 226, 228, 237, 249, 267
  in the Minho 8, 68, 89, 98,
    103, 105
  in the Ribatejo 279, 280, 281
  in Trás-os-Montes 161, 165
Afonso II, King of Portugal 205,
    208, 289
Afonso III, King of Portugal 136,
    214, 237, 280, 301, 311, 330,
    334, 335, 348
Afonso V, King of Portugal 114
Afonso VI, King of Portugal 241
African territories 11, 12, 13–14,
    15, 245
Agdanha 157
agrarian reform 8, 287–8
Aguiar da Beira 180
Albufeira 334–5
Alcácer do Sal 314–15
Alcácer-Quibir, battle of 241, 342
Alcáçovas 310
Alcobaça 19, 215–17
Alcoutim 348
Alegrete 293
Alenquer 225–6
Alentejo, the 9, 287–325
Algarve, the 327–48
Algosinho 159
Algoso Castle 164
Alhandra 285
Alijó 142–3
Aljezur 345
Aljubarrota 216–17
Aljustrel 319
Almansil 332
Almeida 175
Almeirim 283
Almoster 283
Alpedrinha 190
Alpiarça 284
Alter do Chão 294–5
Altilho 150
Alturas de Barroso 150
Alvão Mountains 141
Alvito 320
Alvor 340
Amarante 40, 129–34
Anta da Cunha Baixa 179

Anta da Pêra do Moço 175
aqueducts 70, 260, 298–9, 307
architecture 9, 17–21
Arcos de Valdevez 91
Armação de Pêra 335–6
Arrábida Natural Park 269
Arraiolos 311–12
Arruda dos Vinhos 225
Aveiro 39, 192–4
A-Ver-o-Mar 73
Avô 185
Azambuja 284–5
Azaruja 311
Azibe dam 156
Azinhoso 159
azulejos see tiles, decorative
Azurara 71

Barbadão 96, 173
Barbeita 86
Barcelos 95–7
Barro do Lago 74
Batalha 19, 209–10
beaches
  in the Alentejo 318
  in the Algarve 328, 330, 333,
    334–5, 337, 339, 342, 347
  in the Beiras 206
  in Estremadura 223, 224, 231,
    235, 266, 267
  in the Minho 67, 72, 76, 83
Beckford, William 247
Beiras, the 170–211
Beiriz 74
Beja 9, 18, 289, 323–5
Belmonte 18, 188–9
birdwatching 74, 88, 314, 330,
    344, 348
boats 194–5
boat travel 33–4
boat trips 34, 79, 124, 195, 263,
    280, 330, 331, 333, 336, 337,
    339, 342, 345, 346, 347–8
boatyards 70
Bom Jesus Sanctuary 102–3
Boticas 149–51
Braga 8, 9, 18, 97–104
Bragança 40, 164–8
Bragança, Dukes of
  in the Alentejo 300, 301, 311
  in the Beiras 173, 211
  in Estremadura 214, 241
  in the Minho 105
  in Trás-os-Montes 152, 165,
    166
Buarcos 206–7
Buçaco 197–9
bullfights 49–50, 190, 219, 259,
    285, 310, 335, 342
bus travel 34–5
Byron, Lord George 228, 247

Cabeçeiras de Basto 142
Cabo da Roca 231

Cabo de São Vicente 344
Cabo Espichel 270–1
Cabral, Pedro Álvares 188, 240
Caetano, Marcelo 14, 245
Caldas da Rainha 15, 218–19
Caldas de Monchique 340
Caldas do Gerês 90
Cambarinho Natural Park 179
Caminha 40, 68, 83–4
camping 43–4
Campo Maior 295–6
Cantares Alentejanos 288, 322
Cape Saint Vincent see Cabo de
    São Vicente
Caramulo 179
Carcavelos 235
Carlos, King of Portugal 12, 198,
    244
Carrasqueira 314
Cartaxo 284
car travel 35–6
Carvalhal 157
Carvalhelhos 151
Carviçais 157
Carvoeiro 337–8
Cascais 232–3
casinos 50, 74, 154, 233, 334,
    340, 347
Castelo Branco 189–90
Castelo de Almourol 278–9
Castelo de Bode 279–80
Castelo de Vide 289–90
Castelo Rodrigo 175
castles 137, 143, 152, 154, 155,
    164, 204, 207, 301, 320, 332,
    334, 337, 338, 345, 346, 348
Castro Boriz 95
Castro da Nossa Senhora da
    Assunção 86
Castro de Aire 178
Castro de Alfatima 183
Castro de Castelo Velho 157
Castro de Cigadonha 157
Castro de Sabroso 108–9
Castro do Povoadão 224
Castro do Zambujal 224
Castro Faria 95
Castro, Inês de 202, 215–16, 222
Castro Laboreiro 89
Castro Marim 348
castros 17–18
cathedrals 18
  in the Alentejo 293, 306
  in the Algarve 330–1, 338
  in the Beiras 173, 177, 193,
    201
  in the Douro 118, 136, 141
  in the Minho 98–9
  in Trás-os-Montes 161–2, 166
Cavalos de Ofir 74
Celorico da Beira 175–6
Celorico de Basto 142
ceramics see porcelain; pottery
Cetobriga 313

Chaves 151–3
cheese 47, 182, 322
Chegas de Bois 150–1
Cinfães 139
Citânia de Briteiros 108
Citânia de Lanhoso 103
citânias 17–18, 67, 77, 79
clothing 54
cockerels 95
Coimbra 18, 19, 20, 199–204
Colares 231
Columbus, Christopher 239
Comporta 314
Conimbriga 18, 204
Constância 279
consulates 55–6
cork 288
Cortes 135, 137
Costa da Caparica 266–7
Cova de Lua 168
Covilhã 186–8
Covilhã, Pero de 186–7, 238
Coz 217
craft fairs 71, 234, 332
crystal 53, 209
Cúria 196
currency 54–5

Dias, Bartolomeu 70, 238–9
Dinis, King of Portugal
    in the Alentejo 288, 289, 291,
        296, 299, 300, 301, 302
    in the Algarve 341, 345
    in the Beiras 173, 175, 191,
        207, 208
    in the Douro 140
    in Estremadura 214, 220, 223,
        228, 237, 249, 261, 271
    in the Minho 72
    in Trás-os-Montes 151, 152,
        157, 158, 159, 161, 164, 165
Discoveries, Age of 19, 68, 69,
    238–9, 275, 327, 342, 344
dolmens 88, 89, 129, 132, 143,
    151, 175, 178, 179, 184
Dornes 278
Douro, the 110–43
Duas Igrejas 160

Eanes, General Ramalho 16, 26,
    27
earthquake of 1755 242, 246
economy 27
electrical current 55
Elvas 19, 297–300
embassies 55–6
embroidery 53, 78, 131, 189
Ericeira 227
Espinho 128–9
Esposende 76–7
Estói 330–1
Estoril 233–5
Estremadura 212–71
Estremoz 301–4

etiquette 56
Évora 9, 18, 304–9
Évoramonte 311

fado 10, 50–1, 126, 200, 261, 331,
    333
falcon shows 342
Fão 74
Faro 329–32
Fátima 210–11
Fernando, King of Portugal 114,
    192, 223, 230, 273, 348
Ferreira, Adelaida 117
Ferreira do Alentejo 319–20
Ferreira do Zêzere 277–8
festivals 50, 58–61
Fielding, Henry 247
Figueira da Foz 205–6
first aid 57–8
fishing 52, 72–3, 80, 90, 94, 103,
    129, 132, 213, 328, 336, 339,
    342
Foia 342
Folgosinho 171
folk dancing 160, 162, 163, 335
food 46–7
forest fires 56–7
Forrester, Joseph James 116–17
Foz do Arelho 219
França 168
Freixo de Baixo 132
Freixo de Espada à Cinta 157–9
Fronteira 295
Fundão 190

Gama, Vasco da 239, 255, 317,
    320
Ganfei 85
Gatão 132
glass 53, 209
Golegã 281
golf courses 52, 129, 154, 233,
    328, 333, 342
Gondar 132
Gondomar 95
Gouveia 183
government 25
Grândola 315
Guarda 172–4
Guimarães 20, 105–9

Haute École 274
health 57–8
Henry of Burgundy 98, 105, 158
Henry the Navigator 111, 114,
    121, 210, 238, 246, 275, 327,
    342, 343–4
hitch-hiking 36
horseback riding 52, 90, 234, 333,
    338, 342
horses 273–4, 281, 283, 294
hotels, 41–2
hours of opening 63–4
hunting 52, 288–9

Idanha-a-Nova 190
Idanha-a-Velha 18, 190–1
Ílhavo 195
Inquisition 64, 77, 167, 240–1,
    242, 306, 348
Isabel, Saint, Queen of Portugal
    200, 202, 203, 278, 280, 302

Jazente 132
Jews 77, 165, 167, 176, 188, 240,
    252
Joana, Princess 192, 193
João I, King of Portugal
    in the Alentejo 294, 296, 312
    in the Beiras 173, 175, 176,
        200, 209, 210, 211
    in the Douro 141
    in Estremadura 223, 228, 237–
        8, 246, 270
    in the Minho 86, 87, 105, 106
    in Trás-os-Montes 166
João II, King of Portugal 105,
    192, 218, 238, 239, 299, 302,
    340, 346
João III, King of Portugal 130,
    240–1
João IV, King of Portugal 114,
    122, 241, 246, 271, 348
João V, King of Portugal 189,
    200, 218, 226, 242, 260, 273,
    294, 302
João VI, King of Portugal 115,
    243, 345
John of Gaunt, Duke of
    Lancaster 86, 87, 176, 237
José, King of Portugal 242, 254,
    255, 347
Junot, Marshal Andoche 191,
    223, 280, 284, 323

knights
    of the Hospital of St John of
        Jerusalem 189
    Order of Christ 275, 279
    Order of Sant'Iago 225, 238,
        267–8, 271, 316, 317, 319,
        320, 325
    Templar 159, 189, 190, 205,
        208, 211, 274–5, 279, 285
    Twelve Knights of Portugal
        176

lacemaking 70, 222
Lagoa 336–7
Lagoa de Óbidos 219
Lagos 341–3
Lamego 135–40
Lapa 176
Laundos 74
Leiria 20, 208–9
Lindoso 89
Linhares 184–5
Lisbon 9, 213, 236–66
    accommodation 263–4

districts
Alfama 249–53
Bairro Alto 258
Baixa 256–7
Belém 254–6
immediate outskirts 259–61
Ribeira 253–4
festivals 261–2
history 236–47
links with England 246–7
nightlife 265–6
restaurants 264–5
shopping 262
transport 248–9
Loulé 327, 332
Lourinhã 222–3
Lourosa 18, 185
Lousã 207
Lufrei 132
Luso 196–7

Macedo de Cavaleiros 156
Mafra 226–7
Magalhães, José Estêvão Coelho de 192, 193
Magellan, Ferdinand 93
Mancelos 132
Mangualde 179–80
manor houses 42–3
Manteigas 182–3
Manuel I, King of Portugal 239–40, 275, 320
Manuel II, King of Portugal 12, 198, 244, 301
Marão mountains 111
marble 224, 288
Maria I, Queen of Portugal 172, 235, 243, 247, 344
Maria II, Queen of Portugal 198, 243
Marialva 176
Marinha Grande 209
Martins, Deu-la-Deu 86
Marvão 290–1
Mateus, Solar de 40, 141
Matosinhos 128
Mealhada 199
Meca 226
Medóbriga 18, 291
Melgaço 87
Mértola 18, 325
Mesão Frio 134
MFA (Movimento das Forças Armadas) 14, 245
Minho, the 66–109
Mira 196
Miranda do Douro 40, 160–4
Mirandela 155
Miróbriga 317
Mogadouro 159–60
monasteries 19
in the Alentejo 291, 293, 303
in the Beiras 197–8, 201–2, 209–10

in the Douro 119, 127, 130, 138
in Estremadura 216, 224, 225, 226, 255
in the Minho 85, 101, 107–8
in the Ribatejo 275
in Trás-os-Montes 169
Monção 85–6
Monchique 340–1
Monchique Mountains 328
Mondego, Castles of the 204
Mondim de Basto 142
Monforte 295
Monsanto 191
Monsaraz 310
Monte Gordo 347
Montemor-o-Novo 312
Montemor-o-Velho 204–5
Montesinho 168
Montesinho Natural Park 168–9
motor racing 52, 234
mountaineering 90
Moura 321
Murça 154–5
music 10, 50–1, 126, 148, 163, 200, 261, 288, 322

national characteristics 10
Natural Parks 168–9, 172, 179, 180–2, 269, 285, 313–14, 330
Nazaré 217–18
Nelas 180
Neves 79
newspapers 25, 62
nightlife 50, 80, 126, 232, 265–6, 331, 333, 334, 335, 336, 339, 340, 343, 347
Numão Castle 143
Nun'Álvares Pereira 211, 214, 294, 295, 302, 311

Óbidos 22, 219–21
Odivelas 261
Oeiras 235
Ofir 74
Olhão 345
Oliveira de Frades 179
Oliveira do Hospital 185
Oporto 9, 68, 111, 113–26
Ougela 296–7
Outeiro 164
ox fights 150–1

painting 22–4
Palmela 267–8
passports 55
Pauliteiros de Miranda dancers 160, 162
Pedra Formosa 107, 108
Pedras Salgadas 154
Pedro I, King of Portugal 202, 215–16, 222, 294
Pedro II, King of Portugal 241–2
Pedro III, King of Portugal 235

Pedro IV, King of Portugal 115–16, 192, 228, 243
Pena de Aguiar Castle 154
Penamacor 191
Peneda-Gerês National Park 88–91, 149
Penedono 176
Penela 207
Penha Mountain 108
Peniche 221–2
Peninsular War see War, Peninsular
Peso da Régua 134–5
Philippa of Lancaster 86, 210, 220, 237–8, 246
pilgrimages 76, 88, 128, 131, 176, 190, 211, 218
Pinheiro 314
Pinhel 174–5
Pisões 324
politics and political parties 25–8, 244, 245, 246, 288
Pombal 207–8
Pombal, Sebastien José de Carvalho, Marquês de
in the Alentejo 305
in the Algarve 348
in the Beiras 172, 192, 201, 208
in the Douro 111–12, 134, 136
in Estremadura 213, 235, 242–3, 247, 255, 256
in the Ribatejo 274
Ponte da Barca 91–2
Ponte de Lima 92–5
Porca de Murça 155
porcelain 53, 192, 195
Porches 336
Portalegre 292–5
Portimão 338–9
Porto Covo 318
Porto de Mós 214–15
Portuguese School of Equestrian Art 274
port wine 47–8, 111–13, 126, 136
pottery 53, 96, 138, 141, 219, 226, 336
Póvoa de Lanhoso 103
Póvoa de Varzim 72–6
Praia da Falesia 334
Praia da Luz 343
Praia da Rocha 339–40
Praia de Mira 196
Praia do Guincho 231
public holidays 58

Quarteira 333
Queluz 235–6
Quinta do Lago 332–3

radio 63
railways see train travel
Rates 74
Reguengos de Monsaraz 310–11

religion 8–9, 64, 68
Resende 139
restaurants 45–6
revolution of 1974 8, 10, 11, 15–16, 245
Ria de Aveiro 194–5
Ribatejo, the 272–85
Rio do Onor 168–9
Rio Maior 284
rock carvings 153
Romeu 156
rugs 53, 311–12
rural tourism 42–3

Sado Estuary Natural Reserve 313–14
Sagres 327, 343–4
Salazar, António de Oliveira 12–13, 14, 105, 165, 244–5
Salvaterra de Magos 284
Sancho I, King of Portugal 165, 173, 207, 214, 226, 230, 271, 312, 337
Sancho II, King of Portugal 169, 208, 297, 298, 325, 348
sanctuaries 79, 103, 108, 141, 310
Santa Cruz 168
Santa Luzia Sanctuary 79
Santa Marinha da Costa Monastery 107–8
Santarém 281–3
Santiago do Cacém 18, 315–17
Santo Tirso 73
São Bras de Alportel 331–2
São João da Pesqueira 143
São João de Deus 312
São João de Tarouca Monastery 138
São João do Campo 88
São Mamede, Battle of 68, 103, 105
São Martinho do Porto 218
São Pedro de Moel 209
São Pedro do Sul 178–9
São Salvador de Aramenha 291
São Torpes 318
scenic railways 38–40
Sebastião, King of Portugal 241, 295, 342
Segura 191
Seia 184
self-catering 42
Sem-Pavor, Geraldo (Gerald the Fearless) 297, 304, 311, 321
Sendim 160
Serpa 322–3
Serra da Estrela 171
Serra da Estrela Natural Park 172, 180–2
Serra da Lousã 207
Sertã 191
Sesimbra 270–1
Setúbal 9, 268–9
shanty towns 11, 20, 27, 30

sheepdogs 89, 181–2
Silves 327, 337–8
Sines 317–18
Sintra 20, 227–32
skiing 182
Soajo 89
Soares dos Reis 120
Soares, Mário 15, 16, 25–6, 246, 254
Sobral de Monte Agraço 225
songs 148, 288, 322
Soure 205
spas 44, 86, 90, 152, 154, 196, 196–7, 218, 223, 289
spirits 48
sports 52
stud farms 274, 283, 294

Tagus River Natural Reserve 285
tapestries 293
Tavira 346
taxis 36–7
telephones 64–5
television 63
Templars see Knights Templar
tennis 333
Teresa, Countess of Burgundy 93, 98, 103, 105, 113
Terroso 74
tiles, decorative 21–1, 252–3
time zones 65
tipping 65
toilets 65
Tomar 19, 274–7
Torre de Moncorvo 156–7
Torres Novas 281
Torres Vedras 223–4
train travel 37–40
    scenic routes 38–40
Trancoso 176
Trás-os-Montes 144–69
Travanca 132
Três Minas 154
Tróia Peninsula 312–13

Vagos 196
Vale de Lobos 282–3
Vale do Lobo 333
Valença 68
Valença do Minho 40, 85
Valverde 309–10
Velho, Gonçalo 77
Velho, João 77, 78
Viana do Castelo 68, 77–82
Vidago 153–4
Vila de Mós 157
Vila do Conde 69–71
Vila Franca de Xira 285
Vila Franca do Lima 78
Vila Fresca de Azeitão 269–70
Vilamoura 333–4
Vila Nogueira de Azeitão 270
Vila Nova da Barquinha 278
Vila Nova de Cerveira 84–5

Vila Nova de Famalicão 71
Vila Nova de Foz Côa 143
Vila Nova de Gaia 112, 113, 126–8
Vila Nova de Milfontes 318–19
Vila Nova de Ourém 211
Vila Nova de Paiva 178
Vila Pouca de Aguiar 154
Vila Praia de Âncora 77, 83
Vilar dos Mouros 84
Vila Real 40, 140–2
Vila Real de Santo António 347–8
Vila Verde 95
Vila Viçosa 300–1
Vilharino Seco 150
Vimeiro 223
Vimioso 163–4
Vinhais 169
vinho verde 47, 67, 68–9
Viriato 171, 177
Viseu 176
Vista Alegre 195
Vouzela 39, 179

War, Peninsular
    in the Alentejo 296, 323
    in the Beiras 171, 175, 189, 198, 205
    in the Douro 115, 122, 123
    in Estremadura 214, 223, 225, 229, 243
    in the Ribatejo 280, 285
    in Trás-os-Montes 149–50, 162, 165
War of Restoration 296, 298, 302
War, Seven Years 291
War of the Spanish Succession 161, 291, 292, 296, 302
War of Succession 115–16, 136, 171, 189, 192, 228, 243, 281, 311, 323
water sports 52, 90, 195, 333, 336, 339, 342, 343
weather 32
Wellington, Arthur Wellesley, Duke of 115, 162, 198, 223, 229, 243, 298
wildlife 65, 88, 168, 285
wine 30, 47–8, 136, 140, 140–1, 270, 274
    Alcobaça 214
    Alentejo 289
    in the Algarve 329, 336
    Bairrada 172, 196
    in Boticas 149–50
    Bucelas 213–14
    Colares 214
    Dão 172
    Lafões 172
    Pocarica 196
    in Trás-os-Montes 147–8
    see also port wine; vinho verde
wine lodges 127